T0244286

The US Eighth Air Force in World War II

Ira Eaker, Hap Arnold, and Building American Air Power, 1942–1943

William J. Daugherty

University of North Texas Press
Denton, Texas

Permissions:
University of North Texas Press
1155 Union Circle #311336
Denton, TX 76203-5017

The paper used in this book meets the minimum requirements of the American National Standard for Permanence of Paper for Printed Library Materials, z39.48.1984. Binding materials have been chosen for durability.

Library of Congress Cataloging-in-Publication Data

Names: Daugherty, William J., 1947- author.
Title: The US Eighth Air Force in World War II : Ira Eaker, Hap Arnold, and
    building American air power, 1942-1943 / William J. Daugherty.
Description: Denton, Texas : University of North Texas Press, [2024] |
    Series: American military studies ; Number 8 | Includes bibliographical
    references and index.
Identifiers: LCCN 2024007627 (print) | LCCN 2024007628 (ebook) | ISBN
    9781574419276 (cloth) | ISBN 9781574419368 (ebook)
Subjects: LCSH: Eaker, Ira, 1896-1987--Military leadership. | Arnold,
    Henry Harley, 1886-1950. | United States. Air Force. Air Force, 8th--
    History. | World War, 1939-1945--Regimental histories--United States. |
    World War, 1939-1945--Aerial operations, American. | Air power--United
    States--History--20th century. | Schweinfurt (Germany)--History--
    Bombardment, 1943. | BISAC: HISTORY / Wars & Conflicts / World War II /
    General | HISTORY / Military / Aviation &Space
Classification: LCC D790.22 8th .D377 2024 (print) | LCC D790.22 8th
    (ebook) | DDC 940.54/4973--dc23/eng/20240304
LC record available at https://lccn.loc.gov/2024007627
LC ebook record available at https://lccn.loc.gov/2024007628

The US Eighth Air Force in World War II is Number 8 in the American
Military Studies Series.

The electronic edition of this book was made possible by the support of the
Vick Family Foundation. Typeset by vPrompt eServices.

To the men and women of the
Mighty Eighth Air Force,
United Kingdom
1942–1945

All sacrificed, all persevered;
all gave something of themselves;
all were heroes.

Contents

Photo Gallery

Acknowledgments

First, Dr. Vivian Rogers-Price, director of the Roger A. Freeman Research Center at the National Museum of the Mighty Eighth Air Force, has my deep gratitude. Throughout the time I worked on the manuscript, Vivian offered advice, assistance, relevant but little-known information, encouragement, and support. Vivian read an early draft for accuracy and a grammatical check. As a bonus, Dr. Michael Price, former head of the history department at my university and Vivian's husband, also read the manuscript and made welcome comments. The manuscript is a better product because of these two colleagues, historians, and friends, and I am most appreciative.

I thank my friends and colleagues at the museum, whether permanent staff or volunteer, and especially Judy Roddy and Tiffany Bueno, for their friendship and their dedication to the Eighth and to the museum that represents the 350,000 men and women who served in the Eighth during the war. And my unending appreciation to Teri Bell and all the ladies at Miss Sophie's English Pub, for their cheerful greetings always make my day.

Because of COVID restrictions on travel during much of the research for this work, I looked to the Air Force Historical and Research Agency (AFHRA) at Maxwell Air Force Base as a source of original documents. The ladies at AFHRA graciously and efficiently provided digital materials essential to the book; they have my gratitude for their service.

I am indebted to Ron Chrisman at the UNT Press for his kindness and consideration, and for his willingness to stay with this project as it went through several iterations before it finally gelled into the version that it is today. I must also express sincere appreciation to the two individuals who reviewed this manuscript for the work they put into reading and commenting on various aspects of it. Each commented on different aspects, and from them both I learned much more of the material's substance and focus. I thank them both, sincerely.

Thanks to Dr. Geoff Jensen at Embry-Riddle Aeronautical University, Prescott, Arizona, editor of the American Military Studies Series, for his guidance in moving the manuscript through the key stages as it approached the end of the process.

Ms. Amy Maddox was my assigned copyeditor and in this I truly hit the jackpot; I could not have had a more professional or more helpful person to guide me through the prepublication processes. She cheerfully professed to tolerate my interminable questions and seemed to be always available even from the opposite side of the Mississippi River. Amy has my gratitude and respect for her kind assistance.

And as always, my endless gratitude and appreciation to Ms. Jeanne D. Nelsen for her reviews of the manuscript at various stages and for her never-ending support and friendship.

I reviewed the final manuscript while enjoying the warm hospitality of my high school classmate and his wife at their home in southern California. Toby and June gave me a quiet place to work while I reread the manuscript one last time and saw to it that I was fed, rested, and able to savor a few of the jewels in Toby's magnificent wine cellar. I cannot thank them both enough.

Glossary

AAFIB	(US) Army Air Forces in Britain
ABC Conversations	American-British-Canadian discussions for joint strategy, 1941
ACTS	Air Corps Tactical School
AEAF	Allied Expeditionary Air Force
AEF	American Expeditionary Force
AFHRA	Air Force Historical and Research Agency
ARCADIA	US-British Joint Strategy Summit, Washington, DC, 24 December 1941–14 January 1942
AS	Air Service
ASC	Air Support Command
ASSEMBLY	The gathering of bomber aircraft following takeoff into formations of squadrons, then groups, then combat wings before proceeding across the English Channel in tight, close, mutually supporting elements
AVALANCHE	Codeword for the Allied amphibious landing at Salerno, Italy
AWPD	Air War Plans Division
AWPD-1	Air War Plans Document-1
AWPD-42	Air War Plans Document-42
BA	British Army
BADA	base air depot area, any one of four huge aircraft repair and maintenance facilities in England and North Ireland belonging to the Eighth Air Force, at which major work was done on US aircraft
BCS	British Chiefs of Staff
BDA	bomb damage assessment
BOLERO	The buildup of matériel and supplies in England for an eventual invasion of the Continent in 1942 or 1943

BIGOT	A list of names of individuals who have been told about or "read into" a sensitive intelligence program; a list of people limited to a "need to know"
CBO	Combined Bomber Offensive
CCRC	Combat Crew Replacement Center
CCS	Combined Chiefs of Staff (US and British service chiefs sitting together)
CG	commanding general
CIU	Central Interpretation Unit
CO	commanding officer
CROSSBOW	Operations for targeting and destroying Vengeance Weapons
DBR	damaged beyond repair
D-Day	The invasion of France by British, Canadian, and American forces, 6 June 1944
DSC	Distinguished Service Cross
ETOUSA	European theater of operations, US Army
EUREKA	US-British-Soviet Joint Strategy Summit, Tehran, 28 November- 1 December 1943
GYMNAST	First codename for Operation TORCH
HADPB	high-altitude, daylight precision bombing
HqAF	Headquarters, Air Forces
IP	initial point
JCS	Joint Chiefs of Staff (United States)
JUGGLER	Codename for the joint bomber strikes on Regensburg and Schweinfurt
JUNIOR	Codename for the not-yet-activated Twelfth Air Force in August–September 1942
KIA	killed in action
Luftwaffe	German Air Force
MAAF	Mediterranean Allied Air Force
NOBALL	Operations against specific CROSSBOW targets
OPD	Operations and Plans Division
OVERLORD	Codename for the invasion of France, 6 June 1944

PFF	Pathfinder Force
PI	photo interpreter
PINETREE	Headquarters, VIII Bomber Command, at High Wycombe, 1942–1943
	Headquarters, Eighth Air Force, at High Wycombe, 1944–1945
"Plan Dog"	Memorandum by Admiral Stark for the President, November 1940, advocating a "Europe First" policy and an alliance with the British against Germany and Italy
POINTBLANK	AAF-RAF joint operation implementing the Combined Chiefs of Staff directive known as the Combined Bomber Offensive
PR	photo reconnaissance
QUADRANT	US-British Joint Strategy Summit, Quebec City, Canada, 14–24 August 1943
RAF	Royal Air Force
RE8	Research and Experiments Office 8
RFC	Royal Flying Corps
RN	Royal Navy
RODEO Mission	A fighter sweep, usually twenty or more fighters wing tip to wing tip at low level looking for enemy aircraft or targets on the ground
ROUNDUP	Invasion of the European Continent, spring 1943
Second Washington Conference	Unplanned second summit held, first, secretly at the presidential retreat at Hyde Park, New York, on 19–20 June 1942, thence in Washington, DC, for the CCS, 21–25 June 1942
SEXTANT I and II	US-British joint strategy summit, Cairo, Egypt, 22–26 November 1943 and 2–7 December 1943
SLEDGEHAMMER	Possible incursion/bridgehead in France, November 1942
SOUTHDOWN	RAF Bomber Command Headquarters near High Wycombe, Buckinghamshire

STARKEY   An Allied deception operation to convince the
                    Germans the coming invasion would occur at the
                    Pas-de-Calais

SYMBOL   US-British joint strategy summit, Casablanca,
                    14–24 January 1943

TORCH   Codename of the Allied invasion of northwest
                    Africa, 8 November 1942

TRIDENT   US-British Joint Strategy Summit, Washington, DC,
                    12–25 May 1943

ULTRA   The British top-secret operation where German
                    coded messages sent by the Enigma machine were
                    intercepted and decoded at Bletchley Park
                    estate in England

USAAC   United States Army Air Corps

USAAF   United States Army Air Forces

US Sea Services   US Navy, US Marine Corps, and US Coast Guard

VE-Day   Victory in Europe Day, when German leaders signed
                    the surrender documents, 8 May 1945

WDGS   War Department General Staff

Wehrmacht   German Army

WIDEWING   Headquarters, Eighth Air Force 1942–1943
                    Headquarters, USSTAF 1944–1945

WPD   War Plans Division

Preface

Five generations have been born since the end of World War II. With but very few exceptions, men who were of military age in 1939 have passed on while their great-grandchildren are now approaching maturity. Interest in the war, from the general public and by academics, ebbed and flowed for perhaps four decades after its end. The end of conscription in the United States in 1971 served as a proximate cause of the beginning of a slow rise in interest, as over the next two decades fewer Americans came to have a personal acquaintance with the American military and the war itself.[1] By 2018, even with wars enduring more than two decades in the Middle East and Southwest Asia, no more than 14 percent of living Americans had ever served in the military; contrast that with the Second World War when it was almost impossible to find a family unit that did not have at least one member in the military, and rare was the family that was not touched in some deep sense by that war.

In considering the US Eighth Air Force, as with any part of military history there are always familiar names, often heroes, that at least a plurality of Americans can point to as leaders in this unit or heroes of that war. Jimmy Doolittle is one of those iconic Americans, an inspiring leader in civilian aviation, a genuine military hero, and for the final seventeen months of the war in Europe, commanding general of the Eighth. In measurable part because of his leadership, so, too, did the Eighth earn a well-publicized reputation for the air war against Hitler's Third Reich, flying thousands of missions with hundreds of bombers deep into Germany, accompanied by even more fighter escorts. But what of the Eighth before Doolittle's arrival? What of the Eighth during its first two years of existence when it was not simply the first but also the only US fighting force to take the offensive against Hitler's Germany? At a time when missions struggled to put up even fifty bombers and escorts could accompany bombers barely past the French coast? Those months arguably slid, and did so rather quickly, into near obscurity once

General Doolittle assumed command in January of 1944. Yet the men with the unfamiliar names who came before Doolittle were just as courageous and faced missions that were at least as dangerous in the first seventeen months of air combat as those in the final seventeen months. Yet today they, and the first two years of the Eighth, are approaching obscurity.

During the first seventeen months of air combat, from August 17, 1942, through December 31, 1943, the statistical odds of the average airman in the Eighth living through twenty-five missions and receiving his "ticket" home were nearly zero. While a handful of lucky chaps did beat the odds, most men were casualties of one type or another by their tenth or twelfth mission; some did not live to finish even their first. And yet at mission time, the great majority still climbed into their bombers and flew east to face the Luftwaffe. Not once, not even in the two absolute worst air battles of the war—the Schweinfurt missions of 1943, each of which cost one of every four bombers and six hundred–plus men—did the Eighth ever turn back before reaching their target. On both missions it was said that the aircraft at the tail end of the bomber streams could find their way to Schweinfurt by following the burning Fortresses in the snow twenty-three thousand feet below.[2] And still they flew on, alone. Not until after November 1943 was there a fighter that could escort the heavy bombers, the B-17s and B-24s, much past the German border. Indeed, it was well into 1943 before fighters could escort the bombers as far as Paris.

Nor was the learning gap limited to the flying cadre. In spring of 1942 the Eighth had exactly one air intelligence officer. Months were required to build up not only enough trained personnel and intelligence distribution systems but also the knowledge to understand and interpret the intelligence accurately and in turn to recommend appropriate targets to commanders. "In the process, they honed their analytical skills while providing increasingly accurate bomb damage assessment (BDA) to senior air commanders, who in turn employed it to steer their ever-larger bomber forces against the most lucrative German target sets."[3] Neither movies nor television ever showed the air war like this. The story of the first two years of the Eighth Air Force in some senses presents an even stronger case for heroism, dedication, and self-sacrifice than those depicting events in the final seventeen months. Yet it was the men, their stories, and the raw circumstances in the beginning that are little known today.

The first two years of any war make a good case study, for they are forever calling for creativity, innovation, and intense devotion to duty in response to new and unforeseen circumstances often fueled by great need, danger, and even desperation. For the Eighth this was the time when will was expected to overcome hardship and minimally trained men were driven to climb above difficulty and deprivation to achieve the impossible. It was as though there were two Eighth Air Forces during World War II: There was the early one, in which all experiences were new, too many circumstances were unknown, and too often essential equipment was everywhere but where it was most desperately needed. It was when the unplanned-for arose seemingly nonstop, nothing worked right, and officers and men were trying just to survive in strange environments. By contrast, the "second" Eighth Air Force was staffed with well-trained and prepared men, supported by an established and systematic bureaucracy in which many situations were understood, needs were addressed, and essentials were provided even before leaving the States for England. It was a time when equipment was readily available, so much so that damaged airplanes were not even repaired but simply wheeled to the boneyards and new ones delivered before the next mission.[4]

Few Americans today think about America in 1940, when the population was 133 million and 65.5 percent lived in towns of 50,000 or fewer. The average American 25 years of age and older had completed, at most, some part of the freshman year of high school; 13 million had no more than a grammar-school education, while slightly more than 2,000 had a four-year college degree. It was not uncommon to have traveled no further than the county seat. Few had ever seen an airplane and fewer still had ever flown in one.[5] These were the men who, on 8 December 1941, lined up outside the Army Air Forces recruiting office and said they wanted to fly. Eighteen-year-olds with a high school diploma signed up to fly high-performance single-engine fighters or sophisticated four-engine long-range bombers. The Eighth was soon populated with young men who, on average, had never been outside their home county, much less the country, and were poorly educated by today's standards. Nor was the AAF at all prepared for literally thousands of men to join.

In May 1942 when Colonel Curtis E. LeMay picked up the 305th Bombardment Group (Heavy) at Muroc Army Airfield, California, his group had only three airplanes. Five months later, flying across the Atlantic to Prestwick, Scotland, he noted, "Crews are not coordinated. . . . Pilots came right from basic trainers to B-17s. . . . Navigators . . . we got a lot of 'em two weeks before we started overseas. . . . Most gunners haven't fired. . . . Bombardiers haven't had much practice. . . . And no formation flying. We've never had enough airplanes to fly formation. We'll have to fly our first formation in England."[6] Once in England, the men were living in a country over a thousand years old, where the language was a strange English and life was foreign in many more ways than simply being on the other side of the Atlantic. Every day they flew in an airplane they probably had never seen until operational training, battling enemy fighters and flak at twenty-five thousand feet in temperatures of minus forty degrees because the back half of the aircraft was open to the outside. Even those from Montana had never had a day like that.

Beginning in December 1942, the Eighth was commanded by a man who, because he was the first heavy bomber commander, focused on his instructions received upon departure for England in early 1942. These instructions were, quite simply, to take his command to England, learn what he could from the Royal Air Force (RAF), and when ready commence bombing German targets in Western Europe and the Third Reich. The tension that grew between him and the commanding general of the AAF, inflated until something had to give, was mostly because he worked for a man whose position encompassed many things at once. As important as the Eighth was to the war, it was not the most important thing for this general. Scrutiny of General Ira C. Eaker's two years commanding VIII Bomber Command and then Eighth Air Force, the growth and maturing of the Eighth, and Eaker's ultimate relief is, thus, more than deserving of its own serious and discrete examination—the principal subject of this work.

Organization

Most histories are written chronologically, for good reason: not only is that how life—how history—unfolds, but also the reader tends to become lost more easily when the story flits between and among events that are months or years apart. However, even writing about a discrete event clearly delimited by time and place often presents a challenge to chronological order. The fact is that in war even a single event is comprised of multiple and overlapping decisions, actions, influences, and circumstances that occur concurrently as well as eventuated sequentially in the past. Understanding is only possible if earlier, relevant events are explored and explained as the story progresses. This process then becomes still more complicated if the subject is not a single event but a series transpiring over time, for each iterative event drags along its own history as well. Wars are never simple but inevitably complex, with many facets. The trick is to keep it from becoming complicated at the same time.

This work begins in Washington, DC, but then gravitates to England in 1942 as it follows the life of the Eighth Air Force (if, that is, a large organization at war may appear as a living organism; there are many who would not disagree.)While many men exercised some measure of power within the Eighth during 1942 to 1943, only a few were truly instrumental in its direction. Also affecting the Eighth as an organization were men who never served in it yet exercised influence over it because of positions they had held or decisions they made. Hence, to have some idea of the many different moving parts of the Eighth Air Force as it matured in combat effectiveness—and why, in some cases, it may have taken an overly long time for some very serious shortcomings to be corrected—an occasional digression is necessary.

To comprehend the hold that the flawed theory of high-altitude, daylight precision bombing (HADPB) had on many in leadership positions in the Eighth, a digression reviewing the Bomber Mafia at the Air Corps Tactical School (ACTS) is necessary. The same applies to the failure of leadership to accept that bombers needed fighter escorts all the way to the target and return. The belief that the bombers, as a self-defending force, could fight their way through enemy territory defended at times by literally hundreds of enemy fighters and antiaircraft artillery and safely return had its roots at ACTS as well.

Necessary, too, is a short digression into the SYMBOL Conference in Casablanca in January 1943. Among the significant decisions there, three were especially important for future operations of the Eighth: the eventual formulation and approval of Operation POINTBLANK, the program to destroy the Luftwaffe before D-Day; General Eaker's presentation to Prime Minister Churchill reversing the PM's agreement with the president for the heavy bombers of the Eighth to conduct only night area bombardment missions with RAF Bomber Command; and the president's "Unconditional Surrender" directive. Without this modest excursion to Casablanca, the *why* and *because* of these three influences on the Eighth would be muddled at best, leaving the reader unjustifiably unsatisfied.

With the exception of those few digressions, essential to a fuller comprehension of the Eighth's initial two years, this work will proceed smartly in the chronological style of most histories, keeping in mind this is not an account of individual men who flew and fought in the heavy bombers; important details of some of the more significant missions are given, but omitted for the most part are the airmen's stories. Missions discussed were selected for the emphasis they bring to the moment; the blood, guts, and glory found in the books about the men have been left aside, more appropriate for first-person recitals.

The common thread running through this work is the influence General Henry H. "Hap" Arnold almost constantly brought to bear on the Eighth's commanding general, his own protégé, General Eaker. Arnold lived with unrelenting political, military, and personal pressures, many of which had little to do with the Eighth or with the air war in Europe. Of those pressures that had a direct relation to the war, most at that early stage were unresolvable; for example, only so many airplanes were rolling out of the factories at that early time, yet commanders from every region of the world were crying out for literally hundreds of aircraft to be delivered yesterday. Likewise, Arnold had Congress, as an institution and as 431 individual representatives and 96 senators, barking at him every hour, not to mention the president of the United States. Conversely, Eaker's needs were far more tightly focused: his marching orders were to take the air war to Hitler and the Third Reich, and to do so in an increasingly lethal manner. Unexpectedly, he had to do that while concomitantly giving up his aircraft and aircrews to the operation no American commander wanted, Operation TORCH. Above all else, Arnold was continually measuring how or whether each major event could affect the chances for creating an independent United States Air Force after the war.

Besides coping with General Arnold's influences (or interferences) from afar, after landing in England on 20 February 1942, General Eaker had to: bring the Eighth from only seven officers, no troops, no airplanes, no airfields, and no infrastructure to a planned force of nearly two hundred thousand men (and women) and hundreds of heavy and medium bombers and fighters by the end of 1943; build up the necessary support structure, including four enormous area repair depots, over 120 new airfields, crew training centers, and personnel facilities from medical to barracks to mess halls; deal with the uncontrollable and execrable northern European weather that was very much unsuited for aviation in general and bombardment in particular—and then dispatch his aircraft to fly in it anyway; entertain debates on whether escorts for the bombers were necessary (he thought not); cope with the inability of the precision bombardment theory to fulfill its promise; develop a radar-guided Pathfinder force; and—always—assess whether the Eighth could absorb the casualties or determine at what point the casualties would exceed the allowable. Simply stated the two generals—Arnold and Eaker— had completely different objectives; at times it seemed as though neither of these old friends cared much about the demands under which the other was living. An observer might also have thought that the Eighth was being managed from Washington instead of England. While Arnold was deciding his general was failing him, his general's bosses and allies in England were equally certain that he was doing excellently in fighting the air war. Only with the arrival of General Doolittle in January 1944, and the establishment of the strategic air forces under General Carl "Tooey" Spaatz, did Arnold's presumed attempts at day-to-day management of the Eighth disappear.

Note to Reader

During the war many officers moved quickly up the ranks and/or changed positions frequently. For ease of comprehension, the rank or position of all officers used is the one that the individual held at the particular time he appears in the narrative.

The word *Luftwaffe* is used throughout in lieu of *German Air Force* or *GAF*. The correct terminology for all numbered air forces is to spell out the number; hence, *Eighth Air Force* vice *8th Air Force*. Subordinate components—air divisions, combat wings, bomber groups, squadrons—are designated by digits: 4th Wing, 97th Bomb Group, 362nd Bomb Squadron.

The United States Army Air Corps became the United States Army Air Forces (plural; USAAF) on 9 March 1942. General Spaatz, whether commanding general of the Eighth or of USSTAF, was headquartered at WIDEWING (singular), Bushy Park, Teddington, London. VIII Fighter (or Bomber) Command headquarters was located at Bushey Hall, Hertfordshire. VIII Bomber Command was PINETREE at Wycombe Abbey and remained so after redesignation as US Eighth Air Force in January 1944.

Chapter 1

Harbingers of the Eighth Air Force

Developments in World War I and the Interwar Years

The Wright brothers first powered aircraft flight covered 120 feet in twelve seconds at 6.8 miles per hour, the lower wing barely five feet above Kitty Hawk sands. The birth of the army aviation bombardment probably occurred somewhere during that 120 feet when some quick-thinking observer wondered, How can I make that thing drop bombs on the bad guys? The army established a tiny Aeronautical Division in the Signal Corps in 1908, although the beginning was not greatly propitious: the first army airplane flight was that August, and not quite four weeks later the army experienced its first aviation casualty.[1] Still, fledgling aviators persisted and were rewarded with an "Aero Squadron" in 1913, which became the 1st Aero Squadron in 1916. Based at Fort Bliss, Texas, it was soon attached to General John J. Pershing's "Punitive Expedition" to pursue and capture the Mexican Pancho Villa. In the short run, the 1st Aero's performance seemed to reflect little positive on the future of army aviation: it was equipped with aircraft very much inadequate to the mission, although no one knew exactly what the mission was. The squadron commander, Captain Benjamin O. Foulois, would later tell Congress the squadron was sent to "perform a service we knew nothing about, with no maps and no knowledge of the situation whatsoever."[2] The squadron was given eight dated, underpowered JN-3 Jennys in such poor condition that they were limited to flights no farther than 50 miles from base.[3] But when Pershing was ready to move out to a point 125 miles away in the Mexican desert amid surrounding high mountains, Foulois's squadron and his Jennys were too. The weather—high winds, arid climate, and dust storms—along with a lack of navigation aids, woefully inadequate maps, and poor maintenance capability soon reduced the aircraft numbers to six. After the second week, the Jennys were in such poor states that they were in "questionable condition to conduct military operations." Within a month the aircraft were unable to operate in, much less over, the mountains, incapable even of carrying extra food and water for the pilots. More than once pilots were forced to abandon a crashed aircraft and hike over fifty miles across an alkaline desert to friendly lines. Unable to utilize the aircraft in the role initially envisioned by Foulois and Pershing, the several remaining were of limited utility but nonetheless performed above expectations.

The "punitive" mission was called off in January 1917 with all returning to Fort Bliss. Although Villa was never captured, the deployment of the 1st Aero Squadron was a success in that the future value of the airplane in military operations was accepted, even though that value was still to be defined by doctrine. The 1st Aero Squadron flew "540 flights totaling 346 hours in the air and covered 19,533 miles while performing aerial reconnaissance and photographic missions, and transporting mail and official dispatches." It was an operational testbed for various missions that a squadron equipped with much better airplanes than the Jenny might be expected to perform in the future. The secretary of war later ordered, at a cost of $500,000, twelve Curtis R-2 fast airplanes, armed with Lewis machine guns, automatic cameras, bombs, and radios. Even at that early stage, aviators had proved themselves to be a particularly inquisitive kind of soldier, always looking to do things better or differently, or both. Most important "for the nation was the ultimate realization that the airplane was no longer an experiment or an oddity."[4]

Remaining under the Signal Corps but in recognition of the promise, growth, and permanency of an aviation role in the army, on 18 July 1914 Aeronautical Division become the Aviation Section, with the formal responsibility to "train" army personnel in "matters pertaining to military aviation."[5] What the aviators meant by that, however, could be stated simply: figure out what types of airplanes were needed, push the envelope to see what the airplanes could do, then generate standards and tactics both for contemporary utilization and as a basis for developing the next generation of aircraft. Soon, airplanes were divided into categories based on their capabilities, with bombardment, pursuit and reconnaissance, and observation coming to the fore.

In 1917 the chief of the Air Service (AS) was now Brigadier General Benjamin Foulois, who, upon arriving in France on 12 November, quickly discovered the AS was way behind the rest of the American Expeditionary Force (AEF) in terms of organization since the AEF had arrived some six months earlier. He was frankly "shocked" at the disorganization he found at AS headquarters.[6] Foulois's staff of 112 personnel was headed by a senior staff of three, none of whom had ever attended command and staff college. One of the senior staff was a colonel, soon brigadier general, named William "Billy" Mitchell, with whom Foulois would be immediately and continually in conflict. Foulois spent two weeks inspecting the AS units and facilities in France and then, returning to his headquarters on 27 November, was named chief of the AS, AEF.

Foulois divided his headquarters into eight sections and began setting things right, as he perceived the situation, while dealing with Colonel Mitchell, who thought the reorganization was done all wrong—"the first of many conflicts" with Mitchell. The colonel possessed an aggressive character and was always a strong advocate for air power, tenacious and outspoken in his positions. Ahead of his time, arrogant, and unwilling to listen to most anyone, Mitchell pushed for strategic bombing operations flown by bombers in tight formations and guarded by escorting fighters.[7] The colonel did not carry with his vociferous air power advocacy the necessary patience for essential staff work or the temperament to deal effectively with bureaucratic opponents. Seven months later, with the Air Service falling further behind in keeping aligned with the AEF ground forces, either Foulois requested that Pershing relieve him as chief of the AS/AEF or Pershing took the initiative; it was not completely clear.

Regardless, Foulois was instead assigned as chief of the AS for the First Army, in part because of Mitchell's "lack of progress" in that office. Foulois's new responsibilities included assuming Mitchell's, which Foulois described as "a bunch of disorganized men, a bunch of disorganized airplanes—somebody had to put them together," and now he would do it. Foulois was Mitchell's superior officer, which only deepened the dislike the junior had toward his boss. Foulois faced a "monumental task": he had to "build a world-class air force from scratch in less than year . . . without a pre-existing infrastructure" and work with a staff that was somewhere between disorganized and chaotic, with much of the discord between Mitchell and Foulois amazingly centered around who should be in senior staff positions: aviators who understood flying (but maybe, or maybe not, also understood how to get things done on the ground), or nonaviators who could do staff work but—allegedly—would not understand what it was they were administering.[8] As there were insufficient numbers of both types in the AEF, it was a dispute that needed a different solution than the simple division fervently put forth by Mitchell. Serious problems at the pursuit pilot training command at Issoudun when Foulois had first arrived in France were much more easily put right by replacing the poorly performing commander with Major Tooey Spaatz, who had been with Foulois in Mexico. By January 1918 the school was "digging itself out of the mire" and turning out excellent pursuit pilots for the front.[9]

While the European powers, which had been fighting for three years, had developed various theories and doctrines of air power, the AS had none that was "clearly defined" at the time, although control of the air quickly became a requisite objective once in air combat.[10] "Once in combat," however, was not an immediate event. "About one year was required after the United States of America had declared war on the Central Powers before American air strength of any measurable degree could be brought to bear against the enemy."[11] In the early days of the American experience in the air war, the observation mission developed fairly "simply and harmoniously," but not so others. Bombardment, for example, was looked upon by the War Department General Staff (WDGS) as simply another type of artillery—but without the longer range of the best land-based cannon! In its wisdom the WDGS determined that two bomber squadrons were equal in firepower to one 155 mm gun.[12] Bombardment was considered to be both tactical and strategic, with the former undertaking daylight raids over battlefields while the latter took place at night with bombers carrying heavy bomb loads—except that the Americans (unlike the Germans) possessed no aircraft that were, in fact, capable of true strategic bombing missions. One area in which the Americans were in concurrence not only among themselves but also with their British allies was that the airplane was essentially an offensive weapon that, to be employed correctly, should be unified "under one major command."[13]

World War I provided exactly the opportunity to create an airplane—or airplanes—for use strictly as a bomber and to develop tactics to enable accurate bombing with minimum losses.[14] Flying combat missions from February to November 1918, army aviators and their airplanes were approximately 10 percent of the total Allied air strength. Regrettably, the army's senior level refused to allow the AS's bombardment forces to train and fight with the experienced British and French air forces. Aware that those two organizations had gained independence from ground forces, the American general staff was not about to do anything that might encourage the AS to entertain the same idea, going so far as to warn US Army aviators that thoughts of independence would not be tolerated: to the WDGS, the airplane existed to support the ground forces, period.[15]

Into the summer of 1918 and toward the finale of the war, army aviators by this time had enough airplanes, training, and organization to perform like an air force. Reconnaissance missions were being flown more and more by US Army pilots, then pursuit aircraft were added to the mix, finally joined by the 1st Day Bombardment Group, which was stood up and entered the fight in time for the St. Mihiel offensive. By Armistice Day the army had twenty pursuit, eighteen observation, six day bombardment, and one night bombardment squadrons in action at the front, with army bombers penetrating as far as 160 miles behind German lines in the process of conducting some 150 bombardment strikes and dropping 138 tons of bombs.[16]

The Bombardment Community

The day bombardment community was the first of Army Aviation to see action in the Great War. The first bombardment unit, the 96th Aero Squadron, arrived in England in November of 1917, believing that it was to receive six months instruction from the Royal Flying Corps (RFC); instead, the squadron was quickly dispatched to France for training at the 7th Aviation Instruction Center at Clermont-Ferrand. There, aircrew were given open access to the entire base while learning the two-seat French Bréguet 14-B2 aircraft. Meanwhile, the enlisted mechanics received instruction at the nearby Renault and Michelin factories where the airplanes were built.[17] Six months later, and assigned to the First Air Service, the 96th deployed in May 1918 to the "zone of advance" for more training at Amanty Airdrome near Gondrecourt; among the primary missions the aircrews were to master included interdicting German lines of communication (LoC), bombardment of massed troops, and reconnaissance. The squadron flew its first combat on 12 June, to rail yards at Domary-Baroncourt. Fulfilling the assigned role to hit LoCs, the strike was rated as successful, particularly after the returning aircraft had to fight off three Germans. Thereafter, the squadron enjoyed a remarkable, if short, history.

Save for parts of fourteen days, August was a month of poor flying weather, causing the squadron's first losses. Taking off in late afternoon, six Bréguets ran into closing weather, forcing them down near Coblenz. The Germans captured all twelve airmen and the airplanes. Despite the month's run of foul weather, the squadron still managed twenty missions, in which a total of 42,947 pounds of bombs were dropped on the enemy. The squadron had missed the June battles at Chateau-Thierry and Belleau Wood but flew in the St. Mihiel and Argonne offensives. The squadron's last mission was several days before the armistice; five Bréguets were bounced by fifteen German Pfalz fighters, but not before all their bombs were dropped precisely on target. Grounded afterward by bad weather, the 96th Aero Squadron flew no more combat before the Armistice. Afterward, it continued to fly in France until returning home, leaving behind an enviable record as the army's day bombardment unit of the war.[18] Three other bombardment squadrons in the First AS, late arrivals to the war, also flew combat missions equipped with the de Havilland DH-4.

The two major campaigns of Chateau-Thierry and St. Mihiel saw the commander of the AS, Major General Mason Patrick, station US Army aviation units alongside French Armee de l'Air squadrons in the French sector. Within the AS, First AEF, the total number of combat squadrons was forty-nine, almost evenly split between American and French, with Brigadier General

Billy Mitchell in operational command. Mitchell thus enjoyed command of just over 700 pursuits, 366 observations, 323 day bombers, and 91 night bombers, the largest aviation force in the western sector during the war, with Mitchell utilizing about 500 of the aircraft for ground support.[19] In the final major offensive of the war, the Meuse-Argonne, air superiority was established by the bombardment squadrons simply because the Germans had come to fear being on the receiving end of aerial bombardment. On 9 October a forming German ground attack was hit by over two hundred bombers, including all four squadrons from the First AS, one hundred pursuit planes, and fifty-three triplace airplanes in full view of Allied ground forces. The infantry troops were duly impressed by the consequences of more than thirty tons of bombs dropped on enemy troops and another thirty-nine tons dropped on other German targets, the twenty-four-hour record for the war.[20]

By the war's end, the AS had established three subordinate air services, the rough equivalent of future air forces. The First Air Service had pursuit, bombardment, and balloon groups, and an extraordinarily large observation contingent; the Second AS was composed along the lines of the First but with two bombardment squadrons; the Third AS, assembled after the Armistice, was the smallest. Both the Second and the Third were heavy on pursuit and, especially, observation units; bombardment in the Second and Third AS was represented by one or two squadrons and none made it into actual combat. The numbers of men, missions, and aircraft of the First and Second Air Services at the time of the Armistice was impressive: at the beginning of the war, the entire Signal Corps Air Service had one squadron (the 1st Aero Squadron) flying barely a dozen obsolete JN-4 Jennys and fifty pilots. By the Armistice on 11 November 1918, AS strength was 20,000 officers and 175,000 enlisted flying or taking care of 740 airplanes in American squadrons, not quite 11 percent of the Allied aviation total. But the cost had not come cheaply: the AS lost 289 airplanes, including those airplanes "piloted by Americans flying with British, French, and Italians." Americans shot down "over 780 enemy aircraft and 73 balloons [but taking] 1,233 AS casualties in France." Of these casualties, "164 were killed in action, 319 were killed in accidents, 335 died of other causes, about 200 were missing in action, about 102 were taken prisoners and about 113 were wounded." Fewer would have died except for a "stubborn refusal" by pilots to wear parachutes.[21] If members of the AS could be asked for the statistic of which they were the proudest, it would almost certainly be the more than seventy-five pilots who became aces, with five or more aerial kills.

To Billy Mitchell and other air power advocates, peace was a mixed blessing; it had come too soon for the AS to prove what the airplane could do in air combat if given the opportunity. The Armistice deprived them of that. Without actual combat to validate various "doctrines" they were deriving from their experiences, they could only be recognized as theorists. They felt cheated.[22] Back in Washington, where these officers reverted to their prewar ranks as captains and majors, there was no advocate for their doctrines in the highest councils of the War Department. It was easy for the senior officers, who continued to see the airplane as little more than flying artillery, to ignore the cries from below. Worse, if possible, Secretary of War Newton D. Baker actively worked against the AS, misrepresenting its achievements in the Great War and maintaining that "strategic bombardment" was not an appropriate mission for the US Army.[23] Still, Army aviation, and particularly bombardment, survived, slowly maturing and establishing a record of peacetime achievement.

Air Corps Tactical School

Whether it's medicine, logistical systems, naval ships, or most anything else, war inevitably accelerate advances in design or in application. That was the case with the airplane in World War I, following which came two decades of theorical energy mentally expended on air power for the next war. The ACTS was established in 1920 for the professional development of army aviation officers, and by the time it moved to Maxwell Field in Alabama in 1931, the sense of excitement over the future was equaled only by the intellectual energy that filled the classrooms. The small bombardment faculty came to dominate the curriculum, proud of their unofficial motto, "We make progress unhindered by custom."[24] Time proved that while they did indeed break from the past, they also misread the future.

From the end of World War I through the following decade, notable aviators of different nationalities pontificated on the future of bombardment aviation, giving the faculty at ACTS much to think about. Italian Air Force general Giulio Douhet, critical of the slaughter in trench warfare, believed the way to avoid it was by targeting the enemy civilian work force at home, a softer and more vulnerable target than hardened troops in the field. Sir Hugh Montague Trenchard, head of Great Britain's independent air arm, likewise advocated "terrorizing" an enemy's vulnerable work force as the key to victory by depletion of the enemy army's essential materials. Sir Basil H. Liddell-Hart wrote of the value of killing civilians while a member of Parliament and future prime minister touted the killing of women and children as the fastest way to victory.

American theorists saw bombardment a bit differently, beginning with Colonel James M. Gorrell of the AS, whose copious writings during and after World War I spoke of the destruction of "manufacturing centers . . . chemical plants . . . aircraft engine manufactures . . . commercial centers and lines of communications," all of which would restrict an enemy's ability to continue a war. Notable was a wartime Gorrell essay on "Area vs. Precision Bombing," which, along with other Gorrell writings, would later inform the ACTS staff.[25] General Billy Mitchell pressed strongly for an independent air force that would attack an enemy before the army and navy were even battle ready, destroy an enemy's vital industrial centers, and disperse the government. Mitchell also became such a persistent political voice that he crossed the line into insubordination and was court-martialed. Distilled to its most basic form, his thesis held that bombers would overfly hostile armies and "make devastating attacks" with high explosives and gas on civilians and industries that would "overpower the home front" and end the war. Armies and navies would be unnecessary.[26] Early in his thinking Mitchell seemingly sought to avoid civilian deaths, but then progressed to the bombing of smaller cities with a debilitating gas to "drive out" the civilians, some or most of whom would undoubtedly die. His later positions became even more extreme as his influence waned.[27]

Chapter 2

Air Corps Tactical School and Influences on Bombardment Doctrine

Strategic Air War: an aerial attack on an enemy's capacity and will to sustain military operations, rather than on the operations themselves.
—*Michael S. Sherry,* The Rise of American Air Power

Major Harold L. George, a World War I bomber pilot who had also served as one of General Mitchell's assistants, was assigned to ACTS in 1931 as chief of the bombardment section, then served as director of the Department of Air Tactics and Strategy in 1934–1935.[1] Believing strongly in strategic air power, it was probably inevitable that he became known as "a prophet of air power."[2] Under his leadership, the small bombardment staff was soon christened the Bomber Mafia for their staunch, unrelenting advocacy of strategic air power, with George focused intensely on "determining how air power will be employed in the next war."[3] Underpinning the instruction was the firm conviction, imparted to all students, that strategic airpower would win wars before army ground forces and the navy could even begin to respond. From this grew the untested—hence, unproven—but nonetheless near-sacred doctrine of high-altitude, daylight precision bombardment—HADPB. Although army doctrines, including those of the air corps, were determined by the WDGS, ACTS faculty taught as if they possessed the gift of pronouncing air corps bombardment doctrine. Supporting George were equally dedicated instruction staff, including Hayward S. Hansell, Laurence S. Kuter, Kenneth Walker, Donald Wilson, George Kenney, and Muir S. Fairchild, all future general officers.

Major General James E. Fechet, chief of the air corps from 1927 to 1931, "wanted a doctrine that would give his air force the responsibility for winning wars independently." This attracted the attention of First Lieutenant Kenneth N. Walker at ACTS, who investigated the subject enough for Fechet to make "the achievement of accurate bombing from high altitudes the priority of the air corps on 2 January 1931."[4] When first conceived, the Doctrine postulated a (then nonexistent) modern bomber flying long distances over enemy territories and armies in daytime, high and fast, avoiding antiaircraft fire and enemy fighters, dropping bombs visually by an accurate bombsight (in development but only for the navy) precisely on military targets, and returning to base safely.[5] Target accuracy would be guaranteed while preventing morally reprehensible civilian casualties. Unlike Europeans, who thought it both useful and necessary to kill civilians, America's geographic isolation had allowed its people, over several centuries, to develop a moral compass that swung differently.[6] So strong was the antipathy toward the deliberate killing of noncombatants that members of Congress were convinced that the deliberate targeting of civilians was a war crime.[7] Targeting enough "chokepoints" or "key nodes"—critical objectives that, when destroyed, would "cripple the whole country," so preached Captain Don Wilson at ACTS—would win wars by so much economic destruction that the enemy would be compelled to sue for peace.[8] The enemy's means of waging war would be destroyed and civilian morale undermined, saving the lives of both aircrews and enemy civilians.[9]

This contrasted with RAF Bomber Command's doctrine of flying large bomber formations at night and dropping bombs over a metropolitan area vice attempting to destroy specific targets. In the early stages of World War II, the RAF sought to fly bomber missions during daylight, but their aircraft were too lightly armed for self-defense and took "murderous losses"; very quickly the RAF lost so many aircraft and men to Luftwaffe fighters that it had no choice but to switch to the relative safety of night bombardment.[10] The darkness protected the bomber force while urban zones were easily identified, either visually or with electronic means; precision targeting, though, was impossible. Bombardment in darkness saved the lives of many RAF airmen, but indiscriminately released ordnance killed far more civilians than enemy. Trenchard and others insisted that civilian deaths and concomitant degradation of morale were justified. Any destruction of military objectives was purely serendipitous.[11]

Two budding technological developments appeared in the mid-1930s, giving hope to the air power enthusiasts at ACTS. First, in 1934 the navy decided it preferred dive-bombing and so passed the Norden bombsight to the army. Bombardiers were trained in the still, clear desert skies of Muroc Army Airfield, California, dropping bombs from twelve thousand feet on well-defined, isolated targets painted on the desert floor; similar performance from above twenty thousand feet seemed assured.[12] Data entered correctly into the bombsight would ensure precise destruction of a valid military target while precluding the civilian casualties abhorrent to the American ethos.[13] The second development was the B-17 heavy bomber, designed in 1934 and operational in 1937. The first truly modern four-engine, all-metal aircraft, it could fly above twenty-three thousand feet with a maximum airspeed of 285 miles per hour (mph). Standard cruise speed was 185 mph, slowed to 165 mph when laden with three to six tons of bombs and in long-range formation. With a combat radius in excess of one thousand miles, it was a formidable strategic bomber.

Conversely, the air corps' first-line pursuit (fighter) aircraft of the 1930s, the Boeing P-26, was unacceptable as a bomber escort. All-metal and capable of speeds of 200 to 230 mph, it was so deficient in all other regimes that it was partly responsible for convincing most of the air corps—especially engineering officers at Wright Field—that no pursuit aircraft could ever be designed to fill the escort mission. An open-cockpit, fixed–landing gear airplane closer to fabric biplanes than to the dazzling B-17, the P-26 was woefully under-armed with a combat radius of a meager 360 miles. And if a new pursuit could be designed, once the Depression hit its worst, the military could not afford to build it; bombers were possible only because the military could piggy-back on civilian aviation's investment in long-range transport aircraft.[14]

Given all that worked against the maturation of a fighter having a comparable performance with the B-17, it became essential for the bombers themselves to be so heavily armed as to become "self-defending." Douhet's assertion that "the bombers would always get through" was (wrongly) taken to heart as the Battle of Britain in 1940 proved that bombers would not always "get through."[15] The ACTS staff loftily pronounced that escorting fighters would be unnecessary as B-17s were armed with numerous .50-caliber Browning machine guns (the final G version sported thirteen). But Douhet meant only that bombers would "get through" to a target because they could overfly a battlefield, not because they could fight their way through defended enemy airspace without benefit of an escort, a subtlety that escaped his ACTS followers.

So convincing were the instructors that "faith in daylight bombing [became] the unshakable belief of all the high Air Forces officers."[16] The bomber advocates, in their certitude of HADPB, never did any realistic testing of the Doctrine to verify (or refute) any part of it. This was despite that in developing the Doctrine, few of the early ACTS instructors knew of the Norden bombsight; they had proceeded on the assumption that "if the advantages of [HADPB] could be established in theory, American ingenuity and inventiveness would provide the means."[17] ACTS instructor Captain Ralph Snavely explained that the "best evidence" for HADPB was Adolph Hitler, whose "mere threat of bombing" caused nations to surrender.[18] The Eighth's own air war would eventually vitiate the Doctrine's credibility.[19]

Instruction at ACTS

Lesson plans of ACTS bombardment staff yield insights to staff thinking. Hal George taught "An Inquiry into the Subject 'War,'"—an overview of abstract issues of air warfare punctuated by theoretical discussions of the airplane as a new weapon of war. It was an eloquent presentation given with confidence and certitude, but it was almost all presumption and logic without evidence.[20] Lieutenant Colonel Muir S. Fairchild presented lessons on

"Air Power and Air Warfare," an elaboration of George's inquiry into war specifically oriented to bombardment. Two other lessons he taught dealt with Don Wilson's "chokepoint" or "industrial fabric" theory, reconstructed using historical events and theoretical effects from the notional bombing of American corporations, the air corps then being forbidden to collect information on foreign concerns.[21]

First Lieutenant Kenneth Walker was the "most zealous" among the faculty regarding HADPB; with his insistence "based on faith rather than on evidence," refutation by students was difficult. His lesson "Driving Home the Bombardment Attack" made the case for HADBP, asserting, "A well-organized, well-planned, and well-flown air force attack will constitute an offense that cannot be stopped."[22] In one sense Walker was correct in asserting that "the bombers will always get through," for the Eighth Air Force always did "get through," never once turning back before reaching a target. Walker, though, only thought in terms of a single mission; he never addressed what would constitute an acceptable loss rate or whether there would be enough bombers left after one mission for subsequent missions.[23]

Other faculty who were disciples of Walker and HADPB were Captain Laurence S. Kuter and First Lieutenant Haywood S. Hansell. The latter, called Possum by all because his nose reminded some of that animal's visage (he even signed his memos and personal letters as Possum), became as strong an advocate as Ken Walker for HADPB, to the point that he was fired in January 1945 as commanding general of a B-29 force for an incapacity to jettison HADPB for literally any other tactic that would put bombs on target. The jet stream and normal weather conditions over Japan proved to be beyond computational abilities of the Norden bombsight in the B-29, obviating completely the effectiveness of HADPB; Hansell, intellectually unable to accept this, was soon replaced by the pragmatic Major General Curtis E. LeMay.[24]

Both Generals Spaatz and Eaker, future commanders of the Eighth, attended ACTS but were affected differently. Spaatz, class of 1925, well before HADPB, was influenced by Billy Mitchell and his advocacy of air power. In Europe Spaatz would argue that air power alone would not only preclude a cross-channel invasion but even bring about Germany's defeat. A devotee of the self-defending bomber from ACTS days, Eaker was never able to accept the need for bomber escorts over Germany—up to the German border, perhaps, but not across, for self-defending heavies were sure to survive over the Third Reich. Aware of the engineers' opinion of the "impossibility" of designing a long-range fighter, Eaker accepted the finding without question. Upon learning that mission 1, to Sottéville-sur-Rouen on 17 August 1942, was not subjected to Luftwaffe attack, Eaker expressed disappointment as though a mission of twelve aircraft flown by green crews could have in any manner definitively proven the theory of the self-defending bomber. Eaker perhaps became even more convinced of the incapacity of fighters as long-range escorts when American fighter pilots formerly in RAF Eagle Squadrons were inducted into the AAF. The aviators formed the 4th Fighter Group, flying very short-range Spitfire Mark Vs given by the RAF; even when replaced with Mk IXs, combat radius was not significantly increased, negating any ability to escort the heavies even as far as Paris. Arguably, most reasonable men would reconsider by summer 1943, and certainly after Schweinfurt II, but there is no indication that Eaker did. After the war General Laurence Kuter candidly acknowledged, "We just closed our minds to [long-range escorts]; we couldn't be stopped, the bomber was invincible."[25] Possum Hansell later engaged in some self-flagellation in admitting that "people like me who didn't know enough about the technical factors were weighing technical features when we shouldn't have been; but [later] it was explained to us by the engineers that it couldn't be done, and it sounded perfectly reasonable."[26] A tiny group of inexperienced men had not only taught but more importantly convinced a significant part of the AAF of a doctrine "more as a matter of faith than of knowledge empirically arrived at," in which thousands of lives and millions of dollars were invested.[27] General Arnold, though never an ACTS student, also as chief of the air forces, accepted HADPB as doctrine. Near the end of May 1942, on a visit to England and Air Chief Marshal Arthur Harris's headquarters, the RAF officer gave Arnold a sales pitch on night area bombing, but Arnold was not sufficiently impressed "to abandon the American daylight precision-bombing plan."[28] Ever pragmatic, by mid-1943 he was ready to jettison the idea of self-defending, and later that year radar bombing began to substitute for HADPB.

Flawed Logic

Manifestly, any important program developed on theory and logic alone without serious testing should be examined with a jaundiced eye. This did not occur with HADPB, so certain were the creators of its viability.[29] One critical error was the happy assumption that the bombardier could always visually acquire the target through the Norden bombsight. The ACTS staff had no concept of the northern European heavy cloud cover that could run solid from a few hundred feet to above twenty thousand feet. Even with cloudless skies, precision bombing from that altitude could be defeated by fog, smoke, camouflage, or surrounding built-up areas near targets. Weather was always the principal limiting element in air operations, with every mission element affected, from size and target selection to bomb and fuel loads. No amount of technology could overcome the persistently awful northern European weather.

Errors of assumption occurred that only actual combat would resolve. Crucially, not just Eaker but also the bombardment community in general trusted that fighters capable of matching the bombers' long ranges and speeds were beyond engineering ability. Hence, bombers would be self-defending by flying in close formations that provided mutual protection against enemy fighters. But seldom in the first two years were formations tight, as pilots had little experience with formation flying. In units like Colonel LeMay's 305th Bomb Group, new pilots had gone directly from the slow, clunky, two-place BT-8 trainer right into the B-17 with no formation work. Escort range could be extended by wing tanks, which the French had demonstrated in World War I and the viability of which was tested in the United States in the mid-1930s, but to no interest. Yet American companies were even then engaged in the design and testing of more powerful yet smaller, more fuel-efficient engines suitable for fighters. But application to a long-range escort was ignored. Hansell would later say that the "failure to see this issue through proved one of [ACTS's] major shortcomings."[30]

A deadly error was the near-willful ignorance of radar and its utilization as a key defensive tool. At least eight nations, including Germany, were developing air defense radar systems before the war, with the RAF and Luftwaffe both experimenting with airborne radars in night fighters. The RAF had employed mobile radar nets and ground controlled intercept (GCI) operationally in the western desert war in 1940–41.[31] Once in combat in 1942, the Eighth's heavies immediately found themselves contending with Luftwaffe fighters directed by German ground controllers staffing air defense radar nets with names like Freya and Würzberg, a revelation that should have merited second thoughts about flying without escorts. Concurrently, the United States and Great Britain were developing airborne radars for accurate bombing in heavily overcast skies. Thus, radar was a known entity, and instead of thinking about whether radar could be utilized by the Germans, thought needed to be given as to how it would be.[32] The Bomber Mafia disregarded the menace by clinging to the delusion that bombers would be very tiny targets in the limitless sky and thus undetectable at high altitude. Ironically, air corps senior officers, including both Eaker and Spaatz, had served as observers in England during the Battle of Britain and were exposed to various radar activities by the RAF hosts, while the US Army itself was busy developing early warning radar nets.[33]

More misjudgments would surface only after heavy bombers began flying combat or once an effective air intelligence capability was in place. Most officers had underestimated the toughness and resiliency of German industry and the spine-stiffening effects of bombing on the German citizenry. Factories that poststrike reconnaissance showed to be destroyed or crushed were back producing in weeks, even days, necessitating more repeat strikes than anticipated. Targeteers advocated follow-up strikes within a day or two of the original strike, but the finicky European weather inevitably refused to cooperate. Experience served as the teacher.

Intended as the air forces' supplement to the overall army submission, AWPD-1 managed to elude the usual (and usually antagonistic) vetting by WDGS offices, ending up instead with General Marshall, who sent it directly to Secretary Stimson, where it was approved.

Air Intelligence: The Missing Key

Perhaps the most egregious error was the absence of any air intelligence capability. Not only was this deficiency present during air corps modernization beginning around 1939, but in creating HADPB, Walker, Hansell, and colleagues completely overlooked requirements for detailed knowledge of potential targets, prestrike photo reconnaissance, enemy air strength, defenses, or poststrike BDA—essentials for long-range strategic bombardment. The planners had not "realized what immense demands their air plan would make upon the wholly inexperienced air intelligence office. [AWPD-1] itself made no provision for gathering target information, organizing photointerpretation to support the reconnaissance aircraft, or determining whether targets selected were the correct ones and whether attacks on them had actually achieved the hoped for results."[34] Air Forces planners were forced to deal with many unknowns, not only because this war would be fought with more advanced aircraft but also because there was available little prewar information about potential targets; Army G-2 was the air corps intelligence provider in lieu of any air intelligence organization, but it vastly favored the ground forces while slighting the aviation community. Most important in the spring of 1942 was what, exactly, would it take for the Eighth Air Force to wage a sustained air offensive against Germany?

The Most Important Relationship

Mostly unappreciated until recently was the exceptionally close relationship that developed between the AAF and RAF air intelligence specialists during the prewar years.[35] It was a tense time of learning and experimentation for the AAF as it evolved into a professional fighting force, while the RAF had already been in almost-daily combat with the Luftwaffe for nearly three years. One of the war's ironies was that the RAF had created a broad-gauged air intelligence capability particularly well suited to the strategic bomber mission while concurrently neglecting to create a strategic bomber force that could make use of those intelligence capabilities. Conversely, the AAF, through the work of the Bomber Mafia at ACTS, had developed the complex theory of HADPB while completely ignoring the requisite need for supporting air intelligence, especially in the crucial areas of targeting and BDA.[36] In an act of untold generosity, the RAF ensured that the Americans received or viewed, beginning in 1940, literally everything they had collected, analyzed, developed, and evaluated in all facets of air intelligence, including top secret materials. Once in the war, the British invited the Americans into their secret world as full partners, from RAF Medmenham to the civilian ministries that played major roles in the targeting and damage assessment requirements.[37] The Americans quickly reciprocated, providing officers and other personnel who, after training by the RAF, sat side by side with their teachers while also bringing to England some of the country's finest minds in economics and other relevant academic expertise to refine targeting strategies. A side benefit was the close personal relationships and trust that quickly grew between all the ranks of the US and British air forces, aiding immeasurably the overall UK-US affiliation.

One related issue was the failure of the AAF to produce a mission-specific aircraft for photo reconnaissance (PR). The performance requirements for such an aircraft were difficult but not impossible: unarmed for best performance; with a service altitude of at least thirty thousand feet, well above enemy fighter capability; speed of 400-plus mph; combat radius of 1,100 miles; capable of carrying a variety of cameras. Most of the thirty-three different variations of the British de Havilland Mosquitos met or exceeded these requirements, but only a few flew with AAF PR squadrons. Two squadrons in the 325th Reconnaissance Wing (Photographic) under Brigadier General Elliott Roosevelt flew the Mark XVI Mosquito, but neither performed the PR mission.[38] Unable to develop its own PR aircraft, the AAF in 1941 began modifying versions of the P-38 Lightning fighter into photo-reconnaissance versions. These variants, although unarmed, were unable to fly above or faster than Luftwaffe fighters, leaving them vulnerable to skilled Luftwaffe pilots. And all P-38s, until the last versions, had chronic engine problems that manifested above seventeen thousand feet, unhelpful when reconnaissance altitudes were often required to be in excess of twenty-five thousand feet.[39]

Chapter 3

Preparing for War

U ntil 1940 the United States Army Air Corps (USAAC) was officially and by law limited to the defense of the Western Hemisphere. Americans, captive to their nation's post-1823 history, preferred to look inward, challenged by a continent to tame and comforted by the country's geographic isolation. Protected by two vast oceans, the United States existed mostly in a perceived state of splendid isolation while always ready (but not necessarily prepared) to defend its interests. In his message to Congress in January 1938, President Franklin D. Roosevelt stressed the need to keep America's enemies "many hundreds of miles" from the United States' continental limits; Congress the same month appropriated funds for a "two-ocean navy," giving it both offensive and defensive authorities. As late as 1940, the air corps' assigned hemispheric defense missions included seven objectives: protect the homeland; deny the establishment of hostile air bases in the Americas; defeat hostile air forces lodged in the hemisphere by attacking their bases; defeat hostile air forces by aerial combat; prevent the landing of expeditionary forces by attacking transports and supply ships; cooperate with the mobile army in ground operations; and operate in support or in lieu of US Navy forces against hostile fleets. The air corps was denied strategic or offensive missions, although it was easily seen that some measure of offensive capability was necessary to fulfill the seven objectives. Congress created the air defense command in 1940 as "primarily a planning agency" to establish "unified air defense systems for critical urban areas." Four "air forces" were established with responsibility for designated "strategic zones" through "air defense planning and organization." Tactical aircraft groups (approximately thirty-six to forty aircraft) were located at bases around the interior as well as in the Philippines, Hawaii, Alaska, and the Panama Canal Zone.[1]

Still, President Roosevelt was not quite at ease. That same year—the year of Munich and appeasement, to the delight of the newly selected chief of the air corps—Roosevelt directed the air corps to produce ten thousand combat aircraft. But then, while following the RAF in its fight with the Luftwaffe in the Battle of Britain in May 1940, Roosevelt decided that initial number to be "insufficient" and demanded another fifty thousand combat aircraft: thirty-five thousand for the air corps, the remainder for naval air.[2]

The ABC Conversations

On 12 November 1940, Admiral Harold R. Stark, chief of Naval Operations, submitted an untitled memorandum to the secretary of the navy for passage to the president giving his thoughts on potential "major decisions" relative to "immediate preparation for war." In the first paragraph Stark opined that it was essential the British win any conflict with Germany because, if so, the United States could "win anywhere." But if the British lost such a conflict, then "while the United States might not *lose everywhere*, neither would it *win anywhere*" (emphasis in the original). As the admiral shared his thoughts predominantly regarding Asia in this twenty-six-page document, he gave the president five decision options labeled A through E using the phonetic language of the time (Able, Baker, etc.) Option D (Dog) was to ally with the British against Germany and Italy with Japan "not initially involved." The document, known as the "Plan Dog" memo, was signed by President Roosevelt in mid-January 1941. The paper advocated a "Europe-first thrust, maximum support to the British, and insistence in full equality in strategic decision making. . . . Receiving the presidential imprimatur, [it became] the guiding document for military leaders as they anticipated US involvement in the war."[3]

Thus with the blessing of the Roosevelt Administration, representatives of the United States and British military met secretly during the first three months of 1941 to draft coordination guidance in the event of war, along the lines of "Plan Dog." The sessions culminated with the signing of United States–British Staff Conversations-1 (ABC-1) on 27 March 1941.[4] Nearly simultaneously the Joint Board of the Army and Navy (predecessor of the Joint Chiefs of Staff) was overseeing another iteration of America's own unilateral and comprehensive war plans, the RAINBOW plans.[5] Both ABC-1 and RAINBOW-5 called for the "main effort" of war to be in Europe, where Italy and Germany, along with Imperial Japan, were allied in the Tripartite Treaty.[6] The conference was to "determine the best methods" by which the United States and British Commonwealth militaries "could defeat Germany and the Powers allied with her" and reach agreements on "Military Cooperation" essential to victory.[7] ABC-1 was notable for its foresight and key provisions either to be implemented immediately after a Japanese attack in the Pacific or considered later in overall strategic planning. ABC-1 served as the precursor for many Allied policy decisions once war arrived. "The final report [ABC-1] provided the following assumptions: The European Theater was primary. German defeat would probably entail an invasion of northwestern Europe, and offensive measures would include 'a sustained air offensive against the German military power.' These assumptions then guided changes to the US military's current operations plan."[8] America and Britain would communicate "continuously in the formulation and execution of strategical policies and plans." Particularly, the nations were jointly to "provide for the ultimate security of the British Commonwealth of Nations" and not solely of Great Britain itself. Strategic missions, in addition to the "sustained air offensive," included air offensives in other locales under enemy control and the aggregation of necessary forces to take the offensive against Germany.[9] With Europe as the "decisive theater," the United States would be responsible for the Atlantic and the British for the Mediterranean; war against Japan would be "defensive" until victory in Europe was assured; and "air superiority" was to be attained over Europe as soon as possible.[10]

At the ABC talks the USAAC had no one person specifically to represent air power as did the RAF, although Colonel Joseph T. McNarney, an air corps officer, was a member of the US Army contingent, and the US Navy group counted several "rated air officers" within their membership. Informally, though, air corps officers from the Headquarters Air Staff A-3 (Operations) office and the recently established Information Division's Intelligence Section (there being no independent Intelligence Office in the air corps), met and "worked closely with" the RAF representative Air Commodore John C. "Jack" Slessor and Colonel McNarney.[11] The Joint Board found one particularly contentious point in the air policy (ABC-2) annex, not because of what it required of the USAAC—a sustained bombardment campaign against Germany and Italy— but because it promised half of the US military aircraft production to the RAF.[12] At the time of ABC-2, "The United States was belatedly in the process of building a force of 84 bombardment groups including 24 heavy groups," but was far from meeting that goal. Ceding half of the air corps' power at that moment was not popular with the generals and admirals.[13] The documents were sent to the president on 2 June but were returned unsigned because the British had not yet approved them. The president's military aide noted that "in case of war the Papers would be returned to the President for his approval."[14] Despite the absence of a presidential signature, the accords remained a north star for future War Department guidance. The language of ABC-1 on its face and for the first time ever gave an official and explicit overseas offensive role to the United States Army Air Forces (USAAF, so renamed on 20 June 1941).[15]

In June 1941 Brigadier General Carl Spaatz moved from director of the recently authorized Air War Plans Division (AWPD) to chief of air staff under Major General Arnold, commanding general of the air forces and deputy chief of staff for air. Spaatz's career had been exceptional: following the Great War, his expertise was in pursuit aviation until switching to the bombardment path, always earning praise for his knowledge, leadership, and sound judgment. Strong performances in diverse operational and staff assignments polished his reputation. Spaatz had met Major Hap Arnold after returning from France with three air combat victories and the Distinguished Service Cross (DSC); he soon joined Arnold as his deputy at Rockwell Field, San Diego. Sharing many objectives for the air corps, especially for an independent air force, the two became the closest of friends. The ABC agreements came early the next year, and then events in Europe in the spring and early summer led the president to direct the new Air Forces to generate new aircraft production needs, with minimal delay.

Hal George, now a colonel, had barely begun his tenure as the chief of the AWPD when General Arnold assigned him to respond to FDR's 9 July mandate to develop Air Forces "production requirements for a war that assumed Germany would be the main enemy and Britain the main ally."[16] Lieutenant Colonel Kenneth N. Walker and Major Haywood Hansell, two AWPD officers of superior caliber—and not coincidentally former members of the Bomber Mafia—summarized the task as constructing "a mobilization plan based upon new and unprecedented requirements."[17] Desiring one more full-time participant, George pried Major Laurence S. Kuter (also formerly Bomber Mafia) from Army General Staff S-3 (Operations), where General Arnold had specially assigned him.[18] These officers had either studied together as classmates at ACTS, served together as faculty members, or both. All were exceptionally able officers and proselytizers for the Doctrine. With passionate certitude serenely undisturbed by any scintilla of doubt, and in smoldering contumacy against the War Department's position on doctrine, Hal George's small group was the best able in the Air Forces to weave the Doctrine into a foundation for an air war that would culminate in the defeat of Germany or Japan.[19] Assisted by several colleagues of specialized expertise, these four convened to produce a seminal paper for the president, a strategic bomber force never far from their minds.[20] The result was "straight American air power doctrine as developed at ACTS but with the provision to support an invasion to make the plan more acceptable" to the general staff planners who wanted no independent strategic mission for the air forces.[21]

The First Document for Global Air War

"Guided only by the general provisions of ABC-1 and RAINBOW-5," George's group produced Air War Plans Division-1 (AWPD-1), a "prescient document" that far exceeded the written letter of their tasking—as perhaps intended by General Arnold.[22] The planners, drafting in secret, took advantage of the generous latitude inherent in the literal wording of assignments from the army chief of staff and created a detailed blueprint for defeating Germany in a total air war. It reflected three achievements: it was the "most important document in the doctrine of strategic air warfare against Germany in World War II . . . the first of its kind written in Air War Plans Division . . . [and] the first of its kind written in the world."[23] AWPD-1 detailed the strategies, operational status, and materials required to win a global war by strategic bombardment.[24] And it reflected precisely the needs of HADPB.

AWPD-1 anticipated an air corps of 2.1 million men with 6,834 bombers in 98 groups, 1,708 aircraft in reserve, and a monthly replacement rate of 1,245 airplanes,[25] plus an initial 8,748 fighters with 3,244 replacements, assuming a "production capacity" sufficient "to replace the combat elements every five months."[26] A continual production of 770 four-engine bombers per month and 416 fighters was just for an air war against Germany.[27] The numbers, audacious by any count, "staggered the imagination but proved to be remarkably accurate."[28] Those numbers enabled the USAACUSAAC to conduct a "decisive air offensive against Germany"[29] but with resources also for war in the Far East and defense of the Americas. The air campaign against Germany encompassed four subordinate objectives:

1. reduction of Axis naval operations: the Battle of the Atlantic was still a close-run affair, and active American participation was required to ensure an adequate supply chain for the Allies and the movement of essentials for future amphibious assaults including the cross-channel invasion;
2. restriction of Axis air operations, for multiple objectives;
3. strategic bombing to deprive the Germans of necessary war materials to degrade military operations; and
4. support for a cross-channel invasion leading to a land war with Germany.

War was predicted to last twenty-six or twenty-seven months in five phases: mobilization; training, materials production, and preparation of bases; deployment to England and initial action against the enemy; an air offensive against Germany; and a cross-channel invasion (after which aviation participation apparently would cease). That four staunch air power advocates wrote a remarkably balanced war plan does not detract from their personal beliefs that strategic bombardment alone would, or could, bring final victory.[30]

Auxiliary participant Reserve Captain Richard "Dick" D'Oyly Hughes thought the plan "a magnificent piece of staff work."[31] Aware that US industries, banks, and other financial institutions had underwritten much of the German industrial development and construction, another reserve intelligence officer, Major Malcolm Moss, acquired from business contacts massive amounts of data, including blueprints and engineering specifications on the industries and the electric power generating and distribution systems in Germany. Then, "using these sources, together with scientific journals and trade magazines, it was possible to put together a comprehensive target study."[32] The data was woven into an "infrastructure web"—a concept developed by Don Wilson at ACTS—in which destruction in one sector would "cascade" throughout the entire web to the detriment of all other parts. The web prioritized five "strategic target sets," including "the Luftwaffe, electrical power, transportation centers, and morale," with three subsets of "airfields, aircraft production, and aluminum/magnesium production."[33] The strategic targets broke as follows: "154 industries within the web; 50 electrical power plants; 47 transportation networks; 27 synthetic oil refineries; 18 aircraft assembly factories, six aluminum plants; and six 'sources of magnesium.'" The planners calculated the weight of ordnance needed for destruction, loss rates of aircraft and crews, and number of personnel required to support, maintain, and fly the force.[34] That the estimates were, in the event, almost uniformly on the low side does not detract from the foresight that went into identifying critical targets; the officers were, after all, planning for a war of unimaginable scope.

The officers figured a production run of 11,800 heavy bombers—of which there were two models, Boeing's B-17 Flying Fortress and Consolidated Vultee's B-24 Liberator—would be utilized in both Europe and Asia in the daylight bombardment role. This conclusion was left untouched by General Arnold, who, having determined that neither bomber would be satisfactory for an air war against the Japanese home islands, had already placed orders for the B-29 Superfortress still only in blueprints at Boeing. That aircraft would simultaneously be test flown and produced from factories still under construction, and with each airplane undergoing developmental changes daily. Victory in Europe required over thirty-one thousand Fortresses and Liberators during three and a half years.[35]

Errors and omissions notwithstanding, AWPD-1 was nonetheless a "reasonably accurate forecast of the US strategic bombing effort against Germany," despite being written under the extreme pressures of nine days and for the president of the United States.[36] It would be unfair to be critical of the authors for their errors in calculation and mistakes of judgment, for they were going to fight a war new to world history and do it with new weaponry. A year hence, when Ira Eaker assumed command of the Eighth's strategic bomber force, he was destined to contend with these issues. It was great good fortune that not only did the planners have the foresight to think big but even more so that Generals Arnold and Marshall believed in them. Hansell, in discussing the intense desire of the four like-thinking friends laboring in close collaboration to produce a revolutionary plan, would say years later that "without our previous service together on the [ACTS] faculty it would have been quite impossible to produce a plan of this magnitude in so brief a period of time."[37]

Larry Kuter spent four hours briefing Marshall on the plan; suitably impressed, he had Kuter brief the general staff, some members of which "were vehemently critical." Nonetheless Marshall then had Hal George and the other three brief Secretary of War Stimson, "thereby circumventing the Joint Board where the navy might tear it to pieces." Stimson accepted it as presented.[38] AWPD-1 was indeed a most remarkable document.

Chapter 4

The Mighty Eighth at the Beginning

ARCADIA

Fires were still burning at Naval Base Pearl Harbor on 7 December 1941 as the United States Navy became the first service to take the war to an enemy by unrestricted air and submarine warfare, "to paralyze the Japanese economy and cut off food supplies to the Japanese civilian population."[1] Five months later the two navies met in the Coral Sea, where an American task force suffered a tactical defeat while winning a much more important strategic victory. The US Navy's decisive victory off Midway Atoll came the next month, and then the first US invasion of enemy-held territory when the First Marine Division landed on Guadalcanal and Tulagi islands in the Solomons on 7 August. The navy had also been in an undeclared war against Kriegsmarine U-boats in the North Atlantic since 1940. The navy, battle-tested since the Revolution, became a two-ocean force in the 1800s, adding land- and carrier-based naval air forces in the 1920s, complete with operating doctrines to guide it during the first year of this war. Conversely, the USAAF had little in the way of experience, resources, and history in 1941. It was instructed to create overseas combat air forces literally from the ground up, replete with trained flying personnel, modern aircraft, land bases, and an array of newly required support assets.[2] Building for war while also concurrently fighting it wasn't enough: the air forces had also to face demands from the navy for the lion's share of resources, which it justified because the US Sea Services had been fighting in the Pacific since Pearl Harbor. The air corps could only hope to send its first bombers against German targets, and then just in the occupied countries, by mid-1942.

In General Arnold's first four years of leadership, the AAF had only increased from 2,092 officers and 21,500 enlisted men to 22,000 officers and 270,000 enlisted, while the aircraft inventory showed just 1,100 aircraft "fit for combat service" and another 1,900 tagged indiscriminately as "combat types," rated by Arnold as "unsuitable."[3] The number on 7 December included 159 four-engine airplanes, mostly B-17s, of which 26 were in the Philippines and 13 in California under Hal George preparing to transit the Pacific to the Philippines via Hawaii. Most would be lost, either on Oahu or in the Philippines, by 10 December. In Washington, DC, ARCADIA, the first wartime US-British planning and strategy summit, convened on Christmas Eve 1941, sitting until 14 January. Among the many significant decisions was an agreement for the American military heads to sit as the Joint Chiefs of Staff (JCS), mirroring the British Chiefs of Staff (BCS); the two staffs jointly convened would become the Combined Chiefs of Staff (CCS). The CCS spoke with one voice to the president and prime minister, the political leadership being the final deciding voices on the direction of the war. Guided by the ABC-1 agreements, the two nations concurred on meeting periodically in the future for developing a worldwide strategy, the "Germany First" decision of ABC-1 unchallenged. At General Marshall's suggestion, the president designated General Arnold as chief of staff, AAF, to satisfy Churchill's desire to have an American "opposite member" to the head of the RAF.[4] Soon after, Arnold issued directives to move smartly toward the "rapid buildup of an American heavy bomber force in Britain, striking at Germany itself with a thousand Flying Fortresses and Liberators by April [1943]."[5]

Chancellor Adolph Hitler, honoring the Tripartite Treaty, declared war on the United States on 11 December, presenting the US Army, soon to engage the Japanese on Luzon, with a much greater demand for immediate resources.

The army quickly derived an initial stratagem of landing six divisions in France as soon as practicable—an incursion rather than an invasion. Establishing a bridgehead on either the Cotentin or Breton peninsulas would commit US forces to fight German forces with the immediate objective of compelling Hitler to reposition to France some of the three million Nazi troops then in the USSR and relieving pressure on the Russian army and Premier Josef Stalin.[6] But with "the current rate of [war matériel] production, the heavy matériel responsibilities to Allies, the status of trained units, and, above all, the dearth of shipping, the United States could not at an early date deploy and support in a European campaign any large forces."[7] Army assessments determined just two US divisions could be provided for the bridgehead; four divisions would have to come from the already overextended British Army.[8] Most worrisome, a bridgehead would require fast-response, on-call air and naval gunfire support if there was to be any chance of it withstanding German assaults until a larger force could be put ashore in the spring of 1943.

The British, already at war with Germany for thirty months, were now as consumed in the Far East as the Americans, leaving the British Army (BA) with even greater manpower shortages than the Americans. And Great Britain was soon to lose ninety thousand troops with their impending surrender to the Japanese in Singapore. Hence, the BCS saw this "incursion" as naïve folly, especially for a green, untested army, and raised instead a joint military operation in northwest Africa. A successful operation there would ideally siphon Vichy French colonial forces potentially aligned with Germany to the Allied side while enabling British forces to trap the Afrika Korps between them and the Eighth British Army in Cyrenaica. Most important, it would provide an opportunity for the US Army to meet the Wehrmacht on the battlefield in limited scale and gain needed experience in fighting Germans before facing a more battle-hardened Wehrmacht force on the Continent.[9]

At ARCADIA it was decided that America's role in any northwest Africa operation would be to provide a mobile reserve corps with an air support component. General Arnold, traditionally referred to in the air forces as "the chief," turned to III Air Support Command (III ASC), commanded by Colonel Asa North Duncan at Army Air Field Savannah, Georgia, to fill that role.[10] On 2 January 1942 Duncan was ordered to form an "air task force" drawing from III ASC. Principal subordinate units selected for the command were added on 19 January, and on 28 January Headquarters and Headquarters Squadron, Eighth US Air Force, was activated in Savannah's National Guard Armory. The US Eighth Air Force, in which some 350,000 men and women would serve by V-E Day—and suffer over 26,000 killed in action (KIA), more than the total KIA for the entire United States Marine Corps during the war—came to life with an initial enrollment of ten personnel.

The CCS developed three options for the two political leaders. First, GYMNAST/SUPER-GYMNAST, the land invasion of Northwest Africa, would lead to a pincers operation to snare the Afrika Korps in Tunisia. Second option was the American scheme of a limited incursion into France, codenamed SLEDGEHAMMER, establishing a small bridgehead in an attempt to compel the Germans to redeploy forces from the eastern front where 150 Wehrmacht divisions were grinding down the Russians. Third was a delayed invasion of Europe, codenamed ROUNDUP, which would either be the "expansion of and breakout from" the SLEDGEHAMMER bridgehead in the spring of 1943 or, should that operation be canceled, a larger invasion of France in the same timeframe. The British were insistent on GYMNAST; the Americans pushed hard for SLEDGEHAMMER.

Eaker and VIII Bomber Command

Summoned to Washington from California in January 1943, Colonel Ira C. Eaker entered Hap Arnold's office on Saturday morning the eighteenth to be informed by the chief that he was to leave for England to "understudy the British and start bombardment as soon as I can get you some planes and crews." Eaker, a career pursuit pilot, was stunned at being given a bomber command until Arnold told him that he was expected to instill the "fighter spirit in bombardment aviation."[11] That evening, Arnold invited Eaker to a dinner hosted by Arnold's deputy, Major General Walter Weaver; beforehand, the chief handed Eaker a schedule for combat aircraft arriving in England. Dinner guests included Air Chief Marshal Sir Charles "Peter" Portal, chief of air staff (C/AS) and head of the RAF, already well-known to Arnold and other Americans, and Air Vice Marshal Arthur Tavers "Bert" Harris, the new air officer commanding-in-chief of RAF Bomber Command. Over dinner, the schedule for the new Eighth Air Force's combat aircraft anticipated arrival times in England was passed to the RAF guests; it anticipated 3,500 aircraft and two hundred thousand men in the United Kingdom by April of 1943— barely fourteen months away—with the first tranche to arrive in March, three months hence. Whether the guests accepted these early figures as valid or speculation was soon moot; the numbers were superseded by another set from Arnold's office the next month. That schedule called for the deploy- ment before year's end of fourteen heavy bomber groups and two fighter groups. One heavy bomber group would initially consist of four squadrons of twelve airplanes each plus twelve aircraft in group reserve/maintenance.[12] January of 1943 would see an additional fifteen heavy bomber groups and thirteen fighter groups arriving in the UK.[13] By January of 1944, the Eighth would have 2,016 heavy bombers and 1,500 fighters.[14] President Roosevelt later reviewed the numbers, then conveniently passed them to Prime Minister Churchill. Eaker could be forgiven for believing that he would be bombing Germany with several hundred airplanes before Christmas.

Events moved quickly following the dinner on the eighteenth, with General Arnold on 26 January 1942 recommending to Army Chief of Staff General George C. Marshall that the Air Forces pull together all the disparate Army Air units in the British Isles and create a single command—US Army Air Forces in Britain (AAFIB) and lodge within it the Eighth's headquarters/base component plus bomber and interceptor commands.[15] Marshall concurred. Arnold promoted Eaker to brigadier general at January's end and ordered him to England to assume temporary command of AAFIB. Separately, VIII Bomber Command was activated at Langley Field, Virginia and VIII Interceptor Command, soon renamed Fighter Command, was concurrently activated at Selfridge Field in Michigan. Bomber command would eventually become Eaker's while fighter command would go to Brigadier General Frank O'Driscoll "Monk" Hunter, a fighter pilot in World War I with eight confirmed air-to-air kills and five DSCs and who, like the Eighth Air Force, was born in Savannah.[16]

Before Eaker departed for England in mid-February, Arnold verbally imparted five explicit objectives: establish a "bomber command head- quarters"; locate and prepare airfields for the arrival of bomber groups;

"understudy" the RAF to "insure competent and aggressive command and direction, absorb all you can from them and when ready commence bombing targets in Germany and Western Europe"; prepare training schedules for all US units arriving; and "submit recommendations" for changes in training and equipment.[17] Eaker's assignment was a heavy challenge: ultimately, it "turned out to be the biggest logistical, operational, and diplomatic task in the entire Army Air Forces."[18] The Eighth would be the first US command in the air war against the Third Reich; it would also be, for the foreseeable future, the only US military force taking the war directly to the Germans. Arnold promoted Brigadier General Carl A. Spaatz to major general and anointed him Eighth Air Force commander-designate. AAFIB would then come directly under Spaatz, as well.

Chapter 5

England

General Eaker and six staff officers departed for England at the end of January 1942, arriving in London on 21 February to be greeted warmly by Bert Harris, much less so by Major General James E. Chaney, an AAF officer and commanding general, US Army Forces British Isles. Chaney was aloof and disinterested. Eaker carried with him not only Arnold's earlier verbal instructions but also written instructions from Arnold captioned "Details Which Must Be Accomplished by Bomber Command Advanced Echelon," received before leaving Washington with a copy concurrently cabled to General Chaney.[1] There were at least sixteen separate to-do items beginning with "Report to General Chaney and establish relations with his staff." Several were of a housekeeping nature, including "Prepare General Spaatz's headquarters" and "Work out training schedules and areas." Most were substantive, with one-third concerned partly or fully with the British government and/or the RAF, particularly regarding agreements and technical requirements necessary for US aircraft to operate in British airspace. Several covered the establishment of bases, protocols, operating instructions, and measures essential to enable the AAF to begin bombing quickly after arrival. Eaker's written instructions made no mention of the bomber force he was to command, nor of the AAF units present in England for purposes unrelated to the Eighth. As the war progressed, the Eighth's mission did not greatly change until 1944, although its description received a cosmetic makeover: "The basic mission of the Eighth Air Force [is] to fatally weaken the military economy of Germany."[2]

Major General Chaney

General Arnold's written instructions required Eaker to place himself "under the supervision" of Chaney but gave no elaboration. Quickly, Eaker found that positive relations with Chaney and his staff were hopeless and serving under Chaney's "supervision" would undermine Arnold's verbal instructions. Chaney's icy greeting to Eaker was his way of expressing that he "wanted no part of Arnold's plan to set up a separate air force command," despite it having already been firmly decided by Arnold and approved by Marshall.[3] Chaney was wedded to his interpretation of the ABC agreements as he had discussed them with Marshall and Arnold in autumn of 1941; he seemed unaware of AWPD-1. Discussions the previous fall had intimated that small air corps units coming to the United Kingdom might be placed in areas that mirrored the generic corps districts in the United States, regions in which units from all army components were under the command of one general officer as the corps commander. Now seemingly unaffected by even the possibility of change wrought by war, Chaney intended to order corps-area commands established across the British Isles within which "token forces" of Army Air units would be placed to support the British. He assumed without cause that Eaker's still nonexistent bomber force was the total offensive force arriving in the UK and he meant to parcel out its components among the various corps—and then command them all from his own office. He gave no hint of recognizing the exigencies of the day or that he had ever consulted the British about this plan.

Eaker realized that Chaney's thinking was outdated.[4] Although Chaney was an air forces general, by dint of his assignment he reported directly to General Marshall and not Arnold, allowing him the conceit that he need listen only to the chief of staff. In London he was served by an indolent staff who wore civilian clothes, worked bankers' hours, took weekends off, saw little import in their mission in England, and were happily ignorant of the new direction of the US-British relationship and of Washington's wartime decisions. Once the establishment of a logistics base and the subsequent buildup of supplies and men for a potential cross-channel attack—Operation BOLERO—was ordered by Marshall in April of 1942, Chaney did not much bother with it even though it was a high priority. Perhaps worst for US-UK military relations, neither Chaney nor his staff were held in respect by their British counterparts—and apparently neither noticed nor cared.[5]

Chaney first attempted to corral Eaker and his small staff by presenting Eaker with a separate list of in-house instructions.[6] This list made no reference to Arnold's instructions while giving Eaker just two—make studies and recommendations of RAF Bomber Command procedures and perform reconnaissance of possible British airfields for incoming AAF units. The instructions forbid Eaker from making any agreements with the RAF prior to submitting a reconnaissance report to Chaney's office. Eaker was then admonished not to make any recommendations to AAF headquarters in Washington but to report instead to Chaney. In contrast, instructions in Arnold's letter were specific and focused; Eaker, of course, had no thought of withholding information from Arnold.

Chaney sought also to exercise command authority over Eaker and his staff by making them adjuncts to his own staff. He intended to assign all arriving American bombers to the RAF for night bombing missions, contrary to decisions already made. It was the same for his pending decision to forbid US pursuit groups any mission other than defense of the isles, again contravening prior Washington decisions.[7] By isolating himself from the decision processes on both sides of the Atlantic, Chaney existed in an informational void, removed from both decision and plans loops in a fast-moving process. Little wonder, perhaps, that Chaney's staff, with only four army air members out of thirty-five, were openly "antagonistic to Eaker's mission" and treated the newcomers as a hindrance through inattention. Eaker kept the chief informed of these issues, writing that in Chaney he found "a complete inflexibility of mind." In a gross and unacceptable display of disrespect and incivility, Chaney's staff intended to quarter General Eaker and his officers in tents in a nearby London park rather than spend time locating suitable lodging. Correspondence from Eaker's small group, sent through Chaney's office as demanded by protocol and using the phrase "Army Air Forces," was treated with disdain; Chaney's staff returned it all with a directive to remove the word "air" from Army Air Forces.[8]

By May the principle of "theater air forces of each nation" existing as separate entities under one Allied command had been firmly agreed upon by the national political leaderships at the strong insistence of both the American and British. Chaney, in his hubris, failed to remain current with senior-level decisions, completely missing the implications of the agreement. Arnold and Spaatz, meanwhile, had gained Marshall's concurrence that the US Army's forces in the UK would organize functionally vice divide geographically. There would be no corps areas.[9]

Bert Harris

After Harris's welcome, RAF escorts drove Eaker and his staff to Buckinghamshire and Walters Ash, a tiny residential area in the Chiltern Woods. Scattered among a few private homes, a church, and a manor house, disguised against Luftwaffe raiders, was the heart of RAF Bomber Command. Much of the facility, code-named SOUTHDOWN, was underground and that above ground concealed by heavy forest. Eaker refused the instruction to place himself "under Cheney's supervision," relying instead on Arnold's verbal directive to understudy RAF Bomber Command by deciding it would be impossible to work in London with the RAF as required. His staff officers were lodged in comfortable RAF quarters while Eaker enjoyed the hospitality of Air Vice Marshal and Mrs. Harris. On 23 February Eaker officially stood up VIII Bomber Command headquarters and for the next weeks labored on its immediate needs in anticipation of the arrival of the Eighth's heavy bombers and crews while his staff considered RAF Bomber Command procedures, standards, and requirements. Identifying airfield locations for the many fighter and bomber groups in the Eighth of necessity carried a high priority. One unusual document to come from the joint labors was a "dictionary with translations of the terminology, chiefly of the technical institutions"—necessitated by a shared heritage with "different languages."[10]

Eaker scouted a campus five miles from SOUTHDOWN that fit his requirements for VIII Bomber Command headquarters—a sprawling girls' school named Wycombe Abbey, outside of the village of High Wycombe. It was perfect. Not only was the institution on a lovely, heavily wooded estate in excess of sixty acres, but it was also within a fifteen-minute automobile ride of other important posts: SOUTHDOWN; RAF Medmenham with the Central Interpretation Unit (CIU), photographic and standard libraries, and model makers; the RAF's Photo-Reconnaissance Unit and PR Squadrons at RAF Benson; and (later) the AAF's 7th PR Group airfield at Benson's auxiliary airfield, Mount Farm, along with the 325th Photo Wing (Reconnaissance). Codenamed PINETREE, Wycombe Abbey was also a half-hour drive from future Eighth Air Force headquarters on the capacious grounds of Hampton Palace. The cadre of Eighth Air Force personnel, 1,850 officers and men, departed the United States by ship on 27 April. They would dock at Liverpool on 11 May for transport to PINETREE.[11]

War Department General Staff Reorganization

March was a pivotal month for General Marshall and the WDGS, which affected Arnold and Spaatz, as well as Eaker and the first units of the Eighth. On 3 March the JCS released the Eighth from participation in planning for GYMNAST, implying that it would have no role in a North African invasion, leaving the budding air force unanchored. Six days later, with the intent to prosecute the war much more efficiently, the entire US Army was, by executive order, restructured and greatly simplified.[12] Its previous Byzantine structure (with nearly 350 individual offices, bureaus, branches, etc.) was eliminated and replaced with three principal commands: ground and air forces and service of supply. Instead of requiring the chief of staff personally to supervise a large part of the army, lieutenant generals heading the three commands were given great latitude, authority, and discretion in managing their part of the army. The chief of staff was freed to concentrate on winning the war, guided by the revamped WDGS, itself greatly reduced in size. The "first function" of the WDGS—"strategic direction and control of operations"—was to be sole province of the powerful War Plans Division (WPD).[13]

The blueprint for a reimagined WPD had been sent to Marshall by Arnold before Pearl Harbor, influenced greatly by Army Deputy Chief of Staff McNarney, a "seasoned Air Forces officer [who] had long served in WPD."[14] Within the new army command structure, all deputy chiefs of staff positions would remain positions of power, with responsibilities "mainly in the fields of staff administration, budget and legislation" and all delegated duties. WPD was redesignated Operations and Plans Division (OPD), with orders to "direct military operations insofar as necessary to carry out the orders of the Chief of Staff . . . the powers, duties and organization of OPD were elaborated in such a way that enabled the staff to meet the heavy demands made of it by General Marshall." OPD was viewed as the "Washington Command Post," so it was not surprising that, when the staff under new office chief Brigadier General Dwight D. "Ike" Eisenhower considered new names, almost all had either "Command" or "Combat Headquarters" in the title. While Marshall seemed amenable to any of these on their face, he quietly substituted "Operations and Plans" instead.[15] The director's position was from then on considered as a "command" assignment, vice a staff job: the director was to be "running the war, at least from the army's side." As Ike was departing for a trip to London near month's end, Marshall directed him to "integrate" the AAF units in the UK into the Eighth, whose mission it would be to "attain air supremacy in the skies over northern Europe as a vital prerequisite" for a future invasion.[16]

The UK Buildup

With the War Department streamlining for war, the JCS on 14 March directed the "buildup of US ground and air forces" in the UK as the most propitious location "for an eventual offensive against Germany."[17] Quickly thereafter, the air staff issued its Plan for Initiation of US Army Bombardment Operations in the British Isles on 20 March. This "strategic air offensive" against the Third Reich was followed by OPD's overall scheme for waging war against the Axis in Europe, known as Plan for Operations in Northwestern Europe, to which the air staff's bombardment plan was annexed. OPD's all-encompassing plan called for BOLERO to support either SLEDGEHAMMER in late 1942 (should the Russians appear in danger collapse) or ROUNDUP the follow-ing spring. Regardless, at its most basic, the Americans needed to convince the British that some kind of cross-channel invasion was preferable to an African campaign.[18] SLEDGEHAMMER required the four British divisions now more than ever as the US became even more deeply engaged in the Pacific, with major commitments to Allies in that region. Eisenhower told Marshall that "[the Pacific nations] may excuse failure, but they will not excuse abandonment."[19] At home "aircraft production was in flux" as every army air unit in the world clamored for more airplanes and parts; but even if there were planes and parts, there was as yet no organized air cargo service, far from enough pilots and navigators, and demand for maritime shipping far exceeded hulls. No wonder, then, when the president queried the JCS about sending "1,000 airplanes and 100 thousand troops to Australia," panic permeated the WDGS.[20]

Thinking ahead, on the last day of March, Spaatz—perhaps after infor-mal discussions with Eisenhower, whom he had known since West Point—recommended to Arnold that the missionless Eighth headquarters element be sent to England to "assume operational control" over all AAFIB commands in the United Kingdom. Spaatz thought the Eighth should serve as "the intermediate command headquarters" between the army's European Theater headquarters in London and the other AAF commands in England, relieving the theater headquarters (and General Chaney) of supervising the air forces subordinate units. The War Department required only a week to approve.[21]

General Marshall and principal presidential advisor Mr. Harry Hopkins arrived in London on 8 April to make one more effort at convincing the British of the admittedly few merits of SLEDGEHAMMER. There was still modest optimism among the Americans that the British favored SLEDGEHAMMER, because at times "the Prime Minister seemed to be enthusiastically support-ive" of it. But they were allowing themselves to be fooled as they "missed [Churchill's] signs of cooling toward the idea . . . [the] Americans, unaware of Churchill's sometimes indirect methods, seemed to ignore these signs." Separately, on the seventh the War Department ordered headquarters, Eighth Air Force, to England to serve as the umbrella command of all units in AAFIB, as Spaatz had suggested, with General Eaker as temporary forward commander.[22] This step insured Chaney would have no control over any air forces unit, a measure that Arnold likely had first quietly cleared with Chaney's reporting senior, General Marshall. With the switch from a mobile air task force to the bombardment of Germany, air staff planners also figured the Eighth to receive "twenty-three heavy bombardment groups, four medium bombardment groups, five light bombardment groups, four dive-bomber groups, and thirteen pursuit [fighter] groups." But when firm orders were cut, they were for just two pursuit groups, the 5th Photo Reconnaissance Group, and one B-17 unit, the 97th Bombardment Group (Heavy).[23]

Chapter 6

Spaatz

General Spaatz was officially named commander of the Eighth Air Force—the "first numbered air force created for offensive operations"—on 5 May at Bolling Field, Washington DC, with Colonel North Duncan remaining as chief of staff.[1] Upon departing for England at the end of May Spaatz, too, received something of a letter of instruction from the chief, a short paper concerned with "channels of communications." Although Spaatz knew Arnold's thinking well, he also had his own ideas for the employment of heavy bombardment, developed from his observations of the RAF two years before. Meeting Marshall and Secretary Stimson separately earlier in May, he explained that he intended to "draw the Luftwaffe into combat and destroy it in a battle of attrition"; to force the Luftwaffe to come up and fight, he would destroy economic and military targets of importance that, if not defended, would push the Third Reich toward defeat.[2] Spaatz recognized that any cross-channel operation would require air superiority, if not air supremacy; personally he believed that air power alone would not only obviate any invasion, but could even push the Third Reich into surrender.

Arnold's Letters

In April Eaker responded to a very unofficial inquiry from Spaatz, in Washington and near Arnold's side. The subject of Eaker's cable—which carried no reference—was a bland "Study of General Arnold's Letters," meaningless to casual or inquiring eyes. Eaker began deceptively with "General Arnold's letters to General Chaney and Air Chief Marshall [sic] Portal . . . have been carefully read and studied . . . the following is believed pertinent to the very important questions raised therein." Eaker then continued with deliberate circumspection, giving no hint that he was precisely dissecting each element of Operation SLEDGEHAMMER, which he was likewise careful not to identify in any manner. Yet anyone with access to SLEDGHAMMER details would have immediately recognized that each element of that operation was being sliced into individual issues with application to the capabilities of the Eighth Air Force. In this three-page missive, Eaker provided a detailed critique, written in a formal tone as if he knew it would be presented to or read by officers at the highest levels of the WDGS. Eaker concluded by opining that the "original all-out air plan for the destruction of the German war effort by air action alone was feasible and sound, and more economical than any other method available." In short, don't bother with a small bridgehead or whackadoo invasion scheme but instead proceed with the earlier submitted air plan. The letter closed with an assessment by "the Intelligence Section of this Headquarters" that found "many worthwhile targets" within range of the Fortresses in France and the Low Countries, which would "cripple the German ability to wage war and retain its hold on the occupied countries."[3] Eaker was politely touting the air plan for the first three heavy bombardment groups he had submitted to Spaatz back on 25 March. It would be, like other plans, cast aside for something entirely unwanted.

While decisions by the CCS on the initiation of an air war were pending, the debate among the US and British militaries continued over when or whether the Allies would cross the channel; but there seemed no question that the Eighth Air Force wanted to strike the Germans on the Continent as soon as it could. A vexatious unknown for Eaker and VIII Bomber Command was, When would they receive airplanes and the aircrews to fly the missions?

At home the few available combat aircraft were diminishing as Headquarters Air Forces (HqAF) sent heavy bomber groups elsewhere, Arnold's list of intended units for England notwithstanding; a B-24 group for the Eighth was ordered to the China-Burma-India theater in March, and then a second Liberator group destined for England was redirected to the Southwest Pacific in April. Each diverted group meant a loss of sixty airplanes and crews that could be bombing the Germans. Eaker had been in charge of VIII Bomber Command barely four months and had already been denied more than 150 Liberators, crucial resources for the Eighth.[4] On April Fool's Day, Eaker learned that just 25 aircrews out of an expected 157 had reported to the recently established Combat Crew Replacement Center (CCRC) at RAF Bovingdon, given to the Americans as a training facility. May passed and now June was fading and Eaker still had no airplanes.[5]

Spaatz Assumes Command

Arnold formally installed Spaatz as commander of the Eighth on 10 May at Bolling Field and then sat to discuss the Eighth's deployment to England. Spaatz talked specifically with Arnold about procedures and processes once the Eighth deployed and laid down four desiderata for the chief. As subsequently entered into his command diary, Spaatz: (1) insisted that he "would not be *stampeded into premature action* by political pressure or other influences"; (2) warned Arnold not to exaggerate the strength of the AAF; (3) stated flatly that he would operate with a reserve complement (of 100 percent) of aircraft *until the replacement pipelines both for men and aircraft were reliable*; and (4) wanted Arnold to understand completely that he *would not begin combat operations* until men were trained and airplanes ready.[6] Once Spaatz was in England, Arnold wasted little time breaching three of the four criteria.

Spaatz passed 15 May with Secretary of War Stimson, repeating the briefing presented to Arnold and Marshall, hitting on the most significant points related to the coming air war against Germany. As before, the basic strategy was to destroy the Luftwaffe through attrition by attacking strategically important targets that would have to be defended. Stimson was then in his third cabinet chair, having served as secretary of war under President

Taft, secretary of state in the Hoover administration, and now heading the War Department once again. At age 73, his Ivy League and Wall Street lawyer's mind and memory were as well-honed and agile as ever. Reviewing AWPD-1, Stimson detected that the strategic targets listed by Spaatz in the briefing differed from Army doctrine. Yes, Spaatz acknowledged, the original doctrine "involved the usage of Air Power *supported by ground forces*; but that the present planning involved Air Power *supporting ground forces*. Spaatz then spoke of having two US expeditionary air forces . . . one strategic and one tactical. Both would operate under the same overall commander. Stimson promised his full support to Spaatz" (emphasis original).[7] As the Eighth had, by that time, been deleted from the list of organizations to participate in the North African campaign, Spaatz was most likely thinking in terms of a European ground war. Ironically, he would gain expertise in tactical air support as commanding general of all air operations in the Mediterranean theater, where his operational flexibility and focus on accomplishing the mission were on full display.

VIP Delegation to England, Late May–Early June 1942

With the navy consumed with the looming showdown with the Japanese at Midway, a group of senior officers including Major Generals Arnold and Eisenhower and Mark Wayne Clark (chief of staff to the army ground forces commander), Colonel Hoyt S. Vandenburg (assistant chief of staff for operations at HqAF), and a half-dozen others departed for London.[8] Among numerous assignments, Marshal wanted Eisenhower to assess the abilities of the current commanding general of the European theater of operations, US Army (ETOUSA), which had been activated on 8 June.[9] This was, of course, Major General Chaney. Eisenhower found the command under Chaney nothing less than a complete mess. Upon visiting Chaney's offices, Eisenhower discovered the same problems that Eaker had back in February, with neither Chaney nor his staff having the slightest idea what "revolutionary changes" back in the War Department meant and, worse, were "at a complete loss in their earnest attempts to further the war effort."[10] Eisenhower was appalled to see how befuddled the personnel in Chaney's organization were regarding their mission. The staff was out of touch with both the British and their own War Departments while they seemed oblivious to the seriousness of BOLERO and any cross-channel effort. Clearly, something would have to be done at once to light a fire under Chaney and his officers. The evening of 28 May, Eisenhower, Arnold, and Clark informally convened in a hotel room and, with all concurring that Chaney should be reassigned, debated among themselves potential successors. According to Arnold, the three generals agreed that a new theater commander had to be an officer "who could meet the British senior officers on even terms. We agreed it must be a man who had the experience and knowledge of our ways of doing things, and was fully acquainted with our War Department plans. He must have the confidence of General Marshall and the Secretary of War. We also agreed that the man selected should get to London as soon as possible."[11] Eisenhower then left the other two, who continued to bat about potential candidates of the position; both generals were of a mind that it should be Eisenhower.

Eisenhower had more shocks coming as he learned of the plans and resources available for a late 1942 invasion. There was no "detailed study of tactical plans" for any invasion of the French beaches, no judgements on the numbers and kinds of "troops, airplanes, supplies and equipment" that might be required, no existence of any air force(s) in England for air support missions, and a presupposition of questionable accuracy regarding Royal Navy and RAF capacity for "quick delivery" of materials. The BA was "badly stretched" with forces in India and the Middle East, and in a "precarious position in the Western Desert." He came to believe strongly, and correctly, that even an invasion in the spring of 1943 would be impossible, concluding that it would be the spring of 1944 before a "large-scale invasion" would be feasible.[12]

Before leaving for England, Arnold's staff worked up yet another schedule for Eighth aircraft arrivals in the UK for the general to present to Air Chief Marshal Portal. Now, Arnold outlined, there would be sixty-six AAF combat groups in England by March 1943, of which nineteen would be heavy bombardment. All army aviation units in the United Kingdom were to be the responsibility of the senior airman in the isles and administered by the highest-level aviation headquarters.[13] Arnold returned home on 3 June with the make-or-break battle for Midway Atoll to begin at dawn the next day.[14] After landing, he heard something that most likely struck him as even worse news: there would be more "delays and diversions of combat aircraft and crews" as an additional fifteen medium and heavy bomber groups intended for the Eighth had, in his absence, been redirected to the Pacific.[15]

Spaatz in England

Spaatz landed in Prestwick on 15 June, his mission from the CCS to use the Eighth to "conduct in co-operation with the RAF an offensive against western Europe in 1942."[16] There were numerous questions to be answered in the coming days about the Eighth's missions and overall strategy, the principal of which was whether SLEDGEHAMMER or ROUNDUP would be mounted. Not knowing "made planning difficult for the Army Air Forces [as] its equipment and its role would be determined by the final choice between the two alternatives."[17] Subsumed within directives for either operation was the responsibility for army units to continue BOLERO for whichever operation was selected.

Spaatz would be living under several chains of command. One chain ran from Spaatz up through the army's commanding general for the European theater and thence to Marshall. Spaatz's correspondence intended for General Arnold as deputy chief of staff for air sent through this channel was tagged for passage to the chief. A second chain ran up through the air staff to Arnold as commanding general of the USAAF. A third chain came down from the CCS through the JCS to Spaatz, most often implementing directives received from the national leaderships. Spaatz could only await higher orders while continuing to build the Eighth's infrastructure and see to the thousands of details involved in preparation for combat missions by light, medium, and heavy bombers, plus fighters, along with the myriad support aircraft, maintenance, supply, and basing need across England, Wales, and North Ireland.

Second Washington

In mid-June there briefly appeared a sign providing hope of some movement on a cross-channel decision when the CCS assented to continue accumulating matériel under BOLERO. Then, to the surprise of almost everyone, an unplanned meeting involving all the principals was called to convene quickly in Washington on the twenty-first. Unknown to all, prior to the official meeting the president and prime minister met in greatest secrecy at Roosevelt's home at Hyde Park, New York. There, in two days of private and unrecorded conversations that surely must have been intense and frank, Roosevelt and Churchill agreed to delay any cross-channel invasion and proceed with GYMNAST, the British negative analysis of SLEDGEHAMMER being too acute for Roosevelt to overcome.[18] (The genesis of this secret session was earlier private discussions between the president and Vice-Admiral Lord Mountbatten, RN, in which the president expressed firm intentions for a cross-channel invasion. His Lordship's observation disturbed the PM sufficiently to request a hurried meeting to put his strongly held views to FDR.) Joined with that decision was a subsequent colloquy between the two regarding the selection of a commander for GYMNAST. With that, the two embarked on the president's train to Washington.

On 23 June, following two days of still more frank discussions on GYMNAST, the president and General Marshall met to review a British query on the issue of Allied command, with Marshall afterword sending a note to the president suggesting that his reply to the British say simply that "the US is prepared to furnish a commander, or will accept a qualified British commander. . . . *But unity of command is regarded as imperative.*"[19] This was of utmost importance as the BA did not adhere to the unity-of-command concept. Almost unbelievably to the Americans, the BA gave second-level commanders as a right the ability to challenge a senior commander's decision through reclama to still higher headquarters in London. Also to be settled were measures to aid Stalin and the Soviets, and another Roosevelt-Churchill agreement, this one for both nations to share information on the development of atomic weapons, was included.[20]

Eisenhower

On the twentieth, at the official beginning of Second Washington, Major General Eisenhower of OPD was summoned to Marshall's office, who directed the Kansan to proceed immediately to London, relieve Chaney as commanding general of ETOUSA, and assume command in his place. Eisenhower was then very possibly the most junior major general in the entire US Army, but obviously Chaney would never be able to work with the British with any modicum of respect or comity. Eisenhower's personal qualities, as well as his sense of duty and professionalism, rendered him ideal for the position, despite his lack of seniority. He was to arrive in London before the president and prime minister made their final decision on where and how to go to war. Among Eisenhower's instructions from Marshall relevant to Spaatz and the Eighth was to "integrate all USAAF units deployed in the United Kingdom into the Eighth Air Force." Eisenhower was further informed that the "objective of the Eighth Air Force will be to attain air supremacy in the skies over northern Europe as a vital prerequisite for the contemplated invasion of Occupied Europe by Allied ground forces."[21] Before leaving, Eisenhower made a courtesy call on Admiral Ernest King, whose fearsome personality was legendary. Uncommonly generous with Eisenhower, King advised the general that he "wanted no foolish talk" about his "authority depending upon cooperation and paramount interest." Rather, the admiral "insisted" that there be only one "single responsibility and authority" and encouraged Ike to communicate with him personally should there be any "violation of this concept by the Navy."[22] Hap Arnold wrote a "Dear Eisenhower" letter in which he congratulated Ike on his assignment and gave a "brief summary of the fundamental principles [for] relations with the air forces under your command." Arnold closed by saying, "I feel that our relationship here in Washington has been both pleasant and profitable, and I sincerely desire to do everything in my power to aid you in the accomplishment of the tremendous task to which you have been assigned." The letter ended with Arnold inviting Eisenhower to inform him about "anything that might serve to improve our situation."[23] It was Arnold at his genuine best.

As customary, Eisenhower's last call was to his boss. Ike would long remember Marshall's parting words: "See what needs to be done, then do it. Tell me about it when you can."[24]

Conclusion of Second Washington

Decisions reached during Second Washington fell almost entirely to the British side of the ledger. President Roosevelt had listened intently to a synopsis of the North African situation placed before him by Prime Minister Churchill while the latter had pressed upon him the need to bring desperately required assistance to the British Eighth Army in North Africa, which had just lost its bastion at Tobruk, Libya, with hundreds of tons of supplies and thirty thousand troops captured. The exigency of easing Afrika Korps pressure on Egypt could only be achieved by landings in northwest Africa. Although the USJCS remained focused on Russia and Stalin, the British chiefs argued adamantly against all operations on the Continent throughout the conference. The BCS warned of extreme consequences following a failure to gain an Allied beachhead in France, a near certainty given the limitations of both armies. There was also the manpower issue for the British as well. The Americans acknowledged little chance of Hitler moving any forces from the eastern front to defeat or contain the Allied beachhead, undermining their own rationale for the plan.

Both Marshall and Eisenhower had little confidence in SLEDGE-HAMMER, which mirrored most of the army senior staff. Ike thought an initial landing had about a 50 percent chance of succeeding, while putting ashore successfully six divisions of troops would be only "about 1 in 5."[25] Yet the Americans steadfastly pushed ahead: as Eisenhower wrote in his diary, "We should not forget the prize is to keep 8,000,000 Russians in the war."[26] While believing SLEDGEHAMMER to be "hazardous," Ike still favored it out of fear that any other option, especially GYMNAST, would "deeply involve" Allied forces to a point at which "a cross-channel invasion would be indefinitely postponed, possibly even canceled." He recognized clearly that a foray into the Mediterranean would preclude any cross-channel operation in 1943.[27] It was one of the few but critical times in the war in which the president went against his chief military advisors. His decision distilled to one simple fact: the US military could not meet the Germans in battle in Europe until 1943 and he wanted—indeed, needed—US troops to be killing Germans somewhere before the November 1942 elections.[28] He directed Marshall to proceed with GYMNAST.

Meanwhile . . .

Barely had Arnold's latest schedule of aircraft arrivals in the UK been received by Spaatz and Eaker than the chief told them that they would not be retaining their first combat group—the 97th Bombardment Group (H), intended to be the "nucleus of a Bomber Command"—because it would be sent onward to northwest Africa in the fall. Further, the arrival schedule for other groups was nullified as many of those were also earmarked for GYMNAST. Of eight fighter groups promised to VIII Fighter Command, only one would stay in England: the new 4th Fighter Group. On 29 September 1942, American pilots in the RAF's Eagle Squadron would be discharged and quickly sworn into the USAAF, then formed into three squadrons to become the 4th FG.[29] While flying with the RAF, the Eagle Squadron had recorded 73.5 victories with several pilots becoming aces. Now, the 4th FG was not just the only combat-experienced American fighter unit in the theater, but it would also literally be the only American fighter unit in the theater. Seven other intended groups with their P-38s were on their way to North Africa.[30] Eaker acknowledged later to Churchill and the British contingent at the Casablanca Conference that GYMNAST had "drained resources from the Eighth."[31]

Spaatz Arrives

Delayed by the exigencies of the Midway operation in early June, General Spaatz finally arrived in the UK after a journey beset by delays. However, he was able to experience flying into the "Bluies"—the challenging expeditionary airfields in Greenland—on the way to "obtain a first-hand idea of the difficulties" his pilots would face in flying across the Atlantic.[32] Arriving at Prestwick, Scotland, on 18 June, Spaatz immediately assumed full command of the Eighth, relieving Eaker of his temporary responsibilities, and on the nineteenth began courtesy calls on his RAF hosts, the US ambassador, and General Chaney, who was unaware that Eisenhower would be arriving the next day to relieve him. Ambassador John G. Winant, the US ambassador, had been a navy pilot in the Great War, earning the Navy Cross, and would staunchly support Spaatz and Eaker. Before making his final call of the day on Portal, Spaatz gave a small press conference where he asked that his presence in the UK remain a secret to keep the Germans unprepared for the first raids and to avoid any calls from the American public for "immediate action." The following day, Spaatz held a staff meeting at High Wycombe where he stressed two topics in particular: one was his objective to foster a friendly relationship with the British, for without it the Eighth's "prestige" would suffer not only with Americans at home but also with their hosts, who were "depending on the US effort"; second, it was essential that the Eighth take advantage of British experience—but not British tactics. He then departed to concentrate on filling the organizational structure of the Eighth.[33] Anticipating only a short delay before moving into a heavy combat role, Spaatz worked toward building and staffing every directorate, office, department, and section across the entire air force, while blending into the fold fighter and bomber commands and awaiting the arrivals of air groups and ground support units. A critical gap was the absence of an intelligence directorate and officers to staff it, for the Eighth was "more deficient in its provisions for intelligence than in any other phase of its activities."[34] As a first step, fifty novice intelligence officers had landed in England earlier, on 17 May, to begin training at RAF Bomber Command.[35] Others would soon begin instruction as photo interpreters (PIs) at the CIU, RAF Medmenham. On the twenty-fifth Spaatz established Eighth Air Force headquarters at Bushy Park on the edge of Hampton Palace grounds, although personnel continued to work in Mayfair until suitable headquarters facilities were constructed.

Spaatz and the RAF

Major General Spaatz was well-known to the RAF leadership, among whom he had numerous friends. As a colonel he had been detailed to London as a military observer to the RAF during the Battle of Britain during 1940, making many friends in that service while impressing the highest levels with his willingness to engage in unofficial conversations about US aid to the British and to the RAF in particular. Reciprocating, the RAF introduced Spaatz to their technical assets, especially radar and a "blind-bombing" system called H2S; the variants of IFF (identification, friend or foe) equipment; and GCI (ground-controlled intercept), by which fighter-interceptors were steered to incoming German bombers by ground officers watching radar screens. Spaatz attended RAF aircrew mission debriefings, examined downed German aircraft, spent nine days with an RAF night bomber group taking note of the ineffectiveness of night area bombing, and experienced German air attacks.[36]

Spaatz returned to the States with several unshakable convictions. First, he was certain that the Germans would not beat the British, especially if allied with the United States. Second, in witnessing the strength, perseverance, and acceptance of sacrifice by the bombed civilian populations of Great Britain and Germany, he concluded that neither would "collapse in the face of bombardment." Third, Tooey thought the RAF strategy of night area bombardment was feckless—and when the RAF later arrived at this identical conclusion, they changed to night firebombings.[37] And last, Spaatz discerned that the Luftwaffe's method of escorting its bombers would lead to the loss of both escorts and bombers. The German escorts were remaining with the bombers until the British fighters appeared, at which time the Luftwaffe fighters abandoned their bombers to confront the defenders, thus robbing "the German fighters of their aggressiveness by forcing them to react to British attacks." RAF tactics reinforced Spaatz's strongly held beliefs in HADPB and the invincibility of the self-defending bomber, although he was unaware that the RAF was switching to night bombardment due to excessive losses on unescorted daytime missions.[38]

RAF bombers were far from self-defending, being poorly armored and equipped with only a few light .303-caliber guns, characteristics that left the bombers vulnerable to Luftwaffe fighters. After losing too many men and airplanes in day missions, RAF Bomber Command sought the protection of dark nights. Even after the electronic systems of GEE and OBOE came online in 1943, the RAF had become so convinced that daylight bombardment was both ineffective and deadly for the aircrews that they refused to reconsider it and thought the Americans foolhardy.[39]

Both air forces shared the conviction that air superiority over northwestern France was vital for a successful cross-channel invasion, the Americans arguing that the best way to rid the skies of Luftwaffe defenders was to force them to come up and fight—which is precisely what daylight bomber missions did. Only with the Luftwaffe defeated could the Allies conduct a successful cross-channel invasion, after which the Continent would be open for the heavy bombers of the Eighth to strike the targets in AWPD-1. Spaatz was so convinced of the efficacy of air power that he believed effective bombardment of Germany alone could obviate a land invasion and force the Germans to the surrender table. He was joined by Arnold, who not only supported HADPB, but also in an interview in the *Daily Telegraph* opined that that it was "possible to knock Germany out by bombing alone."[40] (Arnold had rejected multiple opportunities to direct the development of a suitable bomber escort even before the war's beginning, although he later wrote that he "preferred never to send any unescorted bombers over Germany."[41])

The arrival of Spaatz in England was an occasion for Eaker to write a summation of the progress of the Eighth's "advanced echelon" for the commander's background. It was also an opportunity to inform Spaatz about the assistance he and the advanced party had received from their hosts. The British, wrote Eaker,

> in whose theater we have been understudying and operating for the past five months, have co-operated one hundred per cent in every regard. They have lent us personnel when we had none, and have furnished us clerical and administrative staffs; they have furnished us liaison officers for Intelligence, Operations and Supply: they have furnished us transportation; they have housed and fed our people, and they have answered promptly and willingly all our requisitions: in addition they have made available to us for study their most secret devices and documents. We are extremely proud of the relations we have been able to establish between our British Allies and ourselves, and we are very hopeful that the present basis can be continued, and that all incoming staff and tactical commanders will take the same pains we have to nurture and maintain the excellent relations which now exist.[42]

It was a propitious beginning that augured well for the relationship between the Eighth and the British through the end of the war and afterward.

There was much for both the Eighth and VIII Bomber Command to do, even without airplanes. The Eighth Air Force Composite Command activated in Northern Ireland was a necessity as Spaatz knew that Arnold would yield to his chronic impatience and send crews across the Atlantic just as soon as they were experienced enough to make the trip without killing themselves but "well before they had finished their training."[43] Eventually, it would become evident to all that pushing back against Arnold's inability to stick to policy matters was a fruitless endeavor: "Arnold retained a very keen interest in the details of the movement [of aircraft]. He was constantly providing directives and advice, all impatiently aimed at getting the Eighth into combat as quickly as possible. Unrelenting attention from Washington was not always warmly welcomed by Spaatz and Eaker, who continued efforts to educate Arnold, generally without any great success, about the difficulties involved. For the next 18 months, given the diversion of assets from the strategic bombardment effort caused by the Guadalcanal and North African invasions, Arnold was perpetually urging greater effort and quicker success."[44]

Eisenhower relieved a surprised Chaney on 28 June and immediately set to work, including an introduction to the Eighth Air Force. Tooey and Ike had known each other well at West Point and were periodically reacquainted when both were assigned to Washington. The professional and personal relationships between the two would develop into a close affiliation upon which the final fifteen months of the European war would depend. That it was one of complete openness, undiminished two-way loyalty, and mutual trust had everything to do with why the strategic air war in 1944–1945 was pursued efficaciously in providing innovative and unparalleled support to the ground forces from D-Day to VE-Day. Their relationship demanded close collaboration founded on trust and comity in the achievement of a common goal, the defeat of the Third Reich, yet it remains almost ignored by history in this aspect.

Arnold and George C. Marshall

Hidden from almost all, Arnold's most cherished friendship was with army chief of staff General George Marshall. The two had met as lieutenants in the Philippines before World War I; one day on maneuvers Arnold stumbled across Lieutenant Marshall in the jungle working on an operational plan for 4,800 men who had been placed under Marshall's command, normally a job for a higher-ranking officer. Right then Arnold thought that Marshall would one day become army chief of staff.[45] With adjacent office suites in the Pentagon and neighboring quarters at Fort Meyers, Arnold and Marshall communicated privately throughout the day, during the evenings, and on weekends in discussions that, because they were never overheard or recorded, have been lost forever to history. Without knowing these discussions, it is now impossible ever to understand the extent to which the two collaborated, in private, in advance on decisions announced by one or the other that affected the direction of the war, the relationship between the air and ground forces, or the future of the AAF. Indicative of the closeness of the relationship, Arnold was one of the very, very few people to address the chief of staff as George.[46]

The personal closeness and professional trust between the two was ever present but rarely apparent. Arnold worked quietly behind the scenes with Marshall to slow the movement for an independent air force, deliberately holding off his cherished goal until after the war, as the push for independence could do little good for, and stood to inflict harm to, the war effort. Instead, Arnold maneuvered deliberately but silently toward that goal, never losing sight of it. In return for Arnold's unfailing loyalty and support, Marshall allowed Arnold "increasing autonomy" over the AAF and to the extent possible "gave Arnold nearly all that he asked for."[47] Several times during the war, the two generals were able to take vacations together far away from the Pentagon, including once a fishing and camping trip to the remote High Sierras in August 1944. Marshall counseled Arnold to slow down and to delegate

authority in an attempt to preserve his health, thus extending his life; Arnold
was simply unable to do that. Without this unique relationship and different
personalities in the two offices, the history of the war, and the United States
Air Force, would undoubtedly have been altered, almost certainly for worse:
"To many at the time, and later, Arnold was the Army Air Forces. He threw
himself into his work in a way that was both impressive and deplorable.
He didn't pace himself. It was all or nothing at all. Arnold simply couldn't
delegate anything, unlike Marshall, who freely delegated to mere majors and
lieutenant colonels powers that few generals would ever possess. Every day
Arnold got involved in decisions large and small, like a man suffering from
perspective deprivation."[48] This was pure Arnold—never "a deep thinker or
long-range planner," he was instead "decisive and a quick study" in the inci-
sive opinion of Colonel Lauris "Larry" Norstad, an aide who became the
youngest ever four-star general in the United States Air Force.[49]

Tooey and His Staff

Once in England General Spaatz did not forget Lieutenant Colonel Dick
Hughes, who had made a strong impression on him back home and who
had been laboring for Eaker in London's Davis Street in temporary office
spaces. Choosing for quarters a somewhat dark Victorian house near
Wimbledon called Park House, Spaatz moved in three key officers: chief
of staff Brigadier General Edward "Ted" Curtis; Colonel Harry Berliner,
A-5; and Dick Hughes, assistant A-5 and targeting officer.[50] Ted Curtis
had flown with 94th Aero Squadron in World War I, downing six German
aircraft and later becoming aide-de-camp to General Billy Mitchell.
A reserve officer and senior executive for Eastman Kodak, he returned to
active duty as Brigadier General North Duncan's assistant chief of staff;
upon Duncan's early death, he moved up to be the chief of staff for his
longtime friend Tooey Spaatz.[51] These officers were devoted to Spaatz and
committed strongly to him; in return, Spaatz returned their loyalty, having
complete confidence in their abilities.

Chapter 7

June–July 1942

In February 1942 Arnold's schedule had called for three heavy bomber groups to begin arriving in England by 1 May, with the full complement on the ground by 1 July. But none arrived in May, nor in June. July first rolled around and later in the day so did one lone B-17 from the 97th Bomb Group, with one C-47 for company.[1] Although the lone Fortress missed the promised date by two months, at least it was from the correct unit. Several Fortresses from the 97th had departed Washington with Spaatz on 1 June, but the next day had been ordered to the West Coast because of the Midway battle. Released a week later, they should have been delayed ten days at most. The Fortresses of the 97th BG would straggle in by twos and threes, with the last one wheels down at Prestwick on the twenty-seventh, save for three that crashed-landed along the Greenland coast.[2]

It became obvious quickly that all arriving aircraft needed major modifications and the crews much more training before airplanes and men could be combat qualified:

Crews arrived with little or no experience in high-altitude flying. Pilots and copilots had received little instruction in flying formations at any altitude, to say nothing of maintaining tight formations

at the extreme altitudes [where the air was thin] planned for day
bomber missions. Many of the radio operators could neither send nor
receive the Morse code. Worse yet, the gunners proved to be almost
completely unfamiliar with their equipment. Many of them had had
little or no opportunity to shoot at aerial targets, and several had never
operated a turret in the air. This deficiency was especially disturb-
ing . . . the ability of the heavy bombers to destroy enemy targets by
daylight without prohibitive loss would depend in large part on their
ability to defend themselves against enemy fighters.[3]

Priorities

But even before the first B-17 landed from the States, Arnold had begun
pressing Spaatz and Eaker to begin operations "against the Germans as soon
as possible" while ground crews in England were constantly working to
put the Eighth in a combat status as quickly as possible. Spaatz and Eaker
were likewise consumed with tasks as diverse as preparing "a logistics and
base structure" for the command and negotiating to protect the Eighth's
fighters from RAF control.[4] Even now, at this early time, differences in
objectives and priorities between Washington and England began appearing.
"As Commanding General of the Army Air Forces Arnold naturally had
priorities very different from those of a leader of a combat air force like the
Eighth. Arnold had to justify Army Air Forces appropriations to the president,
Congress, and the public. In addition, he had to maintain Army Air Forces
production and strategic priorities in the face of challenges from the British
and the US Navy. All this required a perception of the Army Air Forces as a
successful and aggressive weapon being used against the enemy."[5] Arnold
was working to grow the AAF from a relatively small organization of fewer
than 250,000 officers and men with hemisphere defense responsibilities
into a global combat force, with hundreds of training schools to establish
and staff for hundreds of new job specialties, from basic to advanced levels.
There were airplane manufacturers to beg, plead, and cajole, and thousands
of suppliers to corral. Significantly, Arnold had to allot among all the fighting
units the still-small number of aircraft coming off production lines—a difficult problem when every unit in combat was seriously short of airplanes and

aircrews. There was never any question that Arnold had a nearly impossible task. To expect combat operations when there were no airplanes to send into combat was the hallmark of a man with no patience and high expectations.

Hap

Henry Harley "Hap" Arnold bore the nickname not because he was perennially happy or even usually of good cheer, because he was not; instead, he suffered "a slight anomaly in which a facial muscle pulled the left corner of his mouth into a permanent expression of amusement." Arnold had a sharp, even explosive, temper, and when combined with a perennial lack of patience, Vesuvian results ensued. His impatience was a "characteristic of which he was well aware and that he never earnestly attempted to change."[6] In the bottom half of his West Point Class of 1907, Arnold was a flight student of the Wright Brothers in 1911; there were so few pilots that almost anything he did in the air made him the first pilot to do whatever it was. He would later say, as if to explain his unwillingness to accept an excuse of "it can't be done," that "the Wright Brothers gave me a sense that nothing is impossible."[7] Arnold once wrote to General George Kenney of the 5th Air Force and later the Far East Air Force, "As you know, I am not the kind of fellow who says can't and I don't want such people around."[8] He "reveled in hard work, physical and intellectual," which was unkind to his health once war began.[9] Officers who worked with, near, or close to Arnold would always agree on one point: Arnold's "acute intelligence" gave him the "rare ability to ask penetrating questions on issues he seemed to know little about . . . without ever studying a complex subject closely he could nonetheless go straight to the essentials and leave his staff floundering."[10] Despite these traits, not to mention a reputation as a "notoriously stubborn and maverick spirit" that made him the recipient of more than a few poor fitness reports, his positive qualities such as an ability to quickly "grasp the big picture" served him well.[11] General Laurence S. Kuter, a great admirer who spent much of the war working for Arnold, described him as

> a highly personal leader in face-to-face contact with his subordinates. He was not nearly as well-attuned to the task of guiding the leaders of his large new Air Staff as he struggled to create air power. The general

just had to be doing things himself. He found it difficult to sit quietly
as he projected his thoughts into the future. He had to be talking to
people. . . . Very rarely did anyone go to Arnold and say, "Chief, this
project you directed just can't be done." An officer who said that was
liable to never be given an opportunity to say it again.[12]

Arnold spent a great many hours in the presence of Henry Stimson, the
secretary of war, who not only greatly respected Arnold but also fully
supported him against the criticisms of the secretary of the treasury, Henry
L. Morgenthau Jr. Stimson inevitably found Arnold "brilliant in his presentations and fearless and undiplomatic; a good counterpose for Marshall who is
a little overdiplomatic." Stimson recognized Arnold for his "quick mind, who
doesn't hesitate to make his views clearly felt." Stimson also knew Arnold's
"impetuosity" and "frenetic nature," acknowledging more than once that he
had to "intercede or quash some 'half-baked action'" by the chief.[13] Always
rushed, Arnold refused to read papers more than one page in length and while
admired by many who worked for him, one would say that the general was
"utterly ruthless when he felt that someone let him down."[14]

The View from England

The perspective from across the Atlantic was very different from Washington's.
Eaker and Spaatz had a war to fight, and without needlessly wasting precious
assets like heavy bombers and the ten-man crews. In the first year of the war,
the generals had to be careful not to deplete their heavy bomber inventory or
the ranks of the airmen; it would have been very easy to do—just fly as many
as possible on every mission when loss rates from combat and accidents were
greater than replacement rates, which were highly uncertain at best. But that
would have been unwise for the Eighth Air Force not only as a fighting force
but also because the Eighth, as the representative of the US government and the
AAF, had deep commitments to the British government and the RAF in addition to Arnold's directive to "bomb Germany." Eaker was alert to this every
day. In January 1944, after his relief, he wrote an after-action report in which
he said, "This action [introducing forces into battle as they became available]
had to be carefully controlled so that the forces should not depreciate in either

numbers or fighting edge to the point where effectiveness would disappear."[15] Eaker would, during his tenure, carefully husband his heavy bombers, rarely having much, or any, lead time in knowing when replacements in aircraft or aircrews might arrive, or how many there would be, or which of his present heavy bomber units would be sent to another theater. Without care, just a few missions with losses of 12–15 percent could easily deplete his heavy forces mostly, if not entirely. Spaatz and Eaker would soon also discover that how nearly disastrous it was to lose hundreds of aircraft plus the air and maintenance crews to another command, most never to return to the Eighth. And therein lay a difficult problem for the AAF leadership: how to balance the political and administrative needs of the air forces commanding general in Washington against the responsibilities of the field commanders in England who sent men to battle, with responsibility for their lives, the airplanes, and commitments to allies. It was not a dilemma, though, because in Washington General Arnold evinced little doubt as to what was needed, where, and why.

Arnold, for all the brilliance he brought to his offices as chief of staff and commanding general, had never flown in combat, never sent men to die in combat, and would never fly operationally in the European combat environment. He had attended command and general staff, but never the war college nor even ACTS; instead, he had been—and this became truly a blessing in disguise—enrolled in the Army Industrial College, which served him exceptionally well as chief of staff, especially with the relationships he made with civilian industrialists. But he had received no experience or senior-level instruction as a combat commander, and too, by being promoted directly from lieutenant colonel to brigadier general, he missed out on the learning experiences usually acquired at an important leadership level. Spaatz would probably have finessed Arnold's impatience and demands had he remained in command; Eaker, ten years Arnold's junior, more admirer than contemporary, who also missed the confidence-building leadership experiences as a full colonel, would be a different matter.

By July the European theater's air command structure was in place. Spaatz was in command of the Eighth and Eaker had VIII Bomber Command. North Duncan was ensconced as chief of staff. To the certain relief of all, Ike had taken ETOUSA on 24 June: Spaatz would soon be joined in common cause with Ike while Eaker and the new theater commander would quickly establish a comfortable relationship.[16]

The Independence Day Raid

Arnold wrote to Churchill on 10 June promising that the AAF would be in action by American Independence Day: "We will be fighting with you on July 4th." He did not inform Spaatz of this for almost three weeks, his cable ordering the Eighth into action on July 4 arriving in Spaatz's hand only six days beforehand.[17] As the first, and only, heavy bomber would not be landing in the UK for another two days—with minimum aircrew, no ground crew, no modifications for combat or operations in British airspace, and no crew combat training—Spaatz and Eaker were left scrambling to find both airplanes and American crews for the mission. Spaatz's lecture to his boss back in early May about "not being stampeded into premature action" and "no combat operations until men are trained and airplanes are ready" had had no effect on Arnold: he needed to tell Congress, the White House, and the press that the Eighth was operational, and for that he needed airplanes dropping bombs; it was up to Spaatz and Eaker to make it happen.

Arnold made no mention of the raid in either his diary or his autobiography, despite his intense interest in seeing it executed. With the Eighth devoid of airplanes, Spaatz turned to the RAF, which was training some AAF crews on A-20 Boston light bombers. The AAF's official historians say little about this first "American" mission, noting only that Eisenhower and Eaker visited RAF Swanton Morely airfield on 2 July to "consult" with the pilots and counted the men and aircraft lost after the mission.[18] The editor of Arnold's diaries suggests that Arnold's motivation "was probably a combination of the desire to justify the large investment in the European bombardment buildup, a hope to duplicate the favorable publicity that had resulted from the daring Doolittle Tokyo raid six weeks earlier, and an effort to balance the navy's trumpeted success at the Battle of Midway in early June"—all of which mattered in the arena of Washington politics. The last thing the chief of the AAF needed was to see was the navy rewarded with AAF aircraft production slots. Certainly, it was a time of low spirits for both Americans and British, so perhaps Arnold ancillary's wish was to "let the Germans know that the Americans had really arrived and to give the British a badly needed lift."[19] Regardless, neither Spaatz nor Eaker "liked the idea worth a damn," with Eaker thinking that "someone must have mixed up April Fool's Day with Independence Day."[20]

Both generals held serious doubts over their aircrews' readiness for combat, regardless of the reasons, while Eaker "sensed disaster," calling the raid a "gimmick" that was going to be flown "against his better judgment."[21] He did not believe for one moment that a low-level raid flown by a few light bombers against targets just across the channel along the Dutch coastline was a rational person's idea of strategic bombardment. Eaker wondered, What exactly was the raid to achieve? If the strike were to be flown with a full two groups—or even just one experienced group—of Fortresses, that would be one thing; but this mission would prove . . . nothing. Worse, and critically important to Eaker, men's lives would be risked when the odds of inflicting serious damage to the target airfield were long indeed. No matter which, or how many, reasons Arnold may have had for ordering the mission, he obviously wanted it badly enough that he was willing to promise it to Churchill and to fly it with borrowed light bombers and partially trained crews.

The chosen aircrews, minus airplanes, had arrived in England in May, eventually to man Boston squadrons in VIII ASC; they had been seconded to RAF 226 Squadron, which did have airplanes, for training. For the Independence Day raid, twelve A-20s from 226 Squadron would fly the mission, with six graciously loaned to AAF crews. RAF rondels were hastily painted over, replaced temporarily with the AAF's white star and stripe. The strike was against four Luftwaffe airfields on the Dutch coast, with the twelve Bostons in "four flights of three aircraft each," the novice Americans "in relatively protected positions."[22] Escorted by RAF Spitfires, the mission flew at wave height to avoid detection. But they still managed to mistakenly overfly a Kriegsmarine picket boat, which alerted the German defenses. Duly warned, the defenders threw up dense flak patterns while several Luftwaffe fighters attempted intercepts of the A-20s. The final tally was two AAF-flown aircraft downed and a third severely damaged; one crewman was KIA; seven more missing in action (MIA), all later confirmed dead; and one prisoner of war (POW), the first Eighth Air Force crewman to become a captive.[23]

The 4 July raid was not the most propitious of missions; Spaatz remarked "sourly" in his command diary that "the cameramen and newspapermen finally got what they wanted—and everybody seemed happy." Newspapers reported the raid in headlines of large letters and "grossly exaggerated stories" above the fold. "Everybody" did indeed seem happy—save for Hap Arnold, who said nothing afterward but continued to push Spaatz "for more AAF action and publicity." A laudatory article in the *New York Times* assured readers the raid was not a "Holiday stunt . . . a mere gesture for publicity or propaganda purposes."[24] But there would be no more bomber missions in the Eighth for forty-four days. A January 1944 *Narrative History of the Eighth Air Force* refers to this mission simply as "a rather unsuccessful low-level operation," the euphoria of first combat long since evaporated.[25] It was hardly a promising beginning for what would become, within eighteen months, the most powerful military force in the world.

Chapter 8

TORCH

With the 20 June decision to conduct GYMNAST—now TORCH—before the end of the year, planners in Washington began putting together forces for the landings, including requisite air cover.[1] As combat air units were in short supply, the only place for planners to find aircraft and crews quickly was to look to the Eighth, although if the Eighth were to cede its groups to TORCH, a robust air war in Europe would have to wait. That did not keep Eisenhower, on 21 July, from giving Spaatz a directive to obtain air supremacy in western Europe by 1 April 1943.[2] The very next day Spaatz started losing his airplanes to TORCH. The Eighth was notified that it was not only to send most of its medium and heavy bomber groups to the North African venture, but also fifteen groups initially assigned to the Eighth were being rerouted to the Pacific. Not one of those aircraft had moved one inch toward England.[3]

And yet on 1 August Arnold again pushed his generals to send heavy bombers, of which Eaker had just the 97th, into combat without delay. Afraid that Admiral Ernie King would succeed in obtaining priority in aircraft production, Arnold wanted heavies from the Eighth over the Continent with no further delay. Arnold was also not only attuned to Congress's high interest in the activities of the Eighth but also "maintained an acute ear on the populace," giving the American people's unwavering interest in the war "a high priority." They, along with the administration and the Hill, were eagerly looking forward to results for their sacrifices at home, something to which Arnold was ever alert.[4] The 97th had arrived piecemeal throughout July, the last landing at Prestwick just four days earlier. Only now could the group begin an intensive training program under a new, dynamic leader, Colonel Frank A. Armstrong; the aircrews were so green that none would be fully qualified for combat for weeks. Still, Eaker obeyed orders and scheduled the first strike for 9 August. Criticisms from the British newspapers about the lack of American combat missions had by now burrowed deep under Arnold's skin and, unable to ignore them, he demanded the first of many future "explanations" from Eaker as to why AAF bombers had not already struck the enemy. Meanwhile the 97th, on airfields at Polebrook and Grafton Underwood, suffered from the usual English autumn weather—often unsuited for general flight, much less combat training. With the 97th awaiting better conditions, Arnold informed Eaker and Spaatz that the 97th—and two of the next three heavy bombardment groups destined for England, the 91st and the 301st—would soon be transferred from the Eighth to the budding North African venture. It was the final blow to Arnold's plan "to have a thousand heavy bombers over Germany by April 1943."[5]

Off to War

It would be six weeks after the Fourth of July strike before the first B-17 raid was flown, with Arnold "spurring Spaatz and Eaker to get into action" almost daily. In the interregnum and in deep secrecy, General Marshall and Admiral King, accompanied by the president's close friend and principal advisor, Mr. Harry Hopkins, had traveled to England on 8 April to make one last effort to sell Churchill and his generals on SLEDGHAMMER, the outcome of which was a firm postponement of any cross-channel invasion for the near future; TORCH would have to do for the present. "Arnold knew about it and he desperately wanted the Eighth to show its mettle at once so he could salvage something for the strategic bombing offensive and continue to send it reinforcements." Moreover, the American and British press were both "expressing skepticism" about the American daylight bombing plan and abilities; at one point Arnold was "so fussed" by one British journalist's article that he fired off an angry cable to Spaatz about it.[6]

There was more to the top-secret visit by Marshall and Harry Hopkins, of course, than simply being informed that TORCH was a definite go. The decision also entailed a crucial adjustment in BOLERO commitments: BOLERO (and by extension, the Eighth) was to be reduced by "nine combat, four transport, and two observation groups," which would instead be sent to the Pacific, in addition to one heavy bomber group already diverted and a second heavy group to depart for the Pacific by mid-September.[7] For the next months, Arnold—who had argued determinedly against TORCH—would derisively refer to it as the "European-African Theater."[8]

Mission Number 1

On 17 August the B-17s finally went to work, although neither Spaatz nor Eaker were happy about it. Both sought to build the strength of VIII Bomber Command and then "unleash" a major force on serious targets on the Continent. Arnold, with different audiences to please, wanted bombers in action yesterday, crews trained or otherwise. Late the afternoon of the seventeenth, the first strike was flown, spending seven minutes over target. Eaker was able to cobble together a "force" of twelve B-17s from the 97th to hit the railroad marshaling yards at Sottéville-sur-Rouen, France, and another six to fly a diversionary route. The Eighth's assistant targeting officer, Lieutenant Colonel Dick Hughes, chose Sottéville: "It really did not matter what, at this early stage, we bombed, the marshaling yard was suffi-ciently far from the town so that there was small likelihood of our killing any Frenchmen, and that the target was comfortably within range of Spitfire fighter cover."[9] Railroad marshaling yards were easy to identify visually, even from twenty-five thousand feet, and had few buildings among their twenty to forty parallel railroad lines, which made damage easy to cover by an RAF PR Spitfire. Damage to or destruction of marshaling yards could halt the movement of troops or war supplies for days, or weeks if complete, so yards were always high on the lists of the targeteers. Sottéville was one of the largest yards north of the Loire River: with a location more or less at midpoint between Paris and the port of Le Havre, it facilitated the movement of troops and matériel to and from rail transportation centers leading to all areas of northern France and the Low Countries. With Rouen and Sottéville on opposite sides of the Seine nearing its widest point, the target fell, barely, within the limited range of the 108 escorting RAF Spitfires divided into four squadrons. It was as perfect a target as one could hope for rookies on a first mission—not to mention the thirty members of the US and British press assembled to watch the takeoff.[10]

Lieutenant Colonel Cecil P. Lessig had been a captain in the 20th Pursuit Group when Eaker was the commanding officer (CO) in 1940, soon gaining a bit of fame as the first American pilot to fly a combat mission in Europe, piloting a Spitfire with an RAF squadron on a fighter sweep. Now the operations officer (A-3) for VIII Bomber Command, Lessig wrote the operations order for the 97th and then he and Eaker went fishing.[11]

The 97th group commander, Colonel Frank Armstrong, was the mission commander and occupied the copilot's seat of the lead Fortress, Butcher Shop; the aircraft commander in the left seat was Major Paul W. Tibbets, "one of the best and most fearless pilots the AAF possessed." The second element lead was Yankee Doodle, with Captain Rudy Flack as aircraft commander and General Eaker in the cockpit as an observer.[12] Sottéville, thirty-five air miles from where the Seine empties broadly into the channel at the port of Le Havre, served no challenge to novice navigators. Bombing was "reasonably accurate" with damage—from 18.5 tons of bombs hitting buildings and track, destroying rolling stock and machinery—sufficient only to "temporarily disrupt service." Two bombers were slightly damaged by flak that was at best "sparse"; no enemy aircraft were seen.[13] When only a dozen bombers are escorted by 108 first-rate fighters, incentives for defending interceptors to interfere are few indeed.

Neither Spaatz nor Eaker were thrilled about escorts, believing them unnecessary and seeing the mission as a missed opportunity for the self-defending bomber theory to prove itself. Eaker in later years would write that "he always sought fighter cover" despite the defensive capabilities of the heavies, "convinced that it would be greatly to our advantage and reduce our losses significantly if we could have fighters to protect us."[14] Yet during the war he asserted that he was fine with escorts only to the German border, after which he had full confidence in the bombers continuing to the far reaches of the Reich unescorted, convinced in their ability to look to their own safety. He never, during the war, backed away from his faith in the self-defending bomber.

Events of 17 August seem to have caused Spaatz to experience a temporary state of ecstasy as he cabled the chief, claiming this first daylight raid by heavy bombers "far exceeded in accuracy any previous bombing in the European theater by German or Allied aircraft."[15] This statement may have been true, as far as it went, but compared to the vicious air battles from September 1943 to March 1945, the first mission in a long war did not "go" very far. Still, it was a chance to show the British how the Americans intended to accomplish the bombardment of Germany.

Spaatz followed up on the twenty-fourth with a note to Arnold asserting that with 1,500 bombers—a mix of heavies and mediums—plus 800 fighters in England for airfield defense, he could gain "complete aerial supremacy over Germany within a year," deprecating both flak and the Luftwaffe and appending "bombing accuracy does not diminish under fire, but rather increases."[16] Spaatz neither proffered any evidence to support this counter-intuitive statement nor explained how a bomber, under fighter attack and bouncing from turbulent air, flak bursts, and evasive moves, could bomb more accurately than in still, peaceful air.

There was one deadly consequence from Sottéville unknown to the Allies until later in the war: after Sottéville the Germans realized more American bombers would be coming. Divining all too well that AAF daytime missions would be added to the RAF's night raids, the Luftwaffe high command saw "a need to develop a large fighter strength in the West." At the time, 60 percent of the Luftwaffe's airpower was at the eastern front, including significant numbers of fighters. The Luftwaffe's immediate solution was to increase production of fighters for air units in the west, with long-range plans viewing a production rate of two thousand fighters per month by the end of 1944. But ULTRA intercepts revealed that within three months the Germans begin transferring fighter Gruppen from the Russia to western Europe.

These fighters were "simply folded into the mushrooming Reich air-defense effort" rather than returned to Russia.[17]

Operational Matters

Strategic bomber operations in wartime England, like many operations involving large aircraft and numbers of men, were complex and in no wise simple. One obvious cause for the persistent problems with the airplanes, crew equipment, and training—besides the fact that no one in the Eighth had any previous combat experience, from group commanders to gunners—was that no one had ever before tried to grow a small, defensive air corps into a massive air force with assets waging offensive war on five continents in an almost impossibly short period of time. The command learning curve was almost vertical, supply was always uncertain, and partially trained men were required to learn while doing.

Eaker produced two reports after the Sottéville mission. One, a firsthand report in almost excruciating detail of the 17 August mission to Sottéville was for Spaatz, who then forwarded it to an appreciative Arnold.[18] Additionally, Eaker wrote a critique on and offered suggestions for such problems as the Fortress's oxygen system (which would have serious issues well into 1944), "station keeping" in formation flying, the need for "frequent crew drills" on all aspects of flying the bomber, "air discipline" in operating the aircraft during takeoffs and landings, the necessity for better trained navigators and bombardiers, and more for much of the five-page missive. After the fifth bombardment mission, Eaker submitted a "lessons learned" letter to Spaatz on 25 August, a measurably improved critique in that more issues were covered, in succinct detail, also with suggestions for improvement.[19] The general raised issues like group leadership, the extreme importance of crew training, a need for a greatly improved oxygen system in the B-17E, an in-depth illumination of German fighter tactics, the accuracy of ball turret gunners in general, and the value of attaching cameras to each bomber—something the RAF had already adopted and that Hansell would later promote. Perhaps most interesting was a long section on the training of bomber command head-quarters officers, especially those working in the operations (A-3) section.

Later, astute commanders having gained serious combat experience would themselves write detailed critiques with some of the same critical issues reappearing with some regularity into the autumn of 1943, proving not that HqAF did not listen but instead how long it took to get America's industrial capacity turned from a civilian to a wartime economy.

In Washington the principal source of Arnold's most urgent concerns in late 1942 and into 1943 was the large numbers of bombers and crews originally destined for the Eighth that he was now having to send to northwest Africa. Particularly painful was the loss of most of his heavies when the consensus among generals was that GYMNAST would be little more than a costly distraction. Arnold believed that the campaign presented a true "existential threat" to the Eighth and by extension to proving the viability of daylight precision bombing.[20] He was fearful of losing so much of the Eighth's vital lifeblood—the heavy bomber groups—to the fight in the desert that he would have no choice but to send the rump of the Eighth to the RAF. Such would have been devastating on multiple fronts: besides the threat to proving the viability of daylight precision strategic bombing, it could seriously imperil any possibility of the Eighth becoming a near-autonomous air force in the future—both of which, Arnold was convinced, were essential to the eventual creation of an independent United States Air Force. To Arnold, one event would cascade into another and then another, ultimately ending the dream of independence.

Spaatz and Three Hats

Arnold cabled Spaatz on 30 July with a favor: recognizing that Spaatz was swamped with the affairs both of the Eighth and planning requirements for TORCH, Arnold was dispatching two stellar colonels, Lauris Norstad and Hoyt S. Vandenberg, to lend a hand. However, there was more behind the assignments than a thoughtful provision of extra talent; Arnold included verbiage in the cable to Spaatz that was clear as to what the chief wanted of his air force commander: "Arnold recognized that Eisenhower, because he had Marshall's complete confidence and would soon be a power in his own right, should have the best air advice available, especially if he were in charge of American airpower's most important theater. . . . Arnold wanted Eisenhower to accept Spaatz's [Eighth Air Force] headquarters as his own air planning unit. 'Get him to use you in that way as he is the head of all US Army Forces in Europe. I want him to recognize you as the top air man [*sic*] in all Europe.'"[21] The reality was, though, that there was nobody else to whom Eisenhower could logically turn, even if he wanted. Arnold was of no mind to send out anyone else for the job, and Spaatz was already the senior American airman in Europe. Still, Arnold thought that placing two outstanding colonels with Spaatz would compel Eisenhower to utilize the Eighth's officers as the ETO's air planners, especially as TORCH was subordinate to—not separate from—the ETO.

Arnold waited nine days—barely enough time for the two colonels to travel and find quarters—before poking Spaatz with a sharp follow-up. "I am not satisfied that Ike is using you and your staff to the extent that we hoped he would. Perhaps geographical separation, or other factors not in evidence here lead him toward decisions without the advice and counsel of the air-thought [*sic*] represented in your command."[22] Spaatz, busy, replied two days later, laconically informing Arnold that Norstad and Vandenburg had already been assigned to ETO headquarters as air planners for the future cross-channel invasion and TORCH, respectively. Recently arrived Haywood Hansell, new plans chief for the Eighth, was also to be the theater commander's air plans officer and would reside in the same house as Spaatz and the senior staff. On the nineteenth Arnold sent Spaatz a personal letter acknowledging his "impatience" while making no apology for any premature disruption such might cause nor asking for any understanding for this trait—such was his make-up, he wrote, always had been, always will be, and "that was that."[23] Arnold's gift of Norstad and Vandenburg would be short-lived: the chief would soon detach and "regift" them to Jimmy Doolittle, who would need them more than Spaatz as he took the new Twelfth Air Force to northwest Africa. Norstad and Vandenberg would serve as Doolittle's chief of staff and A-3.[24]

Spaatz and Ike

In England it was apparent that Ike at first had a bit of trouble looking past Tooey's methods of running his headquarters, not because it was inefficient (it decidedly was not) but because the airman's methods were almost alien to the theater commander's strict, rural Kansas upbringing. Ike's attitudes were then possibly heightened by habits Ike might have assimilated while working, twice, for the officious General Douglas MacArthur. Spaatz's work habits were simply an itch that Eisenhower could not scratch. In autumn 1942 the British gifted the Eighth with a new headquarters built especially for the Americans at Bushy Park, sufficiently large to occupy parts of Kingston and Teddington boroughs. Twenty miles from London and on the grounds of Hampton Palace, it bore the codename WIDEWING. But Spaatz's personal residence and offices were at Park House, a "medium-sized country house" (to Ike, a "large mansion") close to Wimbledon. Spaatz preferred to conduct all official business in the comfort and casual atmosphere of a residence instead of the formality of an office; while to an outsider it might at first blush have resembled something of a fraternity house, it was a disciplined military facility that "operated on a 24-hour basis." It probably did not help build rapport with Ike that the Eighth's commanding general "loved poker, bridge, Cuban cigars, and Kentucky whiskey."[25] But there was more behind Spaatz's style of conducting business than comfort and ease. "By keeping his senior officers close at hand, messing, drinking, and even gaming with them, he established a firm and deep rapport with his subordinates. He did not make a habit of issuing long, detailed orders. General Curtis LeMay, who served under Spaatz in both the Pacific and European Theaters of World War II, recalled many years later that he 'never got any direct orders from General Spaatz on anything,' but after a few hours of sitting at the same poker table in the evening, he understood what Spaatz wanted him to do."[26] The house operated around the clock with routine papers brought out to the residents usually at the end of the working day, although one officer could also recall rushing to Park House at two in the morning when "General Anderson came out in his bathrobe and General Spaatz served us tea . . . [during] a big night we were up all night in some cases."[27] In relaxed times the bar was open in the evening and often a high stakes poker game, usually with the general at the table, would be in progress. A former staff member likened the general to "a literary character who was a night worker more than a day worker. The last thing in the world he wanted was an 8 o'clock officers call someplace with everybody sitting down at desks pushing paper around. . . . He just didn't want to be bothered with administration or minor matters. He refused to be."[28] Spaatz later explained that Park House was a system in which, for it to work, "you needed good men that are doing the job . . . and they must be loyal to you."[29]

Eight months after the TORCH invasion, Eisenhower made notes on all of his senior officers in anticipation of a possible later need. He applauded Spaatz as a "fine technician who fits into the Allied team very well indeed." Then he devoted another dozen sentences to Spaatz's style, which had left Ike wondering whether the airman was "tough and hard enough to meet the full requirements" of the mission. Spaatz was "constantly urging more promotions for his forces . . . he wants a liquor ration for his men . . . he apparently picked officers more for their personal qualifications of comradeship and friendliness than for their abilities as businesslike . . . while it is possible that his methods are correct for his particular job, the fact is that I never have great confidence in his recommendations for promotions of personnel." The theater commander closed on a positive note, admitting "this weakness is his only one . . . he does not seek personal glory or publicity, and he is a most loyal and hardworking subordinate."[30] By victory in May of 1945, the supreme Allied commander had come around completely. After the war Eisenhower could not have been more complimentary: "The Eighth Air Force was allocated to our theater, with General Spaatz assigned to me as its commander. From the time of his arrival in London in July [sic] he was never long absent from my side until the last victorious shot had been fired in Europe. On every succeeding day of almost three years of active war I had new reasons for thanking the gods of war and the War Department for giving me Tooey Spaatz. He shunned the limelight and was so modest and retiring that the public probably never became fully cognizant of his value."[31]

Monthly Updates

On 9 August, with the pending Sottéville mission on weather hold, Eaker drafted an update in partial response to a late July letter in which the chief had pushed for earlier bomber strikes and complained about the British press. This cable would become the first of Eaker's eighteen monthly status reports, in addition to many equally long or longer cables that inevitably highlighted the positive, explained—or excused—the negative, and repeated his confidence in the progress and performance of his aircrews.[32] In the beginning Arnold claimed high interest in Eaker's correspondence, being able to devote his personal time to each missive from England. As early as 26 August, with the Eighth having flown but five strikes, Arnold wrote to Spaatz that he had read "Ira's report on his bombing missions with great care [and] hope that you will continue to send me these reports," finding reports with the "personal touch" useful in briefings.[33] But as the AAF grew exponentially from 250,000 officers and men toward an organization of 2.7 million personnel in two years, the chief's continued ability to devote personal attention to correspondence decreased concomitantly. Arnold would have little choice but to use officers on the Air Staff and his advisory council to deal with correspondence from his senior commanders, trusting them to keep him apprised of the more critical issues. Brigadier General Larry Kuter, at age 36, was drafting many of the "personal letters for [Arnold] to send to Air Force commanders in the far-flung combat theaters," an exercise of trust that also "suggests an unusual congruence of thinking" by the two.[34] After Arnold established his advisory council, some of those officers also wrote under Arnold's name and, upon becoming Arnold's chief of staff in October of 1944, Brigadier General Larry Norstad likewise found it both useful and necessary to write in the chief's name.[35]

Eaker's prototypical lengthy cable of 9 August postulating four progressive phases of strategic bombing to the chief was almost certainly too long, too detailed, and too purely theoretical for the chief's complete attention, splintered as it was among the uncountable demands upon him by that time. It also proffered an overly detailed explication as to why he could not do what the chief had been pushing him to do—undertake sustained bombardment of German targets. Even at this early stage of the war, Arnold had already heard the usual reasons—weather, training, shortages of aircraft and crew availability, and more—as to why the bombers were still sitting on their hardstands. As these and other problems would neither be solved quickly nor magically disappear, Eaker would only continue to repeat them in response to Arnold's continuing demands for explanations and growing frustration.

Eaker kept Arnold faithfully current with events in the Eighth, inevitably expressing his points in three to five detailed pages, although half that number of pages might have sufficed for many of the reports. Worse, the bomber commander's first status report was replete with unwelcomed news, leaving the chief not "placated in the least." Victimized by his usual impatience, Arnold sent an acerbic response not to Eaker but to Spaatz, pushing for "immediate or early initiation" of the bombing campaign to foreclose any doubts as to the abilities of the heavy bombers to perform the missions.[36] Attuned to the need to prove the Doctrine, Spaatz replied that in his seven weeks in England there had been only a half dozen days when weather would have allowed for visual bombing from twenty-five thousand feet, but that they would of course bomb when the weather permitted. Nothing more needed saying, but after this Arnold addressed his concerns on the daily operations of VIII Bomber Command directly to Eaker rather than through Spaatz first, despite normal protocol requirements.

Arnold, Spaatz, and Eaker

Arnold met Major Carl "Tooey" Spaatz after the Great War and, upon assuming command of Rockwell Field, San Diego, had Spaatz assigned as his executive officer. Captain Ira Eaker, a pursuit pilot, was already at the airfield, and when Arnold needed a post adjutant, he chose Eaker.[37] Also at the airfield was a remarkable young reserve lieutenant whose military service in World War II would almost rival the other three; his name was James Harold "Jimmy" Doolittle.[38] Arnold recognized Eaker's many outstanding qualities early in their relationship, including his ability to accomplish any assigned task quickly and expertly. Eaker had been born in hard-scrabble West Texas and was attending a small state college in Durant, Oklahoma, as a journalism major before dropping out in 1918 to join the army. Described as "soft-spoken, athletic, modest and retiring almost to the point of shyness," he was inevitably courteous in the way of the antebellum South. As an observer to the RAF in the early days of World War II, he developed a strong affinity for the British, later counting Air Chief Marshal Arthur Harris among his dearest friends. As commanding general of the Eighth, his close friendships and cooperative attitude, and a belief that these traits were integral elements of his assignment, may have unwittingly become part of his problems with Arnold by supporting British positions over those of his own Service once too often.[39]

Eaker was serving as executive assistant to the chief of the AS in 1924 when Arnold reported in as chief of the Information Division and the two reunited with Spaatz, also working for the chief as assistant operations officer (G-3), to participate in the defense of Brigadier General Billy Mitchell at his court-martial.[40] The trio became fast friends despite the age differences, with Spaatz five years younger than Arnold and Eaker five years younger than Spaatz.[41] One historian opined that both Spaatz and Eaker were "selected by Arnold because they had shared with him the struggle to establish American air forces during the years of isolation, and both supported his view of the strategic importance of independent airpower."[42] "Spaatz and Arnold were the closest of confidents from 1918 until the latter's death in 1950. . . . Eaker was almost as close to both."[43]

While Arnold advanced Eaker as well as Spaatz, it was the latter in whom Arnold confided, sought advice, and viewed as an equal. Eaker was different; he saw Arnold as a mentor and, if he did not truly idolize Arnold, he gave a fine impression of it.[44] Eaker, to Arnold, was always the promising protégé to whom the elder gave, but rarely sought, advice. Yet the two nonetheless enjoyed a strong friendship. In the early 1930s, while Eaker was earning a degree at the University of Southern California and Arnold commanded March Field in Riverside, they flew together on the weekends, along with Spaatz and even Doolittle occasionally. Once again reunited in Washington, DC, Arnold and Eaker turned coauthors, publishing three books together; Arnold was the intellectual force, Eaker put the ideas into logical and clear prose.[45] Eaker thought Spaatz was "terse . . . a miser with words" and was fond of saying that "if Tooey had brought down the Ten Commandments from Sinai, there would have been only one, 'Always do the right thing.'"[46] Tooey Spaatz learned experientially and by listening carefully; throughout his career he was well-served by excellent instincts and intimate knowledge of "training, operations, administration, and staff work." His personal make-up of "self-confidence, honesty, loyalty, and courage" and reputation as a "man of action" served to set him apart from the rest.[47]

The Push to Bomb

Arnold, impatient to show Congress, the president, and the American people that American bombers were attacking German targets, evinced little awareness or concern over just how debilitating to flight operations the northern European weather patterns could be, and not for just a day or two, but for weeks at a time and to bomber operations specifically. HADPB—something Arnold sought to prove, although he was skeptical—required a sky at least six-tenths clear of clouds to see, visually, the target through the Norden sight more than twenty-thousand feet below, but weather was frequently too poor even to launch. When the raids did go, the returning aircrews often found that the weather at home was even worse, with many pilots and navigators untrained in or unqualified for the British instrument landing system in near zero-zero conditions. Spaatz and Eaker in England rejected Arnold's orders when they went "beyond what they considered prudent," with the chief usually backing off when Spaatz was correspondent. But with Eaker Arnold could seldom abide more than a few days before beginning his "perpetual questioning, doubting, needling, and puppeteering."[48] There were undoubtedly times when Eaker would have been better off saying "yes, sir" in a one sentence reply rather than demurring in five explanatory pages, no matter how politely stated or elegantly explained. But it seldom happened; Eaker would never learn.

Chapter 9

Ike

TORCH C-in-C

Eisenhower's selection as commander of Operation TORCH was announced
on 8 August 1942 and officially approved by the CCS on the thirteenth.[1]
Significantly, he would continue as commanding general of ETOUSA,
with responsibilities for BOLERO and ROUNDUP. Ike quickly delegated
TORCH responsibilities to his deputy, Major General Mark Wayne Clark, a
strong indication that he did not consider TORCH his primary job. In fact,
Ike thought TORCH was "only diversionary in character, necessitated by
the circumstances of the moment" and requiring his involvement for only
a matter of weeks, after which he would return to England and continue
preparations for the larger cross-channel invasion, now less than a year off.[2]
Spaatz was working with Eisenhower every day on their primary responsibility, BOLERO/ROUNDUP, and although they probably did not realize it at
the time, they would henceforth be joined together until the end of the war.
For Spaatz this date proved to be "the start of an effective, close, working
relationship that did much to advance the cause of the Allies and, to a lesser
extent, the Army Air Forces."[3] Spaatz worked diligently and harmoniously

to ensure that Eisenhower always had the necessary as quickly, efficiently, and effectively as possible. After the war, Spaatz described his relationship with Eisenhower "as a rather close personal relationship, and I think on both sides that mutual confidence made it unnecessary to have long detailed explanations for courses of action." Between 1 July and 31 October 1942, Spaatz's command diaries show that the two "conferred" fifty-five times.[4] A more vocal man might have elaborated on his interaction with Ike, but the brevity was genuine Spaatz.

Rarely did Spaatz have any doubts as to what Ike wanted his air arm to do or what the objectives were, and Ike inevitably left the "how" to do those things to Spaatz's professional judgment. In return, out of courtesy and discretion, Spaatz would privately raise issues that might be problematic for Ike before putting the matters into official channels. In July Arnold had given Spaatz a second command, that of the AAF in the European theater. Now in August Arnold formally requested Eisenhower to name Spaatz as the air officer for the ETO. Arnold sent the request through channels, and after 21 August Spaatz would hold these three commands until leaving for the Mediterranean at year's end.[5] Spaatz, who detested even perceptions of "empire building," much less the actual practice, added the responsibilities for the other two theaters to those of his Eighth headquarters staff rather than create new staffs, impressing Ike, who also looked askance at "empires." These assignments accomplished Arnold's objective of "keeping air power and its advocates in the forefront of the theater scheduled to receive the preponderance of US wartime air strength."[6]

Ike and Ira

As commanding general of ETOUSA, Eisenhower was the direct reporting senior officer for Spaatz, and while Ike assiduously followed the chain of command by sending orders to the Eighth's bomber command via Spaatz, it was inevitable that he would still have personal contact with Eaker. In fact, they had met on and off the usual way, at the War Department working in various staff positions. As with Spaatz, Eisenhower and Eaker saw their prewar friendship develop into something stronger during the conflict in Europe: "The new theater commander and Eaker were well acquainted but they had never served together. Eisenhower and Eaker had many similarities. Both were born in small Texas towns, both had warm, considerate personalities and instinctively courteous manners, both were pragmatic in philosophy, adapting easily to change in military concepts or circumstances. But Eisenhower was far more of an extrovert and with a sharp temper he did not always, like Eaker, keep under control. The two men quickly reached a level of comfortable frankness and became close friends."[7] When Eaker, still a lieutenant general, retired in 1947 as deputy chief of staff of the AAF, he received a "Dear Ira" note from Army Chief of Staff Eisenhower in which were enclosed four coins—one each from Britain, Africa, and France, plus an American silver dollar—that the five-star general had carried with him throughout the war. The handwritten note was signed, "Your devoted friend, Ike."[8]

The Air Forces Men

Spaatz, like Eaker, Arnold, Hansell and others, never lost sight of objectives of import to the air forces, predominantly the need to prove the viability and effectiveness of the Doctrine. Eaker went quickly on the record touting both the Doctrine and the superfluity of fighter escorts, a sign of how thoroughly Eaker, a career pursuit pilot, absorbed the Doctrine while a student at ACTS. On 21 August, after just four missions by VIII Bomber Command, Eaker bragged in a letter to Major General George Stratemeyer, chief of air staff at HqAF, "the boys can do high altitude precision bombing in the daytime" while retaining "confidence that we can do deeper penetrations without fighter support and get by with it."[9] Well! That first raid on 17 August to Sottéville had just twelve bombers but 108 escorts. The second mission was a milk run for twenty-two heavies to the Abbeville/Drucat airfield in Calais on the nineteenth; the third strike was next day, when eleven Fortresses hit marshaling yards at Amiens with no losses but also no Luftwaffe defenders. The fourth mission on the twenty-first was a fiasco, as all twelve B-17s from the 97th BG lost their way over the channel on their way to Rotterdam while missing their escort rendezvous. Two dozen Luftwaffe fighters then jumped the errant Fortresses, resulting in one American KIA and five WIA; the bombers were recalled at the French coast and the mission aborted.[10] Yet Eaker's letter to Stratemeyer reflected unbounded confidence, unleavened by that day's reality.

HADPB was ever present in Eaker's mind and would exert a strong, occasionally exuberant influence, sometimes overtly and sometimes from deep within the shadows. An existential imperative was that the Eighth was the only AAF unit in the world that was positioned, with respect to geography, targets, and weather, to prove the validity of the Doctrine. This was partly driven unknowingly by Churchill, who was steadfast in his conviction that precision daylight bombing would fail from too many casualties. Fortunately, the three most important RAF officers for the Allies pushed their own doubts aside and strongly supported the Americans. Chief of Air Staff Portal spoke at the Second Washington Conference in favor of daylight precision bombardment, having decided to "use all of his influence to stop Churchill from crippling the American experiment." Portal stood fast behind the Eighth even in the worst of times as he "repeatedly and successfully pressed" the Americans to do all they could to quickly bring the Eighth up to its full strength; by bombing during the day, the AAF would become a full partner with the RAF in the air war. The RAF leader believed "from first to last" in the American strategy because, if it were successful, it would be superior to area bombardment "and 'round-the-clock bombing would be more effective" than either daytime or nighttime bombing alone would be.[11] Air Marshall Jack Slessor, arguably the warmest RAF leader toward the AAF, was convinced that the Doctrine would be "prohibitively expensive in casualties" but that it was essential to victory. Slessor was also more forgiving of the Eighth's "rather slow progress" in attaining a proficiency in the business of air warfare; he never failed to make clear to critics that "the Eighth's crews arrived in this country with quiet inadequate operational training [which was] largely due to their generosity in the past in giving us so many aircraft that they badly needed for training themselves." Moreover, Slessor thought any attempt to change the American's minds from a doctrine in which "they held such a passionate belief" could create serious resentment and even cause the Americans to direct their forces to the Pacific.[12]

Harris, who inevitably spoke in such an open, direct, and honest manner that he earned the admiration and respect of the Americans, was as usual clear-eyed about the Doctrine.[13] Before Pearl Harbor Harris ridiculed both the Doctrine and the B-17, telling any who would listen that AAF "could not be counted as among the first class air powers" and that he was unable to comprehend "the myth of American air power." But Harris quickly joined the AAF's staunchest supporters once the Americans were in the game.[14] He argued strongly, along with Spaatz, against using Eighth resources for anything other than operations against Germany, asserting the quickest way to victory was for the two strategic air forces to combine their assets in nocturnal bombardment. Yet Harris told Eaker in all honesty that "nobody will hope that you succeed more strongly than I do, and I am going to do everything I can to support your efforts."[15] And so he did. After the Combined Bomber Offensive (CBO) was approved in spring of 1943, Harris only wished to "see the Eighth Air Force vigorously reinforced and actively engaged over Germany."[16] Which did not mean, of course, that Harris or anyone else in the RAF, for that matter, thought HADPB was a marvelous idea, because none did, so convinced were they of its ultimate failure. Eventually, Eisenhower believed that both services were so certain in their positions that discussions could only be "centered exclusively around the one point of feasibility"—executing the CBO with each service following its own methodology.[17]

Chapter 10

Tooey, Ike, and Hap

Growing JUNIOR

The United States Twelfth Air Force, codename JUNIOR, was activated for TORCH at Bolling Field, Washington, DC, on 20 August 1942 with the job of air officer for TORCH falling into Spaatz's ETO portfolio the next day—one more indication that TORCH belonged to the European theater. On 31 August the Twelfth's advance party arrived at VIII Bomber Command in response to Eaker's invitation to colocate the Twelfth's headquarters with that of the Eighth, a generous act of comity to facilitate the transfer of men and aircraft to the new air force. Brigadier General Jimmy Doolittle, the Twelfth's commanding general, remained in Scotland with his command staff, assembling the pieces until leaving for Gibraltar in Eisenhower's wake.[1] Although Doolittle, after leaving active service, was a test pilot for Shell Oil, both Spaatz and Marshall supported his assignment even though he had literally no command experience, notwithstanding the airplanes and crews of his Tokyo Raiders. Doolittle had never built from scratch a large military organization, but then neither had any other senior officer in the AAF; and certainly neither Doolittle nor his subordinate officers had ever to shanghai thousands of troops and hundreds of airplanes to do it.[2] But he proved to be an exceptionally effective and efficient commander—despite Eisenhower's initial negative impressions and expressed desire for a different commander for the Twelfth—and a greatly respected leader, from Marshall down.[3] Doolittle and Eaker had been friends at March Field in the 1920s but had grown apart after Doolittle resigned to pursue civilian aviation.[4] Doolittle assumed command officially on 23 September, immediately commencing the massive migration of men, airplanes, and equipment from the Eighth to the Twelfth: when the headquarters element departed for North Africa on 24 October, nearly 3,200 officers, 24,000 enlisted men, and 1,244 aircraft had been transferred from the Eighth and more were in the offing. For the next four-plus months, over one half of all the supplies meant for the Eighth and the lion's share of its aircraft maintenance work, from routine to modifications to damage repair, were for aircraft of Doolittle's command.[5] The nascent ability of the Eighth to take the war to the enemy in devastating numbers was crushed as the transfers to the Twelfth had left the Eighth "little more than a skeleton."[6] It would be almost eighteen months before the Eighth would have as many aircraft again. Eisenhower's air requirements for TORCH totaled 1,698 aircraft, with the RAF supplying 454. To provide that many airplanes meant Spaatz would lose his few experienced groups in addition to new arrivals.[7]

The association of Spaatz and Eisenhower was crucial to the development of their relationship for the remainder of the war, and Spaatz entered convinced it was his responsibility to "establish confidence in the initial work of the strategic air forces." This, to Spaatz, meant "giving consideration to Eisenhower's task in Africa" even though Spaatz "had no concern with it at the time." Spaatz never questioned that his first duty was to Eisenhower and TORCH: "I had to weigh in the balance very carefully what I needed to do to make the Eighth operative immediately and what I had to let go with the Twelfth Air Force to make that function . . . I gave greater weight to Africa because that was an imminent thing that had to be a success."[8] Spaatz acknowledged later that he "leaned over backwards in taking care of the requirements for the African campaign," since the air war in Europe was progressing ever so slowly while TORCH was moving quickly.[9]

Still, Spaatz was disappointed, wondering, "What is left of the Eighth after the impact of TORCH? We find we haven't much left."[10] His air force had been gutted, and along with it the anticipated strategic bombing campaign against Germany; suffering one setback after another, his heavy bombers had yet to drop one ounce of steel on German soil. Arnold was even more pessimistic, as he "saw Operation TORCH as a threat to the very existence of the Eighth Air Force . . . [before] it was completed, the depleted Eighth might be absorbed into the Royal Air Force's night campaign."[11] This, he feared, would become a fatal setback in the ultimate quest for an independent air force. As for Eaker, he gave Doolittle all the support possible—with one exception: while losing his experienced heavy groups, he also knew that the heart of any unit is its leadership. With this thought he held back a few of the outstanding officers for the benefit of VIII Bomber Command by transferring them from their groups to the protection of staff positions at Eighth headquarters.[12]

Spaatz's willingness, however reluctant, to build the Twelfth at the expense of the Eighth meant working closely with Eisenhower. It created a deep reservoir of trust and confidence between the two men that transcended rank and position. When it was mentioned to Spaatz in a postwar interview that the "strategic concept [of TORCH] might have failed if it had not been for that close [personal] relationship," the airman replied, "It is quite possible."[13] In continuing a conversation by correspondence begun by Arnold few days earlier, Spaatz did not hesitate to speak his mind. Among other points, he "reiterated the folly" of trying to fight a global war when Germany was the primary threat and the UK was the best location from which to fight them. It was "time for the powers that be" to realize that establishing air supremacy over Germany required a mass of bombers flying in daylight hours, but fighters were unnecessary; past operations, although only a few, had nonetheless proven the ability of the bombers to drop accurately from above twenty thousand feet. When the bomber force "has been built up," operations into the "heart of Germany" without fighter escort would be possible, and nothing else but that held promise for the Allies.[14]

Arnold and TORCH

General Arnold disliked TORCH from the first. Correspondence between
Arnold and Spaatz from mid-August through the first week or so of September
gives a glimpse into thoughts of both about the immediate and near future.
On 19 August Arnold began drafting a long memo to Marshall in which
he stated frankly that the "current dispersion of Army Air Forces aircraft"
not just to TORCH but "throughout the world causes me great concern."
First "Luftwaffe air operations have always been outstanding in all theaters," with an "overwhelming superiority of numbers (1500–2000) in all
major theaters of operation." Yet for North Africa, Arnold told Marshall, the
AAF was planning to deploy only 657 aircraft; the RAF would contribute
another 150 aircraft "supplemented temporarily" by eighty to one hundred
aircraft from the US Navy in the initial stages. The USN-RAF contribution
of "only 166 carrier-borne aircraft" was supposed to seize all the needed
airfields. In support of his position, the chief included a two-page survey of
the problems facing the landing troops and ships in the invasion forces when
arrayed against the aircraft numbers deployable by the Germans. Attached
was a trenchant analysis of what a buildup for additional air assets in North
Africa would or could mean for other global areas, including Alaska, the
Pacific generally, and the Celebes and Solomon Islands specifically, highlighting Arnold's acute awareness of the worldwide strategic problems that
would be affected by North Africa. True to his (and Spaatz's) beliefs, Arnold
reinforced his position that the war in Europe had to be pursued relentlessly
against Germany's great industrial strength; while the conflict in the Pacific
was important, he postulated fighting there would not win the larger war.
Closing, he urged Marshall to "assign the maximum forces to the combined
European-North African Theater [to] ensure tactical success and permit decisive strategic operations."[15]

In a 26 August letter to Spaatz, Arnold wrote that he was "trying to
reconcile" TORCH with what he believed was the "limited" number of
aircraft requested for it, but then followed that with a plea for "someone"
also to ask for enough aircraft for the Eighth's missions. Arnold then opined
that the solution was for that "someone" to be Spaatz, who could request

more planes and men to "properly" take the offensive against Germany.[16] Regarding the "limited" numbers, Arnold was bothered in diverse ways by what he referred to as "The Special Operation," having told General Marshall on the nineteenth that it was "generally accepted that the North African operation has *less than a 5% chance of success* [Arnold's emphasis]." He then shared that with Spaatz in early September.[17] Clearly, at that early stage of the war, Arnold was seeing not only North Africa as a "sideshow" of the European theater but also the fight against the Japanese as something of lesser import than the European war. Separately, there was no daylight between Spaatz's and Arnold's opinions on the wisdom and modalities of prosecuting the air war in Europe, as well as their antipathy for the North African venture. Despite this emphatic disapproval for TORCH, Arnold, with the TORCH decision made, ensured the air forces were fully committed to its success—and that the army chief of staff knew it. Still, his principal concern was the "absolute necessity" for the air offensive against "Germany proper" although no missions would be flown into the Third Reich until 1943 because of the aircraft/aircrew drain for TORCH.

Within the War Department there were concurrent pressures from the navy for an "all-out offensive" in the Pacific now that navy–Marine Corps operations in the Solomon Islands had placed the air forces in what Arnold was termed "a very tight spot." Still, Arnold assured Spaatz, while Arnold was doing whatever was necessary to help achieve success in North Africa, those measures did not also encompass "weakening" Spaatz's mission.[18] Spaatz was equally concerned through the late summer and fall about the "dispersion" of the Eighth's assets and how "easily" the war could be lost if it continued. Conversely, he was certain that it could be "expeditiously" brought to successful conclusion if the Eighth could join its strength with that of the RAF.[19] Regardless of the machinations at higher levels, both Eaker and Spaatz were highly generous, almost worshipful, in their praises of the men of the Eighth, officer and enlisted alike. As Spaatz ended one communication, "This gang of mechanics, pilots, gunners, etc., etc., are the most audacious, intelligent, alert, and eager for combat gang that God has created . . . [add] to them with the necessary numbers [of aircraft] and the war is in the bag."[20]

The generals were also worried about a potential problem should either a German victory occur in Russia or the German and Soviet forces move into a World War I–type trench war stalemate. Either condition could allow the Germans to rejuvenate the Luftwaffe and permit the redeployment of large numbers of fighter groups from Russia to the western front. These units would then be positioned to confront strikes by VIII Bomber Command and, in turn, would permit Luftwaffe bombers to again subject the British Isles to deadly air raids. To their relief, on 24 August the president directed the AAF to revise its requirements for new aircraft first and then other production requirements necessary "for complete air ascendancy over the enemy," the details of which soon became enshrined in another AWPD.[21]

The abuse of the Eighth's aircraft and aircrew inventory did not end with the TORCH landings on 8 November. Not only were other units and men intermittently transferred from England to North Africa for as long as a year afterward, but Eaker was also later directed to send three of his five B-24 groups to the Ninth Air Force in Libya for inclusion in the 1 August 1943 strike on the Ploęsti refineries. The first elements of the new 389th Bombardment Group (H), would be in England for three days, obviously had no combat experience, and would politely be described as "incompletely" trained—an inoffensive way of stating the hard truth that an excessive number of men would likely die for lack of training and combat exposure. Ultimately, fifty-four Liberators and crews were lost on the strike, with seven more forfeited to neutral Turkey and the crews interned; the surviving airplanes would not be returned to Eighth Air Force control until nearly October, two months after the strike.[22]

One letter of the several from the chief to Spaatz on 19 August was manifestly different in tone, written simply from one friend to another, rather than from senior to subordinate. The chief opened with the personal "My Dear Tooey," noting its dispatch by "special messenger for you and you alone." The personal was also evident in one overly long sentence in which Arnold confessed to Spaatz—who undoubtedly was well aware—that "you can't blame me for being impatient, because I have been impatient all my life . . . but that's my make-up and that's that." Several of Spaatz's recent correspondences had obviously resonated with Arnold, for the latter advised his friend that he had broken out various issues and distributed them among the air staff for action or responses that were to be aggregated into one cable so that the air force commander would know "of the actions taken." Arnold also admitted that the "one thing that disturbs me and it disturbs me mightily is the tendency of the Strategic Planners to take aircraft away from the European Theater and throw it in the Southwest Pacific Theater."[23]

Arnold then related his "great concern" that Marshall and King returned from their final attempt to persuade His Majesty's government not to pursue TORCH bearing the "approval apparently of everybody in London for the dispersion of about fifteen groups to the southwest Pacific theater." "I wondered why," mused the chief, still perturbed, "somebody didn't make a formal protest," and even more so how anyone at the meetings could believe that TORCH would be a success with just six bombardment groups and five pursuit groups; he also recounted the numbers of an expected, much larger Luftwaffe presence. Having then "gotten that outburst off my chest," Arnold concluded with three paragraphs covering various situations in seven theaters of war, an analysis of the Eighth's strength vis-à-vis the Luftwaffe, and a plea for the leadership to stand up and get the Eighth all that it needed. The AAF commander was preaching to the choirmaster.[24]

Chapter 11

AWPD-42

A perpetual source of Arnold's disquietude was that pressures from other war theaters for more resources were continually appeased with aircraft and critical assets originally intended for the Eighth. Each time aircrews and aircraft were taken from the Eighth and sent elsewhere, it seriously affected the nascent air war against the Third Reich and the "continuous application of massed air power against critical objectives." A partial resolution was the chief's insistence that the few primary theaters receive the lion's share of the resources while minor theaters make do with the minimum until the domestic industrial machine could catch up with demand. Arnold solicited Spaatz's aid to spread the message, contending that without strong outside support, the Eighth would see its own air assets become so "dissipated" throughout the lesser commands that its efforts to take the war to the enemy would be imperiled.[1] Spaatz, just as concerned, authored a bluntly worded cable that Ike sent under ETOUSA's authority to the army chief of staff for passage to Arnold, a cable path that carried more heft than if it had come direct from the Eighth. The cable made four points: the utilization of the air forces in the UK for any purpose other than attaining supremacy over Germany "jeopardizes the attainment of supremacy . . . and of ultimate victory," any diversion of air forces units intended for the ETO "jeopardizes ultimate victory," the application of airpower comes from "well prepared and well defended airbases . . . which exist only in the UK," and the "new operation [TORCH] can be accomplished only at the expense of present operations" by the Eighth.[2] Bureaucratically, Spaatz made his point; functionally, the Twelfth still rated the highest priority of any unit in the AAF, which continued to work to the detriment of the Eighth.

AWPD-42

Brigadier General Haywood Hansell, billeted in Park House with the senior staff, was abruptly recalled to Washington literally in the middle of the night of 26 August by General Marshall. Marshall's cable informed that: "(a) the president has called for an immediate detailed air war plan; (b) required data is the essential modernization and extension of AWPD 1; (c) basic factors consists of study of objectives the destruction of which will guarantee air ascendancy over enemy; (d) specific data . . . confirming or disproving assumptions in AWPD-1 is of vital importance to this study." Marshall closed ominously: "The results of this [study] are of such far reaching importance that it will probably determine whether or not we control the air."[3] Accompanying Hansell to Washington were Eaker, at Spaatz's direction because of "the vital importance of the forth-coming decisions" for TORCH; Lieutenant Colonel Dick Hughes from Eighth Air Force A-5; and Major Harris Hull, of VIII Bomber Command A-2. Undaunted, Hansell described the mission simply as the president wanting "to know the number of military airplanes that should be produced in 1943 to attain air supremacy."[4]

Subsequently, Arnold referred to AWPD-42 as "an up-to-date version of AWPD-1 [which it was not] and based on the same premise," that Germany was the "principal enemy that had to be disposed of first" (which was accurate). He further emphasized that the "principal objectives of the new plan, as well as the old, were to be attained by *precision bombing* [Arnold's emphasis; Hansell's implication]."[5] The next day Spaatz cabled an appeal to Arnold to return the two generals as soon as possible, for "Hansell is thoroughly familiar with my ideas on overall organization [and] Eaker's ideas of operations exactly parallel mine." Interspersed with lesser issues, Spaatz gave a strong voice to his oft-expressed feelings that denuding the Eighth of heavy bombers was a mistake. He urged Arnold to keep in mind the "vital necessity of continuing our present operations in this theater," expressing concern that TORCH would "prevent the essential blow to the German Air Power" that would "insure the eventual knockout blow"—perhaps another hint of Spaatz's belief that air power alone could bring victory. Insisting once again that TORCH and operations by the Eighth against Germany were "incompatible," Spaatz emphasized that the "idea must be put across that the war can be won against Germany or it can be lost . . . very easily if there is a continuation of our dispersion." He concluded noting that although Japan's defeat might be "soul-satisfying," it would "leave us no better off than we were on December 7."[6]

Hansell returned to WIDEWING in the middle of September, having written AWPD-42 in ten days. As with the predecessor AWPD, Hansell exercised an extraordinary degree of latitude, certain Arnold would approve. The older war plan, explained Hansell, was a "contingency plan" if war should eventuate, while the current plan was "essentially a 'requirements' plan for the current war specifying munitions, bases, and air needs to carry out an agreed strategy." Hansell also used the document to "represent the mature realization of interwar thinking" of the Bomber Mafia, proselytizing within the document itself for the Doctrine.[7] Hansell identified 177 targets in the Third Reich and occupied Europe and stated that, if attacked by heavy bombers for six months flying a total of 66,045 sorties, it would result in the destruction of the Luftwaffe, a "depletion" of the U-boat force, and a "disruption of the German war economy."[8] AWPD-42 made no pretense of defining a strategic, war-winning air campaign, instead maintaining only that air strikes were preliminary to a successful ground assault against "an enemy weakened through air bombardment." Privately, Hansell assessed that "employing strategic airpower was America's only real offensive option early in the war," and in consonance with most air planners "realized the importance of at least appearing to accept the need for action by surface forces"[9] Hansell was "extremely confident" in his target choices and believed that Germany "would have no choice but to sue for peace."[10] He planned for one-third of the objectives to be achieved in 1943, with the remaining two-thirds to be settled during the four months prior to 1 May 1944, the original D-Day. Although satisfied with the document in postwar analysis, Hansell offered that the greatest fault of AWPD-42 was the omission of the "function and possibility of long-range fighters."[11]

A discussion of the war against Japan was so minimal it might well have been an afterthought, while the specificity given the European war was wanting; mention was given only to "air support for surface operations" in the acquisition of bases for future operations against the Rising Sun.[12] The navy simply walked away from AWPD-42: first, Hansell bypassed navy input—instead of waiting for the navy's numbers he simply supplied his own preferences, to the anger of Admiral King—and then committed a lesser malefaction of assigning to the AAF B-24s requested earlier by the navy for submarine patrol bombers, also displeasing General Marshall.

Arnold, Spaatz, and Eaker were all happy with Hansell's handiwork, receiving exactly what they sought: an air strategy with Germany first and Europe as the primary region for offensive operations against the Axis. As war-making industries in Japan were presently beyond the reach of a sustained air campaign, the AAF argued that the Eighth, specifically, should receive priority over the Pacific; Third Reich military and industrial capabilities were accessible by AAF and RAF bombers, while Japan was still a distant target. Hansell's thinking exactly.

The navy's concurrent Pacific air strategy was not without its validity, but it was also not entirely pristine; while it had legitimate aviation needs, its vigorous ship-building program was one cause of essential materials shortages. In the allocation of those scarce resources, the navy's unacceptable solution was always for the AAF to simply stop building airplanes until the needs of the sea service were met at some future time. These disputes could not be resolved even at the JCS level, thus elevating them automatically to presidential level, where FDR's proclivity was to give each side half a loaf.[13]

Chapter 12

Early Missions

Eaker's after-action critique addressed the 17 August 1942 mission in his methodical, emotionless style, commenting that it was "too early in our experiments" with the Fortresses to know with any certainty whether the aircraft could survive "deep penetrations without fighter escorts and without excessive losses." He then proceeded to state with certainty points that were at best problematical and, at worst, either unknown or flat wrong. Eaker ventured that future Luftwaffe defenders "are going to attack very gingerly"—no doubt wishful thinking; how the Germans were actually going to go after the Fortresses was unknown since there had been no Luftwaffe defenders in the air on the first raid.[1] The general was to learn soon enough that there would be nothing "ginger" about attacks from the Luftwaffe. Nonetheless, on the results of the first mission, Eaker declared firmly the Doctrine was "confirmed." The mission was flown in relatively calm winds, and with no need to take evasive action, the bombers were in level flight at bombs away; different circumstances would likely have returned different results. Eaker, ever the optimist, had projected his heavy bombers would place 10 percent of their bombs dead center on target, 25 percent within 250 yards of target center, 40 percent within 500 yards, and all bombs within one mile of the target, to which

Spaatz responded by praising the "extreme accuracy" of the bombers.[2] He was "overjoyed," reporting to Arnold his "opinion and conviction" that the B-17 was "suitable as to speed, armament, armor, and bomb load." Even the theater commander was not immune from the excitement, with Eisenhower writing on 5 September following mission 9, a return to the marshaling yards at Sottéville-sur-Rouen earlier that day, that he was "becoming convinced" that HADPB was "feasible and highly successful"; all that remained to increase effectiveness was a greater "scale" of attack. He added a plea for a "quick buildup" of the air forces in the UK, with a focus on the heavy bombers.[3] All of this optimism from nine missions, and not one bomber had yet come within three hundred miles of the German homeland.

Eaker forwarded a three-page analysis to Spaatz on 9 October, reiterating the four phases of daylight bombing and asserting the validation of phase one based on the first dozen missions. Those dozen strikes ran the gamut of mixed success between mediocre and total failure, and none had flown farther east than Paris.[4] Near the end of September, seventy-five heavies were sent out to bomb airfields just west of Paris, but only sixteen found their targets and none dropped bombs. One group missed its escorts and, by directive, had to return to England, which was standard procedure (and interesting in that it was counter to the official insistence that escorts were superfluous). Poor weather during the period was the norm, with the missions mostly proving that the bomber crews were still far from combat and instrument flight proficient, which somehow escaped evaluation in Eaker's assessment. VIII Bomber Command went after the Avions Potez factory at Meaulte, near Paris, for the third time on 2 October. There was little to distinguish this mission from the first two against the same target save for one deadly augury of the future: some of the defending Luftwaffe pilots eschewed the usual tail-end attacks on the Fortresses and conducted head-on runs against the undefended noses of the F-model B-17s. This was the cause for one and perhaps both Forts downed that day—the first aircraft losses for the Eighth.[5] Of these first twelve missions, only four had contact with Luftwaffe fighters, but overall, Eaker's feelings were just short of exuberant in apprising Spaatz a week hence of the "validation" of phase one.[6]

Eaker's statements quickly lost some luster, though, with even his aide acknowledging the numbers were "somewhat deceptive." That same day the Luftwaffe came out to fight, going after 108 B-24s and B-17s as they bombed vital railway factory targets in Lille on mission 14. Against earlier attacks, the Germans, seeing how small the American formations were and how little damage they achieved, did not bother "to deploy fighter squadrons specifically to counter them. They did, however, snoop around the edges of early flights, studying the formations, noting the limitations of the B-17's defenses."[7] And as the earlier bombing raids were flown with few or no losses, in part because the heavies were often escorted by four to eight times as many Spitfires as bombers, the leadership continued seemingly to miss the connection between safety and escorts. The Eighth's leaders remained universally upbeat in their assessments. Objectively, though, the "sufficient" test of bombing and navigation skills provided by these dozen missions consisted only from being flown against relatively soft targets and among the easiest to locate and strike any crews would ever face. The escorts, superb Spitfires flown by experienced and blooded RAF pilots, were by far the best defenders the B-17 crews would have for months to come. When, on the ninth, the Luftwaffe came up after the heavies, the German pilots did so in the very capable Focke-Wulf-190, using the new tactics to bring down their American prey. While the Spitfires failed to down any Germans, the enemy downed four heavies and damaged forty-seven, including one DBR (damaged beyond repair).[8] There would be much worse to come.

"Full Explanation" versus the Weather

General Arnold, whose fierce temper seemed to escape more frequently, wrote Spaatz and Eaker jointly also in late October demanding a "full explanation" (soon to become his favorite phrase) for the reasons behind the "infrequency of bomber operations" that had allowed only one mission to be flown since mission 14 on the ninth. The query factually required but a one-word response: weather. Colonel LeMay of the 305th, had he been asked, would have told him that there were only two kinds of weather in the ETO, "lousy and worse."[9] Spaatz, having more, and apparently to him more serious, issues than the weather simply shoehorned illuminating weather issues into discussions of other substantive issues in his reply. Spaatz's first, and presumably most pressing, point was to remind Arnold of "the necessity for a full understanding of the conditions of operations in this theater." "Bad weather" was likewise prominent in the explanation of why VIII Fighter Command's P-38s were released to Doolittle's Twelfth without the desired combat experience. Spaatz underscored once again that "requirements for TORCH have imposed a heavy handicap" on the Eighth for both the present and future.[10] Two genuinely serious handicaps were the deployment of all the Eighth's PR assets to Doolittle and the reality that the Eighth, until a just week prior, possessed a heavy bomber force of over one hundred bombers and three fighter squadron for offensive operations. But no longer.

Raids on the Bay of Biscay U-boat pens received a separate focus from Spaatz, who explained extant factors that would "result in much heavier casualties than heretofore," weather again being first on the list. Other factors included absence of fighter support, as the P-38s now belonged to Doolittle and P-47s had yet to arrive in theater; the pens were heavily defended; the Eighth's aircraft gunners were not as seasoned as those in the 97th Group, also now with Doolittle; a strong enemy fighter presence; and the near impossibility of destroying concrete pens absent armor-piercing ordnance. Spaatz then returned to the first, and most prominent, impediment—abysmal meteorological conditions, reflecting on cloud layers that were forcing the bombers to fly at lower altitudes than were conducive to the accuracy of both light and heavy flak defenses. Spaatz referenced a recent letter he had written to "Strat"— George Stratemeyer, chief of the air staff—commenting that, as the "the military situation" regarding Russia and TORCH was improving, with the Russians keeping the Germans engaged, the prospects for TORCH were looking up. However, this good news threatened to require the temporary presence of an outsized portion of the Eighth's bombers in North Africa should TORCH prevail, mentioning of Eisenhower, "*he will use all of the Eighth Air Force in that manner if necessary* [Spaatz's emphasis]." Consequently, the Eighth was reviewing its organizational tables looking at "mobility and temporary operation by limited personnel."[11]

With the favorable odds for TORCH increasing, Spaatz was comfortable adding a topic that he had touched upon with Ike: the establishment of a single air commander. The Eighth's commander and the chief had already become engaged on this subject, which held the prospect of several distinct advantages. Spaatz, the war fighter, saw pivotal advantages to be derived from the ability to shift air units easily between theaters. Opining that these benefits would soon become "more apparent," he mentioned that his conversations with Eisenhower led him to believe that Ike was also coming to that conclusion. As "air commander" Spaatz would be able to "shift our heavy bomber forces anywhere between Iceland and Iraq; but, to 'capitalize on that potential ability we would have to have unity of air command.'" In the last, Spaatz was almost parroting the words of Marshall and Eisenhower. The letter ended with a postscript summarizing discussions with the RAF's Jack Slessor, TORCH and the European weather receiving the most attention, but also mentioning possibly constructing the P-51 in England with a Merlin-61 engine.[12] In all, the correspondence was visionary relative to key requirements for and the difficulties inherent in an air offensive against the Third Reich flown from the UK.

The Eighth began the month of November with just three heavy groups, one of which had only 51 percent of its aircraft operational, and ended the month in an even worse state, as one operational B-17 group (the 92nd) found its effective strength diminished by 50 percent when one of its squadrons was detailed to RAF Coastal Command for antisubmarine patrols and a second was sent to RAF Alconbury to assist in experimental work for the new H2S blind-bombing program. Additional to the chronic infirmity of unsuitable aviation weather, flying in general was hampered by an inadequacy of spare parts and trained personnel able to keep up with the demands of operational maintenance.[13]

Chapter 13

U-Boats

The U-boat menace was a particular worry in the fall of 1942 as "Allied shipping was being sunk at the average rate of 650,000 tons a month, and the pressure . . . was very strong on the Eighth Air Force to attempt to do something about it."[1] Yet it was doubtful that bombing either the U-boat servicing and resupply bases along France's Biscayan coast or the boats' construction yards off the North Sea in Germany proper would effectively retard the menace. Nor was it certain that the heavy bombers of VIII Bomber Command were the mechanism to inflict the damage in the first place.[2]

> But it was believed that the facilities at these bases were so integrated, and the time schedule for repair and refitting so carefully adjusted, that any damage to the installations surrounding the pens would cause serious delay in turn-around and so, in effect, reduce the number of submarines in operation. Locks, floating docks, storage depots, railway yards, powerhouses, foundries, barracks, and submarines not actually in the pens all appeared to present vulnerable targets for bombing aircraft—especially for bombers equipped for precision operations. It was considered very probable that much of the servicing had been put under concrete along with the submarines themselves and that alternative power installations existed which could be used to relieve most emergencies affecting the power system.[3]

In late October, with TORCH approaching, there were no intelligence mechanisms yet developed to collect the essential information that "too often obscured . . . the mysterious activities of that most mysterious of the enemy services."⁴ But attacking the U-boat facilities with heavy bombers meant that Luftwaffe defenders presented themselves to bombers' guns and escorting fighters, and the destruction of each Messerschmitt or Focke-Wulf was one less to face next mission. Nor was this ancillary opportunity the only additional benefit to accrue from the raids even if, as was later found to be the case, the bombings themselves did little to diminish the Kriegsmarine threat. Eisenhower's directive to strike the pens "marked the first USAAF effort, and signaled the first serious involvement of US intelligence personnel, in the targeting and damage-assessment processes, a key initial step in the development of a mature Allied air intelligence organization."⁵ Spaatz also issued a revised directive saying, "Until further orders, every effort of the VIII Bomber Command will be directed to obtaining the maximum destruction of the submarine bases in the Bay of Biscay."⁶

There were five servicing, repair, and resupply facilities—pens—for U-boats and their crews either on or with direct access to the Bay of Biscay and thence to the open Atlantic. Bases were at Brest, settled by Romans between 200 and 300 AD at the tip of the Bretonne Peninsula; Lorient, with nearly fifty thousand inhabitants, was to the south; St. Nazaire was 3.2 kilometers up the Loire River Estuary; La Pallice was the seaport of the tenth-century Aquitaine city of La Rochelle; and the last was sixty miles up the Gironde River by the Bordeaux city docks. With 240 active U-boats in the Atlantic, these five sanctuaries could collectively service or repair "about 100" at a time.⁷ Even without knowledge of the top-secret landing and shipping schedules for TORCH, at least some of the 140 submarines at sea were sure to cross some of the shipping. In mid-September Eisenhower tasked Spaatz with suppressing the U-boat threat: Ike saw the boats posing an existential menace to every Allied ship afloat in the Atlantic. In October alone 119 Allied ships would be sunk by the Seawolves of the Atlantic.⁸

In Washington General Arnold, an early optimist regarding the destruction of the pens, wrote Harry Hopkins, promising to "dislocate or depreciate the German submarine effort by destroying the five U-boat bases in southwestern France."[9] Ten weeks later Eaker sent a letter to Arnold expressing his own "belief" that the program against the submarine pens was going to be "successful." He added that intelligence reports "indicated that they were making progress even with the small force at hand." But just a month after that, with more raids against the pens completed and additional intelligence assessments, Eaker changed his mind, agreeing with both Kuter (now on Eaker's staff, soon to command the 1st Bombardment Wing) and Hansell, who were certain that a "major failure" with the U-boat pens was in the offing and that it lay with the ordnance available. The bombs dropped on the nearly indestructible pens were fine for "industrial targets" but proved to be "incapable" of even damaging the pens.[10]

In A-5/Targeting, Lieutenant Colonel Dick Hughes studied reconnaissance photographs and intelligence reporting on the pens and concluded the heavy bombers could do little to damage them or even "appreciably affect the outcome of the submarine war" with the few types of bombs then available to the AAF. Hughes noted exceptionally heavy antiaircraft defenses surrounding the pens and so "expected that we would pay a heavy price for conducting what were virtually training missions over such targets." Hughes regretted to Spaatz that he had no suitable alternative to "resist the pressure from above."[11] No one disagreed. However, it was also recognized that the Eighth needed "training missions" for its new aircrews and bombing the pens were perfect for this. Excused were AAF Liberators assigned to RAF Coastal Command for antisubmarine patrols over the bay.[12]

On 13 October Eisenhower informed Spaatz that ending the U-boat threat was "to be one of the basic requirements for winning of the war"; he then followed up on the twentieth with a direct order to make the U-boats Spaatz's top priority, to "protect the movement of men and supplies from the United Kingdom to North Africa by attacking German submarine bases on the west coast of France, with shipping docks on the French west coast as a secondary targets for these missions and with German aircraft factories and depots in France as second priority."[13] Ike's problems with the U-boats were not just that they were sinking ships laden with valuable lives and cargo; because significant amounts of matériel destined for North Africa were lost with each sunken ship, "each sinking caused revisions in operational and tactical plans . . . [and all] these things called for constant conferences, usually with members of tactical staffs and services in Great Britain but frequently also with the Prime Minister."[14] The Eighth soon became enmeshed in a "protracted campaign" against a target impervious to the air power of the day and that ultimately had little to no effect against the outcomes sought. The raids simply "had no appreciable effect on the rate of [U-boat operations]"; to the Germans the raids were merely an "inconvenience."[15] If the bombing campaign "did not dramatically alter the course of the war, the Allies did spend considerable amounts of national treasure and lost many lives in their attempts to turn the [pens] into rubble."[16] The French residents soon left the adjacent cities, which were then leveled in place of the pens. Lorient, for example, was almost entirely destroyed by February of 1943, with 80 percent of the Lorientais fleeing the city, "not as an accidental consequence of operations with other objectives, but as a deliberate attempt to diminish U-boat activity."[17]

The pens were constructed with a great deal of innovation, but "the most innovative work . . . was the design of the roof." Roofs would eventually have a thickness of more than six meters (19.6 feet) with a "layer of concrete beams laid across the roof some 3.8m [12.5 feet] above its surface [the FANGROST concept]; the beams were 1.5m [five feet] high and spaced about the same distance apart." Brest experienced more than eighty strikes during the war, eleven of which were raids of more than one hundred planes, with the RAF also dropping four-thousand-pound TALLBOY bombs. It took the US Army over ten thousand casualties to capture Brest in 1944, destroying the town. The pens were, and are still, intact.[18]

Eighth Air Force liaison officers met with RAF Bomber Command to share intelligence on the pens and learned that the RAF had been bombing Germany's North Sea ports and adjacent U-boat construction yards for some months. At the U-boat construction yards, destruction was limited and indiscriminate; damage at parts factories and host cities was, literally, hit or miss—mostly the latter. For night area bombardment by the RAF, "the shipyards presented targets too small, too isolated, from other suitable objectives, and of a type not easily enough put permanently out of action to warrant a major share of the bombing effort [while] . . .

component parts plants were numerous, widely scattered, often inaccessible from the United Kingdom, hard to identify, and of a type difficult to destroy." The RAF did find it convenient to strike cities on or near the North Sea, though, because "their proximity to British airbases made them always useful secondary objectives."[19] Anyway, shrugged the RAF, night area bombardment of the pens would be "ineffective" since they "probably wouldn't hit anything."[20] With that the RAF backed away from any real bombardment effort against the Biscayan pens but continued with harbor mining, a more effective approach.

Daylight bombing was more accurate for the AAF but mostly useless as the bombs were much too light to penetrate the thick concrete of the pen roofs. However, as the bombers were also heavily armed, sporting as many as eleven .50-caliber heavy Brownings for the B-17Fs, and since the Luftwaffe could be counted on to defend vigorously U-boat facilities, the opportunity to destroy enemy fighters made the war against the pens more worthwhile. So that was how the U-boat threat was divvied up: the RAF bombed the port cities at night and, if they were lucky, maybe hit something to do with U-boats. Meanwhile, the Eighth would fly daylight precision missions against pens on the Bay of Biscay and yards on the North Sea coast until the time when analysts could "conclusively determine whether or not they constituted" profitable targets.[21] Both Allies held serious doubts, but proof was not soon in coming.

Four B-17 groups flew the first U-boat raid on 21 October, the day after Ike issued the directive, thus "beginning one of the most bitter, but also, from an experience point of view, most useful campaigns VIII Bomber Command would undertake."[22] Although missions would become increasingly dangerous, they provided an excellent introduction to flying against contested targets. When the heavies began deeper penetrations into the Continent, the violence from flak and Luftwaffe defenders of the pens would already be familiar to the crews.[23] One persistent problem on the Biscayan coast was that even when it enjoyed decent weather days, a deadly combination of icing conditions with thick cumulous clouds was too often present.[24] The icing would force the Fortresses as low as 17,500 feet—5,000 feet lower than planned—often negating the ability of the inexperienced bomber crews to rendezvous with their fighter escorts. On mission 15 to Lorient on the twenty-first, only fifteen aircraft from the 97th were able to locate the target, while seventy-five other heavies turned back, the clouds aiding the defending Focke-Wulf-190s in downing three Fortresses.[25] Poststrike PR cover by an RAF Spitfire showed direct hits on the pens but no resulting damage as the bombs "were unable to penetrate the layer-cake reinforced concrete roofing."[26] Upon return, three of the groups packed up and departed for North Africa. After New Year's, strikes on the Biscayan pens were limited to days when U-boat construction yards in Germany were weathered in. It was known that hitting the construction yards and facilities would not have an immediate effect on the operating strength of the U-boat fleet, as was the case for the pens, but the U-boats were thought to be so "chronically dangerous" that this was warranted.[27]

The assumption that the Luftwaffe would energetically defend the pens was quickly proven true. Antiaircraft artillery, from the smallest to the largest, belonged to the Luftwaffe, and the flak (named after the 88 mm gun that fired it, the Fliegerabwehrkanone) was much more deadly than the Messerschmitt or Focke-Wulf fighters and more feared by the American crews. The Luftwaffe was generous to a fault in flooding the region with the deadly cannon, soon positioning over one hundred of them for the four facilities that were on or close to the bay. One dependable characteristic of war is that human instinct for inventiveness appears almost as soon as the first round is fired. Hence, flak batteries began experimenting with new tactics as the Eighth was able to fly more bombers in each raid. Aware that American bombers would arrive from the western skies over the bay, the flak gunners began tracking them from their initial point (IP) inbound. At a calculated distance from the target, the guns would throw up a box barrage of flak over the pens through which the heavies had to fly. The Messerschmitts and Focke-Wulfs tested different techniques, too. During the 23 November strike on the St. Nazaire pens (mission 23), Luftwaffe fighters attacked B-17 and B-24 squadrons head-on from the twelve o'clock high position instead of the usual aft position.[28]

St. Nazaire's pens would be struck time and again, a consequence of changes wrought by directives flowing from the Casablanca conference. Out of eight thousand structures in the city, only about a hundred were left standing, with 85 percent of the city completely demolished by the bombing; the U-boat pens, however, remained intact and in use.[29] One scholar notes that the bombings of the cities of Brest, Lorient, and St. Nazaire, in an effort to "starve" the U-boat services, instead "effectively annihilated three major Brittany port cities despite earlier policies of limiting civilian casualties and collateral damage." He argues that the "operational approach" used by both British and Americans relied on only "one tool" in attempting to reduce the pens. Had the "operational environment" been better understood and related problems "adequately identified," claims the researcher, perhaps the U-boat campaign would have been executed differently.[30] In point of fact, had much larger bombs been available sufficient to penetrate the roofing of the pens, no further "understanding" would likely have been needed. Regardless, as a training program for green aircrews, the Brittany campaign was close to essential.

The pens remain in existence today, utilized for various activities eighty years after the war, including by France's Marine Nationale.

Chapter 14

Decisions and Actions at the Top

Returning to PINETREE in mid-September, Haywood Hansell gave copies of AWPD-42 to his leadership, to the RAF, and to the air ministry. The secretary of state for air, Sir Archibald Sinclair, was skeptical. Sir Archibald inquired of the assistant chief of the air staff, Air Marshal Jack Slessor, his opinion of the plan. The secretary was at something of a loss with respect to specifics for the Eighth, especially since the Americans had yet to bomb anywhere in Germany. Sir Archibald was apparently mollified after hearing that the Americans anticipated 2,016 heavy bombers and 1,500 fighters by 1 January 1944.[1] Slessor also swayed his boss, Portal, in the direction of HADPB. Portal was still quietly unsure of the Eighth's dedicated strategy, but Slessor mentioned to him that "it might have unfortunate results if we cast official doubts on the day bombing policy just now when the new Air War Plan is before the Chiefs of Staff." Seeing the wisdom of Slessor's thinking, Portal led the rest of the RAF leadership toward acceptance of the American strategy.[2]

One thing Slessor did not do, at Spaatz's request, was to raise objections against more Eighth aircraft being diverted to TORCH. Earlier Spaatz and Arnold had agreed that "one of the principal advantages to establishing a single European Air Theater" (which included northwest Africa) would be a "greater influence in attracting forces to this side of the world, rather than to the Pacific."[3] Hence, the larger the AAF presence in the Mediterranean, the better the chances of securing a single air commander over the air forces in both Europe and the Mediterranean. But as the head of VIII Bomber Command was unrelenting in his criticism of the transfer of "his" airplanes and crews to the Twelfth Air Force, it is doubtful that Spaatz and Arnold shared their thinking with Eaker.

Larry Kuter returned to England from Gibraltar on 6 November with Spaatz and Hansell "to present an air estimate to General Eisenhower" and was soon closeted with Eaker in discussions about his forthcoming position as commander of the 1st Bombardment Wing.[4] Eaker, pressed by the chief for more missions against German targets in the occupied countries, was no doubt anticipating more of the same. With Kuter tied closely to Arnold, Eaker may have seen an advantage in discussing a few issues with someone who also comprehended the problems of flying in northwest Europe. Regardless, Eaker opted to share with Kuter his thoughts on future missions. Eaker

> confided that he had given a great deal of thought to speeding up oper-
> ations by sending his meager forces out in bad weather, but measured
> against doubtful results and obviously higher losses, he was deter-
> mined to hew to a step-by-step policy. He was convinced that the
> course being followed was the correct one. He could not brush aside
> the limiting factors, and he was convinced that his group commanders
> and his reduced staff were working at maximum. He repeated that he
> didn't think that it was very wise to try to conduct operations from
> Washington. As long as he was left in command, he would use his best
> judgment, and that was that.[5]

True to his word, as commanding general of the Eighth Eaker continued to make decisions based on his best judgments for the next thirteen months, even as pressures and criticisms from Arnold mounted. Among these would be the chief's insistence that Eaker fly every airplane available on every mission, leaving no reserve for the next day (or the day after, or the days after that), and for Eaker to fly regardless of the weather. At a time when more aircraft were being shot down in a month (or less) than were being replaced, when the arrival of replacement aircraft was uncertain at best, and with mission loss rates reaching three times the agreed-upon acceptable 5 percent, at times Eaker was certain that it would be just a matter of weeks before there would be no airplanes left in the few remaining groups without a reserve of operational aircraft. Arnold may not have fully understood that, or he simply may not have cared; regardless, he wanted all the bombers in the air. And he was the boss.

Training was inevitably an issue through 1943 as simply being able to fly a four-engine bomber did not automatically make a new pilot proficient in instrument flying—particularly for landings in low visibility and ceiling conditions. Pilots were being rushed to England so quickly that it was not unusual for a second lieutenant aircraft commander to possess only four hundred hours total pilot time, from first trainer flight to B-17, with minimal instrument training.[6] Moreover, running out of aircrews was at least as delete-rious to operations as it was to run out of airplanes. Pilots insufficiently trained in instrument flying remained a problem more than eighteen months after the first B-17 arrived in England in 1942. As late as November 1943, Colonel Fred Castle, commanding general (CG) of the 4th Combat Wing, ordered "immediate steps" implemented for pilots to fly training missions at least four hours a month "in actual instrument weather."[7] Nor was the problem just with pilots: as the adolescent Eighth flew more missions, the command staff noticed that novice navigators were still unable to locate large targets just across the channel in France or the Low Countries, on or near easily identifiable geographic features. Consequently, within the staff there was a growing concern over the abilities of pilots and navigators to fly deep into Germany, find a target under fire, and return home without more training and experience.

ETOUSA

AWPD-42 had multiple annexes with one, *Air Operations in Northwest Africa*, mandating an *Air Forces* responsibility to "provide additional bases for air operations against Germany in connection with the Air Forces stationed in the UK."[8] From this language an inference that the Mediterranean would continue to be subordinate to the European theater received continued credence. This was reinforced by Eisenhower, being still dual-hatted as commanding general ETOUSA with headquarters in London and having primary responsibility for BOLERO/ROUNDUP. He continued to believe that TORCH was only "diversionary in character" while already concluding there could be no invasion of Europe until at least spring of 1943.[9] In late July, a month into his post in London, Ike had cabled Marshall a detailed assessment of TORCH, addressing unknowns such as whether Spain would intervene and the odds of the French opposing the Allies. He ended by giving the initial landings a "better than even chance" but the entire operation considerably less than fifty-fifty.[10] This, at least, was an improvement over Arnold's "less than 5%."[11]

A week following the landings in November, Arnold sent another captious letter to Spaatz and Eaker expressing displeasure with the reduction in the operational level of the Eighth, never mind that he was the officer most responsible for that reduction by having issued the very orders that had, to date, transferred over one thousand aircraft and twenty thousand men to the Twelfth. Included were almost all of VIII Bomber Command's experienced aircrews, which had produced a heavy drag on the training of new crews. Arnold thought, wrongly, "that the [newly formed] groups, often incomplete, he was sending over could go into battle at once . . . [ignoring] the need to train them in British communications, in new American formation procedures and, most difficult of all, in coping with British weather."[12] The responses of Spaatz and Eaker limn a stark difference between the two personalities and their relationships with the chief. Spaatz would flatly tell Arnold that he (Arnold) needed to acquire a "full understanding" of the difficulty of air operations in the Europe theater and leave it at that, letting the chief understand that he (Spaatz) was in charge in England and fully aware of the situation. Spaatz knew well that "personnel that did arrive from the States generally required considerable training [once in England], plus bombers required weeks of final modifications before they could be used in operations," and that was just the way it was.[13]

General Eaker, conversely, wrote not one but two lengthy responses to the chief that were at once deferential and explanatory, relating key points in such precise detail that they almost made for painful reading. In the first letter, Eaker made clear—repeated, actually—the usual points: long periods of poor flying weather, multiple problems caused by the diversion of units to the Twelfth, near-complete absence of replacement groups, first priority on most everything given over to the Twelfth, nearly one hundred new heavy bombers "in the hands of groups not yet operational," the group in England three weeks but without "transport or bomb handling equipment," and orders limiting "target selection to one small geographical area." Eaker's second letter held a distinct warning that sending new groups into combat without being first combat qualified "would be suicide for them and fatal to the daylight bombardment program." He closed by entreating, "Please don't let anyone get the idea that we are hesitant, fearful or lazy. . . . Every human thing is being done every day to make this pace as fast as possible."[14] Eaker's exacting itemization was as moot as it was true; he had attempted to convey the obvious to focus the chief's attention and comprehension. In that Eaker failed. Having known the chief for two decades and survived the writing and editing processes as coauthor for three books, Eaker should have understood Arnold's personality better than he apparently did. Too, Arnold should perhaps have delegated to a trusted assistant the simple duty of summarizing Eaker's long letters, leaving with Arnold his desired one-page synthesis of core problems. But that did not happen either. Whether Eaker's missives were overly detailed and tedious or Arnold was simply overwhelmed with more important matters to plow through it all, the consequences would have been the same: the chief did not have the time to peruse the details, nor did he desire to receive a negative response, no matter how politely stated or reasonably argued; he wanted bombers in the air, period. His criticisms would grow harsher still.

On 13 November Eisenhower cabled Spaatz and "suggested," in that subtle way generals have of giving orders, that Spaatz come to his headquarters on Gibraltar and "confer immediately"; Ike added that "I continue to look to you not only for control of the United States air in the United Kingdom but as my most trusted air advisor."[15] At Gibraltar on the seventeenth, Spaatz met Doolittle, who also had been summoned, and together they "conferred" with Ike—but not on the subject of a single commander as Spaatz had supposed. Instead, unexpectedly strong responses by the Germans to the

Allied invasion caused Eisenhower to question the ability of Twelfth Air Force to get into the fight quickly given its "confused state." After discussions, Spaatz and Doolittle flew to the airfield at Oran, where Spaatz made a two-day inspection of the several airfields where the Twelfth based its airplanes, then Spaatz returned to Gibraltar for more discussions with Ike. One outcome of those discussions was that Ike gave his unqualified blessing to a unified air command over the Eighth and Twelfth and promised to "put in a firm recommendation to that effect," though he needed to wait until the "Tunisian fight" with the Germans was settled. However, as the fight was not settled for another seven months, "this caveat proved the undoing of the unified air plan"—but only for a year. It also proved the undoing of Spaatz as commanding general of the Eighth Air Force as Ike forthwith made Spaatz his "chief air advisor" for air operations in northwest Africa.[16]

Spaatz returned to England on 23 November to inform Arnold of events, endorsed Eaker as his replacement for commander of the Eighth, packed his belongings, and returned to Gibraltar. In another decision that would later prove beneficial to Spaatz, on returning to England in 1944, Ike assigned him as acting deputy commander-in-chief for air of the Allied forces in North Africa, fortuitously melding the command team of Eisenhower, Spaatz, and Air Chief Marshal Sir Arthur Tedder (current air officer commanding-in-chief of Britain's two-and-a-half-year Mediterranean air war), which would later lead OVERLORD. Nonetheless, it would take until February of 1943 before the Allied air power structure for the Mediterranean would finally be constructed to everyone's satisfaction. Spaatz was to find that the principal role for air power in the Mediterranean theater was tactical air support for troops on the ground, with strategic missions second. The American air units had no experience in that sort of work, nor was there any relevant doctrine for air support of ground forces in contact with the enemy. The current standard US Army doctrine, explained in Field Manual (FM)-1-10, put tactical air under the direction of the ground commander, generally kept it overhead ground forces at all times, and forbade it to "engage objectives that would be better engaged by [ground forces]" since "Aviation was poorly suited for direct attacks."[17] The FM was woefully inadequate for the desert war. New RAF tactics for air support of ground forces in the western desert of Egypt and Cyrenaica, and the few isolated AAF squadrons assigned there, were literally being made up under fire; as the fight progressed, so did the skill and proficiency of the British and Allied air units. Unfortunately, no one thought in advance to bring any advisors from the western desert and Cyrenaica to northwest Africa, leaving the US air units in TORCH to begin with a steep learning curve. What Spaatz and his staff would learn about close air support and interdiction during the North African war would not only create a new doctrine for the AAF tactical aviation but would also pay incalculable dividends after Spaatz returned to England and D-Day in 1944.[18]

On the first of December, General Spaatz handed over the reins of command to General Eaker and flew back to Algiers' Maison Blanche airfield to begin his anticipated brief tenure as the air officer for the Allied commander. Before he left, though, Spaatz as ETOUSA air officer made a request of Eaker: could he, asked Spaatz, "borrow" several squadrons of B-24s for North Africa, for "10 days of temporary duty." Of course, Eaker replied, no problem; the Liberators were soon on their way. The airplanes did not return to English soil for three months.[19] One spot of good news had been the arrival earlier, on 1 October, of the Eighth's very first aerial reconnaissance component when the 3rd Photo-Reconnaissance Group (PRG) headquarters and the initial cadres of four PR squadrons set foot on the docks at Greenock, Scotland. It had been earlier hoped that the Eighth would become less dependent on RAF PR, although the only AAF PIs had just recently been trained by the RAF and were now either seconded to the CIU at RAF Medmenham, with RAF Bomber Command, or still in some phase of training. But then General Doolittle requested of Spaatz that the full 3rd PRG be attached to his Twelfth Air Force, and following additional discussions with the 3rd's commanding officer, Major Elliott Roosevelt, Spaatz agreed.[20] It made little difference as two of the 3rd's four squadrons had already been attached to the Twelfth. The third squadron was then also sent to the Twelfth and the fourth was stripped of its aircraft and most of its men. The 3rd PRG then departed on 29 October for North Africa with the 5th and 12th PR squadrons and the B-17Es of the 15th Photo-Mapping Squadron, while the rump of the 13th PRS remained behind with no airplanes and the Eighth still dependent on the RAF for PR.[21]

Shortly before Christmas, the chief cabled season's greetings to Eaker, including good wishes for the holiday and thanks for jobs well done. Arnold wrote, "Ira, we have got a big year in front of us, one that will in my opinion bring about the fall of the axis [sic]: Your bombing raids will determine to a large extent how long it will be before the morale of the German people is broken and the German Army loses its will to fight."[22] Arnold's holiday message to Eaker was one of optimism, arriving as it did when the Eighth had but 80 operationally qualified bombers in a total inventory of 225. Complete ten-man aircrews for the heavies numbered just eighty-five, not all of which were combat qualified. With 88 percent of the Eighth Air Force ground troops and equipment arriving by ship in jumbled cargoes and erratic schedules, everything was "always behind target" as "vital supplies for the Mediterranean [TORCH] and the buildup of forces for the eventual invasion of France" both took precedence over the Eighth's combat readiness.[23]

By November's end the Allied First Army under Lieutenant General Kenneth Anderson, British Army, had fought to within forty miles of the principal objective of Tunis before being driven back by a strong German counterattack. Allied pilots were being initiated into the intricacies of troop support and interdiction missions, and fighters flying combat air patrols were racking up kills of Luftwaffe and Regia Aeronautica aircraft. The landings impelled Hitler to deploy a large part of the German army already in the west to occupy Vichy France, which now placed German forces just across the Mediterranean from the Allies, easily able to reinforce his desert army. December weather in North Africa worsened to the point where General Eisenhower, just before Christmas, halted further Allied ground activity for the remainder of the rainy season, save for the British Eighth Army, which would continue through Libya toward Tunisia. Still, the Allies were in firm control in northwest Africa, though more difficult days were to come. Allied political leaders, looking ahead, agreed that Casablanca was a venue both safe and convenient to meet with military commanders without drawing them too far from the battlefield. The Casablanca conference received the code name SYMBOL and scheduled for 14 January.

Chapter 15

The Eighth Picks Up the Pace

Haywood Hansell took command of the 1st Bombardment Wing on 1 January 1943 and flew a major strike to Lille on the thirteenth with his pilots and navigators successfully adapting to a new "stagger formation" with few problems. More important, air discipline was much improved over the earlier St. Nazaire raid on 3 January, with the crews hitting all of their navigation marks "precisely on time up to the IP . . . the Groups flew in good, close formations in the Combat Wing, and the Combat Wings were close enough together to obtain the benefits of close defensive position." Hansell reviewed attacks by "30 to 40 enemy aircraft," which he observed while flying copilot in the lead aircraft— which he would do often—concluding that his groups held close formation, providing "for a large element of security for the lead group." He noted that he lost only one airplane to enemy contact but two had collided near the target, and while the bombing was not as good as he wanted, nonetheless he opined that most hits would be counted near the center of the target.[1] The true importance of his memo, in retrospect, may be that it showed the first steps of a growing professionalism in the airmen in his wing; their airmanship and combat prowess displayed strong improvement from the green crews of just a few months earlier. The Eighth was becoming a professional fighting organization.

Colonel Curtis E. LeMay

The 305th Bombardment Group (H) took up residence at Grafton-Underwood airfield in October 1942, commanded by a demanding colonel who drove his men hard because he believed training hard was key to survival. The 305th quickly became a first-rate organization. Colonel LeMay already possessed outstanding reputations for piloting and navigating skills; soon he would become recognized for his innovations as a combat leader. Most important, LeMay was thoroughly pragmatic: his mind was always engaged thinking up better methods to accomplish missions; he was far from enthralled by HADPB. Further, he examined any new idea down to the smallest detail before proceeding and once implemented, he never stopped thinking of ways to improve it.

Even before the 305th's first mission, striking the submarine pens at St. Nazaire on 17 November, LeMay began working his aircrews on techniques to enhance bombing accuracy and improve crew survivability. But first the 305th had to learn to fly in formation. Discovering that what passed for formation flying in the Eighth at that early time was "every commander going at his own gait," LeMay insisted the 305th fly a close, tight formation for mutual defensive fire and bombing accuracy.[2] Frustrated at first trying to corral the Fortresses into a decent formation, he realized that he personally needed to see where each aircraft was in the formation. The next day, he left the controls to his pilot and hoisted himself into the top turret from where he was able to see most of the group and give corrective instructions. Soon he was moving from turret to waist window to tail, wherever he could see and talk his pilots into their places in formation. He wanted the wingmen in three-airplane elements almost shoving their wingtips into the waist windows of the center airplane. Using training flights "to advantage in strengthening our formations by constant study and shifting," he eventually derived the "Combat Box," in which three groups would fly as one combat wing (CBW). Each group would fly twenty-one airplanes (which would leave fourteen at home for maintenance or repair) in a formation broken down into those three-aircraft elements. In each CBW the three bomber groups would be in a high, medium, or low formation and staggered to the left or right. LeMay thought an unrecognized advantage was that the box "wasn't too hideously difficult for non-veteran pilots to manage in their positioning and spacing, and speed."[3] The box and variants became the model for the Eighth for the remainder of the war, with proven group or CBW leaders like Brigadier General Frank Armstrong offering improvement suggestions.

Soon after landing in England, LeMay received two pointers that gave him pause. First, he was advised to never fly straight and level for more than ten seconds or the German 88 mm antiaircraft guns would kill you; and from bombardiers he learned that bombing results were often poor at best. Determined to improve accuracy, LeMay focused on the seven-to-ten-mile distance from the IP to the aim point (AP); the bombers would turn to the IP with perhaps four to seven minutes' flight time to the AP. During that time, the aircraft needed to be in stable flight for the bombardier to make an accurate drop using the Norden. But the airplanes never were, as the pilots inevitably took evasive action to avoid the supposedly deadly antiaircraft fire. LeMay began to wonder about the odds, since "[the Germans] weren't shooting everybody down."[4] Before the St. Nazaire raid, he hauled out an old ROTC artillery manual and, after a number of calculations and a bit of estimating, figured that the Germans would have to fire 372 rounds at a bomber flying at twenty-five thousand feet to get one hit. LeMay concluded that his bombers' chances of not being hit during the run were in fact pretty good, even flying straight and level.

Moreover, instead of the bombardier in each bomber dropping according to his own calculations, a method guaranteed to scatter bombs everywhere but on the target, LeMay figured that if the group bombardier was accurate on his drop, and all others dropped when the group bombardier did, chances were much better of massed ordnance hitting on or near the target. After all, thought LeMay, the only reason to fly a bomber was to drop bombs where they would do the most good and not strewn everywhere but the target. When he explained this to the group, there was audible grumbling (LeMay admitted later that was his reaction, too), but he told all that straight and level was better than zigzagging and that he'd be in the lead airplane. Over St. Nazaire the 305th lost only two bombers, both to enemy fighters, but none after the IP, and bombing results were much better. This too became standard procedure for many of the groups.[5]

LeMay's most important innovation was the "lead navigator/ bombardier/crew" concept. Ultimately, it was a matter of identifying the best pilots, bombardiers, and navigators within the group and giving them the responsibility for everyone's bombs on target. The lead crew concept began fairly simply. LeMay corralled "a bunch of crews and divided up the areas in which we might conceivably attack" and then spread the target folders among all the crews.[6] Each crew would spend hours immersing themselves in the details of two or three targets and all aspects of the missions. This ensured that any target announced at a briefing would always have two or three crews who had already soaked up the details, could answer questions from the other crews, and then would lead the missions. Eventually, a lead crew school was established to conduct supplemental training for the selected pilots, navigators, and bombardiers. During a mission, the lead pilot would also be the aircraft commander (regardless of rank) in the left seat while the mission commander, a rated command pilot, would fly in the copilot seat. The lead copilot would occupy the tail-gunner's position and act as flying control officer, keeping the bombers in formation.

By the summer of 1943, there were often two navigators in the lead aircraft: a dead reckoning (DR) navigator who attended to normal navigational duties and a pilotage navigator, a senior navigator seated up with the bombardier and able to navigate by visual reference to landmarks on the ground (weather permitting). The DR navigator would follow standard navigational duties such as maintaining "a constant Air Plot, determining winds aloft and calculating the course by reference to time, ground speed, and drift," double-checked by the GEE set by his desk.[7] When the H2X radar set, called MICKEY, appeared in autumn of 1943, Eaker formed the 482nd BG, the Pathfinders Force (or PFF), to lead the bombers to a target lying under a solid cloud deck and call the drop. Whenever there was a PFF leading a mission, one of the member groups furnished the 482nd with a lead crew. Later, as H2X radar became more available, more non-PFF aircraft would have MICKEY installed and fly with a third, radar navigator sitting in the radio compartment with his scope.

As the Eighth grew, so too did the complexity of the bomber streams. Eventually, when hundreds of bombers flew a mission, each squadron would have a lead crew and a command pilot; each group would also have its own lead crews and there would be a "command-command" pilot; and of course there would also be an overall mission commander who might have a half-dozen groups under his authority with his own lead crew. By then LeMay had transferred to the Pacific, but his concept of lead crews lived on.[8]

Map 1. France, 1942–43

Map 2. Germany, 1942–43

Map 3. Norway and the Netherlands, 1942–43

Figure 1. Lieutenant General Ira Eaker official photograph.
(Harold W. Bowman Collection [2008.0063] / National Museum of
the Mighty Eighth Air Force, Pooler, GA)

Figure 2. Colonel Leon Johnson, wearing the newly awarded Congressional Medal of Honor (CMoH), shows his B-24 Liberator to Lieutenant General Jacob Devers (commanding general, ETOUSA) and Lieutenant General Ira Eaker (commanding general, Eighth Air Force). Johnson was commanding officer of the 44th Bomb Group, one of three groups from the Eighth sent to the Ninth Air Force in Libya for the Ploęsti mission on 1 July 1943. Each bomb on the Liberator fuselage is for a mission flown; the one horizontal bomb represents the Ploęsti mission. Johnson received the CMoH at RAF Shipdham, where the 44th BG was based. (Nancy Luce Van Epps Collection [1997.0078] / National Museum of the Mighty Eighth Air Force, Pooler, GA)

Figure 3. Major General Frederick L. Anderson, commanding general VIII Bomber Command from 1 July to 31 December 1944. Anderson was frequently described as brilliant and aggressive. He was also a personable, fair, honest, and dedicated officer. (William L. Armagast Collection [2006.0207] / National Museum of the Mighty Eighth Air Force, Pooler, GA)

Figure 4. General Dwight D. Eisenhower, supreme allied commander, Allied Forces Europe and General George C. Marshall, chief of staff, United States Army. (Lil Regan Collection [2010.0185] / National Museum of the Mighty Eighth Air Force, Pooler, GA)

Figure 5. Major General Robert A. Williams. Williams, who lost
an eye as an observer in London during the Blitz, led the combat wing
that bombed Schweinfurt for the first time on 17 August 1943.
(306th BGA Historical Collection [2012.0337] / National Museum of
the Mighty Eighth Air Force, Pooler, GA)

Figure 6. Lieutenant Generals Carl Spaatz *(left)* and Henry H. "Hap" Arnold *(right)*. (Landon High School Alumni Association Collection [2006.0085] / National Museum of the Mighty Eighth Air Force, Pooler, GA)

Figure 7. Brigadier General Robert F. Travis, who led the strike on Stuttgart, 6 September 1943. Heavy cloud cover turned the mission into a disaster for the Americans. (Harry D. Gobrecht Collection [1995.0010] / National Museum of the Mighty Eighth Air Force, Pooler, GA)

Figure 8. Brigadier General James P. Hodges, commanding general of the
2nd Bombardment Division (B-24s only). (Charles A. Jones Collection
[2007.0222] / National Museum of the Mighty Eighth Air Force,
Pooler, GA)

Figure 9. Major General Lewis E. Lyle, commanding officer of the 360th BS, deputy CO and acting CO of the 303rd BG, CO of the 379th BG, and CO of the 41st CBW. Lyle was one of the two founding members of the National Museum of the Mighty Eighth Air Force and had three combat tours with the Eighth, including sixty-nine credited missions (and an unknown number of uncredited/unofficial combat missions flown as well). (Lewis E. Lyle Collection [2008.0448] / National Museum of the Mighty Eighth Air Force, Pooler, GA)

Figure 10. Colonel Kermit Stevens, commanding officer, 303rd BG. (Lawrence Friedland Collection [2004.0045] / National Museum of the Mighty Eighth Air Force, Pooler, GA)

Figure 11. Sterling silver punch bowl and cups of Brigadier General Ira C. Eaker and the original officers of the VIII Bomber Command who accompanied Eaker to England in February 1942 to pave the way for VIII Bomber Command and more generally the Eighth Air Force. (Ira C. Eaker Collection [2004.0899] / National Museum of the Mighty Eighth Air Force, Pooler, GA)

Figure 12. General Carl A. Spaatz, USAAF. (Charles A. Jones Collection [2007.0222] / National Museum of the Mighty Eighth Air Force, Pooler, GA)

Figure 13. Brigadier General Haywood S. "Possum" Hansell, commanding general of the 1st Bomb Wing January to July 1943, flew numerous combat missions while commanding general. Perhaps the best air planner in the service, he helped write AWPD-1 and wrote AWPD-42 virtually alone. He admired Spaatz tremendously but was not a great fan of General Arnold. Hansell retired after the war as a BG, was recalled during the Korean War, and was promoted to a justly deserved major general before retiring a second time. (Haywood S. Hansell Collection [2019.0041] / National Museum of the Mighty Eighth Air Force, Pooler, GA)

Figure 14. Major General Curtis E. LeMay. Served as a colonel
commanding the 305th BG and the 3rd Bombardment Division after
Regensburg on 17 August until promoted to brigadier in late 1943.
An innovative thinker and admired leader, he eventually became the
chief of staff of the United States Air Force. (James M. Oberman
Collection [1998.0063] / National Museum of the Mighty Eighth Air
Force, Pooler, GA)

Figure 15. Lieutenant Colonel Lew Lyle of the 360th BS checking out a new ventilation duct in his bomber, caused by some type of antiaircraft artillery round. (Lewis E. Lyle Collection [2008.0448] / National Museum of the Mighty Eighth Air Force, Pooler, GA)

Figure 16. Members of the Womens Army Corps (WAC) in formation for inspection. Recognizing the exceptional efficiency of the women in the British military, Eaker fought successfully for WACs to be assigned to the Eighth. They served honorably and with distinction throughout the war. (Robert L. Bailey Jr. Collection [2007.0319] / National Museum of the Mighty Eighth Air Force, Pooler, GA)

Figure 17. Colonel Edward "Ted" Timberlake, commanding officer of the 93rd BG (B-24s), later commanding general of the 20th Combat Wing. He was CO of the 93rd when he led it as one of the five bomb groups on the 1 August 1943 mission to Ploęsti. Timberlake retired as a lieutenant general. (Alfred Asch Collection [2007.0168] / National Museum of the Mighty Eighth Air Force, Pooler, GA)

Figure 18. Staff Sergeant Maynard "Snuffy" Smith being awarded the Medal of Honor. To his right is Secretary of War Stimson. Smith received the award for heroism on his first combat mission with the Eighth. He was (as was typical for him) unaware that he was to receive the medal and was on KP duty for a week as punishment for a rules violation when an officer was sent to bring him to the ceremony. Known as "obnoxious and stubborn" and in trouble frequently, Smith reduced to private after four more missions and was taken off flight status. (306th BGA Historical Collection [2012.0337] / National Museum of the Mighty Eighth Air Force, Pooler, GA)

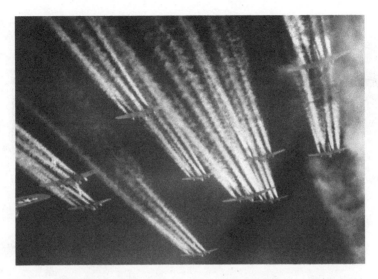

Figure 19. B-17 Flying Fortresses in a combat box formation leaving contrails as they head toward another target. (John D. Leggett Jr. Collection [2011.0132] / National Museum of the Mighty Eighth Air Force, Pooler, GA)

Figure 20. A B-17F from the 379th Bombardment Group (Heavy), the "Triangle K" outfit. (Robert F. Finch Collection [1995.0030] / National Museum of the Mighty Eighth Air Force, Pooler, GA)

Figure 21. (*Left to right*): Lieutenant Generals James H. Doolittle and Ira C. Eaker with Mrs. Ruth Eaker and Air Chief Marshal Sir Arthur Travers Harris, air-officer-commanding, RAF Bomber Command. Eaker was so popular with the British that Doolittle received a cool, aloof welcome from many of his counterparts, especially Harris, and it took some time to thaw before he was accepted as "Jimmy" in lieu of the formal "General." (Earl Wade Henry Collection [2004.0030] / National Museum of the Mighty Eighth Air Force, Pooler, GA)

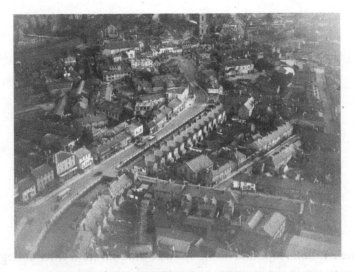

Figure 22. The High Street, High Wycombe, Buckinghamshire, in 1945. (John D. Leggett Jr. Collection [2011.0132] / National Museum of the Mighty Eighth Air Force, Pooler, GA)

Figure 23. B-24s could take a good deal of battle damage and still make it home, unless they were hit in the wing, in which case the chances of survival were slight. (459th Bomb Group Historic Collection [2015.0169] / National Museum of the Mighty Eighth Air Force, Pooler, GA)

Figure 24. Bob Hope and his troupe take time out from entertaining the troops to rest in the company of a couple of commanders. (*From back left*): Colonel Stan Wray (CO, 91st BG), Francis Langford, Colonel Charles Marion (acting CO, 303rd BG), Tony Romano; (*in front*): Jack Pepper and Hope. (Glenn E. Taylor Collection [2006.0403] / National Museum of the Mighty Eighth Air Force, Pooler, GA)

Figure 25. A squadron returns from a mission. (Harry D. Gobrecht Collection [1995.0010] / National Museum of the Mighty Eighth Air Force, Pooler, GA)

WAITING

Figure 26. The Tuskegee Airmen were among the most respected fighter escorts the bombers had. Here, a pilot and his ground crew stand by their P-51B. (Tod Engelskirchen Collection [2012.0010] / National Museum of the Mighty Eighth Air Force, Pooler, GA)

Figure 27. A sky full of flak, as seen from the right waist gunner's position in a Fortress from the 351st BG (Square J). Flak was detested even more than Luftwaffe fighters. (Franklin L. Betz Collection [2009.0332] / National Museum of the Mighty Eighth Air Force, Pooler, GA)

Figure 28. Assistant Secretary of War for Air Robert Abercrombie Lovett (on the right in mufti), a naval aviator in World War I who earned the Navy Cross and a good friend to Spaatz, Eaker, and Arnold. A thoughtful, articulate, knowledgeable man, he was able to influence Arnold like no one else, save perhaps Hap's oldest friend, General George Marshall. It was a note from Lovett that—finally—sparked Arnold to order General Barney Giles of the air staff to get a fighter that could go into Germany with the bombers and come out with them as well, and do it within five months. (306th BGA Historical Collection [2012.0337] / National Museum of the Mighty Eighth Air Force, Pooler, GA)

Figure 29. Arlington National Cemetery. (Ira C. Eaker Collection [2008.0165] / National Museum of the Mighty Eighth Air Force, Pooler, GA)

Figure 30. Major General Lewis E. Lyle Rotunda at the National Museum of the Mighty Eighth Air Force. (National Museum of the Mighty Eighth Air Force, Pooler, GA)

Chapter 16

Symbol

The Eighth Air Force stood down on 14 January 1943 as Roosevelt and Churchill joined the CCS for the third summit, this time in Casablanca. General Arnold faced several issues there, one of which was the pending decision whether to continue with a Mediterranean campaign or plan for an invasion of the Continent in 1943. Also hanging was the prime minister's intention for the Americans to place the heavy bombers of the Eighth—which had yet to bomb German soil—under RAF Bomber Command for joint night missions. After the 17 August raid, the Eighth had flown just twenty-eight missions, all to France and the Low Countries.[1] Arnold cabled Lieutenant General Frank M. Andrews at HqAF that the "207 heavy bombers" that were then in the UK "cannot be held on the ground for any excessive period of time without subjecting [the Eighth and the AAF] to severe criticism" in Washington. The "207 bombers" were being "held on the ground" for good reason from Eaker's point of view. Besides poor weather unsuitable for flying, more than half were not airworthy, either because they were receiving modifications at RAF Langford Lodge, near Belfast, battle damaged and under repair, or undergoing depot maintenance. Modifications were either essentials to aircraft and aircrew combat survivability or those required for operation in UK air space. Without them aircraft would be unsafe

127

either in combat or returning home in poor weather. Spaatz arrived shortly after Arnold and, during a beach stroll, informed the chief that the Eighth would commence "strategic bombing" of Germany "once it had fighter escort for long-range missions."[2]

The PM had written to Harry Hopkins in mid-October that AAF missions to that point "do not give our experts the same confidence as yours in the power of the day bomber."[3] While a veteran air force with seasoned air crews would not have experienced quite as many of these infirmities, the majority of the Eighth's personnel were not seasoned but instead still military rookies. Their willingness to fight was evident; their ability to do so over Germany at twenty-five thousand feet while being shot at by multiple sources simultaneously entailed new skills not quickly acquired. Unknown to General Arnold, Sir Archibald Sinclair had proposed to Churchill a joint RAF-USAAF heavy bomber force of four to six thousand aircraft joined by ground troops, averring that such could "bring the harvest of victory" in 1944.[4] Now Churchill was leaning strongly in favor of placing the heavies under Bert Harris with the RAF's night missions; also unknown to Arnold, the PM had already obtained the president's concurrence.

The Casablanca Directive

SYMBOL held special import for the air war in Europe on at least two counts, one of which was the Casablanca Directive.[5] Haywood Hansell, attending in support of General Arnold, thought the Directive was "one of the finest air documents of the entire war," ranking with AWPD-1 and AWPD-42.[6] Part of the Allied "grand strategy," the directive's objective was "to bring about the progressive destruction and dislocation of the German military, industrial, and economic system, and the undermining of the morale of the German people to a point where their capacity for armed resistance is fatally weakened."[7] Possum Hansell thought that Eaker's "hand was discernible in its formulation" but gave full credit to the "greatly gifted British airman" Jack Slessor. Eaker and Slessor "were eye to eye in terms of air power's contribution to victory and the place of strategic air power in grand strategy."[8] Hansell was certain "air power would take its place with land power and sea power."[9] Slessor was at Casablanca because he was not only a superlative planner but also exceptionally skilled at diplomatic niceties in both civilian and military circles and thus much more suited to the conference than the blunt and occasionally crude Bert Harris.[10]

The directive took a broad cut at establishing targeting priorities "for a sustained and unremitting air offensive against Germany," with Slessor asserting the statement was "in fact a policy, not an operational directive."[11] Indeed, the official history called it as such, saying "it was not a directive in fact at all, but something even more important, a general statement of policy set down by the high personages responsible in the last resort of the conduct of the war."[12] It held something for both air forces: Harris saw the directive as giving him "a very wide range of choice and allowed [him] to attack pretty well any German industrial city of 100,000 inhabitants and above."[13] Harris considered this officially "the undermining of the morale of the German people" to the extent that "their capacity for armed resistance is fatally weakened . . . depriving them of homes, heat, light, transportation, and perhaps food," and not necessarily the deliberate targeting and killing of civilians. But of course, that is what it was.[14] For the Americans, the principal focus would not have been out of place in the ACTS's textbook with its objective of "the progressive destruction and dislocation of the German military, industrial and economic system."[15]

Eaker Wins Over the PM

The second seminal event at SYMBOL for the AAF occurred on the nineteenth: General Eaker's presentation to Churchill on HADPB as applied in the European air war. The British had attempted daylight bombing at war's beginning with bombers manifestly—and fatally—unsuited for daytime missions and fighters designed only for homeland defense, not long-range escorting. The RAF had suffered unstainable casualties until switching to night area bombardment. VIII Bomber Command's twenty-nine heavy bomber missions flown to date had, for the Bomber Mafia if no one else, somehow validated the AAF's unassailable correctness of the Doctrine, even though none of those missions had crossed the Rhine! The reality was that HADPB was a still-unproven hypothesis, a dream, while underpin-ning ACTS's most ardent assertions. Moreover, the Americans rejected as immoral any operation in which civilians were deliberately targeted, which, they were certain, Harris's operations did. The Americans had invested too much intellectual sweat and energy in HADPB to capitulate to the British while also developing the necessary bombsight and airplane: giving in to the British was just not something to which the AAF would ever agree.

Still, it was on the SYMBOL agenda, so to make the case to the prime minister, a very worried Arnold asked Eisenhower—still commanding general ETOUSA, despite a physical presence in North Africa as TORCH commander—to order Eaker down to Casablanca on an urgent basis.[16] Eaker arrived 15 January 1943 and Arnold informed him that "Roosevelt [had] already announced to Churchill that he would go along with the latter's desire to merge the American bombing effort with the RAF's night bombing strategy."[17] Eaker was the right man at the right time; his college yearbook had lauded his debate style as "logic rather than oratory"—a skill the general never lost and that Arnold knew well.[18]

Eaker needed part of one evening to work out his argument, beginning by writing on a sheet of paper, "The Case for Day Bombing," and listing seven reasons in short, crisp, to-the-point sentences—talking points for his half-hour with the PM. Eaker filled another fifteen pages with concise, clear explications of those seven key points, augmented with "answers" to rhetorical questions. At lunch after the presentation, Churchill was highly complementary of the American general's forensic skills, telling him, "Young man, you have not convinced me you are right, but you have persuaded me that you should have further opportunity to prove your contention." Churchill commented that it would be "fortuitous" to be able to "bomb the devils around the clock" and told Eaker that he would "withdraw his suggestion" that the Eighth join with the RAF and instead support Eaker.[19] The same day the British service chiefs approved the AAF's employment of HADPB as complementary to the RAF's night bombing, believing the Americans were certain to lose enough men and airplanes that they would eventually join the RAF's nocturnal missions. The CCS signed their approval on the directive just prior to adjournment on the twenty-first.

Eaker's Notes

Eaker's notes were a combination of the Doctrine blended with practical aspects of the air war. The paper classified secret was subtitled "American bombers should continue to bomb by day for the following reasons:" Seven central points succinctly stated were:

1. day bombing is accurate and small targets (factories, etc.) can be "found, seen, and hit";
2. smaller targets can be hit with fewer bombs, and aircraft will "suffer smaller losses";
3. daytime bombing "complements" RAF night operations; German defenses can't rest, they must be on alert 24 hours a day;
4. it obviates airspace and airfield congestion at home;
5. switching AAF crews to night bombing would necessitate a "long delay" for retraining;
6. AAF bombers are "designed, built, and equipped" for day bombing, are heavily armed, and are able to destroy defending German aircraft, a major Allied objective;
7. day bombing permits "excellent cooperation" with RAF Bomber Command.[20]

Had he been present, Hansell might have interjected that if the Eighth joined the RAF in night bombing "the whole course of the war would have been changed." First, it would have been "impossible to defeat the German Air Force," as the Germans would build up "night defenses that were just as strong as their day defenses."[21] Without Allied air supremacy or superiority over western Europe, there either would have been no invasion at Normandy or, worse, it would have failed. And "without a second front and its drain on German arms, Hitler might have stabilized the Eastern Front." Or, if Hitler failed to halt the Russians at the Elbe or Rhine, Stalin's forces would have gone all the way to the English Channel. "Russia would then have had total domination of the European continent."[22] While speculative, at the time it seemed not just possible but plausible.

Eaker used twelve pages to list hypothetical questions and then "answered" them for the future benefit of the PM. One point left hanging was why did AAF and RAF bombers did not share the same "Strategic Directive and Strategic Targets." Once back in England, Eaker had the opportunity to try to do exactly that in shepherding the Casablanca Directive implementation plan (Operation POINTBLANK) through a four-month drafting process. Were it not for the total independence allowed Harris at RAF Bomber Command, Eaker might have succeeded in accomplishing that very thing. Two pages questioned why the AAF had flown so few missions. The text reflects the same points that Eaker had been sending to Arnold for months (over 1,200 aircraft and twenty-four thousand men to TORCH, terrible weather, few replacements arriving from the States, modifications taking too long at Langford Lodge, etc.). Next, a page with one question: Why had the AAF bombed Lille and other sites in France? The short answer: they were necessary targets. As these locales were within the limited range of RAF fighter escorts, they were the first missions of a new air force with aircrews new to combat, and the weather was usually suitable. Omitted was any mention of the imperviousness of U-boat pens to bombs. Eaker then "responded" to potential queries about the unusually large numbers of individual aircraft aborts for each mission. Unable to answer in just a sentence or two, Eaker managed to cram densely packed, detailed text onto one page. Eaker's final two pages skirted Churchill's most pressing question: Why had the Eighth not yet bombed the Third Reich? Eaker explained, mostly, why and then shifted topics by reviewing what it was the Americans expected to achieve when they did begin bombing Germany.

At one point Eaker assured the PM that long-range fighters were unnecessary as the bombers could not only defend themselves but they could also "destroy quantities of German fighters, which would help pave the way for a the cross-channel invasion." Major General Barney Giles, soon to become the new chief of the air staff and Arnold's deputy, had accompanied Arnold to Casablanca and Eaker took the occasion to advise him that the Eighth's heavies were "knocking the ears off the German day fighters and" and racking up a "six-to-one kill ratio," and if Giles would just give him more bombers "he would achieve air superiority." Eaker is thought to have arrived at this belief because of the inflated number of kills claimed by the air gunners. For just two missions, Lille on 9 October and Romilly-sur-Seine on 20 December, the Eighth gunners claimed forty-two destroyed, fifty-two probables, and twenty-two damaged; postwar Luftwaffe records "admitted to three fighters downed and one damaged."[23]

Despite Eaker's robust performance, Arnold misled most everyone else about the presentation, complaining he had been embarrassed that Roosevelt and the British had "put him on the defensive" over the absence of heavy bomber missions over Germany, even though it was not (or should not have been) a surprise discussion topic. After Eaker's arrival Arnold could have benefited from the former's thinking but instead intimated that his chagrin over being "caught unaware" was Eaker's and Spaatz's fault. Back home, Arnold griped that the two gave him "usual and expected reasons," which he considered "very weak," as though his two friends' truthfulness was suspect.[24] In his memoirs Arnold ignores completely Eaker's crucial meeting with Churchill, writing only that on 16 January "Eaker here and a big help."[25] This is especially odd considering the haste in which Eaker had been summoned and that failure on Eaker's part would have meant the end of daylight bombardment. Arnold claimed full credit for the successful luncheon presentation, writing that he had met the PM on the nineteenth, during which he had "talked long and hard" to Churchill and "outlined to him" why the Eighth could succeed at daylight bombardment. Arnold mentioned almost as an afterthought that he had Spaatz, Eaker, and General Andrews talk to Churchill later and that the PM was "willing to give it a trial."[26]

At a press conference prior to adjournment, Roosevelt surprised all assembled by unilaterally announcing a policy of unconditional surrender would apply to the Axis members. There were, under international law and the laws of warfare, a number of particular requirements for and flowing from unconditional surrender that would make it much more difficult to bring the war to a conclusion while also complicating the process. No discussion followed, although the military commanders were left with a number of questions.

SYMBOL's legacy, the Casablanca Directive and subsequent CBO, mattered greatly. The CBO, when finally written and approved, was a strategy jointly agreed to by the Allied chiefs to prepare for ROUNDUP/OVERLORD by ensuring, to the extent possible, the invasion's success by attaining air superiority over the Luftwaffe. Allied air cover would be over not just the five landing beaches but the entire Cotentin Peninsula and deep into France as far south as Avranches near the Bay of Mont Saint-Michel, then east through Mortain to Argentan. Not only did Allied fighters dominate the skies but RAF Typhoon and AAF P-47 Thunderbolt fighter-bombers flying from expeditionary airfields in Normandy destroyed German armored vehicles and troops by the hundreds. The policy of unconditional surrender has been long debated; many senior military officers were certain that it would deter the German generals from surrendering, thus prolonging the war.

Chapter 17

Back to Business

First Germany Raids

"The large scale bombardment of Germany was delayed many months and the losses of heavy bombers in this theater significantly increased due to lack of numbers and a fighter escort. An operation such as TORCH has been compared to a whirlpool which sucks everything into its depths once started—heavy bombers included."[1] Fortresses of Hansell's 1st Wing struck the U-boat pens at Lorient on 23 January as prelude to crossing the German border. Despite progress since arriving in England, Lorient was evidence that the bomber force was still more amateur than professional, with fewer than half of the seventy-three bombers dispatched reaching the target. In hazardously low visibility, two combat wings managed to get airborne safely but experienced difficulty in assembling; they then arrived as much as forty-five minutes early at key rendezvous points. After departing the English coast, the force found a thick, high cloud layer at the IP, confusing many crews when the lead began a climb through it; half of the bombers of one group became lost and aborted, leading Hansell to note postmission that "the Wing is not sufficiently well-trained at the present time to warrant climbing in formation through an overcast." Another group left the wing formation over France and was immediately "shot up," while too many bombardiers seemed confused during the bomb run. Five heavies were downed and another became lost and "presumably shot down," while "two more were DBR in crash-landings in the UK." Nineteen heavies from one group assigned to strike Brest actually managed to do just that.[2]

Hansell's next mission was to the U-boat construction yards at Wilhelmshaven on 27 January. It was a mission of "firsts": the Eighth's first raid into Germany, the Eighth's longest yet, and the first serious challenge to the "self-defending" bomber while exposed to Luftwaffe fighter attacks for much of that time. Fifty-three Fortresses dropped on the target while two errant Forts struck the U-boat base at Emden. Also dispatched were twenty-seven B-24s but none found the target, victims of "poor visibility and poor navigation." Three heavies were lost, with forty-one damaged.[3] The same day, Eaker informed Spaatz, "We are bombing Germany now, with less than a hundred heavies—something both you and I agree should not be done."[4] But Eaker could still believe that "the mission proved that daylight strategic bombing of military targets could be successful," while Arnold's office in Washington publicized the mission "as if it were a great success." Curt LeMay flew the mission and thought differently: as only 60 percent of the force even found Wilhelmshaven, and with just 1 percent of the bombs actually hitting the target, he believed the mission was hardly better than had been achieved against the pens. The Luftwaffe responded furiously, deploying "hundreds of fighters" from the Russian and Mediterranean fronts to protect Germany proper.[5]

At first the aircrews calculated the odds of reaching twenty-five missions at just one in four. It quickly became worse. Soon, missions would experience loss rates that would leave the Eighth in danger of having no airplanes left to fly, absent any reserves. As he held responsibilities to the British government and to the RAF, as well as to the AAF, Eaker was unwilling to risk completely depleting his heavy bomber force while uncertainty remained with the aircraft and crew replacement rates. By 1 February some heavy bomber groups were operating at half strength, a few with as many as seventy-three aircrews out of eighty-five estimated to be, like their airplanes, "war weary."[6] One bit of good news for Eaker in late January was that transfers of "excess" Twelfth Air Force men who had not shipped out to northwest Africa were to be retained by the Eighth; additionally, new arrivals from the States had now increased the total manpower of the Eighth to thirty-six thousand officers and men.[7]

In November 1942 Eaker had written Arnold "assuring him of the feasibility of bombing Germany without fighter cover, providing the strength was there," meaning a mission required a minimum of three hundred aircraft for adequate self-defense. It was a point Eaker consistently stressed: "Three hundred heavy bombers can attack any target in Germany by daylight with less than four percent losses."[8] Despite the absence of supporting evidence, Arnold, although never a dedicated adherent of the Bomber Mafia, apparently found his protégé's words reassuring. Within just two months the loss percentages would suggest otherwise, the three-hundred-strong bomber force still months into the future. Yet Eaker remained steadfast in the belief of the self-defending bomber. The irony was that, in North Africa, Jimmy Doolittle had months earlier realized the utility of escorts for his heavy *and* medium bombers; the seven P-38 groups formerly slated for the Eighth were now in the desert performing daily what Doolittle considered an essential mission—long-range bomber escort.[9] And the fighter pilots were racking up kills to boot. Doolittle was a practical man, an aeronautical engineer and test pilot; he staunchly advocated the calculated risk and unlike many others, he did not accept the untested HADPB theory. Circumstances made Eaker careful to protect his heavy bomber force in those early days when promised replacements were routinely rerouted elsewhere or turned out to be nonexistent. And like Spaatz, Eaker was dead set against a schedule for which the Eighth suffered "heavier losses than our rate of buildup" could replace.[10] In February Arnold ordered Eaker "to schedule more frequent missions over Germany."[11] Postwar, Eaker told an interlocutor, "But I always said and reported to General Arnold that I would never operate that force at a rate of loss which we could not replace."[12]

Command Change at ETOUSA

With TORCH finally recognized as more than a sideshow or diversion, North Africa became a separate theater on 4 February 1943 under General Eisenhower, while Lieutenant General Frank M. Andrews, an air forces officer of excellent reputation, officially replaced Ike in London. Earlier, Eaker had declined an offer to reside at Park House upon Spaatz's departure, instead seeking a large estate at which he could hold functions from staff meetings to large social affairs to buttress ties between Americans and their British colleagues. Eaker wanted to be able to meet with dignitaries and high officials as well as enjoy the company of American soldiers of all ranks. His aide located Castle Coombe, which just happened to adjoin a golf course, not only suiting Eaker but also his new boss. Like Eisenhower before him, Frank Andrews was conveniently but unhappily quartered in London's Dorchester Hotel in Mayfair, an elegant establishment across from Hyde Park but near the American Embassy and his offices at 20 Grosvenor Square. Andrews would happily spend weekends with Eaker, golfing and engaging in conversations without fear of eavesdroppers.[13] The two generals became more apt to see things similarly than Eaker did with Arnold.

Flying weather over the Continent after Casablanca was so atrocious that the Eighth managed just one mission to Germany in January, that to Wilhelmshaven on the twenty-seventh. Weather in early February upset three attempts to strike Hamm in the Ruhr Valley: the first and third missions aborted early because of impossible conditions either at altitude or at the target, while the second mission had 2nd Air Division B-24s abort as the Fortresses carried on to the secondary at Emden. Finally, on the sixteenth the heavies successfully bombed Dunkerque on France's channel coast. There were two more raids after that: Wilhelmshaven, as the Bremen primary was obscured, and Brest. No strike was greater than sixty-five bombers.[14] Arnold was upset at the limited number of aircraft that flew those few missions, but the simple fact was those were all the operational aircraft that VIII Bomber Command possessed. The average daily combat strength for VIII Bomber Command during February was seventy-four "operating combinations"—that is, seventy-four combat qualified aircrews paired with operationally qualified aircraft.[15]

No one was more aware of the effects of weather on flight schedules than Eaker. Writing apologetically on the fifteenth, Eaker told Arnold that the Eighth had been "unable to show a continuity of operations" during the past three weeks as weather had again grounded the Eighth. After Eaker assured him that Andrews agreed and "we both realize that we must overcome present obstacles," Eaker concluded that he was "equally certain that we shall show you early solutions which will be entirely acceptable."[16] But perhaps after flying combat missions for seven months, it was a little too late to be discussing "future" progress in terms of "early solutions." Possibly part of the problem was Eaker's propensity to explain the usual in detail, offer the same excuses or justifications, and again promise improvement. Perhaps Arnold was simply growing weary of reading the same justifications and promises once again. While the chief wanted "informative letters, he no longer could manage long letters detailing 'minor troubles or problems.'"[17] Unlike prewar days, great issues and problems filled his days, leaving less time for correspondence.

Within a few days Eaker again wrote the chief, citing the cumulative losses of seventy-five heavy bombers and crews in February from all causes, but had "to date received but 24 replacement crews and 63 replacement aircraft." He followed with a lament that the only thing the Eighth required to do its work was "an adequate force." Arnold's response was to ignore Eaker and instead grumble to General Stratemeyer again about being "put on the defensive" at Casablanca and about the absence of heavies over Germany before finally griping about Spaatz and Eaker giving the "usual and expected reasons."[18] Possibly looking to change the subject, Stratemeyer underscored to Arnold that all concerned supported the Eighth in the day bombing mission while the RAF worked at night. Reiterating the importance of "ample force" in the strikes, the air staff chief opined that "two formations of 72 aircraft each" should be the minimum dispatched. Soon enough strikes of more than one hundred heavy bombers would be dispatched, but the high number of individual aborts would keep the numbers reaching the targets below the century mark.[19] It would not be until 17 April that over one hundred bombers—107 B-17s—would reach a target; unescorted, they would suffer a loss rate of 15 percent on the raid.

After SYMBOL Arnold continued eastward, conducting an inspection trip to the China-Burma-India theater and other air forces. Returning home on 17 February, Arnold tended to final trip business and then assaulted some sixty documents that had been held for him since his departure, churning out dozens of responses, including several to Eaker:

- Memorandum criticizing the Eighth Air Force for holding too many bombers idle on the ground. "We had made only two or three raids over Germany in February,1943, while British flyers made seventeen that month." Daytime precision bombing required the bombardier actually to see the target, limiting missions to skies with no more than six-tenths cover; night nonprecision bombardment could be done over solid cloud cover.
- Memorandum to commanding general, Air Forces in England, stating that the Eighth Air Force was seemingly going through a routine repetition of performance and finding alibis for not sending more airplanes out on missions. Suggestion made that more aggressive leaders were needed— perhaps group and wing commanders had been there too long.
- Memorandum to Eaker, expressing satisfaction that the bombing effort had picked up.[20]

Arnold also wrote a personal note to Eaker assuring him of the chief's "faith in his ability."

Changes in the Chief's Office

The growth of the Eighth coincided with the explosive expansion of the entire AAF and in the responsibilities, duties, and concerns of its chief of staff and commanding general, Hap Arnold. In 1940 the air corps numbered four air forces within the United States, two for training, two operational, and a few small forces in foreign regions like the Panama Canal zone and the Philippines.[21] Now there were over a dozen huge air forces and commands spread across the globe flying combat missions while screaming for more men and airplanes, with additional air forces planned for the Far East, India/ China, and the Middle East. As chief of staff, Arnold not only created and fed this huge monster but also had to contend with Washington politicians on matters of policy, budget, personnel levels, and (always) requests for still more aircraft—not forgetting, of course, the War Department and, God forbid, Admiral Ernie King and the navy. Too, there were Arnold's many contacts in the civilian aviation industry, friendships that he had made while at the Army Industrial College that were as important—and time intensive—as his dealings with politicians. He was, it would seem, a perpetual motion machine, pushing, extolling, urging the civilians to build airplanes or to develop new airplanes or create this thing or that device because it was needed by the men and women overseas.

With the AAF increasing from twenty thousand officers to more than four hundred thousand in the blink of an eye, few would be closer to Arnold professionally than Major General Laurence Sherman Kuter. A lieutenant and the youngest in his ACTS class, Kuter was added as a staff instructor after graduation. There, he demonstrated such a "capacity to think big" that Arnold assigned him to the WDGS (G-3) while a major.[22] As a brigadier general after Pearl Harbor, Kuter served for a brief time as a wing commander in the Eighth in the fall of 1942 (but flew no missions), then as deputy commander of Eisenhower's tactical air force in northwest Africa. In May 1943 Arnold brought him back to DC, installing him as assistant chief of air staff, plans, and combat operations. There, Kuter found that "Arnold no longer had the small, tightly knit staff to which he had been accustomed, but now presided over an immense organization. There were branches and sections and offices with hundreds of officers and Civil Servants, far too many for him now to know personally. . . . Thus, after a few encounters with this cumbersome network, Arnold sometimes seemed to regard the Air Staff not as his own personal staff, not as an extension of his own mind and will, but as an obstacle to be hurdled, to be dodged or evaded."[23] As an antidote to the large bureaucracy that had surrounded him seemingly overnight, Arnold created the AAF Advisory Council that reported directly and only to himself. Usually staffed with just two or three officers, Arnold selected each one with care. All the officers were "men with far above-average potential and with recent widespread experience. These were men that Arnold could and did talk to freely and easily. These men were not subject to call or assignments by the chief of the air staff or any member of it. They had no routine assignments and Arnold intended that they were not going to be "'too busy' with the day-to-day business to bat around the new ideas that he might throw to them."[24] Mostly colonels, they included future three- and four-star generals like Emmett E. "Rosie" O'Donnell, Charles Pearre Cabell, Lauris Norstad, Fred Dean, and Jacob E. "Jake" Smart.[25] They became Arnold's think tank

while Larry Kuter moved up to a deputy chief of the air staff slot. Kuter
soon became in many ways the chief's right-hand man, confiding in Kuter
"somewhat as he would in a special assistant and not at all as he related to
most of his contemporaries."[26] In time there came to be a "congruence in
thinking" between Arnold and Kuter, including the same strong belief in an
independent air force. "Eventually, Arnold came to have such confidence
in his 36-year-old general that he set him to such tasks as drafting purport-
edly 'personal' letters for him to send to air force commanders out in the
far-flung combat theaters."[27]

Eaker did not always appreciate receiving letters or cables from
Arnold's staff. Not only had Arnold begun criticizing Eaker and his officers
but he also brought into the situation his advisory council. For example,
in mid-June an ill-tempered cable from Arnold to Eaker over an alleged
event that had never occurred unknowingly presaged a series of increasingly irritating and time-consuming exchanges that would later militate
against Eaker's continuation in the Eighth. Rosie O'Donnell had heard from
"several pilots" criticisms of "fighters not escorting heavy bombers to the
full extent of their capabilities," partly because, he explained in extensive
technical detail, they dropped their wing tanks too early, while eighty gallons
of fuel still remained.[28] Arnold wrote to Eaker, avowing the practice was "of
grave concern" to him and he was "unable to comprehend [its] purpose."
He required three full pages to cool to the point where he could demand of
Eaker, "Desire you give this subject your personal attention and forward me
your comments as soon as possible."[29] As Eaker had previously sent multiple
cables addressing this exact subject, including the fact that the P-47s had
no drop tanks at all but desperately needed them in order to carry the
Thunderbolts to the German border, he thought that the chief was probably
justifying the replacement of his fighter commander, Monk Hunter.

But it was not just Arnold's advisory council that was a problem. When
Major General Barney Giles replaced Major General George Stratemeyer as
chief of the air staff in midyear, Eaker sent a personal letter of congratulations, adding that in wartime the "experience level" of the staff was not what
it had been previously. He continued, "With the wartime buildup there must
be a lot of ardent 'Messiahs' with special hobby horses that are riding them

hard. . . . We get a few amateurish and, frankly, some screwball cablegrams which are signed by the General's name. To my way of thinking . . . it tends to break down confidence in the Office and in the leadership." Telling of a directive to "try out a new experimental device" developed by the British, Eaker explained how he had brought back information on the device more than a year previously and there was now an AAF counterpart in testing. Worse, though, "We get an occasional radiogram or letter which can come under no other heading than 'needling.' It develops the same spirit as a shrewish wife or a scolding mother. . . . People who are working their heads off and doing an outstanding job . . . suddenly get a querulous scolding message or a query as to why they did not do this or that. The messages always show a considerable lack of understanding of the problems in that respective theater." After noting that "in the last war" this situation created in the combat zones "bitter antagonists" against the leadership in Washington, news of which then spread to the news media, Eaker opined that this same sort of thing could happen now to the air forces. He proposed to Giles that no cablegram of the kind just discussed be sent to any air force commander "without being personally cleared by you." He concluded by relating that when General Andrews had arrived to replace Eisenhower as ETOUSA, he gave exactly such a directive, which had a "very wholesome effect."[30] Eaker's request may have received a positive response by Giles, but Arnold's advisory council was beyond Giles's control.

Chapter 18

Late Winter–Early Spring 1943

O n the last day of February, General Arnold suffered his first heart attack, a mild one that grounded him from the office temporarily but soon permitted him to play a round of recuperative golf with his good friend Robert Lovett, the assistant secretary of war for air, at a hospital requisitioned for the AAF in Coral Gables. It was also a chance to celebrate his fourth star, the first in the air forces; days later, Arnold would join in celebrating the promotion of Spaatz to lieutenant general. With Eaker in the States, VIII Bomber Command passed temporarily to Possum Hansell. Eaker was devoted to the men of the Eighth, describing them as "sturdy amateurs," enthusiastic and dedicated— but "simply not ready yet for a major offensive against Germany." Hansell, despite being almost a permanent fixture on Arnold's staff, did not particu- larly care for Arnold, who, though, did want benefit of Hansell's abilities. Hansell was an intelligent and thoughtful officer with polished Southern manners, his mind never seeming at rest. Hansell possessed a deep hatred of targeting civilian populations; hence, it was no surprise that he also had little use for Bert Harris, an aggressive advocate of precisely that.[1] Hansell thought Harris's techniques to be "uncivilized and inefficient [and] resented Harris' criticism of his plan to wipe out key bottleneck industries, which Harris called an 'impractical panacea,'" his favorite bête noire.[2]

During the first three months of 1943, the Eighth's loss rate averaged 7 percent, unacceptable for a force as small as VIII Bomber Command at the time—usually fewer than one hundred heavies—and the cause of "extensive combat fatigue" among the aircrews.[3] One staff victim of January's foul weather was Colonel Henry Berliner, the Eighth's A-5, who, taken seriously ill, was invalided to the United States. Dick Hughes was elevated to assistant chief of staff, A-5 (Operational Planning) and promoted to colonel. Brigadier General Fred Anderson, who joined Eaker's staff prior to assuming a wing command, began an alliance with Hughes, the two becoming close collaborators when Anderson moved up to commanding general, VIII Bomber Command.

March began on a sour note, when Eaker reported to Arnold the contents of a telephone call with Portal, in which the RAF head expressed "grave concern" over the Eighth's inability to create an air force in the theater that corresponded with the numbers on the flow charts that Arnold had earlier provided. This was followed on 5 March by a similar complaint from Harris at bomber command expressing "regret" that the Eighth was still well under the size earlier promised. Although the men and airplanes of VIII Bomber Command were of the best "quality" and fully equal to the task at hand, wrote Harris, unfortunately the force was still too small to undertake its full share of the air war in "day and night" bombardment, leaving "no hope for the enemy . . . who could not long stand against such a weight of combined offensive." These were sharp words from two of the Eighth's most loyal supporters but told Eaker nothing he did not already know. The details of the call and letter eventually ended up on General Marshall's desk. He recognized that the Eighth had been conducting combat operations "with too few airplanes" but opined that, if they could double the number of bombers on each strike, he believed that the effectiveness of the bombing would significantly increase while losses would decrease.[4] It had required two weeks for the issue to percolate up to this level, during which the Eighth engaged in several successful strikes, including one on the eighteenth to the U-boat construction yards at Vegesack that was little short of stunning.

The day following receipt of Bert Harris's letter, Eaker's emotions were raised with a letter from George Stratemeyer, in his last days as chief of the air staff. "Strat" and his pending replacement, Major General Barney McK. Giles, both staunchly supported Eaker and used their position to reassure him and to intercede when necessary with the chief. Now Stratemeyer wrote, "We are doing everything possible to get heavy bombers over to you," adding that "we are stymied" with the still vexing issue of sending the ground crews by ship well after the aircrews had flown their B-17s to England. He then listed the most current data available on the status of both kinds of bomber groups and replacements. Depicted were arrivals by 31 March of 236 Fortresses and 48 Liberators, with another 191 and 52, respectively, showing up by the end of April. Even better news was that not only would all replacement aircraft arrive with complete crews but 75 percent would be combat qualified. Stratemeyer ended writing, "Every time anything is diverted from your theater, Ira, I fight it, but every once in a while I get whipped and that just can't be helped, but please understand that I am continuing my fight to prevent any diversion from UK, particularly of heavy bombers."[5]

"Tactical Lessons Learned"

In mid-March, and responsive to Eaker's request for a summary of "tactical lessons learned," Brigadier Generals James Hodges of the 2nd Wing and Hansell of the 1st Wing addressed problems afflicting the B-24 and B-17 groups from the beginning of operations. The significance is that eight months after the Eighth began flying combat, it was still receiving aircrew with exactly the same training deficiencies. Hodges's submission, while honest in content, was politely deceptive in that most examples were presented not as "tactical measures learned" but as an insufficiency in aircrew training. Under the rubric of ASSEMBLY, one difficulty related to how "low ceilings and layers of cloud covers have complicated the assembly of basic units" resulting in "strung out, disorganized units" from England to the target. Of seven proffered solutions, six were pilot training issues, with one discussion of "leadership" in the experience levels of officers still transitioning and a mindset from civilian life. Such was the case with "tactical issues," including formation flying—of which Hodges felt the necessity to define basic detail such as types of aircraft formations from the two-plane element to group and combat wing, the proper way to climb the aircraft from takeoff to altitude, consequences of a stretched-out formation, and general piloting techniques for maintaining the different formations. Hodges put forth six broad areas with each broken into essential components delving into definitions, causes, and solutions for each. Almost all critiques were elements of advanced flight training that aircrews, especially pilots and bombardiers, should have mastered at training commands before leaving the States.[6]

Hansell's report was much the same, only more direct and longer. His letter began, "Combat crews arriving in this theater, whether as replacements or as integral parts of an organization, have not had sufficient training in the use of their equipment under realistically simulated combat conditions." There followed an itemized critique equal to six single-spaced pages. He pointed to radio operators who could neither send nor receive at the necessary eighteen words per minute, the basic level of competence; only when they could do this competently at combat altitudes of twenty thousand to twenty-six thousand feet "could they then be taught new procedures and the use of the many new radio aids that exist in this highly organized theater." He was critical of gunners who had neither qualified nor even fired at high altitudes and lacked knowledge of the problems to which their guns and turrets were susceptible or of methods to resolve them. Hansell addressed the "tragic results [of] deficiencies in gunnery training," calling "attrition" in the theater "excessive." He explained how gunnery failure was "cumulative," resulting in "loss of airplanes and crews, which in turn causes loss of morale . . . which further reduces the defensive effectiveness of the gunners."[7]

There was criticism of bombardiers who had never dropped from high altitude or under simulated combat flight, navigators who could not read maps, and pilots who had never flown in formation at high altitudes, with long explications of the need and reasons for good formation flying skills in different weathers and under different combat conditions. He returned to the bombardiers and their unfamiliarity with different bombing methods, and more. Hansell imparted expectations on actual combat missions: different flak patterns and penetration of heavy flak areas, degrees of evasive action on bomb runs, long paragraphs on "Air Combat" in general, finishing up with comments and advice for problems with "Communications" and "Equipment." Again, the material centered on basic skills that crews ideally should have learned, or at least been exposed to, in training.

Hansell criticized navigators who lacked Morse code and bombardiers who could not read aerial maps to find industrial targets on the ground or "place the center of the [bomb] train on the target." Not exempt were pilots unable to maintain defensive formations at high altitude or unable to avoid damaging the turbo-charged engines while doing so. He stressed that one learned to fly in combat by doing just that, but training to combat standards would prepare for what could not be taught (flak, enemy fighters, temperatures at minus forty-five degrees, unrelenting cacophony, etc.). Hansell addressed how to react and what to do when the aircraft was damaged or straggling, the use of cloud cover, aircraft maneuvering, and other techniques to survive enemy fighters (e.g., approach and depart land "at 90-degree angles for 50–75 miles because fighter pilots are more determined in their attacks when over land"). He delved into advanced enemy fighter tactics, warning that Fortresses without nose guns invited head-on attacks; the differences in single and multiengine Luftwaffe tactics; and penetration of heavy flak areas, cautioning that flak was usually more accurate in altitude than deflection.

These were problems still extant eight months after the Eighth had commenced bombing the enemy and after three months of operations into Germany proper. Hansell sent his memo to Eaker and then initiated training programs for his wing. Inadequately trained new crews would plague the Eighth for two years—inescapable proof that it took months to establish schools, find instructors, and begin training programs. As the war could not be put on hold for two years, the unfortunate but unvarnished fact was that to fight the war now, airplanes had to have crew members and, though regrettable, the aircrews were as yet imperfectly trained. But they were all the AAF had. The aircrews knew it and worked hard to acquire the necessary skills before the lack of them was the cause of their deaths. Also unhelpful, it would take almost two years before aircraft would undergo combat modifications in stateside factories. Until then they would continue to endure lengthy delays at Langford Lodge.

It is worth underscoring that, four months hence, on 7 July, upon completion of a major inspection of the Eighth, Lieutenant General Delos C. Emmons sent a cablegram to Arnold detailing the exact same deficiencies and problems—and more—mentioned by generals Hodges and Hansell months earlier and urging their quick remediation. Included was the rapid provision of the P-51 Mustang—with the Merlin engine! At the close General Emmons evaluated the Eighth as "well-organized and functioning smoothly" while recommending that Eaker be provided a deputy.[8] On 27 November, finally, Major General Idwal Edwards would at last be moved from deputy at ETOUSA to be the new deputy at the Eighth.[9]

March Operations

Flying weather in the European skies for much of March was adverse, in the cant of the meteorologists, but not enough to cancel a strike on the fourth by Hansell's 1st Wing on the marshaling yards at Rotterdam and on Hamm, the first completed raid into the Ruhr Valley. This mission was followed on the sixth by strikes on the bridge, power plant, and port at Lorient while the Liberators flew a diversionary mission to a bridge and U-boat facilities at Brest.[10] On 8 March, after aborts, Hansell led fifty-four Forts to marshaling yards at Rennes, while thirteen Liberators hit yards at Rouen. At Rennes, photos from PR Spitfires recorded that the heavies had "cut the marshaling yards at both ends and caused a complete standstill for three or four days and a slow-down for two more weeks."[11] The B-24s were not as fortunate. On the way to Rouen, escorted by 4th FG Spitfires, the Luftwaffe introduced yet another new tactic. The defenders attacked in two waves, "the first to engage the escort fighters" while sending "the second to directly attack the bombers." Two heavies were downed, three damaged but repairable, and one landed DBR, to be cannibalized for parts.[12]

The 18 March strike woke up the brass. Ninety-seven Fortresses and Liberators hit the Bremer Vulkan (BV) U-boat yards at Vegesack, a Bremen suburb on the Weser River, with outstanding results.[13] The small size of the BV yards, an "obscure" area 2,500 by 1,000 feet, belied its importance to the U-boat fleet. In exchange for two heavies downed, seven defenders were claimed by American gunners. Damage to the target was assessed as "extremely heavy." Hansell had earlier ordered cameras installed on each of the bombers, resulting in competition that, he believed, had a "salutary effect," as 70 percent of the bombs were assessed as hitting within 1,000 feet of the target. Of fifteen or sixteen submarines under construction, "seven were damaged severely, one capsized, and six others slightly damaged.[14] Photos taken by RAF PR Spitfires confirmed initial assessments, permitting a "jubilant" Eaker to write Spaatz informing that the poststrike intelligence suggested the yards had been "put out for a year by one raid of less than 100 heavy bombers."[15] Despite this successful strike and additional bombings later, seventy-four Type VII U-boats were ultimately constructed there.[16]

The US 7th PR Group, activated in the summer of 1942, finally arrived in England after the new year and were stationed at RAF Mount Farm. On 28 March, Major James G. Hall, CO of the rehabilitated 13th PR Squadron, flew the first Eighth Air Force PR sortie over German-occupied territory, making two photo runs across the Dieppe port and airfield and German installations at Le Treport. The Eighth would no longer be totally dependent on the RAF for photo cover.[17] Following the group's thirteenth sortie on 8 April, General Andrews at ETOUSA was forwarded the grades for the 7th's photos accorded by the CIU at RAF Medmenham. Utilizing both RAF and AAF personnel as photo interpreters and intelligence specialists, Medmenham rated twelve of the sorties as A-level quality and one as B-level. For the remainder of the war, 7th PRG pilots would fly some of the war's most dangerous missions to obtain critical photographic intelligence.[18]

With spring in the offing, the continuing effort by the AAF and RAF to draft a policy for an air offensive, as decided at Casablanca, was accompanied by increased pressure by Arnold for Eaker to fly more airplanes on more missions. Yet the Eighth remained woefully short of heavy bombers because of diversions to Doolittle's Twelfth, and soon the three groups of B-24s would deploy for TIDAL WAVE—Ploęsti. Northern European weather patterns combined with fewer "operational combinations" in the groups to keep mission sizes well below one hundred aircraft. Contemporaneously, for better or worse, Arnold continued to receive periodic written and verbal communications commending Eaker from high-ranking American and British military and political officials who were working closely and frequently with the Eighth. Those voices included every general who commanded ETOUSA, Eaker's commanders of record, Generals Stratemeyer and Giles of the air staff, Ambassadors Winant and Harriman, and Secretary Lovett, from the American side. RAF leadership included Portal, Harris, and Slessor, and lower-ranking operational leaders with whom Eaker worked and who praised his leadership of the Eighth.

Arnold Redux

The cable dialog between Arnold and Eaker during the spring months of 1943 reveal that, at a fundamental level, there was evolving such a consequential difference in perspectives that a resolution suitable to both was increasingly unlikely. The perpetual antagonists that were beyond Eaker's control—the weather in the UK, over the target, or both, and the diversions to TORCH, the Pacific, and missions such as TIDAL WAVE—were personal torments for him. For Arnold, four thousand miles away, there were hundreds of other issues on a global scale that competed for his attention and emotions. There was, though, a personal complication for the chief that lingered in the shadows: How would the series of heart attacks affect him? Would they force his retirement? How would they affect his confidence, judgment, self-concern? One does not simply shake off coronaries, after all. But Arnold returned to his former level of intensity as soon as he was able, although no one in the air forces bore more pressure than he did.

Still, the situation was serious enough that his long and close friend General Marshall advised him many times to ease the burdens of office, even by doing something as simple as rejecting requests for speeches or appearances at affairs unrelated to his immediate official endeavors; he did, after all, have any number of exceptionally competent generals to represent the AAF. Marshall himself firmly declined all such events to conserve his energy, riding horses alone every afternoon to clear his mind. Admiral Chester Nimitz in Honolulu passed weekends at the isolated plantation home of close friends, where the war was a forbidden subject and he especially enjoyed the company of their adolescent children. But Arnold ignored Marshall's pointed suggestions as he persisted in overloading his day, allowing far too many issues of lesser, or no, import to hijack his time and sap his energy. Besides the War Department, the chief spent hours collaborating directly with corporation heads and business leaders, never hesitating to pick up the telephone to cajole, order, argue with, convince, beg, scheme, or employ any other tactics necessary to obtain their compliance or support. Marshall and Nimitz managed to accomplish as much as Arnold, but with far less damage to their bodies. Unable to do the same, Arnold was consequently afflicted with coronaries.

Near March's end, Eaker suggested to General Andrews that he send an updated status cable to the chief on strategic bomber personnel, supplying his latest figures for Andrews on the thirtieth to go out under ETOUSA, vice the Eighth. Eaker was blunt: on 30 March his "average number" of available crews was at 173; but, he added, within the next fifteen days at the present operational rate 90 of those crews (52 percent) would either complete their thirty missions or be casualties (because of a shortage of crews, the "magic number" had recently been raised to thirty missions). And while he had 46 crews then training at the CCRC, 119 replacement crews in three groups promised for March had not been received. Factoring in anticipated operational losses, the consequences of not receiving the promised three groups, then, would be the difference between having 75 bombers for missions in April rather than 300.[19] TORCH continued to be a heavy drain on the Eighth.

Meanwhile, the chief continued to simmer over the "surprise of being put on the defensive," now by Roosevelt and Churchill vice Eaker and Spaatz, in Casablanca more than two months earlier. During his subsequent Pacific trip, he had let fester the perception that the explanations given by the Eighth's commanders were "weak." Yet immediately following SYMBOL, the Eighth had flown eighteen missions against the U-boat facilities directly responsive to Eisenhower's orders, as well as continuing to strike Luftwaffe airfields in France and the Low Countries. Interspersed among these missions, Fortresses had flown five strikes against strategic targets in Germany. Three other missions to Germany were aborted because of weather.[20] In short, Eaker launched missions on average every three days between the last of January to the end of March, an unexpectedly strong number given the usual poor early-spring weather patterns in northwestern Europe.

Eaker must have felt frustrated, or worse, in his exchanges with the chief, for any orders sending bombers across the channel without the British instrument landing system installed and the pilots well-trained in its use would have been little short of a death warrant for the crew of ten when needed. Among the vagaries of British weather, even perfectly clear skies on takeoff would disappear, with heavy fog or low clouds often settling over parts of England with alarming frequency before missions could return, requiring instrument landings for all aircraft. Hansell knew this well:

> The condition of the weather had to be forecast in regard to: takeoff and assembly; route to target; target exposure; return to England; and landing at bases. If the weather at the target was not suitable to bombing, then a whole mission had been wasted. . . . If the weather on return to base was "socked in," disaster could ensue. . . . All our bases were in middle England, and it was quite possible that the entire Eighth Air Force could be lost in a single afternoon by returning to England and finding all bases "socked in." And bombing accuracy was heavily degraded by even partial cloud cover of the target. Weather was actually a greater hazard and obstacle than the German Air Force.[21]

It was not that Eaker lacked awareness of the consequences of remaining grounded: over the first three months of 1943, he followed carefully the growth of the Luftwaffe in France and the Low Countries while the Eighth was sitting because of persistent foul weather. During these months, the correspondence between the chief and his air force commander was frequent and direct in tone and language; still, the two generals somehow managed to talk past each other with increasing frequency.[22]

In the wake of Portal's 28 February phone call and then Harris's follow-up, Eaker made time to craft a lengthy letter to Arnold, unaware the chief had been hospitalized with his first coronary. While the Eighth proceeded with operations, General Eaker, so methodical and calm the greater part of the time, felt compelled to write to the chief out of deeply felt perturbation. The aircraft arrivals schedule Eaker had requested at the first of March finally left Arnold's office at the end of the month. Arnold had earlier promised replacement of damaged or destroyed aircraft and the acquisition of additional aircraft on a regular schedule. VIII Bomber Command was projected to jump to nineteen heavy bombardment groups by 30 June, three months hence. The complement was to increase to thirty-seven heavy groups by the end of the year, and increase yet again by six more groups by 30 June 1944, for a total of forty-four heavy bombardment groups. Disregarding Portal's wishes for a firm schedule, the chief let it be clearly known that the projections were fluid, warning that they "cannot and positively must not" be viewed as anything close to definitive. In this he was correct: the arrival of the new groups rapidly fell behind schedule, remaining about three months tardy through the remainder of 1943.

This was too much for Eaker, whose patience had worn thin as hundreds of bombers promised by various dates went from a few dozen to just a few dribbling in intermittently. He lived with the disappointment of his aircrews and the British day after day; by late March his patience was paper thin. In notable correspondence that counted thirty-one mostly short paragraphs, Eaker said in part:

> The current position of the Eighth Air Force is not a credit to the American Army. After sixteen months of war, we are not yet able to dispatch more than 123 bombers towards an enemy target. Many of the crews who fly this pitiful number have been on battle duty for eight months. They understand the law of averages. They have seen it work on their friends.
>
> The crews know why this command has never dared to set a limit of operational tours until recently. They know that we have been promised replacement crews as often as we have been promised more planes. They have seen the number of planes dwindle until its scarcity has restricted most of our raiding to relatively futile forays on the coast of France. . . . They know that they will have to continue battle duty even after the limit of thirty missions. . . . And they know the reason, which is that after eight months in this theater the Eighth Air Force is still an unkept promise.
>
> This is written with no apprehension of trouble with the crews. They are American and will pay for the mistakes of their superiors as uncomplainingly as the men of Wake and Bataan did. . . .
>
> The purpose of the Eighth Air Force was and is to strike the chief Axis enemy in his heart. No other American military or naval force

was capable of this at the outset of the war. No other will be capable
of this this year. . . .

[Our] men should be returning now, to pass on the lessons and
bring back squadrons trained in our bloodily bought experience. Instead
they will have to remain in dwindling numbers. . . .

To consider the consequence of our unkept promise upon our English
ally is to consider another grave misfortune of our plight. The dream of
around the clock bombing remains, thanks to our numerical weakness in
places, a dream. . . .

The Eighth Air Force is the one tangible combat partner the US
could offer the English and Russians. It was not an offer of charity, it
was self-interest. . . .

It is respectfully requested that the Eighth Air Force be given
sufficient planes to redeem its unkept promise.[23]

His aide described the letter as "twenty-five hundred words filling three single-
spaced, legal-sized pages" with the "impersonal tone of a legal indictment."
While this letter was heading west across the Atlantic, another letter from
Arnold drafted two days earlier was eastbound with an aircraft arrivals flow
chart that, like all others, would soon become moot.

Whether it was because the chief was ill or, as Eaker presumed, Arnold
"would pay attention to strong statements and officers who stood up to
him," the chief's reply was short, even conciliatory. But Arnold also passed
Eaker's long missive to Lieutenant General Thomas T. Handy, chief of OPD
at the War Department, citing the total number of aircraft sent to Eaker since
November of 1942 and commenting that Eaker "thinks I am personally
responsible for taking all of the planes that he didn't get and sending them
to North Africa."[24] Arnold neglected to mention that over 1,200 of all
aircraft that had initially been sent to England had been diverted to North
Africa—at his order, in point of fact. Responding to Eaker, Arnold wrote
that he had air forces in eight different theaters clamoring for airplanes and
was doing his best to service all of the requirements, citing his own problems with the "merry-go-round" that was wartime Washington.[25] Not that
Arnold held Eaker any less to account, but it was also true that in the first
three months of 1943, only sixty-three new heavy bombers had arrived in
England for VIII Bomber Command.[26] A full year after the Eighth had been

created, it was fighting "a war of critical importance with too few bombers for economical operation."[27] While frequently complaining to Eaker about his issues, Arnold rarely acknowledged problems caused by his office.

Arnold, like Eaker, went to war believing in the self-protection abilities of the "300 bomber strike" and had even informed his colleagues on the JCS in February that any formation of heavy bombers penetrating deep into Germany must have that 300 minimum in "supporting distance of each other" for the bombers to effectively protect all in the formation. Moreover, Arnold had added that, for the first 300 heavies "to be really effective," these "must be followed up by a second force of 300." And then, to ensure that 600 aircraft were always kept operational, there must be "a reserve of another 600 bombers."[28] Yet during March of 1943, the Eighth's total inventory of heavy bombers, operational or otherwise, averaged only 281, with almost the fewest number ever on group flight lines. The others were mostly split between those undergoing modifications at Langford Lodge and the heavily damaged being repaired at three BADAs. The average strike during this period consisted of only 88 heavies, with some but not all strikes escorted as far as ninety miles beyond the French coast. At first scheduled to receive three more heavy bomber groups and 157 replacement crews by the end of March, Arnold instead notified Eaker that he was losing all three groups and 132 of the aircrews to North Africa and the Pacific.[29] VIII Bomber Command flew eight "shallow penetrations" of Germany during the month; two had just barely 100 aircraft dispatched, but aborts meant fewer than that number reached the target. The CBO, the formal directive that grew out of the Casablanca Directive, called for the Eighth to have a minimum of 944 heavy bombers in England by the end of June, one hundred days hence. The Eighth could barely call itself an air force.

Chapter 19

April 1943

W hen April 1943 rolled in, VIII Bomber Command counted just six heavy bomber groups, four B-17 and two B-24, with the only AAF escort still the 4th Fighter Group, which had just recently transitioned from Spitfires to P-47Cs, whose short range, while better than the Spits, was still a disappointment. Fourth FG pilots, long accustomed to the small, light, highly maneuverable Spitfire with its feather-touch responsiveness, hated the heavy, barrel-chested Thunderbolt.[1] VIII Bomber Command's inventory improved slightly during the month to seven heavy groups— 198 Fortresses and 66 Liberators—with the promise of twelve new groups to arrive soon. "Regardless of the number of aircraft and crews on hand, the number that could be sent out on any particular mission depended on the ability of maintenance crews and depots to keep the aircraft in operational order, to repair battle damage, and to make such modifications as combat experience demonstrated to be necessary. That ability, in turn, depended on an adequate supply of parts and a force of trained personnel large enough and in a position to devote enough time to this work to keep up with the requirements of the operational units."[2] Viewed differently, the number of operationally ready aircraft always diminished after each mission, with most suffering some degree of combat damage. Many were usually restored within a few days. Several missions within a week's time, though, could drop the number of heavies significantly, with lengthy wait times before any could be replaced or patched up. Throughout spring 1943 the ability of the Eighth to repair battle-damaged aircraft improved significantly despite the large percentage of aircraft suffering damage on each raid and still inadequate maintenance facilities.[3] "But maintenance wasn't Eaker's real problem, it was Arnold. Conversely, Arnold's main problem with the Eighth was his inability or unwillingness to accept weather, limited aircraft and crews, lack of long-range fighter escort, or the need to rest as valid impediments. Hap expected the maximum effort for every mission on every day that weather permitted."[4] Arnold seemed to view weather as an abstract issue: "flying weather" anywhere in Europe meant the airplanes should fly missions, period; while Eaker was always concerned with weather at two places, home and the target. The weather in England had the ability to go from clear to zero-zero quickly, closing most or all the air bases. Group commanders feared having dozens of bombers returning from a mission in a low fuel state to find that, in all of England, only two or three airfields clustered in just one area were barely open. Without radar bombing technology—the H2X radar that would arrive in October for the Americans—there had to be acceptable visual bombing weather either at the target or at designated targets of opportunity; if there was not, it did not matter how fine the weather at home. Yet as far as Arnold was concerned, the weather was just another of the same old excuses not to fly.

If Arnold's plan to have every airplane in the air for every mission was followed to the letter, Eaker's operations staff calculated that a continuous cycle of fewer aircraft and even fewer aircrews would be available for each succeeding strike. A loss rate of just 3.8 percent might look low to those in the Pentagon, but for the Eighth it meant that for every one hundred men present in July, inside of six months sixty-four of them would be dead, missing, prisoner, or too wounded to fly again.[5] And with loss rates for missions running more than double and triple of 4 percent, Eaker needed literally thousands of aircrew. Through the month of April his total heavy bomber strength continued to count six groups, four B-17 and two B-24. In May, however, four more heavy groups would become operational, to be formed into the 4th Bombardment Wing.[6]

Truth to tell, the real limitation on the number of bombers available for dispatch lay not with the airplanes but with aircrews. Replacements just were not available in the numbers required to fly all the combat operational airplanes. Some groups in the Eighth were at 50 percent aircrew strength, if that, with more airmen lost to "war weariness" than to combat wounds.[7] The potential was ever present for physical harm and psychological damage to the aircrews in flying at twenty-five thousand feet while using an erratic oxygen supply in an unheated, open aircraft for four or five hours and facing an enemy trying hard to kill them. There were missions in which half or more of the airplanes in a squadron, or even group, would be lost, leaving the surviving men to deal psychologically with the thought that 150 or more of their friends and squadron mates were now dead, grievously wounded, and missing in just a few hours. Then, in a few days the living would have to go out and face the same all over again. Yet the relationship between operationally available aircraft and the need for matching numbers of qualified aircrews to fly them was basic too. But it often appeared that Arnold did not understand this. In his pushing to "fly every available airplane," Arnold seemed to many to be overlooking the mismatch between operationally ready aircrews and operationally ready airplanes, in addition to the limits on the men physically and psychologically who were flying these missions.

Arnold himself, though, was facing growing demands of a different ilk every day of the week. He had personally "spent considerable political capital making certain that Eaker, above all his other commanders, received the greatest measure of aircraft, crews, and equipment."[8] Eaker owed him more than prudence, Arnold believed. The chief had further concluded that Eaker was retaining too many staff officers who, Arnold was increasingly certain, were incapable of performing at the requisite level of competency. As Barney Giles informed Eaker, the chief "believes that you are weak in your chief of staff and your Bomber Command"—Colonel Charlie Bubb and Newton Longfellow. Arnold was also looking at Monk Hunter as insufficiently flexible, with his persistence in flying fruitless RODEO sweeps.

Arnold cited unspecified reports "from England" relating that fighter pilots only sought "excuses for going to the Savoy"—the bar at London's swank Savoy Hotel occasionally patronized by unaccompanied ladies—instead of hunting the Luftwaffe. Arnold asked rhetorically of General Hunter, "Has he lost his spirit—his dash"?[9] The good news was that Brigadier General Fred Anderson, formerly an ornament of Arnold's headquarters staff, was now with Eaker's staff. Highly intelligent, dedicated to the mission, energetic, and an aggressive bombardment expert, Anderson was preparing to serve an indoctrination stint leading the 4th Wing as a prelude to assuming VIII Bomber Command.

17 April 1943

On 17 April four heavy bomber groups divided into two provisional combat wings flew the deadliest mission yet for the Eighth, with General Anderson as an observer in the lead Fortress.[10] The targets were the U-boat yards and Focke-Wulf factory at Bremen, which had replaced Lorient as "Flak City" for the obvious reason. The strike results appeared significant upon preliminary examination of the target sites, but that did not prevent the chief from levying sharp criticism of Eaker afterward. Following a short, perfunctory comment in which he generously acknowledged the self-evident—namely, that he was not on the raid—Arnold, or quite possibly an advisory council officer in his stead, proceeded to second-guess the attack. Why, the cable's author demanded to know, had the bombers flown in one long column, allowing the lead element to be devastated by the Luftwaffe fighters? Why had not the bombers broken up into multiple elements and approached the target from different points of the compass to "confuse the enemy"?

If the mission had in fact been flown as described, it would unquestionably have been poor judgment. But that was not at all how the raid unfolded. The mission was one of several trial runs with the bombers flying by groups in "well-organized protective formations," another variation of Curt LeMay's innovative "Combat Box." Not only was the route of flight too distant from England for escorts, but as the bomber stream approached the Frisian Islands from the north, it was spotted by a German reconnaissance aircraft that then trailed it, reporting the formation's every move to the Luftwaffe's ground radar and antiaircraft cannon sites. The heavies were soon subjected to yet another iteration of Luftwaffe tactics as the defenders attacked head-on in waves with the fighters deliberately concentrating on the lead elements—which, because those aircraft carried the lead bombardiers, could take no evasive action.[11]

The defenders inflicted serious losses on the bomber force, the most by the Luftwaffe to date on any heavy bomber strike, with the aircrews estimating 150 enemy defending fighters attacking the Fortresses; the defenders picked at the bomber formation until near the IP over Wildeshausen, at which time the Luftwaffe slammed the bombers in full force.[12] Lost were fifteen B-17s to the Luftwaffe, twice as many as on any other mission, and one more to flak— 160 airmen. The Luftwaffe sent up Me-109s and FW-190s as the principal force, with twin-engine Me-110s tracking with the bomber formations at a distance, waiting to bounce wounded stragglers and JU-88s possibly dropping bombs on the formation from above. As memorialized in the tactical mission report, "the intensity of the flak was probably the most severe that has ever been experienced by this Wing, and the huge volume of smoke that overhung the target area . . . acted as a very real deterrent." The intense aerial combat imposed serious losses among the lead bombers between the IP and target, with flak said to have been of a "concentration heretofore unknown."[13] Fortress gunners claimed sixty-three defenders downed, fifteen probables, and seventeen damaged; postwar records showed three downed. The bomber force's loss rate of 15 percent was treble the average for VIII Bomber Command at that time; more important, it was also treble the acceptable loss rate in Eaker's "Four Phase" memo of last October.

The losses at Bremen's Focke-Wulf factory were correctly viewed as a testament to the determination of the Luftwaffe pilots who persisted in the head-on attacks and the ferocity of the air battle. The "fiercest air-to-air fight of the war up to then," the effects of this battle on the aircrews were strongly felt after they returned. After landing, Anderson, Hansell, LeMay, and the lead aircraft crew (commander, pilot, bombardier, and navigator) were driven together to the after-mission critique. En route Anderson asked Hansell whether he had received their report of the sixteen lost aircraft;

Hansell did not reply. Anderson spoke again: "Now I know what you have been talking about. The Germans came at us in waves. They swarmed all over guys like a herd of bees. We need fighter support all the way to the target and back. I didn't see any P-47s."[14] Hansell responded vaguely that "Hap is under tremendous pressure." At the time, the airmen could not be aware of the whole story, as the various intelligence offices required time to resolve the question of damage to the Focke-Wulf factory. Destruction was first determined to have consumed the entire factory; however, on 25 June Dick Hughes in A-5 read a POW interrogation in which the subject claimed that the plant had been "inoperative since August of 1942." An RAF wing commander seconded to the Eighth's A-2 section responded that (a) inspection plates seen on a crashed FW-190 indicated a "recent" date of manufacture, and (b) reconnaissance photos taken of the plant on 10 March 1942 showed seventeen aircraft on the factory ramps. From these two pieces of information, Hughes was assured that the plant was "undoubtedly" in operation on 17 April 1943.[15] But as the photo interpreters scoured poststrike photos over the next weeks, "it became obvious the Germans had not taken any steps to repair the supposedly valuable plant." With this as a "warning flag," intelligence materials were subjected to "extensive analysis" that ultimately led to "incontrovertible evidence" that the equipment that had been at the Bremen plant had been moved to Regensburg in eastern Germany "several months" before the attack.[16]

Despite the loss rate of 15 percent, Eaker "retained his faith . . . that daylight bombers operating in 'well-flown formations' could penetrate enemy air space successfully—with a loss rate of five percent or less—in their missions against the German aircraft industry."[17] As a major, Eaker was first indoctrinated in HADPB and the self-defending bomber at ACTS in 1935. Colonel Eaker in 1941 would no doubt have been aware of AWPD-1 and its reliance on HADPB. That same autumn he had participated in a joint AAF/ RAF board on the future of pursuit aircraft, agreeing with the RAF that there was "no solution" to the escort "problem."[18] As commander of the Eighth's heavy bombers, his assignment included proving the viability of HADPB once in England. Efforts there were supported by AWPD-42, written by his own planning officer. Most importantly, at General Arnold's order he had delivered an impassioned defense of HADPB to the British prime minister at Casablanca. By then Eaker was so psychologically bonded to HADPB and associated issues, like the supposed inability to develop a long-range escort, that it is difficult to imagine him thinking differently.

Eaker's exasperations had been relentless since arriving in England: every morning when he woke up, the war was still there but his airplanes were somewhere else. Fifteen months later, when he should have been sending hundreds of heavy bombers on punishing daylight raids deep into the German homeland and validating the Doctrine, he had only just managed to send out the first strike in which more than one hundred planes had made it to one target thirty miles into Germany proper. And he had been hit hard. Weather grounded VIII Bomber Command for the remaining two weeks of April, making a total of just four missions in thirty days, obviating the desirable repeat strike within seventy-two hours of the initial raid. Europe in 1943 was far different from the ACTS classrooms of a decade earlier.

Arnold's Letter to Andrews, 23 April 1943

Eaker traveled to Washington on 23 April for ten days of presentations to the JCS and War Department on the CBO, which had become known as the Eaker Plan because of the general's leadership in its development. The day Eaker flew to Washington, Arnold chose to send to General Andrews at ETOUSA a letter that Haywood Hansell would later describe as a "petulant" and "somewhat irrational" message negatively comparing Eaker's performance as commander of the Eighth to the earlier tenure of Tooey Spaatz. The letter ignored the different circumstances between the summer and fall of 1942 and the spring of 1943. Arnold began by "attacking just about everything in the Eighth Air Force: its fighter and bomber commanders; its tactics, its pilots, and its leadership," although only one individual was mentioned by name—Brigadier General Newton Longfellow of VIII Bomber Command. About bomber command Arnold asked "Does it not lack an aggressive commander? Is the staff what it should be?" Particularly, Arnold complained that VIII Bomber Command was stagnating, standing down from missions because of weather "which, with more aggressive commanders, more might be accomplished." These accusations were not shared with Eaker despite his temporary presence in the very same offices in which the letter was drafted. Arnold asked the ETO commander for his "frank reactions" to these and other, similar comments about other of Eaker's staff officers, including Colonel Charlie Bubb.[19] Like Longfellow, Bubb was another of Eaker's longtime friends and had been recommended for promotion to brigadier by Eaker—a promotion Arnold was dead-set against.[20] Whether there was any specific instigating factor behind the letter was unclear to Hansell, although there were thoughts at the time that there might have been one too many derogatory stories from Arnold's staff about the Eighth.[21] In his reply Andrews opined tactfully that perhaps the leaders of fighter and bomber commands should be more aggressive but asked to reserve judgment as he was still new to the ETO. Although in command only since 4 February, Andrews had become a supporter of Eaker and was on the record as such; he gave no indication of doing anything before meeting with Eaker after his return to WIDEWING.

Newton Longfellow was Eaker's oldest friend, the two going back twenty-five years to service in the Philippines, but he was disliked by many in the army. He had joined the Eighth in the summer of 1942 as a colonel commanding the 2nd Wing, then was elevated by Eaker to lead VIII Bomber Command on 2 December, the day after Eaker assumed command of the Eighth. Longfellow's assignment was due at least as much to friendship with Eaker as performance, for it came despite a slew of negative feedback from group commanders and the presence of two more senior brigadiers able to take VIII Bomber Command (Kuter and Hansell).

In truth, Arnold was correct with respect to Longfellow: the bomber commander was ill-suited for combat command. Among other inadequacies, he was too high-strung, "tense and irritable . . . [with] the general attitude of a British sergeant-major . . . constant criticism and domineering attitude." After joining the Eighth, he soon earned a reputation as a tough guy because of his bombastic leadership style, leading the troops to refer to him as "The Screaming Eagle."[22] In one officer's opinion, "Eaker covered for Longfellow, serving in effect as both air force and bomber command commander, treating Longfellow [more as an] operations officer than a commanding general."[23] Longfellow flew his first combat mission ever on 6 September as an "observer," standing behind Major Paul Tibbets of the 97th BG, who was both aircraft and mission commander that afternoon. The strike against the St. Omer / Longuenesse airfield a few kilometers inland from the Calais coast ran into some exceptionally aggressive Luftwaffe defenders (the "Abbeville Boys" in their yellow-nosed FWs). When Tibbet's aircraft received 20 mm cannon hits, the new wing commander panicked and the "bravado that had struck fear into the hearts of [his] subordinates" deserted him.[24] Longfellow irrationally yanked back the throttles and turbo controls, immediately endangering the aircraft. Tibbets, busy flying a shot-up airplane with one wounded hand while keeping his copilot from bleeding to death after a shell blew off much of his hand and then bored a hole through the instrument panel, found the only way to dislodge Longfellow was a sharp elbow to the colonel's chin, temporarily cold-cocking him. Eaker promoted Longfellow three months hence to brigadier general and VIII Bomber Command, to the apparent joy only of himself and Eaker; the troops soon changed his sobriquet to "The Shouting Star."[25]

P-47s had first flown escort in early April with the Eagles of the 4th FG, quickly followed by the new 56th FG. On 15 April in a fight over the coast between Knokke and Ostend, Belgium, 4th FG pilots downed three FW-190s, the first Thunderbolt kills of the war.[26] And now the number of missions on which the heavies were splitting task forces to hit multiple targets was also increasing.[27] Despite Bremen, April was a better month than March.

Chapter 20

TRIDENT

May began tragically with the death of General Andrews on the third when his aircraft flew into a mountain in Iceland. The general was making a stop on the way to the States when the pilot—perhaps the general himself—became disoriented in heavy fog while executing an instrument approach to an airfield. Andrews was soon replaced at ETOUSA by Lieutenant General Jacob Devers, an armor corps officer who quickly proved to be a supporter of the air forces. Devers and Eaker soon became good friends, a relationship that rapidly translated into a strong professional relationship. Beneficially, Devers's chief of staff was Major General Idwal Edwards, an air forces officer, another longtime and loyal Eaker friend. Hansell thought it "doubtful that any officer in any guise, with or without pilots wings, could have equaled Devers' contribution to the Eighth Air Force. He quickly absorbed and embraced Eaker's strategic airpower concepts and backed them to the limit of his authority. Eaker and Devers became a unified command team."[1]

The first two weeks of May brought a welcomed increase in both men and aircraft to the Eighth as the AAF's training programs and the productivity of America's war machine were attaining a full wartime footing, the point at which bombers and trained airmen began to flow more quickly and in increasing numbers to England. On 5 May six heavy bomber groups joined the Eighth, five new ones fresh from the States plus the return of the 92nd, which had been utilized as the training cadre at RAF Bovingdon. On the thirteenth, with new crews coming out of the CCRC in larger numbers, qualified aircrews jumped from 100 to 215 almost overnight. As significant, on that same day all Nazi forces that could escape from Tunisia to Sicily had done so, leaving 267,000 Axis forces to surrender to Allied troops under Eisenhower's command.

In Washington the TRIDENT Conference (Third Washington) convened on 12 May; sitting through 25 May, it produced notable decisions affecting the prosecution of the war in Europe. But two days before the opening gavel, General Arnold suffered a second heart attack, less than three months after his first. Hospitalized for ten days of this conference, Arnold was replaced by Lieutenant General McNarney, the air forces officer serving as Marshall's deputy. The CCS met daily in the Federal Reserve Building off Constitution Avenue, apart from the other attendees, to debate and achieve consensus, if not unanimity, on the various issues. One was the CBO, with Peter Portal supporting Arnold and particularly Eaker's proposed operational plan. As before, destruction of the Luftwaffe's fighter force received highest priority, followed by U-boat yards and bases, the aircraft industry, ball bearings, and oil production and distribution facilities. The twenty-four-page document was supported with eight pages of graphs, charts, and maps dissecting the current state of the joint bomber offensive. The document also brought focus to the American strategy of precision daylight bombing to illustrate how multiple Allied working groups had, while meeting over four months, arrived at the suggested target priority.[2]

Since SYMBOL in January, General Eaker had been shepherding the Casablanca Directive from policy statement to the CBO. References to Eaker barely touched upon the months he put into the guidance and development of the operational plan. This was not the action of an indolent commander waiting to be told what to do or how to do it but a leader committed to determining the best way to destroy the enemy. Yet for some reason, Arnold's staff used the project as license to pester Eaker with "needling criticism" despite being the officer most involved with and most knowledgeable about its substance.[3]

The CCS did settle the Americans' anxiety by approving a cross-channel invasion of the Continent a year hence, with a target date of 1 May; the commander could select landing beaches either at the mouth of the Seine opposite Le Havre or the Cotentin Peninsula west of Caen.[4] The CCS specified overwhelming troop strength of twenty-nine divisions, sufficient time to acquire enough landing craft and air superiority, if not air supremacy; the troops were not to be subjected to Luftwaffe attacks while crossing the beaches.[5] As there had been no discussion of Roosevelt's "Unconditional Surrender" doctrine at Casablanca, this time voices were heard, with Eisenhower of the US Army and General Henry Maitland "Jumbo" Wilson of the BA prominently against it. President Roosevelt listened politely to their objections, but as before there was no discussion and no revision.

The final CCS decision for TRIDENT was the approval of the strike on the Ploęsti refineries, the planning for which Arnold assigned to Colonel Jacob E. Smart from his advisory council. Ploęsti irritated Eaker, especially upon confirmation that the Eighth would have to contribute two of the Eighth's combat-tested B-24 groups and a third group so new that it was still en route to England with crews so fresh they had received no combat training.[6] Eaker argued again that Germany ought to be the focus of the air war, with the Eighth receiving every heavy bomber that could be sent to England But having lost this fight, Eaker exerted every effort to give Jake Smart everything he asked for or would need with this difficult mission.

On the eighteenth of May, Eaker took time to write Arnold to register his concern over the chief's latest cardiac bout. In it he suggested that Arnold name a "hatchet man or deputy" to carry some of his load—a point to which Arnold apparently never responded. Importantly, Eaker also lauded the presence of Bob Lovett among his troops on a recent visit. The Eighth's commander mentioned specifically that the "frank and free attitude and discussions" conducted with the troops, combined with the assistant secretary's assurances and detailed knowledge he possessed of the problems, "has been a boon to our morale."[7]

Robert Lovett

Assistant Secretary of War for Air Robert Lovett, through various circumstances, had come to know Arnold, Spaatz, and Eaker between the world wars. He was the one person who had an "effective, calming voice" on Hap Arnold, as the general acknowledged.[8] In his early adult years, Lovett had been a naval aviator, flying combat missions in the Great War, first with the British Naval Air Service and then with the United States Navy, and like the US Ambassador to England John Winant, earned the Navy Cross for heroism.[9] Before Lovett joined the War Department, he had been a successful New York City banker and a director of the Union Pacific Railroad, where he developed a recognized expertise in logistics. Lovett possessed "wisdom, warmth, and wit," which is perhaps why General Marshall took time to be briefed by Lovett every day of the week, including Sundays, permitting Lovett to "influence Allied strategy so it reflected the AAF's ideas, capabilities, and interests."[10] He became one of the six "Wise Men," the architects of Cold War policy after World War II, and served as undersecretary of state and as the fourth United States secretary of defense.

Lovett had come to know the triumvirate of Arnold, Spaatz, and Eaker very well—certainly well enough to "admire greatly" Spaatz, whom he referred to affectionately as "a scamp if I ever saw one." He saw in the taciturn general an officer who "was warm at heart, always mindful of the welfare of people working for him . . . his humor was sardonic, his attitude toward sanctimony irreverent." Lovett thought Eaker was "over-awed" by Arnold, whom the junior officer considered "a genius . . . a non-conformist, the reason he [Arnold] was such a tremendous success." But it was Eaker whom Lovett considered "the only general who never made a major mistake."[11]

Lovett and Arnold had become friends in the summer of 1941 when Lovett supported Arnold on three points of signal importance to the air forces: the heavy strategic bomber, an independent air force in the future, and "saving the Air Corps from the RAF."[12] Lovett spent much more time with the chief than the other two and considered him a leader who was "often a bull in a china shop" (others perhaps saw Arnold as a bull who carried a china shop around with him).[13] Lovett believed the chief to be a "fine leader in an inspiring sense . . . [there] was something flamboyant, almost boyish about his enthusiasms." [14] Of Lovett Arnold would say, "I found in Bob Lovett a man who possessed the qualities in which I was weakest, a partner and teammate of tremendous sympathy, and of calm and hidden force. When I became impatient, intolerant, and would rant around, fully intending to tear the War and Navy Departments to pieces, Bob Lovett would know exactly how to handle me."[15] Lovett's position was purely political, not vested with inherent power; but when he occupied the chair, he exercised a good deal of influence solely derived from his moral and intellectual authority. Given carte blanche, Lovett was able to "delve into anything, and was not limited in scope."[16]

Numbers

Perhaps due to the psychological imprint of two coronaries, Arnold was becoming increasingly contentious in his professional relations with RAF senior leadership, senior AAF officers, and even with the British Air Ministry. Arnold never hesitated to express his mind as he saw every situation, even if it meant that his cable and letters to Eaker, his friend of two decades, were growing harsher. Returning to duty in less than a month after his second coronary, he wrote to Eaker that he expected the Eighth to have nineteen groups of heavy bombers by 30 June, two months hence. At the time the Eighth was again at seven heavy groups, and Eaker was left wondering from where the additional twelve groups were coming.[17] May's end found VIII Bomber Command with five more groups, short of the promised dozen but still most welcome. The new groups raised the inventory to 337 heavies in bomber command, of which 231 aircraft were operationally qualified. The daily operating average was a respectable 153 aircraft. Ten months after combat operations began, missions were being now escorted halfway into Belgian and France by fighter groups flying Spitfires and P-38s.[18] May's final mission, number sixty-one on the twenty-ninth, a return to the naval depot at Rennes and the pens at St. Nazaire and La Pallice, saw the largest bomber force yet, 279 heavies dispatched with 241 reaching the three targets. Losses were fourteen Forts—6 percent—on the mission plus ninety-eight damaged, including two DBR.[19] Afterward, General Eaker declared the "testing period" for the Eighth finished; he now had the force he thought sufficient to carry out his vow to "bomb day and night." Determined now to carry out his promises at Casablanca for round-the-clock bombing, he remained certain that long-range escort fighters remained unnecessary.[20] By that time the Eighth had lost approximately 1,900 men in 188 heavies over the Continent plus more men back in England, the dead and wounded whose shot-up airplanes made it home. The percentages were staggering: of aircrew who arrived in the summer and fall of 1942, 57 percent were KIA or MIA/POW, while another 16 percent had been killed in crashes in England, were too seriously wounded to fly again, or were permanently grounded through physical or psychological disability. Still, aircrew morale was higher at the end of the month than at the beginning, paralleling the increase in force size.

Importantly, also at the end of the month, Major General Follett Bradley, AAF inspector general, sent to Eaker (through General Devers at ETOUSA) the results of a detailed inspection his team had conducted of the Eighth. Among the more salient points was that "an important consideration to the success" of the Eighth was its cooperation with the British, which he described as "excellent." In addition to the expected encomiums, Bradley pointedly detailed the number of American awards for heroism and Legions of Merit that had been bestowed on RAF officers. But good news is usually followed by bad, or at least the not-so-good. Bradley noted the "operational handicaps" under which the Eighth had been flying, focusing on one of serious consequences but which had received little relief: the inability of new groups to become operational quickly because of the "failure to receive organizational equipment coincidentally with the [arrival] of ground echelons"— something Eaker had been trying to get HqAF to focus on for months.[21]

The problem was the ground crews and equipment had to travel to England by ship, turning up weeks after their aircraft and crews. Too often the ground crews were embarked on one ship while parts, supplies, and equipment were sent on several different ships with different schedules. Consequently, once the aircraft were finished with the numerous modifications at Langford Lodge and posted to an airfield, the ground crews could still be at sea with the needed maintenance gear who knew where. The current solution was for ground crews from the older group at the same airfield to double up; men who were already worn out from doing their own jobs for twelve hours now chipped in to help maintain and fix the airplanes of the new group. With tons of material coming across the Atlantic for BOLERO, Lend-Lease, TORCH, and the Eighth, the latter of which was initially at the bottom the priority list, even the most careful planning would not have completely resolved these problems for the Eighth. Plus, in late 1942 to spring 1943, much of the shipping for Europe was being redirected, sent instead to offensive operations in northwest Africa, Burma-India, and the Pacific.[22] It was a mess indeed.

Early on, deployment planning had consisted mostly of shoving people and stuff on whatever ships were available rather than careful staging by priority. Nor did U-boats sinking cargo vessels in the Atlantic help. Eaker wanted his airplanes, but he also desperately needed his ground crews and their equipment. Because it hindered Eaker's ability to put more airplanes into the air more quickly, this bottleneck became another source of friction between Eaker and Arnold. In one letter to the chief, in which he threw in a few awkward analogies (e.g., having an infantry company's attack against an entrenched battalion fail and concluding that infantry attacks are ineffective), Eaker wrote that the "one thing we require here to do a job—the job that will hurt the enemy the most—is an adequate force." But for this problem, Arnold's hands were tied; in late winter he had cabled Andrews not to expect any easing of this bottleneck until April, at the earliest.[23]

One positive consequence of delays at the large repair facilities known as base air depot areas (BADAs) was that bomber group line mechanics eventually began learning how to do more higher-level repair work and even add factory modifications on the group hardstands. Instead of damaged aircraft being hauled off for lengthy repair periods at the BADAs, they were either repaired on-site or placed to the side and cannibalized, the parts used to fix the aircraft on the aprons. This significantly increased the availability of aircraft for missions, with many mechanics becoming masters in the care and mending of their aircraft. Only after mid-1944, when England was flooded with new airplanes, did practices change; airplanes that required major rework and would have demanded hours upon hours to bring to flying condition again were simply set aside and replaced with new ones. Deliberately, General Bradley chose a point in the middle of the letter to comment pointedly, "I think Ira is doing a superb job. He needs all the backing that that you and weight of the War Department can give him . . . [he] has a tremendous job and is doing it well . . . [he] needs no needling."[24]

Chapter 21

June 1943

With Arnold returned to full duty, the confrontational correspondence between Eaker and his mentor resumed, persisting throughout June with diminishing congeniality in almost every exchange. Cables between the two, which before had always softened frankness with civility and courtesy, began expressing impatience and vexation more openly and absent the customary luster of politeness. After the second coronary, Arnold returned to the office still convinced Eaker was unnecessarily holding back airplanes from combat missions. In early June the chief repeated anew an inability or unwillingness to comprehend the full nature of air warfare in Europe, especially differences between the numbers of men and airplanes on the inventories compared with those available for combat.

In the first ten days of June, Arnold sent several queries to Eaker so heavy-handed that Eaker's aide thought them "gruff"—messages in which Arnold took no notice of, much less offered positive words for, the appreciable improvement in the size and frequency of missions flown by the Eighth the past two months. Instead, he brought attention to the number of replacement heavy bombers recently supplied to the Eighth—"Never less than 595" in May and a "high of 722 near the end" of May; "never less than 368 combat crews"—yet the maximum number "sent on any combat mission was 279 and that only once!" Cabled the chief, "Why have so few heavy bombers been sent into action in view of the substantial reinforcements? This is not rpt [repeat] not satisfactory. . . . Your frank comments on this subject are desired together with what steps you will take to remedy this situation." Separately, Arnold shuffled through a roster of "suitable names" to replace those he believed needed to be sent home, particularly Longfellow at VIII Bomber Command and Eaker's chief of staff, Colonel Charlie Bubb. Arnold wanted Bubb, Longfellow, and Monk Hunter replaced with leaders who could "organize attacks in a highly efficient manner."[1]

Eaker was still digesting that cable when another sharp wire followed, this time sent through Jake Devers at ETOUSA, referencing the "low percentage" of operationally ready aircraft and questioning the ability of the Eighth to deal with the "supply and maintenance problems" associated with the "very large number" of aircraft that would soon be arriving. Arnold concluded with an admonition that he was "reserving full decision" and solicited Eaker's "frank comments"—as though Eaker's earlier messages had been cloaked in obfuscation. Devers, in full support of Eaker, insisted the reply go back through ETOUSA for his comments and signature.[2] Eaker answered Arnold by acknowledging that there were indeed 664 heavies in the theater, but 123 were in reserve or nonoperational, and of the remaining only 385 were actually available in the Eighth for combat.[3] Wrote Eaker, "VIII Bomber Command is responsible for keeping in commission and employing in combat only the aircraft [specifically detailed to] him . . . BC [Bomber Command] in May had total of 11 combat groups (35 a/c per group) would be 385 airplanes . . . (but) five of these groups arrived in theater without their ground echelons and without organizational equipment." He explained in detail the problems caused by these factors (e.g., "heavy bombers not assigned to operational groups not included— depot reserve or undergoing modification or repair"). Eaker noted that aircraft "are not reported as available unless it [sic] is completely ready to go on a combat mission." It had become very clear that combat flying was hard on the airplanes, even more so than had been anticipated: to cite one example, the bombers were flying at much higher altitudes than in any prewar exercise, which strained the engines and all the aircraft systems. If Arnold approved additional personnel and equipment to repair battle damage, it would do much to improve availability.

Arnold did not. Apparently touched on a raw nerve, he retorted on the fifteenth with "Your cablegram . . . was not entirely what I had expected," apparently having interpreted the language as Eaker blaming him for the problems. Instead of attempting to ease an escalating situation, Arnold wrote two acerbic pages, nitpicking each of Eaker's itemized explications and criticizing anew the Eighth, its operations, and the need for modifications for the airplanes, adding, "on the other hand I am not so sure that all of these changes are absolutely necessary" and "somebody may be leaning over backwards trying to get 100% perfect airplanes when 90% perfect would do the trick." Arnold closed by telling his protégé that "my wire was sent to get you to toughen up—to can those fellows who cannot produce—to put in youngsters who can carry the ball. . . . In any event, a definite change seems to be in order but you have to be tough enough to handle the situation."[4] While allowing that Eaker had "performed an excellent job," Arnold told his general, "I want you to come out of this a real commander." Arnold wrote almost as though he had placed Eaker in a position above his abilities as a personal favor, blindly hoping that he would grow into the job. Literally everyone with any authority in England had been supportive of Eaker—"Andrews, Devers, [Hugh] Knerr, Harriman, Portal, Harris, and even Churchill had told Arnold so."[5] Indicative of his anger, Eaker did not write again for two weeks.[6]

Also in the mail of the twelfth was a letter to Eaker from Barney Giles of the air staff. Sympathetic like Stratemeyer, Giles attempted to mitigate the deepening conflict. After several general paragraphs, Giles related what the air force commander already knew: that Arnold had sent "two or three cablegrams" referencing "the small number of heavy bombers reported ready and actually used" on missions. The chief had been "much concerned" about the small number of heavies sent on missions, an apprehension Giles had tried to squelch by discussing with Arnold the newness of the groups and aircrews to the UK. Giles also told Eaker that he had attempted to defend Charlie Bubb, reminding Arnold that a commander "should know more about how to employ the officers available than anyone else."[7]

Eaker wrote once more to the chief, first addressing why no replacements for Longfellow were currently ready to take over VIII Bomber Command; he expected Fred Anderson to assume the job by 1 July, once he had acquired more experience as a Wing commander. Curt LeMay was to replace Possum Hansell with the renamed 4th Wing on the same date. Eaker took the opportunity once again to urge the promotion of LeMay "as recommended two months ago" and pointedly mentioned (again) that there would have been more bombers available except for the five groups that just arrived, minus their ground personnel and maintenance gear, yet the Eighth had still flown missions on eight of the last nine days. Eaker finished by letting his temper loose: "You are not satisfied with conditions here . . . [n]either am I, and I am not satisfied with the support I have had . . . I can do this job if I get the same support from you that am getting from Theater Commander."[8] Devers tried to help in his forwarding comments and also by informing Arnold separately that certain information reported to his staff at headquarters was carried to Washington by "transient observers" and was simply "not true."[9]

Eaker knew well that the Eighth "had to be engaged" with the enemy but also that the Eighth's "loss rate had to remain acceptable to the American public, its aircraft and crews had to be continuously replenished, and it had to devise an effective defense against enemy fighters." There were also the uncompromising weather patterns at different times of the year; the effects of the stress of flying, the loss of comrades, and the heart-stopping fright of combat on the aircrews; the limited amount of rest permitted by the necessary training flights beyond the combat missions; and the hardships endured by the ground crews. The ground crews were the true heroes: they daily dealt with parts and personnel shortages, shot-up airplanes, and performing maintenance in the open, in all kinds of weather, twenty-four hours a day.[10] Although he had sent Arnold letters and cables explaining all this many times over and had briefed him on these issues when they were together, Arnold never seemed to absorb the points. But then, "[it] was not written answers that Arnold wanted—excuses, to his way of thinking—but action." Whether it was bombers in the air or personnel he thought needed changing, what Arnold wanted—needed—was movement and action.[11]

At mid-June Devers was directed by the CCS to transfer still more heavy bombers to Doolittle's Twelfth Air Force. Asked for comments, an angry Eaker sent a suggested reply to Devers's deputy, Major General Idwal Edwards, on the nineteenth: "They approved our Combined Bomber Offensive and they are rapidly making it impossible for us to accomplish it by taking our force away from us. We lost one-third of our present operational strength on [Ploęsti] and now we have a further diversion in prospect. I believe we are duty bound to point, as I endeavour to do in this cable, to the serious consequences which must invariably flow from this and any other diversion of our present effort."[12] And too, intelligence reports had now made clear the wisdom in not scheduling a cross-channel invasion for 1943. Since the first Sottéville raid eleven months earlier, setbacks on the eastern front had allowed the Germans to move air combat units to the west while new aircraft production had ramped up to a degree not thought possible by the Allies. One Allied source "at the close of 1942, estimated that the amount of air power which the Luftwaffe could mass against a cross-channel operation was approximately 3,700 aircraft." US intelligence estimated early in 1943 that the Germans had 1,248 "combat and miscellaneous" aircraft in the Mediterranean region, another 732 in "Central Germany," and 2,460 on the Russian front, most if not all able to reinforce the aircraft on the western front. Allied production estimates for June 1943—the fruits of a much-improved intelligence process over what existed even six months previously—predicted 550 Me-109s, 230 FW-190s, and a "wide array" of other aircraft "suitable" for defense coming out of the factories just in that month alone. These new aircraft were in addition to those the Luftwaffe had already "steadily shifted" from the eastern front to the west while also creating a new fighter wing in the west just to counter Allied bombers. These factors made it clear that concerted action must be taken by both British and American air forces to drive the Luftwaffe out of the skies to pave the way for an invasion of Hitler's Festung Europa.[13]

Earlier, in April, Eaker had presented to the TRIDENT Conference a targeting schedule blending his original four phases with the priorities of the CBO. With nine months of experience behind him, Eaker maintained, as he had told Arnold multiple times, that to dispatch three hundred bombers on one strike he needed at least eight hundred airplanes in theater—three hundred on the strike, three hundred in reserve, and two hundred in repairs/modifications—and until those numbers were attained, he could not feasibly undertake a sustained precision daylight bombing campaign against the Luftwaffe and the aircraft industries. Now, in late June, just when he was ready to begin phase II, slow aircraft deliveries and a maintenance backlog at Langford Lodge and the three BADAs once again delayed his ability to meet the requisite aircraft numbers, even though he had sent out six three-hundred-plus aircraft strikes in June.[14] Moreover, the three B-24 groups promised to the Ploęsti mission were close to deploying to Libya.

Eaker received in mid-June initial notice that Arnold was going to take yet another fifteen heavy bomber groups originally slated for the Eighth and instead send them to the Mediterranean to form the backbone of another new air force, the Fifteenth, activation of which was tentatively set for mid-October. Concurrently, Arnold designated Major General Jimmy Doolittle of the Twelfth Air Force to lead the Fifteenth. And now, on 26 June, the chief cabled Eaker through Devers to mention two problems that Eaker had already, in several of his lengthy missives, discussed: acquiring drop tanks for the recently activated P-47s, which, he had reminded the chief, were short-range, and exchanging Major General William Ellsworth Kepner for Monk Hunter at fighter command.[15]

Serious Disagreements at the End of the Month

More letters between Arnold and Eaker again crossed in trans-Atlantic mail on 28–29 June. On the twenty-eighth, Arnold initially complained of reporting that command channels in the Eighth had become too complex, as evidenced in the "time lag" and "delay in hours" of communications such as mission orders, while the RAF "takes only 45 minutes." Foregoing a solicitation of a response, Arnold simply told Eaker what the problem was: "too many headquarters for our organization . . . the American way of doing business wherein we compound one headquarters upon another just to get [officers] promoted." Arnold intended to solve the problem by tabling the requested promotions of Colonels LeMay and Ted Timberlake, although he would happily "review your [Eaker's] arguments and findings."[16]

Meanwhile, headed toward Washington was Eaker's "EYES ONLY" to Arnold, also from the twenty-eighth, his first since Arnold's cable of the fifteenth. As usual, the cable was not short—five pages, as though Arnold's time was unencumbered. Eaker opened with the recent visit to Washington from the president's friend and roving trouble-shooter W. Averill Harriman, who resided in England and visited Eaker upon occasion. Harriman had talked with Arnold twice in Washington and returned to England feeling that the chief wanted to fire his protégé. Because of this news, Eaker segued into a personal note about how he viewed his personal relationship with Arnold, now over two decades old. He then moved on to more immediate issues: Longfellow and Bubb would be out as of 1 July, replaced by Fred Anderson and Colonel John A. Samford. Eaker further acceded to the replacement of Monk Hunter; VIII Fighter Command would be taken by his old friend Bill Kepner, the former Marine.[17] Next was a brief reminder of wing tanks for the P-47 (Arnold seemed to have forgotten) and then the CBO and how it was being jeopardized by the loss of the three Liberator groups (120 B-24s) to TIDAL WAVE—"it depreciates our effort here by approximately 20–25%." Hoping to help his case, Eaker included some BDA photography of a recent raid on the Renault plant in Paris taken by an agent on the ground showing "vast damage."[18]

The final business points had Eaker opining that the Germans had now figured out that their industries were primary targets and concurring with an agreement with Washington to annul the YB-40 program. Eaker had advocated for the YB-40, an up-gunned B-17, as another layer of protection for his bombers, but it had far too many flaws, a major one being the additional guns, ammunition, and armor plate made the aircraft much too heavy for escort work. The extra weight gave the YB-40 "different flight characteristics" from standard Fortresses, including a lower rate of climb and an inability to hold formation at altitude. Besides, the Germans would wisely still attack mission leaders while ignoring the gunships. Nor did anyone want to fly the YB-40s because the men were, after all, bomber crews. Eaker closed the letter by returning to the personal, with a paragraph his aide thought was risking his career: "I shall always accept gladly and in the proper spirit any advice, counsel, or criticism from you. I do not feel, however, that my past service which has come under your observation indicates that I am a horse that had to be ridden with spurs. . . . We have been through a dark period and we are not entirely out of the woods yet, but I think we will make the grade in one of the toughest spots imaginable if I can maintain your confidence and support."[19] The five-page letter ended with Eaker saying, "I know this letter has been long but I think we will make the grade in one of the toughest spots imaginable if I can maintain your confidence and backing."[20] Even though he had been a combat commander for nearly a year now, Eaker's closing more resembled that of a newly commissioned officer with no past record instead of a seasoned field commander working his way through problems.

Arnold waited a week and sent a one-page reply, saying in part, "I see no reason in the world for any fears or suspicions as to [our] relationship entering your mind." Eaker was to "always remember" that Arnold ended by writing, "that if there is anything serious [between us] you will be the first one to hear of it and it will come from me direct."[21] When the time came, Eaker remembered; whether Arnold did also was perhaps a different matter. One point was becoming manifest in Arnold's notes to Eaker: inevitably polite, friendly, and courteous in his correspondence to others, no matter the issue or their rank or position, in communications to Eaker, Arnold's frustration and anger came through loud and clear.

The Forgotten P-47 Wing Tanks

The P-47 "problem" Eaker had mentioned in passing in the 28 June cable was a reminder to Arnold of the delay in acquiring wing tanks for the P-47s months earlier. As background, in August 1941 Eaker had been sent to England as an observer, and one assigned task was to obtain the RAF's opinion on "fighter escort protection." He reported that "without exception" RAF flight leaders possessed a "keen desire" for long-range escorts and accompanied the finding with a ten-page memo listing the usual "desirable but unattainable" characteristics for an imaginary escort. He suggested a committee to generate "operational requirements," which would then be forwarded to "technicians for accomplishment." Returning to Washington two months before Pearl Harbor, he was appointed to "fighter board" with five other pilots and chaired by Spaatz to consider exactly that. The board produced two papers, one suggesting night-fighter qualities that that later appeared in the P-61 Black Widow and a second describing Air Chief Marshal Portal's unrealistic concept of a "convoy defender," a heavily armored airplane that would accompany bomber missions. Eerily similar to the pathetic YB-40, the idea was tagged "a matter of considerable doubt." The board adjourned bequeathing a bland statement reiterating that survivability of deep penetration bomber missions depended on long-range fighter escorts; unsurprisingly, there was no recommendation for the development of an escort. After all, Generals Arnold, Frank Andrews, Spaatz, Eaker, and "most of the bomber enthusiasts" remained certain that heavy bombers on future deep penetration missions (there of course having been none flown at the time) required no escorts. Besides, fighter escorts "with long-range and top combat performance" could never be designed, anyway.[22]

Belly Tanks for the P-47s

Once the Eighth was established in England it did, however, become apparent that bombers did need escorts across France and the Low Countries, but only to the borders of the Third Reich at Aachen, a distance for which wing tanks were essential. It may not have made much sense, frankly, to escort bombers over western Europe but not deep into Germany, but at this time (January–July 1943), the Eighth had not flown any deep penetrations of the Third Reich, and it may have been that commanders simply underestimated the degree of violence that would accompany future missions. From 27 January to the start of Blitz Week on 24 July, the Eighth would fly only nine missions across the border into the Third Reich, entering German airspace either over Aachen or down from the North Sea over the Frisian Islands. Targets were either close to the western border (Huls, Hamm) or the North Sea (Bremen, Wilhelmshaven, Vegesack, Kiel, Emden). It was not until Blitz Week at the end of July that they struck even as far east as mid-Germany (Hannover, Hamburg, and Kassel). Regardless, once Eaker assumed command of the Eighth in December 1942, he became increasingly anxious first for the delivery of the Republic Aviation P-47 Thunderbolts as replacements for the short-legged Spitfires and then for suitable wing tanks. Expected to be excellent fighters, when the early versions (the P-47C) arrived in early 1943, their combat radius was disappointing: around 340 miles or about to Antwerp, hampered in part by the lack of the "paddle-blade" propeller that became available in early 1944.[23] The Thunderbolt's first drop tank was an unpressurized, conformal belly tank made of a substance not unlike paper mâché and designed for ferry flights. Holding 115 gallons, the fuel flow slowed to a trickle by eighteen thousand feet and stopped above twenty thousand. As fighters always dropped all tanks when moving to a fight (and the P-47 did its best work above twenty-two thousand feet, anyway), the value of the extra range more than offset the tank deficiencies.[24] The fighter groups also tried an oversized two-hundred-gallon centerline tank filled two-thirds full; the pilot would climb the airplane using the fuel in the tank. Upon reaching altitude, it would be jettisoned; with full internal tanks and clean wings, the Thunderbolts were then able to pass Aachen with gas enough to fight and still make it home. The P-47's first escort missions were 4 May, to Antwerp and Paris. This was the situation on 29 June 1943 when Eaker wrote Arnold. Everyone, including especially the fighter groups flying the Thunderbolt (the 4th, 56th, and 78th), was awaiting improved all-metal drop tanks.

It was a short wait. By July the desired wing tanks had arrived; each held 108 gallons, almost all usable and adding 150 miles of range. Hanging tanks under each wing permitted the Thunderbolts to range far ahead of the bombers instead of yoking them to the slower bomber stream—a practice useful only as a demonstration of how to waste gas—and allowed them to protect their flock of heavies well across the Rhine.[25] On 28 July, the fifth day of Fred Anderson's Blitz Week, fifty-eight heavies dropped on Kassel while thirty-seven more bombed either Oschersleben or targets of opportunity (initially, 302 bombers were dispatched into lousy weather).[26] As the bombers neared the Rhine on the trip home, sixty Luftwaffe Me-109s, circling like vultures awaiting the heavies, were hugely surprised when they were bounced by P-47s "flying much deeper into enemy territory than they ever had before."[27] The P-47s unquestionably saved damaged heavies and their aircrews that day given the Luftwaffe delight in attacking wounded or unprotected bombers.[28] The success of the drop tanks at Kassel was doubtless greeted with joy at PINETREE, but there was no sign that they changed the minds of anyone already against long-range escorts, like Eaker. Arnold, though, had become a different story.[29]

Bob Lovett

Eaker's most effective defender to Arnold was Bob Lovett, in Washington again after another trip to England. Once settled, he made a point to talk with Arnold about the Eighth and Eaker. Lovett, articulate, thoughtful, highly intelligent, and held in highest esteem by Arnold, conveyed "very strong assurances" that Arnold had a competent leader in England taking the fight to the Germans. Going beyond the personal, Lovett itemized for Arnold some of Eaker's important but unmet requirements to reinforce their validity as much as their importance. Among them were better trained replacement aircrews so they could be dispatched on combat missions sooner after arrival; modifying new aircraft in US plants to meet British and Eighth requirements before sending them across the Atlantic, so the aircraft also could be sent out sooner; and ensuring that ground crews and all maintenance equipment, including spare parts, arrived in England "prior to or concurrent with" their assigned combat groups. Resolving these issues and others would, Lovett opined, improve the efficiency of the Eighth by at least 50 percent.[30] With Lovett's comments in hand, Arnold called the persistent arguing with his subordinate quits with a short, friendly note dated 7 July expressing his confidence. Eaker had been in England almost eighteen months and commander of the Eighth for seven. He had presided over the growth of the Eighth in England from seven officers and no airplanes to over 150,000 men and 1,500 combat aircraft of multiple types. In just over ten months his heavy bombers had gone from mission 1 with twelve airplanes to mission 63 and 183 bombers. Eaker never forgot that he was responsible for the lives of men he often met; he knew what it was like to write letters to their survivors.

Arnold's requirements were even more intense and extensive now; he needed as many bombers in the fight as possible, on as many days as possible. He had to answer for the money and results to the politicians and American people; he believed he had to push the Eighth to prove the daylight bombardment program to counter the perpetual threat to the Eighth from the RAF's night operations, absorption into which was always looming. Above all, he had to show the Eighth could perform as promised or the elusive goal of independence and standing as an equal with the army and the navy would be delayed or lost. Perhaps he talked past Eaker's problems of weather, ground crews, and aircraft modifications, not because he did not understand but instead because they simply did not matter to him. Arnold wanted and needed bombers in the air. Period.

Chapter 22

The Combined Bomber Offensive

Casablanca Directive to CBO to Operation POINTBLANK

At the Third Washington Conference—TRIDENT—on 18 May, the CCS reached agreement on Eaker's strategic bombing design, the CBO.[1] Negotiations had required numerous sessions with representatives from different offices within the AAF and the RAF, bolstered with civilian economists and members of Arnold's committee of operations analysts, economists from the OSS Enemy Objectives Unit (EOU) in the US Embassy in London, the Air Ministry, RE8, the Ministry of Economic Warfare, and elsewhere. CCS approved it, to become effective 10 June to give air planners enough time to write an implementation order. Because of Bert Harris's single-issue focus, his contribution throughout the negotiating period was limited to continuing night strikes on targets his aircrews couldn't miss—metropolitan cities. Hence, RAF Bomber Command submissions remained unchanged as Harris pursued his own priorities.

Separately, Eaker sought to refine the objectives of the directive into something that would "make sense" to AAF aircrews and, more important, materially "contribute to making the invasion of Europe possible"—above all, the elimination of the Luftwaffe and establishment of air superiority over the invasion area.[2] Assisting were Brigadier Generals Hansell and Orvil Anderson, along with a team of AAF and RAF officers. These men understood that eliminating the Luftwaffe from skies west of the Rhine required bomber operations much more focused—more precise—than nocturnal bombardment of urban areas. Air supremacy was an absolute requirement, for defeat on the beaches had no fallback option. The BCS shared this position equally with the Americans, having asserted since early in the war that "the main aim of the air offensive must be to weaken Germany to the point where she could neither avert nor defeat the Allied invasion."[3]

Earlier, in April, Eaker had shared a working draft with Harris as a matter of course, in which Harris mentioned no less than four times that his contribution would be "concentrated attacks against related areas and cities." After that the Americans simply assumed RAF Bomber Command was to support the Eighth and not the reverse: "Unlike Harris, Arnold and Eaker wanted to build on the Casablanca Directive to produce a strategic directive that made greater sense."[4] Near the end, Harris wrote to his close friend Eaker that he had no objections to any of the last several drafts of the document, as it gave both the Americans and the British everything each wanted. Eaker's team then wrote the American plans specifically for the Eighth's heavy bombers with its Norden bombsight. Arnold received Eaker's final draft for his approval in early April, and on the nineteenth Eaker flew to Washington for a masterful presentation to the JCS on the twenty-third. The final version, fully supported by Portal (although a little piqued at Harris), received approval from the CCS in May. On 10 June the terms of the CBO were implemented as Operation POINTBLANK, commencing with the RAF undertaking an extensive series of raids in the Ruhr. A bit of fine-tuning occurred on 14 June with the POINTBLANK Directive, which slightly modified the terms of the original. The priorities for the air war were now effectively sculpted in stone until the program officially concluded on 1 April 1944. An observer laying the target priorities of AWPD-1, AWPD-42, and the CBO side-by-side would see over 90 percent congruity among the three, with focus on primarily the Luftwaffe fighters and secondarily their factories and maintenance facilities.[5]

The CBO and POINTBLANK, with the objective of air supremacy, were inextricably connected to the invasion of the Continent. Portal "saw the bomber offensive strictly in relation to the re-entry into Northwest Europe" and later viewed the CBO objectives as "reaffirmed" at QUADRANT in Quebec later, in August.[6] The CBO required a series of regular progress reports as well as a monthly report from both nations' air forces so that the CCS could better assess the timing of the landings. Progress toward air supremacy was the primary element. Eaker was to send a "British Isles-Weekly Assessment" to Arnold. At Quebec the CCS referred to the CBO as "the prerequisite for Overlord," to be accorded the highest priority: air supremacy was "the key to successful invasion and bombing was its instrument."[7]

Once approved in Quebec, Eaker did not wait to begin pursuit of the CBO objectives. The next day, 19 May, 103 heavies hit the U-boat yards at Kiel while 55 bombed the Flensburg yards. On the twenty-first, 77 heavies raided the yards at Wilhelmshaven and simultaneously another 47 Fortresses struck the Emden yards, although not one bomb landed on the target. For this, five Forts with fifty men were downed and eleven made it home with damage, including two DBR. Three separate missions struck different targets on the twenty-ninth: 57 Fortresses bombed the Kriegsmarine storage depot at Rennes, 147 B-17s dropped on St. Nazaire's U-boat pens, and 34 B-24s hit the pens at La Pallice. Thirteen Fortresses were lost for a 12 percent loss rate, eighty-nine damaged, and two DBR. All Liberators came home undamaged.[8] There was one glaring problem: none of these targets did much for achieving air supremacy over Normandy.

Operation POINTBLANK was focused intensely against the CBO's "intermediate objective," the Luftwaffe fighter world. It was, by dint of the necessity for precise bombardment, generally the province of the AAF while the RAF undertook the reduction of the Ruhr and other industrial zones by night. The American accuracy at Wilhelmshaven was negatively affected by a "blanket" of smoke at the yards. Worse, German fighter pilots took advantage of the absence of escorts and conducted near-fanatical head-on attacks, with numerous near-collisions and one actual, when an FW-190 mistimed his head-on attack and simultaneously occupied the same airspace as his B-17 target. Despite copious flak and FW-190s, only eight heavies were downed for a loss rate of 3.5 percent.⁹ But as the same group had lost six aircraft on the previous mission, the effective consequence was that one entire squadron was lost in two missions. The same day, though, a new B-17 group with three squadrons and a B-24 group headquarters with one of its squadrons arrived at Prestwick. Finally, it began to look as though replacements might be arriving in greater numbers than were being lost.

Fortune did not favor the brave two days later when Bremen and Kiel were again the targets for mission 63. At Kiel, which was to have been merely a diversionary sideshow of seventy-two heavies, the Luftwaffe, notably ignorant of the diversion scheme, began attacks in force while the heavies were still out over the North Sea. It was a vicious battle in which sixty aircraft made it to the target: twenty-two were downed, twenty-four suffered damage, and one returned DBR, a total loss of nearly one-third of the strike force. Among the dead was Brigadier General Nathan Bedford Forrest III, grandson of the Confederate raider, who was observing prior to taking command of the 4th Wing. Nine of fifteen Fortresses from the 95th were lost to the Luftwaffe. Though the acme of the fight was directly above the target as the heavies dropped their bombs, the Luftwaffe attacks constituted such unrelentingly head-on assaults from the IP until the heavies regained escort range over the channel that one official historian remarked that "it would be churlish" to criticize them for "less than precision bombing," especially as, at the critical moment, the lead bomber was "mortally damaged."¹⁰ Fortress gunners claimed thirty-nine defenders downed; the actual score was eight. Meanwhile, the main force of 102 Fortresses hit Bremen; just four were lost but the bombs completely missed the intended targets. "Serious damage" was caused nonetheless since it was "pretty much impossible not to hit something of military value" in such a large port.¹¹ Mission losses were 16 percent overall, three times the acceptable level. Neither of these two missions, Kiel and Wilhelmshaven, were deep penetrations of the Reich, yet without escorts to the target and return, only officers blindly dedicated to the self-defending bomber concept could any longer believe that long-range escorts were superfluous.¹²

Unintentionally fostering that misconception over the months were gunners claiming and receiving credit for vastly more enemy fighters shot down than were in fact splashed. Identifying who should receive credit was too often an impossibility when twenty or thirty defenders, or more, were attacking a large Fortress formation. A dozen gunners on multiple Forts could be shooting at the same fighter, and if the bandit began smoking, maybe it was hit by one gunner or maybe by twelve; or maybe it was not hit at all, instead experiencing an engine problem at that moment, creating a smoke trail. If the fighter dropped away, was it "shot down" or, since it would be over Germany, did it make it safely to one of the numerous airfields east of the Rhine to be fixed and fly again? Or was it just low on fuel? If the cause was fuel shortage or engine failure and not bullets, then it was not even damaged in battle, although some gunners might mistakenly receive credit for that. While most command-level officers understood that numbers were exaggerated, there was a reluctance to cut them back—lending unintentional credence to the viability of the self-defending bomber.[13] Regardless, Eaker was sure that "the destruction of the enemy's air force was the prerequisite for a successful bomber offensive," yet he also maintained an iron mental grip on the certainty that he could gain air supremacy for his bombers over German without fighter escorts.[14] For whatever reason, General Eaker persisted in believing in the self-defending bomber longer and stronger than almost anyone else. Too long, perhaps, for General Arnold, whose negative attitudes were reinforced when counting the many strikes that were not against CBO objectives.

Operation POINTBLANK made it clear that "the highest strategic priority" was to defeat the Luftwaffe prior to the Allied invasion."[15] Fighters were to be destroyed in the air or on the ground; second priority was facilities like airfields, hangars, and operations buildings; and third was support activities such as repair depots, overhaul installations, and production and test facilities. In short, everything that flew, helped them to fly, or supplied what they needed to fly was to be destroyed. Other targets could be struck when opportune but the Luftwaffe was the principal objective. For Portal at air staff, it meant RAF Bomber Command was still to work for "the general disruption of German industry" but to do so in consonance with the operations of the Eighth Air Force. While Harris could continue to attack large, open urban areas, he was also to attack specific CBO targets such as

"German aircraft and aircraft component (including ball-bearing) factories."
Harris remained adamantly unwilling to do so, until he had to accede—
but just a bit, which began to "disturb" Portal. Harris remained staunchly
"reluctant" to hit targets that the "Ministry of the Economic Warfare and the
Air Staff had declared to be of outstanding importance, such as Schweinfurt."
While the Eighth Air Force struck Schweinfurt twice, Harris made no corre-
sponding move and Portal began to wonder whether he needed to replace
Harris.[16] Still, he continued to forego strikes on targets that he considered
either too difficult for his area tactics (i.e., targets that required "precision"
or were "difficult to locate" at night) or that were "panacea" targets. Panacea
targets, Harris declared, were those whose destruction were only for political
or "feel good" purposes but which would have (in his judgment) little or no
effect on the course of the war.[17]

Spaatz, too, felt differently about POINTBLANK and the CBO but
withheld comment. He now believed that an inevitable cross-channel
invasion could bring Germany to the surrender table simply by the USAAF
targeting resources vital to the German war economy. But now that he
was in the Mediterranean under Eisenhower, his position did not conduce
to criticizing bombardment policies in another theater in which he held no
responsibilities.[18] Eaker saw it yet a third way, certain as always that only
a combined air-ground-naval campaign would compel the Third Reich to
surrender, and the Eighth's role was to destroy the German economy in line
with the Doctrine. But before that could be accomplished, it was necessary to
destroy the Luftwaffe and obtain air superiority over the Continent.[19]

As difficult and frustrating as the period between summer 1942 and
June 1943 frequently may have been, it was never a wasted or ineffective
time. Rather, it was a time for the Eighth of learning, gaining experience,
and experimenting; a time to develop tactics for fighting the Germans in a
new environment; a time for bombardiers and navigators to gain proficiency
at their craft; and a time for the pilots to master skills and techniques like
instrument flying, formating, and holding tight formation while under attack.
Above all, these months were for ACTS's theoretical classroom teachings to
confront the harsh reality of European combat.

In the six weeks between 1 July and 13 August 1943, Eaker and his new bomber commander, Fred Anderson, would dispatch seven missions, each with the magical number of three-hundred-plus heavies. But just as the Americans were becoming much better at their craft, so were the German pilots and the radar-equipped air intercept controllers.

Chapter 23

A Productive Summer

Foggia and the Fifteenth

Allied forces landed on Sicily on 10 July 1943; thirty-eight days later, with the invasion a success, the CCS sought to exploit the victory quickly to eliminate Italy from the war. They appended to the TRIDENT directives a draft recommendation to the president and prime minister affirming the continuation of a Mediterranean strategy. The USJCS of course opposed the draft, arguing as expected for an invasion of the European Continent at the soonest possible moment. Arnold, in hospital with a third coronary, remained concerned that a Mediterranean operation would continue to pull resources from the Eighth Air Force as it had for TORCH and the Pacific theaters, not to mention the "loan" of the three B-24 groups for Ploęsti.[1]

The JCS reversed position, however, with the realization that a move onto mainland Italy would give the Allies the huge air base complex at Foggia, with fourteen subsidiary airfields and better flying weather than the UK, compensating for abiding the delay in the cross-channel invasion. For Arnold the most important justification for taking the Italian peninsula was an ULTRA report headlined "German Decisions to Increase Production

197

of Single-Engine Fighters," a circumstance that provided a new opportunity: with the Eighth now bombing western Germany, the Luftwaffe's
fighter production facilities had relocated to southwestern Germany.
Persuasive was another cable reading, "ULTRA evidence suggested that
factories in Regensburg and Wiener-Neustadt [Austria] are now producing
about 55 percent of all German single-engine fighters and further expansion
is to be expected."[2] The cities were within flying distance of Foggia for
AAF bomb-laden strategic bombers.

When the anticipated collapse of Benito Mussolini's Fascist regime mate-
rialized on 25 July, General Marshall was further impelled to seize the port of
Naples with an amphibious landing at Salerno, asserting that the dictator's fall
"had made such an operation almost inevitable." The CCS validated Operation AVALANCHE and granted Eisenhower the authority to land at Salerno
in September.[3] The lure of Foggia as a base for strategic bombers had been
irresistible to the air forces chief and the other air generals, except one: Major
General Ira Eaker in England remained opposed, worried that operations in
Italy would once again diminish the ability of the Eighth to pursue the destruction of the Third Reich. Nor were the RAF leaders sanguine about Foggia.
This "no" from Eaker placed him clearly on the side of the British against his
own service. It was exactly what Arnold did not want to hear.

Eaker relieved his friend Longfellow on July first and sent him home, a
colonel again. Fred Anderson assumed command of VIII Bomber Command
the same day, beginning not only six months of aggressive bombardment of
the Third Reich but also an enduring professional relationship with Colonel
Dick Hughes of A-5, who had proven his expertise in planning and targeting
many times over.[4] Possum Hansell was also replaced, requesting and receiving
an assignment with the RAF in North Africa, but unhappily—given his less
than happy opinion of the chief and a desire for a combat slot—he was shortly
ordered to return to Arnold's staff in Washington. Hansell had "always had a
far higher regard for Spaatz than for Arnold, whom he saw as more of a driver
than a leader."[5] Now he was back under his direct authority again.

From July through September, VIII Bomber Command significantly
increased its mission count, particularly those to Germany, flying thirty-three
missions in ninety-two days; with better weather, even more missions would

have been flown and more still would have been deeper into Germany. Despite the slowness of aircraft delivery from the States, the number of heavies flying each mission also gradually increased. The three months collectively posted a net gain in aircrews, too, although in July Anderson received 159 crews from the States while losing 171. August was better, with 164 replacement reporting in against 120 lost, and September recorded almost 210 new crews for only 104 lost.[6] On 30 September Generals Eaker and Anderson could look at the status board and see that they had 604 total operational heavy bombers and 450 operational aircrews; they were determined to fly as many of them as possible every day that was feasible.[7] In response to Arnold's most recent complaints about the low number of aircraft dispatched on missions, Eaker wrote, again, that it would be helpful if the bombers could be modified before leaving the United States rather than relying on Langford Lodge. The heavies were still arriving in the United Kingdom in need of extensive modifications, and just recently five bomber groups were wheels down at Prestwick after a trans-Atlantic crossing, but without any of their ground service crews or equipment and no idea when any would show.[8]

Blitz Week

In July the heavies flew strikes on ten days of the month, including multiple missions launched on six days of the final week.[9] Dubbed Blitz Week, it was conceived by General Anderson with the intent to "mount seven major bombing missions on seven consecutive days in order to stress the [Luftwaffe] fighter defenses."[10] After nearly three months with the weather wholly unsuited for flying on many days, six of the seven days of Blitz Week were "spectacularly glorious," and Anderson was so exuberant about the prospects of the Eighth "destroying Germany's economic resources" that he wrote George Stratemeyer that he had "come to believe that no invasion of the Continent or Germany proper will ever have to take place, with the consequent loss of thousands, and possibly millions, of lives . . . this bomber command will be the greatest striking force the world has ever seen."[11] More realistically, Blitz Week served as an unintentional test run for Big Week (Operation ARGUMENT) in February of the next year, which grew from the combined fertile minds of Fred Anderson and Dick Hughes.[12]

An Allied Intelligence Report, issued two days before Blitz Week, began with an "assessment of the efficacy of the Combined Bomber Offensive," judging the CBO's first phase results as "good." A product of the British Joint Intelligence Committee (JIC), it asserted the CBO "caused Germany to adopt a defensive air strategy resulting in more than half its fighter strength being employed on the western front at the expense of the eastern and Mediterranean fronts as well as causing considerable damage to transportation, the synthetic rubber industry, and the fuel, iron, and coal industries of the Ruhr." Further, the report "indicates that half of the [Luftwaffe's] fighter strength is deployed in the defense of the bomber routes from the UK to targets in Germany and Occupied Europe." The JIC concluded that Luftwaffe fighter deployments to the west "are being made at the expense of the other fronts and theaters where active ground fighting is under way."[13] All the better for the aggressive, offensive-spirited fighter pilots in VIII Fighter Command who believed heartily in Baron Manfred von Richtofen's mantra, "Find the enemy and shoot him down; anything else is nonsense."[14]

Blitz Week began Sunday, 24 July, with a 1,900-mile round-trip to Norway: 208 bombers to strike the U-boat base and pens at Trondheim, the IG Farben nitrate processing plant at Heroya, and Bergen's port. No losses were incurred by any of the three elements on this, the longest mission to date, although one Fortress diverted to neutral Sweden because of flak damage and one flew with a smuggled "stowaway"—a cocker spaniel.[15] Trondheim results were "impressive," with serious damage to the docks, although the U-boat pens were unscathed. Heroya had twelve thousand tons of aluminum destroyed, but the Germans used so little of it that they abandoned most of the plant after the strike.[16] Thick cloud cover at Bergen sent eighty-four B-17s back to England with their ordnance. Despite civilian casualties, the strikes boosted morale among the Norwegian population. After the war it was determined that attacks on transportation systems and electrical grids were much more effective than bombing the plants.[17] This strike also saw the first operational use of innovative devices called "splasher beacons," which permitted pilots to formate above solid cloud, over water, well separated from other assembling formations. They proved so successful that they became standard procedure for the remainder of the war.[18]

On 25 July 100 heavies of 123 dispatched made it almost to the diesel engine plant at Hamburg before thick clouds sent them looking for the local shipyards and targets of opportunity—in this scramble 15 bombers were downed by flak and the Luftwaffe for a disappointing 15 percent loss rate. A second element of 59 heavies aborted while still over England as dense clouds made it impossible to formate. Foul weather precluded 118 heavies in a third element from locating the Arado and Heinkel aircraft plants at Warnemünde; the bombers dropped instead on the Kiel yards and U-boat pens, losing 4 Fortresses. Weather was better the next day, allowing Anderson to launch another three-pronged strike. First, 94 Fortresses struck two rubber factories, including "Germany's largest tire factory" at Hannover, where heavy flak and Luftwaffe fighters downed 14 Fortresses, for another 15 percent loss rate; two ditched in the channel, with the RAF's Air-Sea Rescue Service rescuing both crews. A second element of 49 B-17s, launched hours later against the same target, found it covered with thick clouds, so instead it hit the U-boat yards at Wilhelmshaven, targets at Wesermünde, and a convoy in the North Sea; 5 Fortresses were lost, and 1 successfully ditched. The final wave looked for "the extensive Blohm and Voss shipyards" at Hamburg but, as with the earlier waves, was stymied by weather. So 54 heavies dropped on random targets with none lost, although dropping bombs in this manner was scarcely different from that used by the RAF and Bomber Harris. The day's total losses were 24 aircraft out of 197, an overall loss rate of 12 percent.[19]

English weather caused a stand-down on the twenty-seventh, thwarting plans to "stress" the Luftwaffe for seven straight days; but on the twenty-eighth, 302 sorties were intended against the German aviation industry. Weather caused almost one-third of the force to abort while attempting to formate, leaving a still-formidable 182 B-17s to continue. German weather was not much better: just 58 Fortresses hit at Kassel and 37 more at Oschersleben, the farthest penetration yet into Germany. Oschersleben was particularly attractive because Focke-Wulf built the deadly FW-190 there. At first the cloud layers looked as forbidding there as everywhere else, but a sharp lead bombardier spotted a landmark through a small hole in the cloud layers and, zeroing in on the Focke-Wulf plant, dropped exactly on target. Gunners in the 58 Fortresses claimed an unrealistic 56 Luftwaffe fighters shot down, with 19 probables and 41 damaged. However, a very real twenty-two Fortresses were downed, for a staggering 23 percent losses for the combined missions, with 121 damaged. Heavy flak accounted for most of the harm, although the defending fighters effectively employed wing-mounted rockets for the first time.

The Germans were especially lethal, with the "first known use by Luftwaffe fighters of aerial rockets, whose firing [was] observed and even photographed with a gun camera by a 78th Fighter Group P-47 pilot." The rocket-firing German interceptors, Me-109s and FW-190s, carried devices called Werfer-Granate, a projectile jerry-rigged from the Nebelwerfer ground weapon so detested by infantry troops.[20] Although wildly inaccurate, the warhead could easily bring down a Fort unlucky enough to be hit by one. One of the rockets slammed into a B-17 from the 385th Bomb Group, which blew apart, sending pieces of airplane into two other Fortresses, bringing down all three.[21] The rockets could be fired from outside machine gun range, and when or if the bomber formation scattered because of rocket hits or aircraft damage, defending fighters would bore in for a guns kill. This deadly tactic would be further perfected against future missions.

On the thirtieth the Eighth returned to Kassel with 134 bombers out of 186 dispatched, with Hanover as the secondary. The loss rate was 9 percent, with twelve Fortresses downed by the enemy. In what would become standard practice, the 56th FG's Thunderbolts flew cover for the heavies up to the German frontier, while the Thunderbolts of the 78th FG and 4th FG were responsible for early and late target withdrawal covers. The Thunderbolts were only generally effective below twenty thousand feet, but above twenty-two thousand they were unmatched. The 78th P-47s, using ferry tanks for the first time, joined with the bombers as they exited the target, once again giving the Luftwaffe pilots a shock as they rolled in on the bombers, expecting them to have been abandoned by escorts. The Thunderbolts totaled at least twenty-four confirmed victories on this one single mission, more German planes than they had been able to knock down in dozens of Monk Hunter's fighter sweeps or even on escort missions in the preceding two months. Because of the extra gas provided by the ferry tanks, this mission was the farthest penetration of Germany ever by escorting fighters. Thirty-three victories were produced "in just two missions in Blitz

Week—the first long-range bomber-escort missions ever flown by Eighth Air Force fighters." Soon, aerodynamic, aluminum wing-tanks became available in the thousands and "forever changed the tenor of daytime air war in Europe."[22] While always enthusiastic about his work as head of VIII Bomber Command, Fred Anderson was "not blindly dedicated to the self-defending bomber"; an independent thinker while chief of bombardment on Arnold's staff, he was even more convinced of the need for escorts after Blitz Week. He told the departing Hunter that "fighter escort was the key to victory."[23]

When VIII Bomber Command stood down at month's end, the "effective" heavy bomber inventory showed 275 aircraft operational, with "88 B-17s and their crews [880 men] gone—dead, POWs, or the few in the hands of the underground."[24] The loss rate for Blitz Week was about 8.5 percent of all heavies that reached the target, not a disastrous statistic but for self-defending bombers it still exceeded the maximum allowance of 5 percent. Yet as Eaker would say, the Americans were now winning, because although the Eighth would suffer large losses on some missions, "the German knows he cannot replace his losses but he also knows that we can and will replace our airplanes and aircrews."[25] One statistic was definitely negative: VIII Bomber Command had received 159 new crews but had lost 171.[26]

VIII Bomber Command Intelligence Memorandum of 3 August began by bluntly stating, "As VIII Bomber Command's formations penetrate deeper into Germany, enemy defenses are proving more effective."[27] One bit of evidence cited was the loss of 392 heavy bombers from mission 1 through mission 80, 17 August 1942 through 30 July 1943—roughly equating to four thousand aircrew lost as well, not counting the wounded and dead who made it back to England in damaged aircraft. As frightening as attacks by the Me-109s and FW-190s could be, it was the flak that bothered the aircrews the most. The memorandum next elaborated on three recent German innovations: Luftwaffe air-to-air bombing of Eighth formations, "German B-17s" joining AAF bomber formations, and "Rocket Guns." While "air-to-air bombing was reported on practically every mission flown" in July, details were given for three missions, two during Blitz Week. At Hamburg one Fortress exploded and a second went down after several "bombs" exploded near it. Over Hamburg several FW-190s dropped "slender objects like pieces of stove-pipe," but without losses. Dropping on Kassel on the thirtieth, heavies were attacked by six silver aircraft, either JU-88s or Me-210s, which "operating singly, dropped silver-colored pieces of stove-piping." The bombs exploded below the Fortresses, probably due to time fusing.

The second innovation involved six missions in July in which mysterious B-17s either shadowed a B-17 formation from several hundred yards' distance or, twice, joined the Fortresses in formation for several minutes. Only once did one of the interlopers open fire, with a 20 mm gun from a waist position, but no harm done. The German Fortresses were painted different colors, from a bright silver to a darker olive drab, than the US aircraft. This section concluded with the comment, "Exactly what purpose the Germans hope to accomplish by the use of salvaged B-17s intruding into our formations is not known."[28] Fertile imaginations doubtlessly generated a few ideas.

The third innovation, "Rocket Guns," was probably the most worrisome and referred to "rocket bombs" from German fighters, which "stand off 1500–2500 yards and, singly and in group abreast, raise their noses and lob their shells into the [B-17] formation." The rockets were fused to burst in the formation. The memorandum ended by noting that although carrying the projectiles under the wings of FW-190s and Me-109s caused a loss of about 20 mph in airspeed, it was nonetheless safe to assume that the Germans would continue to "experiment" with both rockets and aerial bombs as an antiaircraft defense.

One inextricable problem was that while the crews of the Eighth were gaining precious combat experience and learning valuable lessons, so were the Luftwaffe fighter pilots, ground intercept controllers, and antiaircraft gunners. War is seldom a static enterprise, and as was seen at Kiel on the twenty-eighth, the Luftwaffe improved the lethality of the fighters while its pilots were altering tactics, such as attacking in larger formations and from different sectors of the sky. With the rockets, the fighters would remain astern of the bomber formation, out of range of the bombers' tail guns, and fire salvos into the formation. Odds were small that the rockets would hit anything, but when they did, the consequences were usually disastrous. Still, those six days "saw strikes aggregating just over a thousand bomber sorties launched against fifteen targets all over northern and western Germany [and] there is no doubting that the German fighter forces were worn down somewhat, at least operationally, by the unrelenting appearances by the bombers."[29] Disturbingly, if the Norwegian missions with no losses were excluded from the count, the loss rate for Blitz week would have been significantly higher than otherwise. Not that any aircrew would have had the slightest question about survivability, at least not at this point in the air war: had one bothered to do the math, he would probably have been dismayed, but not surprised, to discover the odds were still against finishing twenty-five missions.[30]

One positive from Blitz Week was sourced to ULTRA and thus unknown to almost all Americans. After the Germans had evaluated the damage to aircraft factories and so forth, the Führer ordered Minister for Armaments and War Production Albert Speer to remove the remaining facilities and disperse them much farther east, creating serious problems for the Germans. First, the resupply of new aircraft to the combat units removed the slack in current aircraft supply, which in turn created a lag when production of new aircraft resumed. Worse, new parts had to come from separate factories to a central production facility: the inability to ensure that these disparate individual parts fit as necessary at one discrete factory, instead of all parts being made and fitted at the same plant, created quality-control issues that then affected flight safety. Speer himself thought Blitz Week was a great loss for the Reich, as the twenty thousand 88 mm antiaircraft guns left in Germany would have, if shipped to the eastern front, doubled the number of antitank guns, "reversing the tide of battle there."[31] German minister for aviation Feldmarschall Erhard Milch determined to advance his objective of turning out two thousand airplanes a month from the summer of 1943 to the end of that year. The Eighth never ceased destroying Luftwaffe plants, facilities, and aircraft, rendering Milch's plans continuously moot to the end of the war.[32]

Chapter 24

Summer's End

Robert Lovett and the Long-Range Fighter

When Bob Lovett returned to Washington, DC, in mid-June of 1943 from a trip to England, including to the Eighth, he detailed his findings in a memo to Arnold and urged action on several priority issues—especially "immediate attention to the production of a long-range fighter."[1] Taking time first to give Arnold "very strong assurances about Eaker's command competence, he explained the justice behind Eaker's pleas" for additional crews and aircraft and the delivery of operational equipment and ground units prior to the arrival of the combat groups. Importantly, the secretary for air pressed Arnold to tone down his "wild statements about what the B-17 could do" while mentally opining that Arnold was, "inside of himself, angry that the Fortress just couldn't do all that he had been claiming, and so irrationally took his acrimony" out on Eaker. The chief's "hands were tied by his mouth," thought Lovett, because he had been telling folks that "very few fighters" could keep up with the Fortresses. But, Lovett remembered, the Messerschmitts "had no difficulty at all."[2]

The history of wing tanks for army air units was not especially encomiastic. The French first attempted to increase aircraft range by attaching fuel-carrying "droppable" wing tanks in 1918 with DH-4s.[3] American engineers experimented with various iterations of drop tanks in the 1920s, but these attempts were attended by problems such as restricted aircraft maneuverability and, particularly nettlesome, the tendency to catch fire.[4] Spaatz himself was introduced to nascent drop tanks at Selfridge Field in 1920, but he failed to "fit the piece into place." The ascendant Bomber Mafia at ACTS decided that range and endurance were "the least important" pursuit characteristics, which immediately rendered drop tanks irrelevant despite valid and vociferous counterarguments from the pursuit community. Still, engineers began a decade-long trial of "hanging auxiliary fuel tanks from bomb racks," which limited speed and maneuverability, so the idea was dropped in favor of "auxiliary tanks inside the aircraft (the results were hardly better)."[5] Consequently, in May 1939 the air corps shelved the idea of expendable drop tanks.

In 1940 Arnold convened the Emmons Board to "make recommendations on research and development projects." First priority was "a very long-range bomber"; fourth was an "escort fighter with a 1500-mile range." As the B-29 was already in development, Arnold switched first and fourth priorities. Thus, roughly three years before Arnold ordered production of a long-range fighter, he had made it number one on at least one priority list. As he was also the chief in 1940 when the P-51 had first flown, he (theoretically) could have directed experiments with the Mustang thirty-six months before the Eighth had lost hundreds of airplanes and thousands of men—especially so, as he was aware of developments in 1942 when the British fitted the Merlin-61 engine to the front of the Mustang and saw a top speed of 440 mph with extended range.

Regardless, by early 1943 General Arnold had begun to revisit drop tanks under growing pressure from an increasing number of both fighter and bomber squadron and group commanders, influenced especially by those who had flown in air combat. When his percolating doubts over the viability of a self-defending bomber collided with Lovett's memo, he ordered "the all-out development of auxiliary tanks for the P-51, P-38, and P-47." As for Lovett's memo, Arnold knew the engineering branch at Wright Airfield was convinced that it was impossible to build a fighter that could fly the distance

with the bombers without wing tanks, but Arnold was as intellectually flexible as he was stubborn. And too, he had never been exposed to the sway
of men certain of the impossibility of creating such a fighter. Arnold took
Lovett's memo, attached to it another memo that he sent Barney Giles on
the air staff, emphasizing "the absolute necessity for building a fighter plane
that can go in and out [of Germany] with the bombers. . . . Within the next
six months, you have to get a fighter that can protect our bombers. Whether
you use an existing type or have to start from scratch is your problem. Get to
work on this right away because by January '44, I want a fighter escort for
all our bombers from the U.K. into Germany."[6] Giles, both a command
pilot and an engineering officer, knew immediately the boss was dead serious
and within twenty-four hours was on his way to see the president of North
American Aviation (NAA) in California, like his boss unwilling to take "no"
from anyone.[7] Concurrently, Arnold corralled Major General Bill Kepner at
HqAF and, aware he had long been an advocate of developing expendable
fuel tanks, thought Kepner might want to have some involvement in the
solution. Some years prior, when Lieutenant Colonel Kepner was CO of
8th Fighter Group, he approached the navy about some of their drop tanks;
his boss, a colonel named Eaker, chewed him out in front of a general named
Arnold and ordered the fighter pilot to desist. Asked now what he was going
to do, Kepner replied, "Well General, I think I'll go hang some gas on an
airplane," and went off to California.[8] Against the advice of the president of
NAA, Giles insisted on adding another two hundred gallons of internal avgas
(aviation gas) to the P-51's wings and center fuselage; when he was told it
was impossible, Giles blandly replied, Well, let's give it a try. It worked, and
the P-51 Mustang was on its way into military and aviation history.

Eaker on the Wrong Side

By late summer and early autumn 1943, Eighth Air Force combat losses were
approaching unsustainable levels, for HqAF and for the American public.
Escorts were now able to penetrate as far as thirty miles into Germany by
dint of new wing tanks, but for deeper missions Eaker doggedly clung to
the now-weary myth of the self-defending bomber and despite far too many

missions with loss rates triple and quadruple the "acceptable" 5 percent. And while the escorts were with the bombers, he, and Hunter, insisted they remain tethered to the bomber stream until low fuel required them to drop off. Despite a mix of several hundred fighters now escorting each strike, the escorts were not permitted to range ahead and attack the enemy before they ever came near the bombers. Monk Hunter was both in full agreement and continued ordering pointless RODEO sweeps across France and the Low Countries looking for fights even though the Luftwaffe rarely accepted the challenges.[9] When Arnold had earlier sought to publicize VIII Fighter Command successes, Eaker had demurred, insisting that the destruction of enemy fighters was "a secondary mission." He argued that highlighting the "primary job of the Eighth—the dropping of bombs on the Germans" was better. But these arguments aside, the simple fact was that Hunter's tactics contributed little to the destruction of the Luftwaffe and nothing to air superiority. As a career pursuit pilot, Eaker's obtuseness in missing this point is difficult to explain. By summer of 1943, Eaker had much to lose by standing fast against the chief and nothing to be gained by it. Yet he never wavered, as though his mind was embedded in concrete.

August: The First Two Weeks

It may have appeared to General Eaker that the Eighth had turned the corner by August: more trained crews were arriving from the CCRC, bombers had been flying the Atlantic nonstop from Goose Bay to Prestwick in larger numbers for months now, and with the Ploęsti mission now executed, Eaker was hoping for the speedy return of what remained of his three borrowed B-24 groups; of the 176 Liberators that had hit the refineries, only 88 well-shot-up airplanes returned to Libya.[10] Before QUADRANT, the first Quebec meeting the week of 17 August, General Arnold informed the CCS that his objective was to have "1,900 heavy bomber aircraft with two crews for each plane in the [European] theater by 1 January 1944." But this was purely aspirational. He had promised just three months earlier at TRIDENT, the Third Washington Conference, to have 1,068 heavies in England by mid-August; instead, the Eighth was short 147 heavies, with 921 bombers total in its inventory, including nonoperational aircraft and 100-plus airplanes still in Libya on loan to Louie Brereton.[11] With the 15 groups of heavy bombers initially ordered to the Eighth but now transferred to the still inactive Fifteenth, Eaker and staff had little faith in, or chance of, seeing 1,900 heavies before 1944.

The pending activation of the Fifteenth in Italy was, very possibly, a consequence of Arnold's frustrations with Eaker. Initially opposed to the buildup of heavy bombers in the Mediterranean theater and unwilling to slow the growth of the Eighth as the only American force fighting Germany, the air forces chief soon recognized advantages accruing from the presence of two strategic air forces. Spaatz, believing that bombing alone could force a German surrender, argued in a letter to Bob Lovett that such "could be speeded up" with suitable bases in the Mediterranean with its better weather and shorter distances to critical areas of Germany.[12] A pressing motivation for Spaatz was that it would force Germany to divide its limited fighter squadrons and antiair-craft artillery batteries. Coincidentally, at QUADRANT the CCS had agreed generally to promote "strategic bombing operations from Italian and Central Mediterranean bases." Arnold, no longer hesitant, agreed to bases in Italy. As usual, one or two of his reasons were hidden under his overt support for Spaatz's logic. Immediately important to him, it would make a stronger case that an overall American air commander would be on a par with anyone in the RAF, regardless of rank (specifically, the equal of Air Chief Marshal Harris, effectively a four-star rank; Spaatz was three stars).[13] And, always significant, it would demonstrate to Congress that an air commander could successfully manage a war involving air forces on two continents against a global enemy. Hence, the air forces would have earned the right to independence from and equality with other United States military services. There were so many posi-tive points to the Fifteenth in Foggia that it is difficult to understand how Eaker could not have comprehended at least one or two.

When the Eighth returned to work in mid-August, it flew missions to France and the Low Countries until, on the twelfth, 133 heavies dropped on manufacturing and synthetic oil targets at Gelsenkirchen, Recklinghausen, Bochum, Bonn, and targets of opportunity. This large mission was unes-corted, and the strike force suffered accordingly. Twenty-three heavies were downed by flak and fighters for a terrible 17 percent of the force, while another 105 were damaged to one degree or another; only 5 returned to base unscathed. There is no count of the wounded and dead that returned to England, but the number would have been frightful. One historian judged this mission to have "by far the worst losses inflicted on any US bomber force so far in the war."[14] A second force of 110 Fortresses struck Bonn and nearby targets. For the first time, escorting P-47s from three fighter groups carried pressurized, steel wing tanks with enough gas to enable them to stay with the bombers during both the penetration and withdrawal phases; just two B-17s were lost while the P-47s were able to kill four German fighters. In the early evening of the fifteenth, 290 heavies raided Luftwaffe airfields across the channel, also losing two Fortresses. The next day, Luftwaffe airfields in France were hit by 237 B-17s with P-47s as escorts. Even with the protective Little Friends (the protective fighters), four heavies were still downed; all the fighter cover in the world couldn't protect against flak. Collectively, these last three raids caused the Germans measurable damage, with the American bombers suffering an aggregate of only 4 percent losses.[15]

By mid-August Generals Eaker and Anderson, and Air Chief Marshal Harris, were all upbeat, despite VIII Bomber Command losses, believing that "German fighter opposition will collapse within a matter of weeks . . . contingent upon the 8th Air Force continuing their attacks at the present rate."[16] As before, AAF and RAF officers remained convinced the CBO was "the only means by which the war could be won"; and while the Allies "can sustain their heavy losses, the Germans cannot."[17] Bolstering those opinions, Anderson had now 650 (542 operational) heavy bombers in his inventory, while his force and Bert Harris's together were facing more than a million Germans soldiers manning 8,100 heavy and 31,000 light antiaircraft guns. In short, the fifty-two thousand airmen of VIII Bomber Command plus those of RAF Bomber Command were facing six times as many Germans and guns as opposed to the Sicilian invasion—and any "activity that brings forth such tremendous defensive effort cannot be classified as anything other than a major offensive operation."[18] Still, the Eighth limited its operations in August in preparation for JUGGLER, the two-pronged deep penetration mission to Regensburg and Schweinfurt.

Chapter 25

Schweinfurt I

T he origins of the Schweinfurt-Regensburg raid—Operation JUGGLER—of 17 August 1943 have a murky parentage, beginning with the fact that the ball-bearing factories at Schweinfurt were not initially a target for this mission. Hansell's account is the outlier; he has written that Fred Anderson, upon taking VIII Bomber Command, "at once went to work preparing for the first assaults upon the ball-bearing factories at Schweinfurt and, separately, the Me-109 assembly plant at Regensburg"—but not Wiener-Neustadt, Austria.[1] One historian asserts that when Eaker traveled to Washington in early August for discussions on other issues, HqAF gave him the surprise mission to strike the two Messerschmitt plants at Regensburg and Wiener-Neustadt.[2] Another accepts Dick Hughes's claim that it was he and Fred Anderson who came up with the idea of a "three-pronged attack"— both aircraft factories plus the ball-bearing plants.[3] Yet another story was that Allied planners in the UK cobbled together a scheme in late summer of 1943 to coordinate operations from the UK and Mediterranean by attacking the two Messerschmitt plants simultaneously since, it was believed, neither factory was "aware of its vulnerability."[4] Regensburg factories were estimated to be producing two hundred Me-109s monthly, while Wiener-Neustadt was churning out that number plus twenty more in the same period.[5] Another account has Portal suggesting to Eaker in midsummer that he and Spaatz conduct a joint operation against the fighter plants in Regensburg and Wiener-Neustadt; Eaker followed with a "Dear Tooey" letter to Spaatz in the Mediterranean saying he needed to "discuss one of the most important projects now confronting both of us." He mentioned "two fighter factories" that produced almost half of all Luftwaffe fighters and asserted their "destruction was of the highest priority." Eaker proposed that they develop a joint plan, for which he suggested the codename STILETTO, in which each would "wipe out" the one closest to them, ending with a promise to send one operations and one intelligence officer to meet jointly with Spaatz's staff.[6] Among Eaker's limitations was that only about half of his Fortresses had the long-range Tokyo tanks in the wing; he could send all B-17s to Regensburg if Liberators from Italy could strike the Austrian site.[7]

Regardless, at PINETREE planning for a two-phased mission commenced in earnest: B-17s from England would bomb Regensburg, then cross the Alps to North Africa; the Eighth's B-24s still in North Africa after Ploeşti would depart Libya and bomb the aircraft plants at Wiener-Neustadt, near Vienna, and then continue to England. But a spate of poor weather in the British Isles delayed the participation of the Eighth, so on 12 August Eaker sent a BIGOT-restricted cable to General Brereton, recommending, "9th Air Force attack their JUGGLER Target when weather permits regardless of operations 8th Bomber Command. We will attack our JUGGLER Target when weather permits."[8] Never shy, Brereton sent sixty-one of the Eighth Air Force's B-24s to Wiener-Neustadt the very next day; they struck the Messerschmitt complex and a ball-bearing plant—and then returned to North Africa and Brereton instead of flying on to England! Flak and fighter defenses were light, with two B-24s downed; "the output of Me-109 airframes [was] reduced by one-third . . . and the ball-bearing plant [was] severely damaged." The raid and its positive results left Eaker still without his Liberators and with the choice of either attacking just Regensburg or selecting a surrogate for the Austrian site.[9] Opting for the latter, Schweinfurt in Bavaria, was substituted—as the story goes. Home to five ball-bearing factories of the Swedish SKF company, the city produced as much as 45 percent of Germany's total output of ball bearings.[10]

The Mission

Mission 84 was flown on 17 August, the date perhaps or perhaps not "chosen deliberately" or because it was on or "commemorated" the anniversary of the Eighth's first mission against the Nazi regime.[11] However, it had been planned for earlier and canceled twice on account of poor weather, so probably the seventeenth was the first decent weather date available. Anderson dispatched 376 heavy bombers from sixteen groups, divided into two combat wings, relying on a plan in which timing and weather were of signal import.[12] The Regensburg element was commanded by Curt LeMay; the Schweinfurt leader was Brigadier General Robert B. Williams, an unexcitable, highly competent commander who lost an eye while on observer status during the London Blitz of 1940. LeMay would strike Regensburg and then swing south, crossing the Alps and skirting neutral Switzerland to land in French Algeria, while Williams would hit Schweinfurt and immediately head for home.

LeMay's wing had only a 150-minute window for all aircraft to be off, for the distances to Regensburg and North Africa were so great that the last aircraft had to be airborne by 0830 to complete the mission in daylight. An unforgiving factor was that the East Anglian and English Midlands regions, homes to the B-17 bases, experienced extremely dense morning fog in August and, as standard, for the B-17s to take off, horizontal ground visibility had to be at or above minimums for the pilots. A crucial complication was that operational plans allowed for just nine minutes between the departure of LeMay's last aircraft and the beginning takeoff roll of the first aircraft in Williams's wing, so that the two formations would cross the German border separated only by a ten-minute gap. The German air defense radars would show two huge formations seemingly heading for the same target, while the circling Luftwaffe interceptors would see the last of the P-47 escorts drop off. At the last minute, General Williams would turn and head for Schweinfurt.

By then Colonel LeMay's wing, having drawn the defending Luftwaffe fighters, would be under attack, and would be for perhaps ninety minutes as they flew to and then beyond Regensburg, leaving the Schweinfurt wing to fly on to their target unmolested—so the thinking went. After bombs away on Regensburg, the B-17s would then surprise the Luftwaffe by heading south vice reversing course to England, finding safety over the Alps and Mediterranean to land in Algeria. As the enemy fighters were refueling and rearming, the trailing wing would already have dropped at Schweinfurt and be turning for home. Thus, General Williams's component would be open to air assault only for the time it would take them to fly from target egress to the reunion with their escorts at Belgian air space.[13] Each combat wing would be escorted to and from the Belgian border but would be alone over Germany, thus dependent upon the self-defending concept. General Eaker was "confident" that the bombers would fare just fine without an escort; according to the Doctrine such a large force "would be able to operate without fighter cover against material objectives anywhere in Germany without excessive losses."[14]

The plan fractured literally at the beginning. On mission day the thick Anglian fog did unmitigated violence to the rigid takeoff schedule, with zero-zero conditions lasting so long that even LeMay's pilots—who had trained extensively in instrument takeoffs—barely managed to get their seven groups off in time; each aircraft even had to be guided to the taxiways and runway by "follow me" units with flashlights and lanterns.[15] LeMay, piloting the lead Fortress, was airborne at 0715. Williams, new in the job, had turned to his group commanders to schedule takeoff practice at their discretion. The groups, more recently arrived and with pilots less well-trained in general, did not train as hard and failed to attain the proficiency of LeMay's wing; they launched about three and a half hours later, as the fog partially lifted. Fatally, instead of Williams flying just nine minutes in trail of LeMay, his wing instead crossed the channel hours behind the first.[16] The plan had fallen apart literally at "start engines." Each wing would not only fight its way to the target but also out again, with no cessation in air combat. Fred Anderson had four options: scrub the mission totally; scrub, reschedule, and hope the good weather at the targets remained for another three days; ignore the fog and launch both forces as scheduled, without regard to lack of instrument takeoff or assembly skills in General Williams's force, risking accidents on takeoff or collisions while climbing out through the overcast; or send LeMay as scheduled and Williams later, when fog permitted.[17] He explained, "Inasmuch as the importance of these targets increased almost daily, the risk involved in dispatching the two bomb divisions individually was felt to be commensurate with the results which the destruction of these two targets would achieve."[18] Then, too, the question of the late summer weather over Germany, often unsuited for bombardment missions, was primary. The flying and bombing conditions en route to and over the target on the seventeenth were "the best that had been forecast in two weeks."[19] Anderson could have passed the buck up to Eaker, but as commanding general of the strategic bombers, the call was his to make. And so he did.

The attacks on LeMay's wing while inbound to Regensburg were equal in ferocity to those on Williams's force later in the day; LeMay's wing eventually reached the safety of the Alps after its egress from the Regensburg area, although pursued most of the distance by Luftwaffe fighters. LeMay's wing was "from Antwerp to the Alps under almost constant attack from about 200 German fighters drawn from all parts of the Reich, with one group coming into the fray as fast as another withdrew." Williams's wing lived through over three hours of ferocious attacks on the way to Schweinfurt; near the end of the runup to the ball-bearing factories, aircrews at the rear of the bomber stream saw what looked like large flares on the ground leading to the factories—the flaming wrecks of Fortresses from the lead groups. "Lieutenant Colonel Lewis E. Lyle of the 303rd Bomb Group would later comment, 'We followed the burning Fortresses all the way to the target.'"[20] The bombers were subjected on egress to another 150 minutes of the worst kind of destruction that the Luftwaffe could rain on the Fortresses. Head-on attacks were both ruthless and relentless as the Germans, able to tell easily that the Fortresses were F versions lacking forward-firing chin guns, persisted in the deadly frontal attacks.[21]

Of the 315 aircraft that made it to both targets, 60 were downed—a 19 percent loss rate that, regardless of its size, was not reflective of the absolute hell the aircrews experienced from air defenses. The Germans dispatched every type of fighter and multimission aircraft flown by the Luftwaffe and hundreds, if not several thousands, of antiaircraft cannon were firing once the escorting American fighters left the bombers at the German border.[22] Approaching Regensburg, aircrews even spotted Luftwaffe twin-engine fighters in desert camouflage.[23]

The Luftwaffe unleashed every trick and device in its repertoire. The Me-109's and FW-190's attacked from all directions, singly and in Groups. . . . Occasionally the enemy resorted to vertical attacks from above, driving straight down at the bombers with fire concentrated on the general vicinity of the top turret, a tactic which proved effective. Some enemy fighters fired cannon and some rockets. Even parachute bombs were employed in a desperate effort to stop the bomber formations as they droned on toward their targets. Both AAF elements suffered in roughly the same proportion. It is probable that the Regensburg Groups might have lost even more heavily in the air battle had they returned to their English bases, for they appear to have taken the Luftwaffe by surprise when they continued on toward the Mediterranean. It was the most intensive air battle as yet experienced by the American daylight bombing force, and certainly one of the worst in the memory of the Germans.[24]

General Arnold would later write, "No such savage air battles had been seen since the air war began. Our losses were rising to an all-time high, but so were those of the Luftwaffe, and our bombers were not being turned back from their targets."[25]

Colonel LeMay "believed his bombardiers had done an excellent job and he was right." His seven groups dropped 299 tons of bombs, obtaining excellent hits at Regensburg and killing over four hundred Germans. The bombs inflicted destruction or severe damage to much of the target, with "every important building in the complex damaged" to some degree. Approximately 18–20 percent of the Me-109 production was lost to the Germans for over six months while "37 brand-new Messerschmitt Me-109s lined up neatly on the tarmac" were also destroyed.[26] Had the Fortresses dropped heavier bombs with greater destructive power, much more damage would have been done. LeMay and 122 bombers exited Regensburg; 10 were downed en route to the Alps, 2 were interned in Switzerland, several ditched in the Mediterranean, and the remaining landed not in Algeria but at three "inadequate and scattered" airfields in Tunisia.[27] The Fortresses were so low on gas the engines were sucking fumes. There, the men found no quarters, mess facilities, or repair stations.[28]

Eaker, concerned about just how much of a bomber force he had left, ordered up his single last available B-17 the next morning and flew to Tunisia, stopping only at Marrakech to refuel. LeMay had lost twenty-four

Fortresses and "another 40 more were seriously shot up." Nonetheless, on 27 August, by dint of some impressive feats of mechanical skill, LeMay and eighty-five B-17s headed back to England, losing three more while depositing ordnance on Bordeaux's Mérignac airfield while en route. Left behind to appease the desert gods were some twenty hulls, abandoned as no longer airworthy, the crews eventually returning to England by ship.[29]

At Schweinfurt, success was initially thought to be more than satisfactory, as over 424 tons of ordnance from General Williams's groups scored eighty direct hits with high explosive bombs on the two factories, damaging about 40 percent of the factory and killing 121, at the cost of 36 of the 118 B-17s that reached the target; two of the lost 36 had ditched in the North Sea, where the crews were rescued.[30] William's wing saw 121 Forts return to England, all with some measure of battle damage.[31] Unfortunately, the German aircraft industry was barely inconvenienced by the damage: despite the German Armaments Commission finding a 34 percent reduction in production of ball bearings, the Germans had dispersed more than a six month supply of bearings into rural areas and increased orders from the Swiss and Swedish suppliers.[32] At least, that was the initial reading. Research and Experiments Office 8 (RE8) within the Ministry of Home Security assessed the raid as causing a 15 percent loss both in production and at the three factories that dealt with the finished products, what was about 70 percent of all of Germany's ball bearings.[33] But RE8 was also in error, unaware of the dispersal programs as well as earlier purchases of ball bearings from Sweden and Switzerland. Thus, the factories were back in business faster than RE8 had thought possible.[34] Because few incendiaries were dropped, there was no fire to inflict damage on surviving machines under collapsed concrete roofs.[35]

A total of 552 American flyers were killed, captured, or wounded on the mission, although 16 airmen who were shot down evaded capture, eventually to make their way back to England. The Regensburg factory, a parts source for the new Messerschmitt Me-262 Schwalbe, was destroyed, retarding production and, hence, the introduction of the jet a year later.[36] Each element was subjected from five to six hours of continuous air battle from the time they entered Germany until either reaching the Alps or exiting Germany; 71 percent of LeMay's bombers were damaged to some degree,

from destroyed to slightly hit, including being abandoned in the desert.[37]
On the ground at Schweinfurt, the factory buildings suffered serious
damage while the fabrication machines inside were barely touched, if at all.
The high-explosive bombs utilized were set with contact, not delay, fuses;
the exploding ordnance "smashed" the top floors of the five-story buildings,
collapsing them onto the lower floors but doing little to harm the machinery.[38]
It was learned later that the bearing machinery did not need to be destroyed,
or even damaged; if the bombs had been fewer but more powerful and able
simply to knock the machines off balance on their mounting blocks, the factories would have been finished for the war. The Americans' largest bombs
weighed one thousand pounds; the smallest bombs the British were using at
the time were of four thousand pounds.[39] A more thorough Allied intelligence
assessment of Schweinfurt was soon published.

Although doctrine called for a return strike within two or three days,
reality intervened to delay a return for two months. First, there was "the
need to recuperate and replenish" the B-17 force considering the losses
experienced; second, for days the weather was too inclement to fly; third, the
estimate was that damages were more extensive than they were. Given the
losses suffered by VIII Bomber Command that day, one point was salient:
"On just two missions into Germany in August—the strikes on the twelfth
against five targets in the Ruhr and JUGGLER—eighty-five bombers had
been lost since Blitz Week."[40] These losses grounded VIII Bomber Command
for a full three weeks.[41] While initial damage assessments may have been
overly optimistic, the results were still impressive indeed, as determined
by RE8. Although the bombers were escorted only to and from the German
border at Aachen, P-47s from four fighter groups still had nineteen confirmed
kills.[42] This high number of Luftwaffe kills left yet more commanders
believing that the presence of escorts for the entire mission length was at
once safer for the heavies and more lethal for the defenders. One officer who
had already changed his mind was Hap Arnold.

There could have been a second strike on Schweinfurt just hours after
the American strike had it not been for uncommon circumstances. Portal,
as head of the RAF, had been as direct as protocol permitted in pressing
Bert Harris of bomber command for a follow-up mission that night. That

Harris was unable to comply distressed Portal, nonetheless. Portal had been increasingly frustrated by Harris's refusal to go after POINTBLANK objectives and pushed for Schweinfurt as hard as sensitivities permitted. Harris routinely avoided targets smaller than a metropolitan city area, the panacea targets. Harris asserted that Schweinfurt was such a target, plus it was too far away to reach and too small for his bombers to find. Harris may or may not have been correct, but in this one instance it was also irrelevant, for he was under orders from Churchill to conduct a top-secret strike on the island of Peenemünde that same night, the first against German vengeance weapons—the Vergeltungswaffen—site. In his memoirs Harris discusses the two issues separately, thus avoiding linkage deliberately or otherwise. The Peenemünde raid clearly was a priority for Churchill, whom Harris considered to be his immediate supervisor, not Portal; but even if there had been no Peenemünde, Harris would not have gone to Schweinfurt. He finally, much belatedly, did but only after Portal at last gave him a direct order to do so. Striking the night of 24–25 February 1944, he did "lay waste to the town"—which he had previously claimed his bombers could not find—but by then Speer had moved out the remaining ball-bearing machinery, allowing Harris honestly to claim then that Schweinfurt was, indeed, a true panacea target.[43]

Vergeltungswaffen

A large clearing near Watten, in the Pas de Calais, had been routinely photographed by RAF reconnaissance Spitfires and watched by the resistance for some months as a major construction project for purposes unknown proceeded; by 17 August 1943, it was strongly suspected that the site was part of Hitler's vengeance weapons program. A construction engineer on the D-Day Mulberry Harbor project was consulted and advised that any attack should take place soon after concrete was poured but before it fully hardened. That time came on 21 August, so, despite the large number of B-17s lost or grounded by the Schweinfurt raid, on 27 August Fred Anderson dispatched 224 Fortresses on the first AAF strike against a V-site (vengeance weapons were the V-1 and V-2 unguided rockets built by the Germans to destroy English cities and civilian inhabitants; the Eighth Air Force and the

RAF had an intense program designed to locate the hidden launch sites—V-sites—in the French woods). Although uncompleted, the site was exceptionally well protected by flak cannon; of the 187 heavies that dropped on the target, 4 were downed,1 ditched in the channel, and 98 received damage.[44] The intelligence report from the PIs at Medmenham CIU described a scene of heavy damage and a "jumble of steel reinforcing girders and cement set into a rigid mass." Engineers estimated the site had been set back at least three months. By the first of the year, the site had been abandoned and "new construction commenced to the south."[45]

VIII Bomber Command then rested, mostly. In four strikes during the ten days from 4 to 14 August, the Eighth had lost 148 heavy bombers; put in perspective, only four months earlier for the 17 April mission to Bremen, the Eighth could dispatch 115 bombers total. Now, in five missions over two weeks, more than 200 bombers were destroyed yet the Eighth was still operational.[46] In a three-week operation subsequent to JUGGLER, the Eighth undertook six raids on targets in France—four in late August and two in early September—most in support of a disinformation plan to convince the Germans the coming invasion would occur at the Pas-de-Calais (Operation STARKEY). Taking charge at VIII Fighter Command on 29 August was Major General Bill Kepner, a pre–World War I enlisted Marine (1909–1913) who joined the National Guard upon expiration of his enlistment. He was later wounded in hand-to-hand combat at Chateau-Thierry in 1918 as an army infantry lieutenant when a German bayonet penetrated his jaw and hand. After flight school he became the epitome of a USAAC fighter pilot. In June of 1936, between ACTS and the command and general staff school, one Major Ira C. Eaker set a record by flying blind from the West Coast to the East Coast, completely under "the hood." To validate this achievement, his classmate Major Bill Kepner flew on his wing the full distance. As the CG of VIII Fighter Command, he wanted to fly every mission and fight in every dogfight. Kepner, ever the Marine, would fly over thirty combat missions with his fighter squadrons before the war ended in 1945.

Chapter 26

Supreme Air Commander

On 1 September Arnold arrived in England for an eight-day visit. One agenda item was final discussions with the RAF about a single strategic air commander. It was one year since the chief and Spaatz had begun to think in terms of one supreme air commander under ETOUSA commanding all AAF components operating in European and North African skies.[1] The catalyst then was the new Twelfth Air Force. The possibility had attracted Spaatz the pragmatist, but more particularly was vintage Arnold, "the flexible man, more a fixer than an ideologue."[2]

The plan's virtues included the advantages of "flexibility and mobility inherent in air power," as air assets could be transferred between the two theaters when situations required, with "little administrative difficulty." Spaatz's position was that a supreme air commander should be in command of all air assets "from Iceland to Iraq," as explained to Arnold in his letter of 31 October. Eisenhower hinted at such when he cabled Marshall in early September, noting that England was a locale from which the US forces could support TORCH while simultaneously striking "at the heart of the principal enemy."[3] Thus when Spaatz discussed the tangible aspects of a supreme air commander with Eisenhower during a conversation on 29 October, he found a receptive theater commander. For good measure Spaatz also mentioned that having just one all-encompassing air force presented one additional advantage: it would serve as a "greater influence in attracting forces to this side of the world rather than to the Pacific."[4] This last was, at the moment, a crucial point, as back home Admiral King and the navy were hounding the JCS and the White House for possession of all the air assets then coming off the production lines, and more. The Marines had invaded Guadalcanal and two close-by islands in the Solomons on 7 August and, with the fight nearly done there and more operations prepared for the Solomons, King and the navy wanted every bit of the national war production for a struggle they continually asserted was more important than Germany. It would be months before Arnold felt comfortable with the division of aircraft with the navy. Meanwhile, Arnold and Spaatz were also fighting Ike who was threatening to take all the Eighth's heavy bombers for TORCH. Ultimately, Ike conceded while the Marines in the Solomons gained the upper hand and the strategic objective of "Germany First" as expressed in every iteration of US war planning, prevailed.[5] Arnold, who could look farther into the future better than anyone, could see that having an air officer in command of multiple air forces on two continents would go far in justifying an independent, intercontinental United States Air Force—the elusive objective that was never out of mind.

In fact, Spaatz was so confident of its inevitability that he had convened his WIDEWING staff on 23 November to expound on the "general function of the new theater air command"—singular "theater" still operative as North Africa remained under the ETO. Spaatz "saw its chief duty as strategic control, not operational or administrative control." The commander would be over the Eighth in England, the Twelfth in North Africa, and the AAF detachments in Greenland and Iceland, and would "exercise technical supervision and control of units attached to ground forces." Intuitively aware that northwest Africa would be more a tactical than strategic air war, Spaatz opined that "general directives would be issued on strategic bombing, on allocation of units between the Eighth and Twelfth Air Forces, and on the readiness of heavy- and medium-bombers in each air force to support operations throughout both theaters."[6] Spaatz ended his talk by advising that details would be settled once the invasion (TORCH) was successfully concluded. The general probably thought the change was but a few months down the road. Moreover, he could rightly assume that he would be the commander. The concept would mature over the months, accented in Spaatz's mind by the prospect of adding air bases in Italy.

Arnold had also concluded that there would be positive benefits if the supreme air commander were an Allied position with British air assets also joined under the umbrella of one commander. With the Twelfth Air Force and the northwest African air war increasing in size and complexity by the day, Arnold, seeking RAF membership in the larger united command, had written to Portal on 10 December 1942 saying, "The recent air operations in North Africa have confirmed my opinion that the United Nations air effort against the European Axis should be unified under the command of one supreme [air] commander." He followed with a letter to Spaatz giving an enlarged concept, concluding that if such a "unification" were to be denied, it would "prove a seriously deterring factor in the effective employment of our air arm as a striking force."[7] Arnold had envisioned the general in command having a joint command with strategic bombers from both the RAF and the AAF, facilitating coordination between the two services. The idea had merit from the American perspective; whether the British would agree remained to be seen.

Arnold resurrected his plan in summer of 1943, when at TRIDENT in Quebec he had taken the opportunity to discuss it in greater detail with Portal. The RAF chief had listened politely but stated frankly that he and the RAF would both be against the idea. Regardless, now in August Arnold took his first step in formally moving the proposal ahead, first presenting it to Air Marshall William L. Welsh, the RAF's Washington liaison officer, as an act of courtesy to an ally, an opportunity to show respect to the British and to his relationships with his RAF counterparts. Welsh accepted the paper also in the spirit of comity and promptly sent it on to London and the air staff. The contents were no surprise, of course: in addition to the more formal instances of notification, Arnold and Spaatz both had routinely kept their primary RAF contacts current on an informal basis, and in return the British dealt similarly with their American allies, both sides open and honest. The RAF never wavered from intense opposition to anything of the sort, especially Arnold's proposal to include RAF Bomber Command within the new strategic air force. During his early September visit to England, Arnold once more raised the potential value of a single strategic air commander "in generalities," this time with Bert Harris the evening of 5 September. He met again with Portal the morning of the ninth for the same purpose, although Portal heard nothing new, certainly nothing that would change his determined mind. Arnold was accompanied to both meetings by General Eaker, who remained quiet for the most part.[8] Arnold was certain that with "one man directing all operations, night and day, regardless of who the man was," better results would accrue and it would "allow more efficient use of aircraft." Moreover, that man "would be able to throw more planes into an emergency bombing situation" than could be done "under the organization as it then existed." The concept of one general having the ability to transfer aircraft and crews without having to go through different theater commanders was, to the chief, imperative during war.

While Arnold's reasons and reasoning were limited and simple, the British military air establishment, the RAF in general, and RAF Bomber Command each had shared and individual concerns that militated heavily against Hap's plan. Some objections would have been fairly understandable, while others might have left their American counterparts somewhat (or a lot) perplexed. But to their holders, they were all serious. It should have been, and perhaps was, instructive to General Arnold that no one on the British side, no matter position or status, was in favor of the single air commander and that, as an institution, the RAF found it impossible to support the proposal for several basic and straightforward reasons:[9]

1. Bert Harris had not been shy in making it known that he would not agree to any command change unless the commander would be British and that, Harris was certain, would not be him since RAF Bomber Command would soon be eclipsed in size by the American bomber force. Too, the supreme air commander would fall under the direct supervision of the CCS just as the commander-in-chief did—and it was doubtful Harris would ever give up his direct access to the prime minister or willingly cede his freedom of independent action.[10]

2. To an officer, the British air establishment thought it unwise to upset an Allied arrangement that was and had been from the war's beginning working exceptionally well.[11]

3. RAF Bomber Command "was Britain's only independent contribution
   to the war effort and the Air Ministry wanted to retain exclusive
   control of it."[12]

4. The Americans had benefited hugely from the RAF's air intelligence,
   PR, communications, and weather services, as they in fact had almost
   none of these, either on an air force level or at all.

5. Although the CBO lacked a joint structure (just two different air forces
   with different methods) and while there had been occasional hiccups,
   the system had proven more than satisfactory. Even the targets were
   different: the AAF went after aircraft and oil industries while RAF
   Bomber Command sought the "de-housing and morale objectives."[13]

6. What mattered greatly to the RAF as a whole, not just bomber
   command, was that present command and liaison arrangements had
   passed the double tests of time and stress and were working excellently.
   Now senior RAF officers were fearful that a new command arrangement would destroy those arrangements.

7. Undeniably, the current arrangement collaterally served the RAF's
   institutional interests, which they argued should not be underestimated.
   In existence for only slightly more than three decades, the RAF had in
   that time developed into a professional bureaucracy that was not a slave
   to regulations but was nonetheless one in which established procedures
   and protocol were preferred to questionable risks that might or would
   upset a functioning equilibrium.

8. External considerations included the fact that the CCS controlled
   the execution of the CBO, which it did in part by using Portal to
   effectuate coordination between RAF Bomber Command and the
   Eighth. This protocol also kept bomber command independent of the
   Americans—which pleased Harris and the Air Ministry.

9. Britain was undeniably in a serious manpower shortage after four years
   of fighting on multiple continents, and accepting Arnold's proposal
   would—from their perspective—surely necessitate the creation of yet
   another headquarters staff. This would, they were certain, create more
   demands on the RAF personnel levels and no doubt place the British in
   a minority position in staff membership.

10. Some RAF officers had become at least partially convinced that the Americans would move the new air organization's headquarters to Washington, which would mean the abandonment of London and the outstanding intelligence and communications organizations and their personnel who now possessed over a half decade of experience and had developed extensive practical expertise.

11. Finally, on an operational level, RAF strategic bombers would be unable to bomb targets in southern Germany and then proceed on to Foggia because they had no repair or maintenance facilities there.

For the Americans to absorb all of the objections was no doubt a bit of heavy lifting, yet the points were either wholly or at least partially accurate. What should have mattered most to the Americans was that it all mattered significantly to the British. Everything considered, the British positions were both broad and deep. Arnold would proceed without the RAF. The AAF chief was supported by Generals Devers and Edwards at ETOUSA, both agreeing there might be "better results with one man directing all operations."[14]

On Arnold's next-to-last day in the UK, 6 September, Anderson sent the heavies to Stuttgart with ball-bearing, industrial, and aircraft factories as targets in the largest mission yet of the war. It was no milk run; indeed, it was literally a bloody mess. A total of 338 B-17s and 69 B-24s launched; after aborts 60 Liberators split off early for a diversionary raid—which was completely ignored by the Germans—while 117 B-17s flew on to strike Stuttgart and another 151, unable to work their way through the heavy clouds, went looking for targets of opportunity between the channel and the Rhine.[15] The main force, upon arriving at the Rhine, lost its escorts, leaving the heavies to defend themselves alone against the Luftwaffe. Large areas of thick, heavy cumulus and stratocumulus clouds left the formations ragged, chaotic, disorganized, and confused. Only 46 of the Fortresses made it to Stuttgart, which was covered by a heavy ten-tenths undercast. The mission leader, Brigadier General Robert F. Travis, the son of a general, made a pass over the city, then circled three more times waiting for opening in the undercast. Each circuit took more than ten minutes, consuming precious fuel. The leader's aircraft would make a tight, close-in circle, but those farther behind had to make wider turns in a "pinwheel" effect, burning commensurately more fuel to keep up with the lead aircraft. All bombers were under attack the entire time by over one hundred fighters and rocket-firing night interceptors before finally dropping on "the center of the city" while looking for any possible target.[16] Radar-controlled flak was "moderate to intense, and accurate." Forty-five heavies were lost, either at Stuttgart, at targets of opportunity, or when ditching in the English Channel from fuel exhaustion. Air-Sea Rescue plucked 118 American airmen out of the cold water.[17] Seventeen percent of the force was lost and many bombers suffered serious damage—mostly for naught as little destruction was inflicted on the enemy.[18]

General Arnold was not informed of this strike until that evening while at an official, formal dinner given by General Eaker with the top American and British military brass in attendance. The chief was told only that the results were "excellent" but that "more than 30 aircraft were lost and ten missing," Fred Anderson having no desire to give a complete story and thus perhaps sink Eaker. Eaker's staff knew that Arnold had for months been sending those increasingly critical, often snarky, cables to Eaker, more than a few concerning mission losses, and there was no sentiment to see Arnold distress the boss on what was otherwise a cheerful evening. Arnold learned of the actual results after his return to the United States several days later; although angry over his deception, he wrote in his memoirs only that "certain features of the operation never did find their way into reports sent up through channels. Of the 338 B-17s dispatched to hit the VKF ball-bearings plant at Stuttgart, not one saw its assigned target."[19] Whether Anderson was culpable of anything more than dissimulation to protect his boss, he did not apparently receive any negative attention from the chief's office, all of whom he knew well.[20] VIII Bomber Command lost 105 B-17s and over one thousand men to enemy action at Stuttgart; when combined with the losses of Schweinfurt-Regensburg in August, including the hulls abandoned in the North African desert, 165 Fortresses disappeared from bomber command's inventory on just two raids. Only now, the bombers and crews could be quickly replaced.

Before leaving for home on 8 September, Arnold cabled General Marshall, "Operations over Germany conducted here during the past several weeks indicate definitely that we must provide long-range fighters to accompany daylight bombing missions."[21] In a second cable, Arnold requested another two hundred bombers for Fred Anderson, followed by a third in which he reversed a previous decision to send a number of P-38 groups to Eisenhower in Italy and instead rerouted them to England, aware that while the Lightnings were not perfect—the Allison engines on all but the latest model were negatively affected by the deep cold and high humidity of the European weather—their long range offset other infirmities.

The Arnold-Eaker Split Grows

By fall of 1943 the Arnold-Eaker rift had widened, with Arnold's unhappiness with Eaker and his unfavorable perception of the performance of the Eighth magnified by the expedited activation of the Fifteenth Air Force. From Italy the Fifteenth's strategic bombers would be able to easily reach targets in southern Germany that were a stretch for the Eighth.[22] In moving to command the Fifteenth, General Doolittle would acquire the Twelfth's strategic bombers and to them add the recently reassigned fifteen new heavy groups—those that Eaker had expected for the Eighth. Eaker's near intransigence with regard to the self-defending bomber and his "misunderstanding of the day-fighter program" indisputably added to his problems with Arnold. Still believing the heavies could take care of themselves given large enough formations, he saw little value in fighters that could fly to Berlin. His immediate subordinate, Fred Anderson, had quickly realized what Jimmy Doolittle had always known—that "bombers would be 'bait' for the Luftwaffe"—but to exploit the firepower, agility, and range of the AAF fighters they had to be untethered from the bombers, free to range ahead and seek out the enemy. The new strategy was simple: shorter range fighters—P-47s and P-38s—would take the heavies to the German border on the inbound leg and meet them again at the border on the way out, while the long-range P-51s, much better than anything the Luftwaffe had, were to accompany the bomber streams across the Third Reich; when then freed of the escort mission, the Mustangs would seek out targets on the ground or in the air for as long as they had gas. Eaker never displayed any awareness of this potential. Ultimately, one historian has argued, General Arnold kept Eaker as commanding general "far longer than deserved," but the chief "had his limits."[23]

Significantly, following Arnold's departure for home, three events allowed Eaker to believe all was well between himself and the chief, if he had any doubts. First there was his promotion to three stars on 13 September, with warm congratulations from the chief. Second was his additional assignment as commanding general, US Air Forces in Europe, which soon more than doubled the number of personnel under his command with the addition of the Ninth Air Force, soon to arrive from Libya. The Pentagon had decided that September was the time to reunite the Ninth Air Force in the UK, which had earlier been split between England and North Africa, under Major General Brereton. The Eighth would transfer its light and medium bombers—its air support command—to the Ninth, changing it into a tactical air force, leaving the Eighth as a strictly strategic bombardment force. Eighth Air Force retained VIII Fighter Command, which would see its fighter groups divided among the three heavy bombardment air divisions, although Eaker still lacked all enthusiasm for freeing the fighters to pursue POINTBLANK's Luftwaffe objectives.

Third, any officer watching for signs of a breach in friendship between Hap and Ira would have seen the two continuing their collaboration on two of their previous books as they carved out private time in Arnold's busy agenda during the recent trip to revise the two volumes.[24] From Eaker's viewpoint disagreements were just strongly voiced differences of opinion, nothing more. However, the editor of Arnold's diaries reached a different conclusion, albeit retrospectively. "It seems probable," retired Major General John W. Huston wrote some fifty-five years after the war, "that Arnold felt without articulating it that Eaker's days as Eighth Air Force commander were numbered." After empathizing with Eaker for having to "endure with inordinate patience the hectoring" from Arnold while trying to build the Eighth, Huston opined that "Arnold's concept of strategic bombing as the raison d'etre of a current and postwar air force overshadowed Eaker's vision as a theater air commander."[25]

If Arnold were still not sure whether to replace Eaker, the Eighth's commander's next move could very easily have been the episode of the camel and the piece of straw. Without informing Arnold, Eaker wrote to Spaatz on 11 September saying he had privately "suggested to Portal" that there be a meeting with Portal, Harris, Tedder, Spaatz, and himself to discuss further the issue of one "Strategic *Allied* Air Commander [emphasis added]."[26] It is uncertain what was behind Eaker's thinking, but he may have been looking for a compromise that would be acceptable to Arnold but would not exclude his British colleagues, of whom the Eighth's commander was always solicitous. Of course, Portal had already, both informally and officially, rejected RAF participation beyond any doubt. Regardless, Eaker must have been surprised when he received Spaatz's rejection, phrased as a need for himself and his deputy, Tedder, to look further at things "in their neck of the woods."[27] Eaker bided his time for a month, solicited thoughts from his own senior generals, and then—in a second mistake obviously born in the confidence of a man who was certain of his position—sent his ideas directly to Arnold. Eaker neither supported nor argued against the single air commander concept; rather, he engaged in another of his academic compositions, centered predominantly on how it might affect the Allied relationship, a bow to ensuring that the British did not sustain damaged feelings or a sense of omission. Possibly his most anodyne thought was to delay the creation of an overall air commander until after D-Day, when the need for close coordination with air forces in Italy would be more acute. There was no response from Arnold.

Arnold's position had been straightforward: he wished no further discussion. He had given the British the opportunity to cooperate or at least to submit written opinions for consideration, but they had chosen not to avail themselves of these opportunities. He would push for the position because he thought it was the right thing to do at that point in the war. It was collaterally the perfect opportunity to prove the viability of and necessity for an independent United States Air Force. Such would be undeniable if he could demonstrate that the AAF could manage a massive air war, prosecuted by two strategic air forces based on two continents, under the leadership of one commander. An independent United States Air Force was never absent from Arnold's mind, a consideration in most major decisions Arnold confronted. He was finished negotiating over this position. Spaatz understood; Eaker did not, or worse, was looking out for his British friends.

In addition to receiving kudos from Arnold for Schweinfurt I, there was a spurt of criticisms from Arnold's office to Eaker throughout September with the usual complaints. In that thirty-day month, sixteen missions were flown—more than one every two days—and despite Stuttgart the thirty days were seen as "a month of greatly of increased operations" with 2,085 bomber sorties reaching their targets, a loss rate of 4.7 percent, and 5,743 tons of bombs dropped on the targets. [28] Cables from headquarters, whether from Arnold or a staff member, were sent to "Dear Ira" and mostly expressed concern about the number and the size of missions compared to the number of aircraft available, or that the author perceived as available. Perhaps thinking of aircraft with combat damage being repaired, one cable's author continued, "We obviously must send the maximum number of airplanes against targets within Germany, now that the German Air Force appears to be at a critical stage . . . we must indoctrinate our personnel through all ranks with this principle so as to cut down on the time required to put the planes back into operation . . . I know that you will agree that the minimum number must be kept on the ground at our bases or in reserve." On at least one cable, the author confessed to being puzzled as to why "massive" numbers of heavies were not used in missions since Eaker now had enough to put "500" against Germany. "To us here in the United States, it looks as if the employment of large numbers of heavy bombers has not been followed through by your headquarters and staff . . . the impression in my mind is that you still figure on employing small numbers of 300 or 400 or maybe a third of 300 or 400."[29]

That cable then discussed the "necessity" of developing "an entirely new technique": a "planning technique," or "airdrome technique," even an "actual air operations technique." The day after, another cable arrived asking for data on German aircraft production in light of the August bombings. Because the assessment would, as always, rely heavily on intelligence collection and analysis, it was way too soon for a mostly definitive or accurate estimate of the August data. But Eaker still rendered polite answers: he "believed" the raids had "materially" reduced German fighter production in August and gave "an educated guess" that this would be the case in September. He mentioned that a number of aircraft factories had been relocated to areas farther east, which "might offset" the destruction of some plants; German pilots were less experienced; and in any case the Germans would "mask the decline" in production.[30] It was, so it appeared, business as usual.

Chapter 27

Air Combat

Münster

In the first two weeks of October, the Eighth struck Germany four times before hitting Schweinfurt again on the fourteenth. On 2 October the heavies raided Emden with 339 B-17s after ten aborts, guided by two H2S-equipped Fortresses of the 482nd Pathfinder Bombardment Group (H), referred to as the PFF. The Fortresses dropped 953 tons of bombs through cloud cover—on the mark of a radar officer, the essence of "blind, area bombing"—and returned home with but two losses.[1] Writing to Arnold, Eaker highlighted a "weak" Luftwaffe response to the attack, which he attributed to "a shortage of single-engine fighters caused by our attacks on German fighter factories."[2] Two days later 282 Fortresses went after five targets in Germany with twelve losses, but it was not a stellar performance. Most of the force sent to Wiesbaden ended up a hundred miles away, leaving only 15 Fortresses to hit the target; the lost 77 merged with the element assigned to strike aircraft factories at Frankfurt, but many just dropped on the city itself; only Fortresses from the 3rd Division found and hit the correct targets—marshaling yards at Saarbrucken and aircraft factories at Saarlautern.[3] The next mission to Germany was the first of three straight days of pounding the Third Reich when, on 8 October, 314 Forts hit shipyards and aircraft factory targets at Bremen and targets of opportunity at four other cities; 27 B-17s were shot down (an 8.5 percent loss rate) and 207 damaged. The next day 202 Forts and 41 Liberators flew the longest mission yet of the war to hit POINTBLANK targets at Danzig and Gdynia in Poland, and Anklam and Marienburg in eastern Germany; the heavies were in the air for over ten hours and 1,500 miles at a cost of 12 percent losses. The heavies were not, of course, escorted.[4] Eaker cabled Arnold, "Have just seen the photos of yesterday's attacks; most encouraging. Fighter factory at Marienburg undoubtedly destroyed . . . better concentration than Regensburg. Looks like a perfect job. Fighter factory at Anklam received excellent concentration and principal buildings burning. Believe you will find October 9th a day to remember in air war. Prime Minister sending message to crews."[5] And then it was the tenth, with Münster's railway yards by the city center and canal network as the primary target for 206 B-17s.

Münster consisted of two task forces of three combat wings each, totaling 206 Fortresses at the target. There was also a diversion force of B-24s sent to the Frisian Islands.[6] When the aiming point for Münster, alleged (possibly in mission mythology) to have been the steps of the Münster Cathedral at high noon, was identified at the mission briefing, reactions were mixed, divided mostly between new and old crews.[7] The newer men were aghast at the idea of bombing civilians, some on moral grounds, others alleging it was un-American or "not what they signed up for." Older crews, who had seen the Germans bomb civilian targets in England and on the Continent, and who had lost friends to German flak, fighters, or worse, were ecstatic at the thought.

The air battle was as deadly as any, the two Schweinfurts excepted, with 29 Forts downed from TF1 and one from TF2, for a 15 percent loss rate. There were 216 P-47s from six fighter groups escorting the heavies matched against 300 enemy aircraft. The 100th BG was particularly hit hard: only one of its 14 Forts dispatched from Thorpe Abbotts returned there.[8] Of 140 air officers in the 100th who had arrived in England with the group just a few weeks earlier, only three remained on flight status after Münster.[9] The chief wrote the Eighth's commander once again, hitting the usual: "Candidly, I think your whole bomber effort is picking up. As you know, I was worried because, in my opinion, we're not getting enough airplanes [into combat] out of the total number we had in the 8th Air Force."[10] The first task force was hit hard while the second, following the same track some twenty minutes later was not, perhaps because it sent one wing to Münster and the other to Coesfeld. As the escorts could only take the bombers up to or just across the German frontier, the escort pilots watched helplessly as the Luftwaffe defenders circled in the distance, awaiting the bombers.

The Eighth's busy first week of October was sufficiently successful to have delighted Arnold, who congratulated Eaker for the accomplishments of the month plus the Bremen raid. He then spoiled it for Eaker by confirming that the Fifteenth Air Force would be stood up, despite Eaker's protestations. Larry Kuter, overloaded with the business of the air staff, still found time to write multiple cables as well as a letter or two to Eaker in attempts to spur the Eighth's commander to fly more often, weather notwithstanding. Kuter, bizarrely, also drafted a critical letter intended for Portal. Incredibly, the idea was to "obtain greater results for the Eighth and the strategic bombing initiative . . . by making both Eaker and Portal 'mad' through the tone and nature of [Arnold's] correspondence with them."[11] In the midst of the drafting, a letter arrived from Portal congratulating Eaker for Schweinfurt II; Kuter's own letter was shelved and Arnold instead reworded the cable to Eaker, urging him to adopt "new techniques" that would require "scrapping some outmoded tactical concepts, closer coordination between all elements of command, and more effective use of our combined resources." It was a directive to a general officer who had been commanding an air force— successfully, in the opinions of key generals in England and the US, including his direct commanding officers—serving in combat for over a year, written by an officer in Washington telling the combat commander how to do his job. Brigadier General Haywood Hansell, back on Arnold's staff, thought that the chief "treated Ira very badly. . . . He was not creating the miracles that Arnold wanted to report; Arnold just never understood what Eaker was up against."[12] To Hansell, Arnold had found it "infuriating" to keep informing Marshall at staff meetings that the Eighth had done "nothing" the day before; Arnold did not possess the "type of personality who could stand up under that kind of thing," even if the missions were axed because of execrable weather.[13]

Schweinfurt II

In early September Generals Eaker and Anderson realized that Schweinfurt would have to be hit again. Intelligence had alerted them to activities involving the factories there, the diversity and seriousness of which led them to the decision to send the bombers again.[14] From diplomatic and business sources, Allied intelligence learned the Germans were engaged in intensive efforts to purchase more ball bearings from Switzerland and Sweden; from ULTRA it became known that the Germans feared follow-up attacks on the factories; from PR it was obvious that the Germans were "frantically" engaged in making "intensive repairs"; and other intelligence indicated incendiaries and high explosive (HE) bombs fused to explode after penetration vice on impact with the concrete roofs would be much more effective. The efforts by the Germans to purchase bearings from the Swiss and Swedes were serious concerns despite a half year's supply of bearings in caches away from the factories—of which in any case the Allies were unaware. On October first Eighth Air Force A-2 received reporting that Luftwaffe aircraft production was increasing—despite six months of POINTBLANK bombing by the Eighth—and that the Third Reich was now defended by more Luftwaffe fighters than ever in the air space between England and Germany.[15] Planning for Schweinfurt II began in earnest.

PINETREE was in something approaching controlled chaos on 12 October. First, Louie Brereton had just returned from Washington with the news that in three days the Ninth's change of station from North Africa to England would be executed. Not only was it going to be much more work for Eaker, who had administrative control of both air forces, but there was also the transfer, physically and on paper, of light and medium bombers from VIII ASC to the Ninth. Second, planning for Schweinfurt II reached final stages. The most recent intelligence analyses considered comprehensive reports from intelligence sources including PR, ULTRA, human reporting, economic analyses, and civilian sources in the ball-bearing business in Sweden and Switzerland: all indicated the Germans were quickly rebuilding the plants at Schweinfurt while attempting to locate sources outside Germany from which to purchase ball bearings. A sense of urgency about the strike permeated PINETREE, especially since they now knew that General William's strike back in August, robust though it was, had nonetheless been insufficient to halt production for as long as initially predicted.

Eaker pondered the advantages of delay but saw none, while also assessing that if this mission was not unambiguously successful, the British might well again raise the frailties of daylight bombing and press for the Eighth to join in the night area raids. Anderson, ever aggressive, was urging Eaker to go without delay. In the previous two months, new B-17Gs with twin .50s in a chin turret had arrived on the Eighth's flight lines, giving the Fortresses a formidable forward defense and increasing the number of .50-caliber M-2 Brownings to thirteen.[16] In the background was the knowledge, reflected in other intelligence reports, that despite all of the CBO missions flown by the USAAF and RAF over the past six months, German aircraft production was actually increasing and "that there might be more Luftwaffe fighters than ever before defending the bomber routes from England to Germany."[17] No one at this point would have believed they could fly to Schweinfurt and not find the fight of their lives—but somehow the fact that the increasing production of German aircraft was being slowly but steadily obviated by the devastating losses of experienced German fighter pilots was somehow overlooked not only by many Allied intelligence officers but also by operations personnel and senior commanders. It's not clear why this was so, although one knowledgeable historian has written that Operation ARGUMENT in February 1944 was actually the onset of a "long decline" for the Luftwaffe, possibly a decline sufficiently shallow as to be overshadowed in the eyes of the Americans by the enormous destruction in Luftwaffe aircraft (two thousand just in the three months after ARGUMENT). Afterward there were never sufficient pilot trainees nor "fuel or time to train properly." Consequently it became a "vicious cycle" in which inexperienced pilots were thrown into air combat way too early, facing increasingly better-trained and experienced American pilots, and which, then, "forced the employment of even more hastily trained replacements, [many] of whom died in accidents." The historian ends with the little recognized statistic that the "most dangerous occupation in World War II was being a German fighter pilot."[18]

Weather on the morning of the fourteenth found a dense fog hanging over Britain, but once airborne it was clear over the channel and Germany. The mission included 60 B-24s and 291 B-17s; but only 29 Liberators managed to formate and so were sent on a diversionary mission toward Emden. The Fortresses took off in two elements with 229 making it to Schweinfurt, after 62 aborted, for the strike. As usual, German radar observers saw the formations assemble over the United Kingdom and turn toward the Continent. By the time the bombers were over the Netherlands, dozens of single- and twin-engine defenders along the projected routes of flight were alerted and hundreds of 88 mm flak guns made ready.[19] The First Division escaped heavy flak both en route and while at target, but the Third Division was shot at most of time over the Continent, with fire "meager and inaccurate" en route and moderate but accurate over the target. Luftwaffe fighters attacked with "tremendous ferocity," creating a hellacious air battle from which another sixty bombers and 640 casualties did not return.[20] "In some groups, whole squadrons were almost decimated" with "burnt out wrecks . . . marking a trail hundreds of miles long, soiling the autumn landscape." The air battle lasted over three hours and eight hundred miles; the airmen saw everything in the Luftwaffe inventory from the new Me-210 to the outdated Stuka.[21] The losses were 26 percent, one of every four Fortresses that crossed into Germany, plus 138 damaged and seven DBR. It was a day in which the Luftwaffe "gave every evidence of increasing rather than declining strength."[22]

P-47s from four fighter groups, 196 total with belly tanks, were to provide cover. But the vaunted 4th FG was recalled after becoming lost in the clouds, while the 352nd FG joined with the lost twenty-nine B-24s of the Second Bombardment Division as they motored to Emden.[23] The two remaining fighter groups, the 56th and the 353rd, were all there was to protect the entire strike force as they headed into what many later believed was the "greatest air battle ever fought." To the east, just beyond Aachen where the escorts had to turn 180 degrees and head for home, the loitering Luftwaffe defenders had a field day against the heavies all the way to Schweinfurt and back.[24]

An assessment produced by RE8, where fourteen AAF personnel worked alongside of some sixty-eight RAF staff and British civilians, classified the destruction as "severe," including the complete decimation of "the ball-bearing-forming and heat-treatment buildings and the top two stories of the assembly and storage building." A report from the newly created Allied CIU read, "Very heavy and concentrated damage is visible within the target area, due probably as much to fire as to HE. . . . In many cases, buildings damaged in the previous raid have now been destroyed or received further damage."[25] RE8 estimated that ball-bearing production was completely lost for a period of three months and that of roller bearings lost for seven weeks. Omitted from the report was any mention or assessment of the dispersal of the equipment and machinery; instead, it was anticipated that the sites would be rebuilt and production started again. In the event, the Germans again returned to production quicker than estimated.[26]

Eaker, in his first cable to the chief the next day, wrote of the "perfectly timed and executed" German defenders' attack on the B-17 formations: "A screen of single-engine fighters flew in from the front very close, firing 20mm cannon and machine guns . . . closely followed by large formations of twin-engine fighters in waves, each firing large numbers of rockets suspended under wings."[27] Eaker further depicted how one combat wing was destroyed and a second almost so, but with "excellent bombing results." He concluded by requesting another 250 replacement fighters "at least" to be sent immediately.[28] Eaker's second cablegram to Arnold asserted that "this does not represent disaster; it does indicate that the air battle has reached its climax"—a questionable assessment if more deep penetrations were to be flown without escorts. He followed with a short list of things Arnold could "do to help," including expediting replacement aircraft and crews, sending "every possible fighter here as soon as possible," especially more P-38s and the new P-51s, and eight thousand drop tanks immediately—and then the same number every month thereafter.[29] "We must show the enemy we can replace our losses; he knows he cannot replace his. . . . We must continue the battle with unrelenting fury. This we shall do. There is no discouragement here. We are convinced that when the totals are struck yesterday's losses will be far outweighed by the value of the enemy material destroyed."[30] Arnold responded with an echo about showing the Germans that "we Americans not only intend to replace our losses but will send our bombers into Germany with an ever increasing strength; that with our numbers and determination there is nothing the Germans can do that will stop our precision daylight bombing; that we will change our ideas, our technique, our equipment just as often as is necessary to secure the maximum effort from the airplanes we have available." The chief closed asking for Eaker to tell all in his command "that the cornered wolf fights hardest and that the German Air Force has been driven into its last corner."[31] Having promised P-38s and P-51s to General George Kenney, commander of Allied Air Forces in the Pacific, Arnold now cabled Kenney to tell him that those fighters would instead be sent to England and the Pacific would receive P-47s as substitutes.[32]

Autumn Redux

If anything were "proven" by both missions to Schweinfurt's crucial ball-bearing factories, it was this: deep-penetration raids could no longer be flown unless and until long-range escorts were available that could go with the bombers to the target and fight with the enemy until the bombers were safe over the channel. A later operational assessment disagreed sharply with Eaker's positive outlook, concluding that, at Second Schweinfurt "the Eighth Air Force temporarily lost air superiority over Germany" as initial glowing damage assessments proved to be overestimated.[33] To many it was debatable whether the Eighth had ever had even one day's air superiority before then. One statistic told the story: just three missions—the two to Schweinfurt and one to Stuttgart—flown in less than sixty days produced a tally of 185 aircraft lost in or directly because of air combat, with some two thousand men KIA, MIA, or POW. To be fair, when coupled with other, much less deadly missions in the same two-month period, the blow to the Eighth was not crushing; but neither were the losses easy to absorb. It was evident to Arnold that the Luftwaffe was still a force of great strength and that the Eighth could not continue to accept losses of this magnitude for long. Realistic tests had shown that the "dearly held precept—unescorted, daylight bombardment of Germany—was untenable . . . that the Eighth had been sorely beaten over Schweinfurt."[34]

Eaker maintained long after the war that "he and Anderson would have gone right back into the heart of Germany, even without the long-range fighters, if weather had permitted." But this is at odds with Anderson's statement to his wing commanders. It was also perhaps a sign that Eaker still had confidence in the self-defending bomber concept, even though its validity was now beyond question for most. Regardless, by August 1943 General Arnold's doubts about Eaker's leadership of the Eighth had either congealed or were close to doing so, no matter how successful the air strikes were becoming or how large the size of the force. One factor had to have been the lengthy letters from WIDEWING, paragraph upon paragraph explaining, excusing, challenging, pontificating, pleading, even at a time when Arnold was so overloaded (or had overloaded himself) that he had worked himself into coronaries. Almost as harmful as implying something could not be done or was impossible were the instances of persistently disputing issues after Arnold had made final decisions. Eaker's secretive and eminently inapt exertions to corral the Allied air commanders into a meeting over the single air leader to save RAF participation bordered on insubordination and must have rankled Arnold no end, while the inability of the Eighth's commanding general to recognize (or at least admit to) the deficiencies in unescorted bombardment missions would have been maddening. The increasing tempo of criticisms from HqAF that began in early spring of 1943 should have indicated problems to Eaker, enough so that even if he thought he was 100 percent correct, it would have been prudent either to have attempted a compromise or simply saluted with a "yes sir" and moved on.

While Arnold had urged Eaker to think of new ideas and new methods, Eaker had sent Monk Hunter back to the United States but then allowed Bill Kepner's fighter groups only a slightly freer hand, still keeping the escorts close to the bombers, insisting they stay above eighteen thousand feet and never to be unleashed to hunt down the Luftwaffe. His persistence in believing that German fighters would ignore the bombers and go after the escorts was simply wrong; the Luftwaffe ignored the escorts and went full-force against the heavies. And when they had broken up the bomber formations—which were rarely as tightly flown as necessary for self-protection—they would pick off the stragglers one by one. The chief also had become convinced by now, rightly or not, that Eaker would not put a bomber back on flight status until it was repaired to near-perfect condition, just as he believed that Eaker was "unwilling to challenge the weather." Worse, though he may have never raised it, Arnold probably concluded that Eaker was too quick to stand with the British in interservice disputes. As head of the AAF Arnold wanted, indeed needed, to hear from the Eighth's commander on issues of importance, but brevity was not in Eaker's soul; nor did Eaker's near-constant repetition of the same problems win over Arnold, no matter how valid. And while Eaker could recite the mantra of the three-hundred-bomber minimum necessary for self-protection, he was never able to justify this calculation.[35]

Bombing by Radar

The usual appalling autumn weather over central Europe after Second Schweinfurt put an end to further deep penetrations of Germany until the new year, although the Eighth flew twenty-three missions against CBO and other targets until the last day of December. The missions included shallow penetrations like Münster, but all with P-47 and P-38 escorts. In early November General Arnold approved Pathfinder use of the H2X radar system for blind bombing, which effectively turned the heavies into an "area bombardment" force.[36] Radar bombing was an admission that "precision was impossible" when the weather precluded visual bombing.[37] Even though contrary to the American and USAAF ethos, the alternative was not flying missions for days, which of course was unacceptable to Arnold. Mission 127 to Münster on 10 November sent one Pathfinder with H2X and 59 bombers to strike the marshaling yards while the other 111 B-17s aborted because weather over England prevented assembly; the meager force was escorted by a record 342 P-47s and P-38s.[38] Four other B-17 groups—175 heavies—from the Third Air Division aborted over the Dutch coast because of a navigational error and inoperability of the H2X in the Pathfinder. That only 58 heavies could carry out the mission while 286 aborted because of weather underscored the value of radar. Better news arrived on 5 December when 39 P-51s performed their maiden escort service for the Eighth. But of 548 heavies scheduled for a vital mission to take out NOBALL vengeance-weapons sites, only 4 managed to reach the targets, so awful was the Continental weather. In the solid clouds and goo, 9 heavies were lost in collisions over England or France, or while attempting to land.[39]

The War between the Generals

Throughout autumn of 1943, the carping between the two generals lingered on, only now there was more of it with Arnold's patience tested frequently. Now Arnold—or his staff—had begun complaining about Eaker to people not only outside the high levels of the air forces but also outside the army altogether. For each positive cable Eaker received from Arnold, there might be several, or more, that were kicks in the butt. Staff intrusion endured; the difference of two stars did not inhibit Larry Kuter from (as he stated it) "building a fire" under the combat commander. It was Kuter who wrote the cable to Portal in Arnold's name bluntly putting forth the accusation of "[Eaker] not employing our forces in adequate number . . . I am pressing Eaker to get a much higher proportion of his force off the ground and put them where they will hurt the enemy." Arnold signed the letter and off it went. It was to be a follow-on to an earlier letter to Eaker that month questioning why the commander had not been sending "massive flights of aircraft against a target now that we have planes and pilots in sufficient quantity to put over 500 planes in the air."[40] But this cable was sent after Blitz Week, Stuttgart, and Schweinfurt I, among missions with significant loss percentages when the Eighth did not have "massive quantities" of heavies on the hardstands, there being so many charred hulls on European farm fields. Even if VIII Bomber Command did have five hundred aircraft, they were by no means all at home airfields; the BADAs at Burtonwood, Warton, and Langford Lodge were busy day and night working on the Eighth's heavy bombers, many badly torn with battle damage from the first days of October.

Offered silently as proof that the Eighth was still a fighting force, on 20 October Eaker dispatched 282 heavies—212 B-17s and 70 B-24s—to strike industrial targets at Düren, in the close-in Ruhr Valley. Once again a solid cloud layer stretched from just above the surface to 29,500 feet, yielding abysmal results for VIII Bomber Command. At Duren the lead radar navigator was using the British OBOE system for the first time in Pathfinder aircraft; when it failed, 212 Fortresses aborted, save for 86 that hit the target blindly from above thirty-thousand feet. One group still managed to drop forty-two tons on Woensdrecht airfield in The Netherlands on the way home and another 11 Fortresses struck Aachen when they missed the primary. Two days later Eaker sent a three-page letter to Arnold telling of his intention to send a five-hundred-plane mission on a deep penetration mission to yet-to-be-named major targets in Germany, "the biggest force the Americans have ever sent against a German target." While massive destruction was always the primary purpose of any raid, this one was to have been a conspicuous counter to Nazi propaganda that the United States could not accept any losses inflicted by their defenses. Eaker intended the strike force to fly either four simultaneous attacks of at least one hundred aircraft each against separate targets or send eight wings composed of fifty-four heavies each to eight different targets listed on the CBO and "scattered through an arc of 90 degrees" because of how the OBOE system operated. All targets, whether four or eight or four thousand, would have of necessity been area targets just the same as those struck by the RAF—nonprecision area bombings—because OBOE was a navigation tool rather than a bombing aid, neither designed nor intended to be a precision-bombing tool.[41]

At Düren the doctrine of precision bombing was (again) defeated soundly by something as basic to flight as clouds. VIII Bomber Command flew no more missions in October after Düren. Central European weather patterns had prevailed against man.[42] OBOE was abandoned by VIII Bomber Command after mission 134 to Gelsenkirchen on 19 November because of perpetual equipment failure and given to the new Ninth Air Force, whose medium bombers working in the middle altitudes were much better suited to the system. VIII Bomber Command returned to the H2X radar in the PFF force which, while much more wide-area than precision, was better for high-altitude work.

RAF Bomber Command's Night Area Bombing Results

Without long-range fighter escorts to protect the bombers to targets deep in Germany and back, it was almost moot whether there would be enough of a bomber force remaining to conduct the missions essential to ensuring the success of the invasion of France planned for the next spring.[43] More important at this point, after Schweinfurt II it was questionable if the Allies were even going to make good on the requirement to clear the skies of the Luftwaffe by D-Day. The Eighth, after sixteen months of flying combat missions, "was far from achieving any of its goals and it was most certainly far from securing the skies over the D-Day beaches."[44] RAF Bomber Command was no further along either: Bomber Harris was destroying cities and killing many civilians, but it was pure serendipity whenever his bombers actually hit a militarily viable target. The damage done to the Luftwaffe and POINTBLANK targets by RAF night bombings was only a tiny percentage of what needed doing by this time. Factories required direct bomb hits to be destroyed or seriously damaged, which the area bombings rarely achieved, and with Speer and Göring dispersing the aircraft parts and assembly factories to the smaller burgs and towns, the RAF was missing them entirely. "Whatever else Schweinfurt II proved, as if it still needed proving, was that the bombers could *not* go it alone . . . [it] was a recogniztion hard to come by, because the opposite view had been held so long, sustained in part by Eaker's unyielding optimism [emphasis original]." Anderson bluntly told his wing commanders, "We can afford to come up only when we have our fighters with us."[45]

On November the first, limited deliveries began of the airplane that did what everybody said could not be done—the North American Aviation P-51 Mustang with the Rolls-Royce Merlin engine, the airplane Jack Slessor wanted to build in England in 1942.[46] It was episodes such as this that showed Arnold's practicality, his willingness to redirect his thinking on important issues to find solutions to critical problems.[47] Years later, Lieutenant General Ted Timberlake, Medal of Honor holder for Ploęsti, opined that "the major lesson of the war was the Eighth Air Force's overestimate of its major weapon, the B-17." Before the war, he continued, the "average air corps officer" would have laughed if he had been told it would require "repeated raids of 1,000–1,500 heavy bombers to put out a particular target." If Arnold had ever doubted the need for the P-51, it had evaporated after First Schweinfurt.[48]

Chapter 28

Autumn 1943

The Fifteenth Stands Up

The CCS gave their approval to create the Fifteenth Air Force on 22 October, cabling Eisenhower the authority to stand up the new strategic air force on 1 November.[1] The same day Arnold ordered the 15 heavy bomber groups to the Mediterranean: Eaker had now suffered the loss of over 40 strategic bombardment groups—160 individual squadrons plus reserves—either detached or diverted from his command in little more than a year. Eaker penned another five-page memorandum to the chief, succinctly enumerating once again six salient points in his favor: the principle of concentration of force favored England; of 113 key industrial targets in Germany, only 10 percent were within reach of Foggia; although the weather in Italy might be better than in England, it was the weather in the target area that really counted; the Eighth now utilized the H2X radar blind-bombing system, which obviated cloud cover issues at the target, a capability that did not exist in the Fifteenth; England had extensive maintenance/repair facilities and all-weather runways while Foggia was little more than a sea of mud and minimal repair capabilities; and finally, aircraft from Foggia suffering battle damage over the Third Reich still had to return over the high Alps while England was all "downhill" from Germany. Eaker closed the admittedly cogent arguments favoring the Eighth by asserting it was "axiomatic" that as a bomber force grows, "its loss rate goes down."[2] Perhaps Eaker's years in the military should have taught him that if anything was "axiomatic," it was that when stubbornness confronts impatience, what inevitably wins the day is whatever the boss wants. Eaker committed three sins with that cable: it was at least four pages too long, it repeated arguments that Arnold had already heard, and, worst of all, it came well after the chief had made his final decision. Arnold could not have been pleased to find a cable wishing to continue discussions on an issue that he firmly considered a closed matter occupying his inbox again.

In 1942 Eaker's new air force had been "a continuously pilfered piggy bank of aircraft and material" taken piecemeal to support TORCH or "borrowed" for operations like Ploęsti; now it was subjected to grand larceny so that "a complete and separate strategic air force—in essence, a competitor—could be built."[3] The difference in perspective between the two generals could not have been starker: Eaker's consideration was operational exigencies in fighting a one-theater war while Arnold's long-term objective was leveraging the Fifteenth Air Force as an argument for creating a strategic air commander over two theaters. Eaker looked for victory over an Allied enemy and what an additional fifteen heavy bomber groups could bring to that objective; Arnold thought of establishing strategic air power as a force independent from any theater control. If that were successful, the door to an independent air force would be kicked too far open to be closed. Eaker never understood Arnold, who might have avoided much of the tension and final consequences had he taken the time to explain the larger objectives to his air force commander; after all the discussions over the years on so many related issues, it's possible that Arnold assumed that Eaker understood his intent. If so, he must have been disappointed on this point, as Eaker never evinced a glimmer of comprehension. Regardless, Eaker would have been wise to have acceded to the inevitable, ceased complaining, and got on with the business of doing as much as he could with what he had. Once again, Eaker argued too much, too hard, and especially too long against a decision already made.

Let the Record Show . . .

Fred Anderson compiled pages of statistics for Eaker in October using data from the eighty-three missions flown from 1 April through 30 September, data that unmistakably highlighted steady improvement for VIII Bomber Command. Summarized, the heavies flew 9,603 sorties against eighty-three CBO targets plus another 835 sorties assigned or diverted to other targets, most often due to weather. Fifty-three of the eighty-three missions were considered "successful," a rate well within the CBO plan.[4] Results graded satisfactory or better once the weather was factored in indicated the missions had been accomplished with fewer bombers and crews than had been calculated beforehand as the minimum necessary to achieve the same results. Said differently, 22 percent fewer bombers and 37 percent fewer aircrews than the calculated bare minimum had taken the war to the Third Reich and done well indeed. Those figures did not encompass another 4,513 sorties flown against non-CBO targets, whether intentionally or as targets of opportunity. There was no way to determine how many missions could have been flown if the Eighth had not been periodically stripped of its heavy bombers. November 1943 found the Eighth with far fewer airplanes than had been promised in the spring of 1942; in the chief's office, though, the expectations for the Eighth had not lessened.

In December 1942, of 225 heavy bombers assigned to the Eighth, only 80 were operational, with 85 aircrews operationally qualified to fly them. Six months hence, July 1943, the numbers had effectively quadrupled, with 800 heavies in the inventory although still with fewer than half— 378 aircraft—operational and 315 aircrews combat qualified. But by the end of 1943, the numbers would be impressive: 1,630 heavies in the inventory, of which 842 aircraft and 1,113 aircrews were combat ready.[5] Eaker at last had his full-scale fighting force, despite the large losses in September over Münster, Stuttgart, and both Schweinfurts. The surge in numbers in the second half of 1943 were due to several reasons, including large numbers of men graduating from training commands, American industry approaching its maximum efficiency, and in England the ground crews of the Eighth gaining exceptional expertise about and knowledge of the airplanes, how to maintain them, and how to repair them.

Anderson was also able to demonstrate the destructive power inflicted on German targets by the Eighth by analyzing the growth of the strike forces and the progressive professionalism of the aircrews. The Eighth's first mission had put twelve B-17s against an undefended target barely 115 miles across the channel in such a recognizable location that the most novice of navigators could easily find it, and then achieving only modest results. Seven months later, mission 45 on 18 March 1943 struck inside the borders of the Third Reich when seventy-three unescorted heavies flew over 450 miles to the U-boat facilities at tiny Vegesack and dropped 76 percent of the bombs within one thousand yards of the aiming point under heavy attack. The final strike of 1943 would be flown on New Year's Eve Day when 464 bombers, escorted by 548 fighters, would drop 14,486 tons of bombs on four different targets in France.[6] By any standard General Eaker had made laudable progress, maybe more than a reasonable observer would have expected under the circumstances. The cumulative record was a chronicle of steady, if not lightning, growth accompanied by increasing proficiency and professionalism over a sixteen-month period.

The record of the Eighth Air Force by the end of 1943 under Eaker belied that of an air force commander desultory in the performance of his duties or hesitant to send missions into Germany; it limned a commanding general who performed well with the little he had and under less-than-ideal conditions. Most important, not once—not even when confronting the very fiercest of air battles with the Luftwaffe—did enemy action ever cause the men of the Eighth Air Force to abandon a mission; the men and airplanes never once turned back before dropping on the target. The record presents a fair argument that it was not Eaker's results or command decisions that necessarily brought about his relief.

During the same time period, Arnold was under tremendous pressures from innumerable sources: simply attempting to fulfill the thousands of requirements—for airplanes, matériel, leaders, thousands of officers, tens of thousands of enlisted men in hundreds of specialties, and on and on—presented by a dozen (and growing) overseas air forces from jungles and deserts to tundra and isolated locales, and everywhere in between, would have driven most men from office. Arnold spent at least sixteen hours a day trying to expedite everything from rivets to airplanes to mechanics and pilots while also having to correct problems so basic a sergeant could have resolved the issue. The commanding general of the AAF should not have been the individual to physically show, in his own office, an airplane manufacturer why it was, exactly, that one four-man life raft was unacceptable for an aircraft with eight crew members. But Arnold did exactly that, after which the manufacturer very quickly began equipping his airplanes with two five-man and one four-man rafts—an extra just in case one happened to be punctured.[7] While directing a global air war, Arnold pushed the airplane companies not only for the next iteration of a current plane but also for research and development into the next generation, like Bell Aircraft working on the first jet aircraft. And behind the curtain was always the B-29.

In the Pentagon on 9 October, the same day as the Eighth's heavy bombers raided Marienburg, General Arnold submitted a proposal to designate the Twelfth Air Force as a tactical command and send its few heavy groups to the Fifteenth as its strategic cadre. These, plus the fifteen heavy groups that Eaker was losing, would complete the Fifteenth.[8]

Eaker's Job on the Line

If one of the summer months was the time that Arnold began to seriously contemplate Eaker's replacement, by October his frustrations were impossible to hide. Although aircraft and aircrew availability had ceased to be a problem, marginal weather remained a serious impediment for the Eighth—as it did for any military air command operating from the British Isles. No matter how or how often Arnold cajoled, badgered, or directed him, Eaker was always conservative; although he later expressed comprehension of the pressures the chief faced every day, there were times with the Eighth that he was perhaps too focused on his own immediate circumstances. Eaker's prudence grew more than tiresome now; Arnold wanted him just to get on with the business of war. Eaker's lengthy letters and cables, which must have seemed endless as the chief's time became more in demand from myriad new sources, no doubt frustrated the boss, who would read no more than one page. Perhaps Eaker saying "no" too many times, or seemingly taking sides once too often with the

British against the air forces, or just being too negative and, thus, appearing as "can't do" finally became more than the chief was willing to tolerate, even from a friend and protégé. One can only speculate what Arnold thought upon learning that Eaker had tried an end run with Spaatz to keep the dialog open about the single air commander even though the British had rejected it and after Arnold had made his final decision to move forward, but it could not have been welcomed. More than anything else, though, Arnold had expected Eaker to achieve *something*, to find some way to bomb the enemy with as many airplanes as possible, regardless of impediments, rather than send repetitive cables saying why he could not. It may not have been the most rational expectation, but Arnold wanted something. But whatever it was he wanted, he did not get.

Chapter 29

Sextant

By departure date for the SEXTANT summits in the second week of November, General Arnold had accepted that Portal's "no" on British participation in the strategic air command would be the BCS's final word. Being then essentially a plan only for the reorganization of American forces, the British would not be positioned to thwart moves in that direction. Included in Arnold's paper for the JCS were discussions of and recommendations only for the future of four affected air forces, two strategic and two tactical—the Eighth, Ninth, Twelfth, and Fifteenth.

Summoned by the chief for a series of meetings earlier in October, Spaatz had landed at Gravelly Point on the ninth as Arnold was submitting the final draft of his strategic air command program to the JCS. Arnold also hand carried a copy to Harry Hopkins, who would sign and pass it onward to the president.[1] The proposal was rather simple for a decision that would directly affect roughly three hundred thousand men and upward of ten thousand airplanes. The Fifteenth Air Force would be activated as a strategic air force and the Twelfth would become, for a brief time, a headquarters-only unit until it could be converted into a tactical air force. These two US air forces, the strategic Fifteenth and the tactical Twelfth, would be distributed among the fourteen airfields in the Foggia complex along with the Mediterranean Allied Photographic Reconnaissance Wing. Both US air forces would fall, along with British, French, and other Allied units, under the command of the future Mediterranean Allied Air Force (MAAF) commander, although the Fifteenth would from time to time be tasked by the CCS to execute strikes on selected targets under the operational authority of the strategic air commander.

During the next ten days, Spaatz and Arnold engaged periodically in discussions over the bombardment groups assigned to the Fifteenth: Devers wanted them in England while Ike wanted them in Italy; neither of the generals wished to cede control of these strategic forces, which would happen should they be removed from his theater. Marshall was caught in the middle between his two theater commanders while Arnold held on to his own wild card, the new strategic air commander. The dispute was becoming heated to some extent as Eisenhower was still fuming over Arnold's refusal just a month earlier to give him more P-38s until later in the year and now Ike's well-known hot temper was approaching volcanic levels over possibly losing control of the strategic bombers. One point was crystal clear: if each of the theater commanders exercised full control over a strategic air force within their domain, then the whole point of an overall air commander would be obviated.[2] It fell to Harry Hopkins to put it succinctly to the president: "It is essential that there be one strategic air force and that our bombers not be frozen in either England, Italy, or Africa."[3] There was not much time during Spaatz's visit to Washington for him to talk with Arnold about the two-theater strategic air command proposal in and of itself, but presumably such was not necessary.[4] The two had been in agreement on this matter for most of a year, and there had been other opportunities during that time to delve into it further in personal meetings. When Spaatz left the Pentagon for Italy, he had one request: place the strategic command headquarters either in Italy or North Africa. Arnold wanted it in England, which settled that issue.

The Memorandum: December 1943

General Arnold was an oracle regarding the future of the air forces, as evident in a document formally issued by the JCS on 18 November 1943, while at sea onboard USS Iowa on the way to SEXTANT. With the imposing but unambiguous title "Integrated Command of US Strategic Air Forces in the European-Mediterranean Area," the memorandum recommended the establishment, as soon as 1 January 1944, of the United States Strategic Air Forces in Europe, with Spaatz as commanding general and charged with "the strategic direction of the US Strategic Air Forces." In this capacity General Spaatz would "assign missions" to the two strategic air forces while keeping the theater commanders apprised of these actions. Further, the commanding general would be required to coordinate his operations with those of RAF Bomber Command through the RAF chief of air staff.[5] Arnold had exposed Eaker to the general concept of the strategic air commander position in September when the two called on Harris and Portal during Arnold's trip to England. Now, in November, with the final draft in the hands of the JCS and Harry Hopkins, and previously conveyed to the BCS, everybody who mattered was now current with the precise details—except for General Eaker. Arnold deliberately did not notify Eaker either that the draft was finalized or that it was to be considered for final decision by the CCS at SEXTANT. This extraordinary, deliberate act of omission breached usual military protocol that required a general officer to be regularly informed when major decisions related to his command were pending and given the opportunity to participate in the process. Beyond protocol and professional courtesy, Arnold's lack of personal consideration to a friend and protégé of two decades was a sign of "Arnold's persistent dissatisfaction with the performance of the Eighth Air Force," just as had been his decision to accelerate the activation of the Fifteenth Air Force.[6] An alert Eaker, upon becoming aware of at least some of this, might have recognized the obvious, that he had lost the confidence of the chief. But he had been promoted to a rare third star just two months earlier by Arnold and his command doubled in size with the addition of the Ninth Air Force. Eaker may have heard nothing related to the strategic command, but he certainly knew whom to thank for his promotion and increased responsibility with administrative control of all USAAF personnel in the UK. He may surely be forgiven for having thought his job was secure.

Meeting on 17 November in Flag Country aboard the Iowa, the JCS concurred generally with the unity of command concept and offered several alternatives to be considered when faced with the future British reaction.

At the conclusion the service chiefs inserted into the documents an enclosure summarizing their thoughts and let it percolate overnight. Reconvening after a relaxing dinner and movie the previous evening, the chiefs and the president formally approved both Arnold's plan and Spaatz for command. The key lay with the last word of the document title, which was "Area," in the singular rather than the plural "Areas," despite the inclusion of two geographical regions. The core of the document was that all strategic air operations for the two theaters—as though within one geographic region— should be combined under one man. Otherwise the USAAF would soon find that its resources were strewn piecemeal throughout both theaters, its power attenuated proportionately. The resemblance to the Pacific was obvious for both the navy's fleets and the Twentieth Air Force, where the ocean's vastness and widely dispersed targets effectively precluded consolidation within individual theaters. With all forces under the control and authority of one commander, he could "move the mass of his air where it will be most effectively employed and use the rest to support the ground arm"—a crucial concern to army ground forces that required some mention in this plan to reassure, or at least mollify, them that their needs would be met. Air and ground forces comity was no small matter, for the new command would continue to take advantage of the excellent Allied air intelligence capabilities that had matured since 1939 and now included several thousand American officers plus two USAAF air reconnaissance groups with seven operational squadrons.[7] Of course, the Eighth Air Force's headquarters at High Wycombe would facilitate the excellent coordination that already existed between the two national strategic air forces.[8]

As Spaatz had been earlier informed, it was "Arnold's intention to ensure the Army Air Forces a position in Europe equal to the Royal Air Force Bomber Command under its independent-minded commander, Sir Arthur Harris."[9] Eaker, as he had many times in the past, was at this point was still siding with the British in their combined opposition to the creation of the new command, although Arnold was seemingly unbothered. With the US strategic command on equal footing with bomber command, it was foreseeable that Spaatz might receive a fourth star, which would elevate the American command to the level of bomber command in "prestige and stature." Although this maneuver over "prestige and stature" could be construed as a matter of ego to some, the plain fact was that there were now more American forces in Great Britain than British, and within just a matter of a few weeks the AAF would have four thousand more aircraft in the islands than the RAF did. In this respect, rank and stature did matter. To Arnold a four-star general in command would not only "reflect well on the AAF" but also allow the component air force commanders—Doolittle and Brereton in England, Cannon and Twining in Italy—to receive their third stars.[10] By early in 1944, the British were almost at the near-total depletion of their available national resources, especially their uncommitted manpower reserves, as well as their financial resources and so Americans would merit the command positions.

At home American efficiency in building and training a military of millions of men and thousands of women, the civilian population's effectiveness in transforming the nation's abundant natural resources into armed might, and the seemingly unlimited depth of its financial resources were just reaching full exploitation. American troops and airmen were showing they could outfight the Nazis and the Japanese concurrently, and Arnold was not about to play second fiddle to the British at this stage of the war. The ability of the USAAF to operate on a large, twin-theater scale while also conducting operations in the China-Burma-India and the southwest, central, and northern Pacific areas would make it impossible for any sentient being to argue for keeping the air forces as part of the army and against turning it into an independent service equal to the army and navy after the war's end. All the pieces were falling to place for Hap Arnold.

The final JCS at-sea discussion was held the next day, on the eighteenth, one day out from the Strait of Gibraltar and two days before docking at Oran, Algeria, where only slightly more than twelve months earlier a green, callow US Army and disjointed AAF had first landed to confront the combat-blooded Soldaten of the Afrika Korps. In that short period of time, the United States had built the second largest but most powerful and most effective military in the world. Perhaps because it was not expected to require much debate, Arnold's proposal was last on the agenda. General Marshall and the JCS each added a few cautionary comments. Marshall advised against raising the approval issue with the CCS until after the pending decisions (a) pertaining to a British proposal of a unified Mediterranean command, and (b) the naming of a supreme allied commander for all American and Allied forces fighting the Germans had been disposed of.[11]

The final plan received approval by the JCS and the president and was transmitted to the CCS plus the prime minister also on 18 November. All were familiar with the contents, beginning with the "Problem":

- a directive to ensure the most effective utilization of the USAAF's strategic bombing capabilities from all available European-Mediterranean bases in the accomplishment of POINTBLANK objectives.[12]

The advantages and modalities were addressed in "Conclusions":

- that control of all US strategic air forces in the European-Mediterranean area, including the control of movement of forces from one area to another, should be vested in a single command in order to exploit US heavy bomber aircraft capabilities most effectively; that these forces should be employed primarily against POINTBLANK objectives, or such other objectives as the CCS may from time to time direct; and that such a command should likewise be charged with the coordination of these operations with those of the RAF Bomber Command;
- that the responsibility for overall base service and administrative control of these strategic air forces should remain with the appropriate commanders of US Army forces in the United Kingdom and in the Mediterranean area;
- that provision should be made to assure the assignment of resources, supplies, and other services between tactical and strategic operations so as to bring the required support to POINTBLANK as the air operation of first priority;
- and that the headquarters of such US strategic air forces should be established in the United Kingdom because of the facilities available, the existing weight of the respective bomber forces, and the necessity for continuous integration of operations with the RAF.[13]

The paper's "Recommendation" to resolve the "Problem" was the CCS agreement to establish a "US Strategic Air Force Command" to be headquartered in England to conduct all "US Strategic Air Force operations in the European-Mediterranean area."[14] Several of the points in "Conclusions" could, with slight modification, be applied to the future 20th Air Force.

Cairo

Once in Cairo but before SEXTANT convened, the president and Harry Hopkins took some time off to assess the two generals under consideration for the two most important jobs in the European war: Eisenhower to command all the Allied forces and Spaatz as commander of the US Strategic Air Forces. While Roosevelt and Ike toured the ancient battlefield at Carthage, Spaatz hosted Mr. Hopkins at his headquarters, where the general was queried about his thoughts on the "entire war strategy" and specifically on the CBO. Regarding the CBO, Spaatz candidly opined that "once the weather cleared over Germany in April and May, thus allowing continuous operations from Britain and Italy, Germany would give up in three months. OVERLORD [Spaatz believed] was neither necessary nor desirable. From the point of view of air power, further gains in Italy would bring the bombers closer to Germany and represented a better investment in men and material than the cross-channel invasion."[15] Hopkins was a member of the "George Marshall school" that believed in the conclusions of the War Department's OPD, "which upheld the primacy of the cross-channel invasion over all other operations" and was far from convinced that Spaatz's view would eventuate. However, he appreciated "Spaatz's personality, sincere advocacy of air power, and determination to get the job done at any cost," qualities that sold the advisor on the taciturn general. Playing tourist with the president worked out for Eisenhower, too, but then Roosevelt had known him professionally and occasionally socially ever since the Second Washington Conference early in 1942; as the president had by this time decided against Marshall, it's difficult to imagine the president would have turned to another general. Beyond the necessary and perfunctory first meetings between Roosevelt and Spaatz, which would happen over dinner that evening and on the flight to Tunis the next day, the top two American generals responsible for the defeat of Hitler and the Third Reich had been chosen.[16]

The paper proposing the CCS create a strategic air force was surprisingly short given the authority and responsibilities that would befall the commanding general, its conciseness evidence of the many hours of thought and debate General Arnold must have had with the sharp minds on his advisory council. With British concurrence out of reach, the purpose and jurisdiction of the single air commander could be focused solely on the authorities General Spaatz would exercise when he took command. Of all that Arnold had in terms of duties and responsibilities at this moment, the strategic air commander would have been one of the top, along with the B-29. Arnold was so strongly committed to it, not only for the present need but also because it opened the door much wider to an independent air force in the future, that he had no interest in compromise. The British chiefs were left with but two choices: either fight approval, a battle that they were certain to lose, or acquiesce in dissent. After two days of internal discussions and document drafting, the British circulated their reply on 26 November, which began by stating unequivocally that they—meaning His Majesty's government and not simply the RAF—were "diametrically opposed" to the proposal. What followed was both an acquiescence and a dissent, acknowledging that "this proposal affects directly only US heavy bomber forces and we recognize the ultimate right of the United States Chiefs of Staff to decide the organization of US forces in any theater of operations." The British chiefs went on to say that they "felt bound, however, to record our view that the adoption of this proposal would entail serious disadvantages far outweighing any advantages to be derived from it."[17] The British concerns were consistent with those raised at every previous opportunity:

- the proposal would upset established, existing agreements and rules between the two forces;
- coordinating strikes from two theaters would be too difficult to achieve and result in "effort wasted";
- although moving bombers between theaters was "attractive," full benefit could not be achieved because of infrastructure and facilities limitations;
- and a "potential conflict of interest" could develop between the two governments over requirements necessary for the "transfer of force."

Although unwritten, the possibilities of "serious" disadvantages developing—meaning disadvantages to the British—was keenly felt by the British. The RAF especially perceived a threat to the "present arrangements for the close coordination" between the two services, entailing the RAF operational and support staffs and essential British government agencies (e.g., Air Ministry and those like the Ministry of Economic Warfare, etc.) located in close proximity or nearly so in the UK while the US forces would be spread out between two theaters. Further, the RAF maintained, the agreements at Casablanca would have to fall, as the direction of the US bombing effort would henceforth be "effected" in Washington, DC, vice London where it was at present. But this was blatantly a red herring, as the US "bombing effort" would still be "effected" from London by the CCS, and after D-Day the CBO would of necessity have to be discarded anyway for new joint targeting operations and agreements given that the focus would in part change from a strategic air war to a land campaign supported by tactical air power.

Back in Cairo the evening of 2 December following meetings with Soviet leader Josef Stalin (the EUREKA sessions) in Tehran, Arnold gathered his staff—Kuter, Vandenberg, and Hansell—to review his presentation for the 4 December CCS meeting. Arnold told the three, although they were doubtless familiar with the criticisms of Eaker already, that he "was not satisfied with the number of bombers being used in England out of the available total, or with the number of bombs being dropped on targets, since the objectives themselves were apparently not being destroyed."[18] Little import that the targets were often not destroyed because of small bomb sizes rather than number. That the Eighth had not yet been provided with the size and type of munitions it would ultimately take to destroy some of the harder targets was never the issue. Arnold intended to cite these arguments and more during the CCS meeting two days hence, weaving in the firing of Eaker in support of a unified strategic air command. The British would of course recognize the inaccuracies of more than a few justifications while also being aware that the Americans, with their seemingly unlimited resources, would soon correct the present physical limitations at the Foggia airfields.[19] But this was not the forum to engage on those issues.

At the 4 December meeting, soon-to-be Marshal of the RAF Sir Charles Portal, who remained as close a friend to the USAAF—and to Lieutenant General Ira Eaker—as any British officer would during the war, simply could not support Arnold any more than could the other British chiefs. Normally possessed of a temperament marked by composure, equanimity, and especially civility, on this day the discussions came "close to acrimony as Portal again expressed the RAF's objections" to Arnold's proposition. Portal first offered a point-by-point reclama to Arnold's list of advantages to be had by the creation of a single air commander. He then presented a spirited defense of his friend and colleague General Eaker, beginning by declaring that he did in fact comprehend why Arnold had come to his position, although pointedly stating that "the Eighth had done everything that was possible under the circumstances." Portal recounted that General Eaker had "done his utmost to keep his plan to schedule . . . [and] in spite of his smaller resources he had penetrated deep into Germany and accepted the consequent losses . . . in no other part of the world were our bomber forces up against some 1,600 German fighters over their own country." Portal expressed admiration for Eaker by highlighting that his record was "as satisfactory as possible without the full resources envisaged in the bomber plan . . . General Eaker had only some 75 percent of his full resources and was therefore achieving only some 54 percent of the results expected," but was also obliged to acknowledge that the Eighth's bombardment "program was, in fact, some three months behind." Concluding, Portal was not just unable but also manifestly unwilling to support the American proposal.[20]

Arnold recognized the unchanging British stance about an Allied air force and one supreme Allied air commander, officially abandoning the pursuit of both.[21] He then proceeded to levy an aggressive rebuttal to Portal's arguments, a good part of which was constructed around one overarching point of attack: sustained criticism of his subordinate and protégé, placing Eaker in almost the worst light possible. Arnold made clear that he wanted a "new commander divorced from day-to-day routine" at the helm of the Eighth as Eaker's "intolerable failure" made his continuance as commanding general unacceptable. Arnold asserted that General Eaker had shown a "lack of flexibility in operations despite numerous inspections and reports," leaving the Eighth with only a "50 percent availability rate." This was, he argued, unacceptable "in an industrialized country"—especially when rates of other units in "primitive locales" were 60 and 70 percent. In fact, he continued, Eaker had failed to dispatch up to 70 percent of his force on a regular basis, despite having the ability to do so; he had "dispatched only one 600 aircraft operation" in the thirty days of November, and the Eighth's "failure to destroy targets was due directly to the failure to employ planes in sufficient numbers." Arnold wanted a more aggressive commander, one who would put up "more and larger missions, even in pernicious weather, and one who had a greater sense of urgency about the need for long-range fighter escorts. Arnold was particularly angered by Eaker's decision to launch only two very large missions, with over 500 bombers, against Germany in the entire month of November."[22] There was more. Arnold alleged that "the proper priority of targets" was not being followed and bomb loads had been too light, overlooking the basic fact that the farther away the target, the more the fuel/bomb load tradeoff favored the former. Arnold asserted anew that the "failure to destroy targets was due directly to the failure to employ planes in sufficient numbers. . . . Training, technique, and operational efficiency must all be improved. . . . Only a new commander divorced from day-to-day routine could achieve this."[23] Arnold found those failures "to be intolerable."[24]

Such criticism of a subordinate by a service chief, especially of an officer well known to, very well-liked by, and most important highly respected by each of the British officers present, must have been shocking to all, even the Americans. As Portal's comments had indicated, he possessed intimate knowledge of Eaker's and the Eighth's circumstances. Most insulting, perhaps, Arnold's blistering criticisms were a clashing breech of protocol: it has never been acceptable, in military service, to severely criticize a subordinate before others, especially before members of another service and particularly so openly before allies. Arnold's behavior far exceeded mere impoliteness; all Arnold needed to say was that it was time for a change at the top and the British, as well as the Americans, would have found that acceptable. Only Arnold would know why he chose to attack Eaker's reputation as he did, but it was arguably unnecessary, especially given the positive light in which the Eighth's commander was held by the Allies.

At the conclusion of Arnold's remarks, none present needed to be told that Eaker would not be retaining his position. Arnold assured Portal that coordination and cooperation with the RAF would continue, regardless of "any future changes" and then presented one final criticism of his former protégé. "At present, the necessary drive and ideas" were coming from Washington (i.e., from his office), which would have been a surprise to General Fred Anderson at VIII Bomber Command. The chief reiterated that more aircraft were being sent to the UK than were being effectively used and "unless better results could be achieved no more planes should be sent."[25] After more than fourteen months of practically begging for more aircraft while seeing nearly 40 promised groups—almost 160 squadrons and over 5,000 individual heavy bombers—taken away for another theater, this might have been more hurtful to Eaker personally than almost anything else that could have been said.

Portal, "dignified though deeply indignant" and no doubt seeking to provide some defense of Eaker, who had been a loyal and true colleague as well as a stalwart friend, responded that any commander "who insisted on keeping the bomber force rigidly to a program" would "undoubtedly" have flown even fewer missions and that he—Air Chief Marshal Portal—"for one could never permit his own fighters to escort bombers on missions that he did not believe to be sound." Before Portal could go further or the exchange deteriorated further, General Marshall, always as much diplomat as soldier, seized the floor. Speaking with his usual eloquence, clarity, and calmness of voice and character, he said that he "believed" that daylight precision bombing was being conducted by the USAAF not only in Europe "but from bases all over the world." And that in those other locales, "twice the results" were being obtained—but left unsaid was that the weather almost everywhere else was also at least twice as good, especially the two huge theaters of the southwest and central Pacific, each with over 330 flying days a year. Continued Marshall, "Flexibility of thought and imagination were required. . . . A huge force could not be allowed to collect in the UK unless it was employed to the maximum possible extent." Even if the two strategic air forces were not "integrated," opined the army chief of staff, that one single commander, based in England, "who could give full consideration to the many problems involved and impart the necessary drive" was nonetheless still "required." The general then recommended that further discussion on this subject be "deferred to provide additional time to consider the views put forward by Sir Charles and General Arnold."[26]

On Tuesday, 7 December 1943, two years after Pearl Harbor, the CCS reconvened for the final time at this conference, with but one agenda item before them: a document titled "Integrated Command of US Strategic Air Forces in the European- Mediterranean Area."[27] Only three American principals were present: Generals Marshall and Arnold and Admiral King. Among the "Also Present" was Major General Richard K. Sutherland (General MacArthur's chief of staff) and, from Arnold's staff, Major General Muir S. Fairchild and Brigadier General Haywood S. Hansell Jr. Air Chief Marshal Portal spoke but briefly. He began by reminding all that the British chiefs' views were well known and there was nothing to add. The British "could not signify their approval of the proposals but recognized the right of the United States Chiefs of Staff to issue such directives to their own air forces as they might see fit." He added that if the measure were approved, for his part he was "prepared to accept the responsibilities" that might be required and would carry them out to the best of his abilities. Arnold, in response, said only that he was "anxious to implement the proposals as soon as possible" and that he would have further discussions with Marshal Portal.[28] And so it was done. Now Arnold was obligated, by position as commanding general of the AAF, if not also by professional courtesy and custom, to inform his decades-long friend and protégé that he was being dismissed from command of the Eighth. Whether Arnold had previously given much thought about how to tell Eaker about his relief, the time for that was now.

In a "Discussion" addendum to the final SEXTANT meeting memorandum, the JCS began with a statement that they "consider the air war in Europe" has reached the point where "command direction over the components of the Strategic Air Forces is imperative" and concluded, "The one effective method is to insure the rapid, coordinated employment of the two components of our daylight striking force on a day-to-day basis, in order to take advantage of weather conditions in the United Kingdom and in the Mediterranean. Unified command over the Eighth and Fifteenth US Air Forces must, therefore, be established without delay."[29] A few more minor points were touched upon, but the JCS had made clear the crux of the matter and intended to say no more. The paper concluded with an appendix, a draft of a proposal to give the Americans the final item of Arnold's wish list—an inclusion of the verbiage "Lieut. General Carl Spaatz is designated Commanding General, US Strategic Air Forces in Europe."[30]

Chapter 30

Eaker to the Mediterranean

The morning of 8 December, Arnold flew to Sicily for a meeting with President Roosevelt and Generals Eisenhower, Walter Bedell "Beetle" Smith (Eisenhower's chief of staff), and Spaatz. The generals had flown to the island with the president in his modified C-54, the thought of which must have given those who knew of it a great deal of pause. While Spaatz and the president used the occasion to become better acquainted ("another job interview," thought Spaatz), Arnold solicited approval from Ike and Bedell Smith for Spaatz as the air commander. Both were solidly in favor, much preferring the "known and friendly quantity" of Spaatz, a general with whom they had by now worked closely for a year and who, conversely, knew the needs and overarching intentions of the ground commanders— which Eisenhower and Smith knew would be essential once the Allies were ashore on the Continent. While neither general, by their own admissions, comprehended the need for a strategic or supreme air commander or what it was he was to do, they were more than supportive of Spaatz serving in that amorphous position. Both Ike and Beetle spoke generously of the airman, with Ike adding that he "wouldn't take anyone else, not even Tedder" in place of Spaatz.[1] Arnold soon thereafter obtained the final approval of the president, who had not only his own recent opportunities to become acquainted with "Ike's airman" but also the presumed endorsement of Harry Hopkins, whose opinion was paramount.[2]

The morning of the ninth, Arnold and Spaatz flew to Foggia, where they were joined by generals Jimmy Doolittle, Joe Cannon, and Edward J. House, and Colonel Rosie O'Donnell of Arnold's advisory council, to review the conclusions and decisions of SEXTANT. At dinner that evening, with Arnold as guest of honor and all but O'Donnell present, a discussion centered on "personnel to be utilized in the new set-up [single air commander]" with Spaatz stating his intention to take his staff from Northwest African Air Force to England with him and "repeated again" that he did not want his new headquarters to be in England (and again he lost). Spaatz then pushed Doolittle for the Eighth, certain that Eisenhower would enthusiastically welcome Doolittle in England—and in this he was correct. The absent Louie Brereton received Spaatz's vote to remain as head of the Ninth Air Force, although Portal had hinted strongly the British would gladly accept Nate Twining sight unseen in lieu of Brereton. Cannon received Spaatz's vote for commander of the Twelfth Air Force and to head the Allied North African Tactical Air Force.[3] Spaatz suggested to Arnold that Eaker become commander of the MAAF, a position of significantly greater responsibility than the Eighth.[4]

The chief may have been puzzling over Eaker's future, although at the moment he seemed consumed by other matters. But at some point he must have realized that sending Eaker home as an officer who had failed in his job would be out of the question, even without a demotion. The chief may have been angry and frustrated with Eaker's performance, but there were many senior officers and high-ranking civilians like Robert Lovett and Averell Harriman, American and Allied both, who strongly disagreed with Arnold on this. One officer who would not have accepted demeaning treatment of Eaker was Carl Spaatz. While in command of the Eighth, Spaatz had experienced the same "frustrating and peculiar weather conditions in England and Western Europe" as well as the initial diversions of heavy bombers to North Africa. Moreover, Spaatz "believed in Ira Eaker's great ability, especially as a military diplomat, and wanted him in the Mediterranean to advance the war effort and the AAF's cause."[5] Devers was also a strong supporter of Eaker's, although Arnold paid the armor officer little heed. On 15 December Devers would write to Eaker, praising the latter's "leadership" and the "fighting, ruthless, daring attacks" of the Eighth. Devers assured Eaker that when the weather gave the chief a break "suitable to see the target, I am sure even Arnold in his ignorance will be convinced."[6]

Once Spaatz had learned that Air Chief Marshal Sir Arthur Tedder, the present air officer commanding-in-chief, Mediterranean Air Command, was departing with General Eisenhower as his deputy for OVERLORD, and that a senior, combat-experienced flag officer was needed for a replacement, he was certain that Arnold would realize the post was perfect for Eaker.[7] Eaker was a lieutenant general who had taken the Eighth from a unit with just seven officers to an enormous organization of two hundred thousand men and women in just eighteen months and was bombing deep into Germany despite all of the diversions to North Africa and elsewhere. He may not have done it the way Arnold would have done it had the latter been the commander, but that did not mean that he had failed. It meant only that Arnold would have done it differently and perhaps not as well. And, too, the move to the Mediterranean would be a promotion, as Eaker would be commanding not one air force but collectively two American air forces, two RAF air forces, several smaller national air arms, a large, multinational PR wing with over a half dozen specialized reconnaissance squadrons from six nations, and a fully integrated photo-interpretation center, plus all the supporting ground units from US and European services.

Arnold had savaged—there is no other word for it—Eaker's efforts in the leadership of the Eighth at SEXTANT before his strongest supporters, although he must have been aware of how favorably Eaker stood in the eyes of these and other important men, American and British. Arnold never explained why he was so openly critical of Eaker when much less was required to direct a change; Arnold was, after all, the commanding general of the AAF in addition to chief of staff and could change out commanders for any logical reason. But at some point he had to have realized that Eaker needed a suitable follow-on position equal to the three-star rank that Arnold had bestowed on him just three months earlier, and Spaatz's thoughts about the benefit of having Eaker in command of the MAAF evidently struck the right chord.

Spaatz's suggestion may have been a creation of the moment, but perhaps not. Back in February, when Eisenhower was commander of the Allied forces in northwest Africa and attempting to instill some measure of order in the mishmash of Allied air combat units, he had "made a startling request" in the opinion of General Andrews at ETOUSA. In a cable on 17 February, Ike had written to Andrews, saying, "We are anxious to provide a qualified American deputy commander for Tedder, who is Commander-in-Chief for all Mediterranean air forces, and believe that Eaker is most suitable man in sight for such position." Spaatz surfaced the idea also to Bedell Smith who was unhappy—as was Ike—with the air command structure and touted Eaker as the ideal "high powered Air Force officer" to work under Tedder. Spaatz had not yet come to trust Tedder's ambitions and loyalty but "knew that he and Ira working together would assure a strong US air presence" as something of a brake on the RAF commander. Eisenhower proffered "a trade": Eaker for Doolittle, whom Ike described as "essentially a man of action" and who had, in Ike's eyes, become in that short period of time "a highly qualified commander of an American Air Force." Ike closed the cable touting the swap as something that would "work for the benefit of the whole." Eaker, quite naturally, was less than enthused by the idea but no less so than Andrews, who needed in England at the time "an air commander whom the British knew and liked and whom he knew possessed keen organizational and administrative abilities." In short, he needed Eaker. Andrews cabled Eisenhower and asked him to withdraw the request. Ike did.[8]

Now Spaatz again had the opportunity to take care of both Eaker and the newly reorganized MAAF by arguing for Eaker to move to the Mediterranean as its commander. Spaatz certainly knew that he could work well with Doolittle in England and that Eisenhower, holding complete confidence in the Spaatz-Doolittle team, had no desire to break it up when he was planning the most crucial event of the century. Arnold must have recognized this was the answer to a potentially thorny problem, for he quickly agreed. But he then undermined the positive aspects of the assignment in the unmistakable manner in which he first delayed notification to Eaker and then sent it in a cold, impersonal cable devoid of any cordiality or personal feelings. It was a far different style from the polite but friendly and personal style that was a hallmark of his correspondence with his generals and friends.

Arnold flew home the morning of the tenth, leaving Spaatz to contend with pressing local issues. Tooey was, after all, still the commanding general of NAAF with the Mediterranean air war to fight while preparing to hand it to a replacement. Meanwhile, in England Eaker had no idea that he was to be replaced at the head of the Eighth. He learned of the chief's breach of protocol before the CCS when meeting with Portal on the fourteenth; the RAF chief inquired if had any responses to his boss's criticisms. Portal then cabled Arnold with the substance of his conversation with Eaker, pointing out that Eaker was "thoroughly alive to the need" to energetically attack POINTBLANK targets with "maximum force available." Portal gave assurances that Arnold would "see great achievements as soon as the weather gives him a chance."[9] Arriving in Washington, DC, on 15 December, Arnold discovered that Ruth Eaker was in hospital with a mild case of pneumonia. The chief cabled Eaker on the sixteenth and seventeenth with reports on Mrs. Eaker but wrote not a word either time about the new job in the Mediterranean.

Eaker was, hence, literally stunned when he received word of his removal on 19 December, two weeks after the CCS meeting.[10] The eyes-only cable "was an absolute bolt from the blue," not only because of his removal but at least as much by the cold, dispassionate style in which it was written. Drafted in impersonal bureaucratic style, the cable in part read, "Conference at SEXTANT provided for changes in command of Mediterranean Theater and a commander for OVERLORD. If existing slate goes through there will be a vacancy in the Mediterranean Air Command. It has been decided that an American will take over Command of Allied Air Force in the Mediterranean position now held by Tedder. As a result of your long period of successful operations and the exceptional results of your endeavors as Commander of Air Force in England you have been recommended for this position."[11] There followed a brief summary of the command changes approved by the CCS for both the European and Mediterranean theaters and concluded by asking Eaker who he would like to have for his deputy "if the above goes through."[12] Eaker was extremely hurt, believing that his removal was "grossly unfair" and left feeling "let down" not only over his removal—which he, if no one else, saw as being fired—but also because it was contrary to the earlier promise Arnold had given to him, that "if I am ever dissatisfied [with your performance], you will be the first one to hear of it and it will come from me direct."[13] Parton believes that if Arnold had been "thoughtful or considerate enough" to have kept that promise and explained to Eaker in a personal letter all the "positive" aspects of the move, Eaker would have accepted it, no matter how unhappy he would have been about leaving the Eighth.[14] But both promise and personal note were ignored or disregarded by Arnold. Others later excused Arnold, who may have believed his lengthy run of criticisms for a year or more had given Eaker plenty of warning that he was skating on thinner and thinner ice,[15] and not only over the number of bombers dispatched and the missions per month, but also because of other unmentioned contretemps. Or, perhaps, Arnold had simply become tired of Eaker's constant arguing with him.

Instead, Eaker learned of his transfer in the most disinterested manner possible, in an impersonal cable lacking any sense of friendship.[16] Coffee, a former Eighth Air Force pilot, maintains without providing evidence that Arnold really "tried to break the news gently . . . but he was a victim of his notorious inability to convey bad news gracefully."[17] Eaker wanted very much to remain in England, to finish the war where he had begun it, telling Arnold the next day that it was "heartbreaking to leave just before the climax."[18] While Arnold wished to inject new blood into the direction of the Eighth, and not discounting the differences that he had with Eaker, the chief did think Eaker was a sound choice for the MAAF assignment. Moreover, Spaatz did as well, and Eaker had no reason to distrust the word of his closest friend. For a deputy Eaker selected Air Marshal Jack Slessor.

Attempting to hold on to his command of the Eighth, Eaker immediately remonstrated strongly, sending cables to every senior military or civilian officer he thought might plead his cause. General Arnold was not moved, despite their decades-old friendship; Devers, Lovett, Ambassador Winant, and retired General James Fechet all assured Eaker he was the best officer for the Mediterranean position.[19] Eaker also asked both Spaatz and Eisenhower to intercede with Arnold, prompting Spaatz to write an immediate cable to the chief explaining that Eaker wished to stay with the Eighth, providing that was "acceptable" to Spaatz. Before answering Eaker, he wished Arnold to review the text of his (Spaatz's) response, which was mostly a reiteration of his earlier expressed opinions—namely, "[I] believe that best interests of the war effort, so far as the American Air Forces are concerned, necessitate your assignment as Air Commander in this Theater. I consider it essential because of close relationships with other services and nationalities in both theaters and for other reasons that American Air rank and experience be distributed between UK and Mediterranean."[20] Spaatz expressed the point that command of an air force was of lesser importance than the "overall requirements" to be found in the Mediterranean and closed by mentioning that the Eighth was going to be modified into an "operational headquarters" similar to VIII Bomber Command, implying that remaining at the Eighth would be beneath him both personally and as a three-star.[21]

That correspondence did not end the matter. Two days before Christmas, following the War Department's announcement of the forthcoming command changes, Spaatz discussed Eaker's assignment with Bedell Smith. Smith told of "strong objections" arising in some circles over Eaker's transfer, to which Spaatz reacted very strongly: "I told him that unless this is done, I would not consider the overall Strategic Command with headquarters in UK" and that Eisenhower was at that moment preparing a cable to General Marshall saying precisely that. Both Spaatz and Ike were highly concerned about the absence of a very senior American officer in the Mediterranean command and remained convinced that Eaker was the perfect officer to command MAAF. Spaatz fretted that Arnold may have weakened the original recommendation for Eaker to Marshall: "Feel that Arnold has slipped out from his original decisions so that he has not stated them firmly to Marshall but has thrown it all into the lap of Eisenhower."[22]

Which raises the question, Did Arnold try to disassociate himself from Eaker's assignment to MAAF after criticizing him at SEXTANT with such personal venom? Regardless, Spaatz expressed his personal thoughts about Ike, saying, "My original estimation of Eisenhower's fairness has been strengthened by the way in which he is taking this, and the way he is standing by me in my decisions."[23] In additional exchanges with Marshall, Ike remained insistent that his recommendations were sound. On Christmas Day Ike cabled Eaker to tell him that he would be "delighted" to have the airman in England with him but he supported his assignment in the Mediterranean because "of the absolute necessity of finding an outstanding man for the post of air king." Further, Eisenhower informed Eaker that it would "be a waste to have both you and Spaatz in England . . . [for] both of you I have the highest regard and feel quite frankly that if Spaatz goes to England as commander of the American Strategic Air Force, an assignment which leaves me somewhat puzzled both as to purpose and position, then you should come here." Eisenhower concluded by telling Eaker that he should remain in England only if Spaatz would stay in the Mediterranean; otherwise concentrating both generals in one locale was inadvisable as "we do not repeat not have enough top men."[24] At day's end Eaker went off to the Mediterranean command where, excellent soldier that he was, he set about doing the utmost in his new position to win that part of the war. But he "never got over the humiliation of being replaced and of the way he had been initially notified."[25]

Between 21 and 26 December, cables flew back and forth across the Atlantic. On the twenty-first, Arnold finally wrote personally to Eaker about the difficulties of leaving an organization that "has been built and most successfully operated under ones personal direction." After a somewhat lengthy justification for the move, the chief closed by sending his "heartfelt thanks for the splendid cooperation and loyalty" and then emphasized one more time that he "could not see my way clear to make any change in decisions already reached." Also on the twenty-first, Arnold wrote a short cable to Devers reflecting the near-absence of friendship between the two. He opened saying that all the reasons that Devers gave for Eaker staying in England are the same for "why he should go to the Mediterranean." Following another sentence about loyalty and confidence, Arnold concluded, "CANNOT agree with you that a change of commanders would be disastrous at this time. . . . Inconsistent with your viewpoint but move is necessary from world-wide air operations." On the twenty-fourth Eaker wrote Arnold, "Orders received and will execute promptly 1 January." On the twenty-sixth Arnold wrote his now former protégé to wish him good luck and congratulate him again for the "record of the 8th [*sic*] achieved through your resourceful leadership." But perhaps most meaningful, to outsiders at least, would have been the closing: "Your new assignment in replacing such an outstanding RAF airman as Tedder pays tribute to your talents. . . . Good luck and best wishes."[26] Indeed.

On Eaker's last day of command, Jake Devers penned a "Dear Ira" letter, noting that the "story of aerial combat in this Theater is one to which all of America will always point with pride." In short paragraphs Devers mentioned the rise of the Eighth from a "small, depleted organization to a mighty force," asserted the "menace of the U-boat is almost conquered," and, praising Eaker personally, called his leadership "inspiring" and extolled the "great accomplishments" of the Mighty Eighth, especially the "reduction in strength of the German Air Force." Importantly, Devers took time to applaud Eaker's leadership "behind the actual combat flying" with the "establishment of training centers, replacement depots, rest homes, and air bases." The general closed with a genuinely heartfelt "Very Sincerely Yours."[27]

Chapter 31

Aftermath

Business as Usual for the Eighth

Throughout SEXTANT Fred Anderson at PINETREE kept the heavies flying what missions it could, given the usual weather patterns over central Europe. Anderson had put up eleven missions during November: eight to Germany (none were deep penetrations), two to Norway, and one to France. Mission 130 of 13 November was of the kind that gives nightmares for decades thereafter. An initial 272 heavies from all three bombardment divisions were dispatched to Bremen as a primary, with secondaries in the Kiel-Flensburg area. Flown in the usual abysmal weather, the cloud cover over the British Isles was so appalling that the 1st Division Forts simply could not assemble and so aborted, save for two that somehow escaped the milling mess, broke away on singleton missions, and dropped on targets of opportunity after miraculously finding cracks in the clouds. Most of 126 aircraft from the 2nd and 3rd Divisions managed to assemble after a fashion and head for the North Sea. They found Bremen protected by a cloud bank solid from the surface to twenty-five thousand feet, so most aircraft dropped instead on whatever targets of opportunity they thought they might be over once they found openings in the cloud layer. The German weather was the cause of two collisions between heavies, with more downed near Bremen by antiaircraft fire and Focke-Wulfs. Even before crossing the channel, two Forts had crashed during assembly at a cost of seventeen aircrew; another Fortress had to be abandoned after takeoff because of an in-flight fire; two more Fortresses collided over the North Sea, although all aircrew were saved; yet another pair of B-17s ran into each other over Bremen; and one Liberator crashed upon returning to England while a second merely crash-landed. Forty-five P-38s and 345 P-47s gave the escort mission their very best, but seven Lightnings and three Thunderbolts were shot down by very good Luftwaffe pilots. In return the Americans claimed seven FW-190s and two JU-88s in "running battles" across the Netherlands to Bremen. The final act was two more P-38s DBR after crash-landing at home. All fighters were badly affected by severe winds aloft, reducing range and rendering dog-fighting a supreme test of skill or luck, but mostly both. Bomber casualties were 21 KIA, 26 WIA, and 162 MIA, while the fighter squadrons suffered 9 MIA.[1] The other ten missions of November were walks in the park by comparison.

Eighth heavies flew ten missions in December. Seven were shallow penetrations into Germany, to old targets like Bremen and newer sites of Ludwigshafen, Solingen, and Osnabruck. Fortresses and Liberators struck three times in France, once at CBO targets around Bordeaux and Paris, and twice to hit NOBALL targets—launching sites for the V-1 "Buzz Bomb" near the channel coast. The raids were part of Operation CROSSBOW, the project codename for infrastructure, support, research, supply, and laboratory facilities for the vengeance weapons programs. Unsurprisingly, NOBALL and CROSSBOW soon were incorrectly used interchangeably.

In the final days of 1943, General Spaatz returned to England to stand up the United States Strategic Air Forces in Europe on 1 January 1944.[2] While the prospective commanding general was en route, the chief of the AAF drafted a letter on 27 December that would finally catch the general moving once again into WIDEWING: "You know my apprehension over our not destroying the German Air Force. I believe that we must use every effort to secure the maximum use of our tremendous air power—an airpower so vastly superior to that of the Germans. Without destroying the

German Air Force, we can never secure the maximum benefits of our Air Force in their operations against objectives assigned. As a matter of fact, we may reach a stalemate in the air. Hence, we must destroy the German Air Force in the factories, depots, on the ground, or in the air, wherever they may be."[3] Spaatz's reply was, as usual, short, direct, and to the point; it could be summed up in two words: I understand.

Postscript

Lieutenant General Ira Clarence Eaker was honored at a last dinner on 7 January of the new year by the RAF's most senior persons—Marshal of the RAF Portal and Air Chief Marshal Harris among the most senior, the prickly Harris having long ago thought of Eaker and his family as the very dearest of friends. Two hundred guests were present to say Godspeed to quite possibly the best liked and most respected American in the country. Quietly informed by Portal that "Colonel Holt" desired to see him on his way through North Africa, Eaker soon learned this was the pseudonym under which the PM traveled when abroad. That evening Churchill was in Marrakesh and of course Eaker would be pleased to drop in on the morrow. He departed England the next morning with an RAF color guard and band rendering honors. The final farewells were delivered in person by Air Chief Marshal and Lady Harris in a rare display of from-the-heart sincerity. Following a half-hour chat later in the day in Morocco, the PM, recovering from pneumonia, told Eaker that he understood his disappointment at leaving the Eighth, but added,

> I want to remind you that we're entrusting to you two of our favorite British units, the Balkan Air Force and the Desert Air Force. If we didn't have great faith in you we wouldn't have placed them in your charge. You'll also have RAF Coastal Command, the French Air Forces, and your very own considerable Twelfth and Fifteenth Air Forces. All in all, it will be a much larger command, with more responsibilities, than you had in the United Kingdom. The prediction you made to me in Casablanca last February about our combined bomber missions, including "round the clock bombing," are now being verified. I no longer have any doubt that they will prove completely valid.[1]

General Eaker received countless letters of appreciation, friendship, and gratitude after his departure from England, but the note from Brigadier General Curtis E. LeMay said all that needed to be said: "You are missed here. While you may be absent in body, the spirit of Eaker rides in every bomber to Germany."[2]

Endnotes

Notes for the Preface

1. The US Census Bureau in 2018 found only 14 percent of Americans had ever worn the military uniform. United States Bureau of the Census, *Those Who Served: America's Veterans from World War II to the War on Terror* (Washington, DC, June 2020), 4.
2. Donald L. Miller, *Masters of the Air: America's Bomber Boys Who Fought the Air War against Nazi Germany* (New York: Simon & Schuster, 2006), 199. Major General Lewis Lyle, USAF (Ret.), is a former director of the National Museum of the Mighty Eighth Air Force.
3. Robert S. Ehlers Jr. (Colonel, USAF [Ret.]), *BDA: Anglo-American Air Intelligence, Bomb Damage Assessment and the Bombing Campaigns against Germany, 1914–1945*, (PhD diss., Ohio State University, 2005), 4.
4. In the first year, a damaged bomber would be transferred to a base air depot for repairs, where it might sit for weeks. Group mechanics at home airfields soon learned to make many depot-level repairs locally to avoid losing an aircraft to a lengthy downtime.
5. Bureau of the Census, *Those Who Served*, 4.
6. Curtis E. LeMay (General, USAF [Ret.]) with McKinley Kantor, *Mission with LeMay: My Story* (Garden City: Doubleday and Company, Inc., 1965), 227.

Notes for Chapter 1

1. Thomas H. Greer, "Appendix 2: Redesignation of the Army Air Arm, 1907–1942" in *The Development of Air Doctrine in the Army Air Arm, 1921–1941* (Washington, DC: Office of Air Force History, 1985).
2. Karl R. Schrader, *A Giant in the Shadows: Major General Benjamin Foulois and the Rise of the Army Air Service in World War I* (Maxwell AFB, AL: Air University Press, 2013), 28.
3. Carroll V. Glines (Colonel, USAF [Ret.]), "In Pursuit of Pancho Villa," *Air & Space Forces Magazine*, February 1, 1991, https://www.airandspaceforces.com/article/0291villa/.
4. Glines, "Pancho Villa."
5. Greer, *Development of Air Doctrine*, 149.
6. Schrader, *Giant*, 48.
7. Carman P. Felice (Major, USAF), "The Men and Machines, Part V: Air Operations in World War I," *Air Power Historian* 5, no. 1 (January 1958): 37, 42.
8. Schrader, *Giant*, 50, 68, 76.
9. Schrader, *Giant*, 75.
10. Felice, "Air Operations," 38, 41.
11. Felice, "Air Operations," 37. The Eighth Air Force required eight months to go from concept to the first B-17 strike in German-occupied France. In both instances the US military's lack of preparedness for war was evident.

12. Felice, "Air Operations," 39.
13. Felice, "Air Operations," 39–40.
14. While initially desirous of finding one airplane, as a matter of economy, that could perform the three necessary missions—observation, pursuit, and bombardment—it "quickly gave rise to specialization"; Felice, "Air Operations," 39.
15. Schrader, *Giant*, 77.
16. Air Force Historical Research Agency (AFHRA), *The Birth of the United States Air Force*, 9 January 2008, 2; Schrader, *Giant*, 88.
17. Bruce C. Hopper, PhD, "American Day Bombardment in World War I," *Air Power Historian* 4, no. 2 (April 1957): 88–97. Hopper flew Caudron bombers with the Armée de l'Air before the arrival of the Americans. He then joined the 96th Aero Squadron, ending the war with more bombing missions than any other American pilot. In World War II, he was unit historian for the US Strategic Air Forces in Europe under General Spaatz, a former squadron mate.
18. Hopper, "Day," 88–89, 91, 96–97.
19. Felice, "Air Operations," 50.
20. Felice, "Air Operations," 52.
21. Felice, "Air Operations," 52–53.
22. Greer, *Doctrine*, 14.
23. Greer, *Doctrine*, 15.
24. Malcolm Gladwell, *The Bomber Mafia: A Tale of Innovation and Obsession* (Dublin: Penguin Books, 2022), 33–34.
25. Conrad C. Crane, *American Airpower Strategy in World War II: Bombs, Cities, Civilians, and Oil* (Lawrence: University Press of Kansas, 2016), 15–17.
26. This paragraph is a distillation of various ideas on postwar air bombardment theory. Stephen L. McFarland, *America's Pursuit of Precision Bombing, 1910–1945* (Washington, DC: Smithsonian Institution Press, 1995), 23–24, 76–80; Kenneth P. Werrell, "The Strategic Bombing of Germany in World War II: Costs and Accomplishments," *Journal of American History* 73, no. 3 (December 1986): 4; Michael M. Trimble (Major, USAF), "Air Force Strategic Bombing and Its Counterpoints from World War I to Vietnam," *Joint Force Quarterly* 91 (2018): 82–89.
27. Crane, *American*, 20.

Notes for Chapter 2

1. McFarland, *Pursuit*, 263n35.
2. Haywood S. Hansell Jr., *The Air Plan That Defeated Hitler* (Atlanta: Higgins-McArthur/ Longino & Porter, 1972), 23.
3. Gladwell, *Mafia*, 34; Miller, *Masters*, 38.
4. McFarland, *Pursuit*, 85.
5. Gladwell, *Mafia*, 36–37, cites four explanatory "tenets" that create this "hope."
6. McFarland, *Pursuit*, 81–82.
7. Crane, *American*, 22.

8. Phil Haun, ed., *Lectures of the Air Corps Tactical School and American Strategic Bombing in World War II* (Lexington: University Press of Kentucky, 2019), 29.
9. Haun, *Lectures*, 139–40.
10. Miller, *Masters*, 5.
11. RAF Bomber Command "in fact caused crippling damage to the German war economy and the Reich's larger war effort." The "crippling damage" was, however, more a "creator of friction in the German war economy" than it was the destruction of military targets. Robert S. Ehlers Jr., "Bombers, 'Butchers,' and Britain's Bête Noire: Reappraising RAF Bomber Command's Role in World War II," *Royal Air Force Air Power Review* 14, no. 2 (Summer 2011): 8.
12. Gladwell, *Mafia*, 23–24.
13. Haywood S. Hansell Jr., *The Strategic Air War against Germany and Japan: A Memoir*, USAF Warrior Studies (Washington, DC: Office of Air Force History, 1986), 10, 12–13, 6–7; John T. Correll, "Daylight Precision Bombing," *Air Force Magazine*, October 2008, 2.
14. Haun, *Lectures*, 29.
15. Miller, *Masters*, 42; Werrell, "Strategic," 703.
16. *Narrative History of the Eighth Air Force*, A-2 Section, Eighth Air Force, A5803/592, 595; Gladwell, *Bomber*, 39.
17. McFarland, *Pursuit*, 90.
18. McFarland, *Pursuit*, 263n33.
19. Daniel L. Haulman, "Precision Aerial Bombardment of Strategic Targets: Its Rise, Fall, and Resurrection," *Air Power History* 55, no. 4 (Winter 2008): 28.
20. Haun, *Lectures*, 33–39, 44–45.
21. Haun, *Lectures*, 46–53, 140–79.
22. Tami Davis Biddle, *Rhetoric and Reality in Air Warfare: The Evolution of British and American Ideas about Strategic Bombing, 1914–1945* (Princeton: Princeton University Press, 2003), 142.
23. Haun, *Lectures*, 89, 90–95, 98. The question of enough bombers for a "next" mission was always a concern of General Eaker's in his first eighteen months with the Eighth.
24. LeMay, *Mission*, 338–52.
25. Miller, *Masters*, 42.
26. Miller, *Masters*, 144.
27. Biddle, *Rhetoric*, 209.
28. Thomas M. Coffey, *Hap: The Story of the US Air Force and the Man Who Built It, General Henry H. "Hap" Arnold* (New York: Viking Press, 1982), 275.
29. Crane lists nine "faulty assumptions" that bedeviled HADPB in *American*, 25.
30. Hansell, *Air Plan*, 22. See also Miller, *Masters*, 41–42.
31. Robert S. Ehlers Jr. (Colonel, USAF [Ret.]), *The Mediterranean Air War: Airpower and Allied Victory in World War II*, Modern War Studies Series (Lawrence: University Press of Kansas, 2015), 13, 102–3, 104, 274, and *passim*.
32. Miller, *Masters*, 41, from Williamson Murray.
33. William M. Cahill, "Technology Not Realized: Army Air Forces Radar Employment in the Early Pacific War," *Air Power History* 56, no. 2 (Summer

2009): 18. US Army early warning radar detected Japanese airplanes approaching Pearl Harbor at 0750 on Sunday morning, 7 December 1941.

34. John F. Kreis, ed., *Piercing the Fog: Intelligence and Army Air Forces Operations in World War II* (Washington, DC: Air Force History and Museums Program, 1996), 3.

35. See generally: Robert S. Ehlers Jr. (Colonel, USAF [Ret.]), *Targeting the Third Reich: Air Intelligence and the Allied Bombing Campaigns*, Modern War Studies Series (Lawrence: University Press of Kansas, 2009); Kreis, *Fog*; Paul D. T. Stewart (Group Captain, Royal Air Force [Ret.]), *Medmenham: Anglo-American Photographic Intelligence in the Second World War* (PhD diss., University of Northampton, England, 2019). For details and personal insights into the work of the photo interpreters, analysts, and model makers at RAF Medmenham, see: Ursula Powys-Lybbe, *The Eye of Intelligence* (London: William Kimber & Co, 1983), and Constance Babington-Smith, *Air Spy: The Story of Photo Intelligence in World War II* (New York: Harper and Brothers, 1957).

36. See Ehlers, *BDA*.

37. Included would have been joint offices in war-specific ministries, like the Ministry of Economic Warfare, to singularly focused offices such as the Railway Research Service. For an excellent summarization of the nature of the work done at RAF Medmenham and with RAF-AAF photo-intelligence organizations in general see Kreis, *Fog*, 84–87, and Ehlers, *Targeting*.

38. The 653rd BS (L) (Wx Rcn) and the 654th BS (Sp) (Rcn) of the 25th Bomb Group (Rcn).

39. For life in PR units, see: Roy M. Stanley (Colonel, USAF [Ret.]), *World War II Photo Intelligence* (New York: Charles Scribner's Sons, 1981); Tom Ivie, *Patton's Eyes in the Sky: USAF Combat Reconnaissance Missions, North-West Europe, 1944–1945* (Surrey, England: Classic Publications, 2003); and Patricia Fussell Keen, *Eyes of the Eighth: A Story of the 7th Photographic Reconnaissance Group, 1942–1945* (Sun City, AZ: CAVU Publishers, 1996).

Notes for Chapter 3

1. Wesley Frank Craven and James Lea Cate, eds., *The Army Air Forces in World War II*, 3 vols. (Chicago: University of Chicago Press, 1952), I:68, 117, 119, 153, 289, 154.

2. Joseph E. Persico, *Roosevelt's Centurions: FDR and the Commanders He Led to Victory in World War II* (New York, NY: Random House, 2013), 86; John T. Correll, "The Air Force on the Eve of World War II," *Air Force Magazine*, October 2007, 63.

3. Memorandum of 12 November 1940, Admiral Harold R. Stark for the president, via the secretary of the navy, http://docs.fdrlibrary.marist.edu/psf/box4/a48b01.html. See also Ehlers, *Mediterranean*, 48.

4. Memorandum by the United States Chiefs of Staff, Basic Strategic Concept for 1943, CCS 135, Washington, December 26, 1942, in Frederick Aandahl, William M. Franklin, and William Slany, eds., *Foreign Relations of the United States, The Conferences at Washington, 1941–1942, and Casablanca, 1943*

(Washington, DC: US Government Printing Office, 1958) (hereafter *FRUS*), https://history.state.gov/historicaldocuments/frus1941-43, document 399.

5. Mark E. Grotelueschen, "Joint Planning for Global Warfare: The Development of the Rainbow Plans in the United States, 1938–1941," *Army History* 97 (Fall 2015): 8–27.

6. Germany and Italy signed the Pact of Steel on 22 May 1939; Japan joined the renamed Tripartite Treaty, creating the Axis, on September 27, 1940.

7. ABC-1, 27 March 1941, para. 3(a) and 3(c).

8. T. W. Beagle, *Operation Pointblank: Effects-Based Targeting, Another Empty Promise?* (Maxwell AFB, AL: Air University Press, 2001), 23.

9. ABC-1, paras. 8, 6, 11(b), 12 (b) (c), (f), and (g).

10. ABC-1, paras. 13 (a) (b), (c), (d), (g).

11. Hansell, *Air Plan*, 57.

12. United States-British Staff Conversations; Air Policy (ABC-2), 29 March 1942, para. 8(b). ABC-1 held five annexes, plus ABC-2.

13. Howard David Laine, *AWPD-1: America's Pre–World War II Plan for Bombing Germany*, master's thesis, Virginia Polytechnic University, May 1991, 34.

14. The United States was technically neutral at the time, hence under international law the president was unable to sign. Maurice Matloff and Edwin M. Snell, *Strategic Planning for Coalition Warfare 1941–1942* (Washington, DC: Center of Military History, United States Army, 1990), 44–47. Jay A. Stout (Lieutenant Colonel, USMC, Ret.) is mistaken in saying that Roosevelt signed the documents; see Stout, *The Men Who Killed the Luftwaffe: The US Army Air Forces against Germany in World War II* (Lanham, MD: Stackpole Books, 2010), 23–25.

15. United States Army Regulations 95-5 of 20 June 1941.

16. Laine, *AWPD-1*, 41; Phillip S. Meilinger, "The Prescient Planners of AWPD-1," *Air Force Magazine*, July 2011, 1; Richard G. Davis, *Carl L. Spaatz and the Air War in Europe* (Washington, DC: Center for Air Force History, 1993), 59–60.

17. Hansell, *Air Plan*, 61.

18. Hansell, *Air War*, 31. General Marshall, impressed by Kuter, promoted him to lieutenant colonel while concurrently sending his name to the president for promotion to brigadier general, which occurred fifteen days later.

19. Meilinger, "Prescient," 2. Laine, *AWPD-1*, 37–41, 55–58, 65, 75–76.

20. Hansell, *Air War*, 31.

21. Crane, *American*, 29.

22. Hansell, *Air Plan*, 67; Meilinger, "Prescient," 72–74.

23. Laine, *AWPD-1*, abstract.

24. Meilinger, "Prescient," 2–5.

25. Meilinger, "Prescient," 4.

26. Hansell, *Air War*, 37. See also Stephen L. McFarland and Wesley Phillips Newton, *To Command the Sky: The Battle for Air Superiority over Germany, 1942–1944* (Washington, DC: Smithsonian Institution Press, 1991), 82 and 269n4.

27. Hansell, *Air War*, 37. AWPD-1 omitted mention of providing US aircraft to the British.

28. McFarland and Newton, *Command*, 74.

29. Arnold, *Global Mission*, 265.
30. Hansell, *Air War*, 38; additional elaboration courtesy of Dr. Ehlers.
31. Richard D. Hughes, untitled memoirs, reel 40505/188-258, AFHRA, 8.
32. Hansell, *Air Plan*, 51.
33. Richard S. Hallion, "The USAAF Role," chap. 5 in *Air Intelligence Symposium Bracknell Paper No 7.* (London: Royal Air Force Historical Society and Royal Air Force Staff College, 1997).
34. Meilinger, "Prescient," 73.
35. Hallion, "Role," 16.
36. Meilinger, "Prescient," 9.
37. Haywood S. Hansell Jr., "General Laurence S. Kuter, 1905–1979," *Aerospace Historian* 27, no. 2 (June 1980): 92.
38. Geoffrey Perret, *Winged Victory: The Army Air Forces in World War II* (New York: Random House, 1993), 52.

Notes for Chapter 4

1. Anthony Gaughan, "Execute against Japan," *Faculty Lounge*, 7 December 2018, https://www.thefacultylounge.org/2018/12/execute-against-japan.html.
2. The air corps was renamed the Army Air Forces on 20 June 1941.
3. Arnold, *Global Mission*, 175, 267.
4. Hansell, *Air War*, 45. In June of 1941, Arnold was designated chief of the AAF and acting army deputy chief of staff for air. On 9 March 1942 he was appointed commanding general of the AAF.
5. Arnold, *Global Mission*, 321.
6. Dwight D. Eisenhower, *Crusade in Europe* (New York: Doubleday, 1948), 70.
7. Craven and Cate, *Army Air Forces*, I:115.
8. Craven and Cate, *Army Air Forces*, I:563.
9. *Proceedings of the American-British Joint Chiefs of Staff Conferences, Held in Washington, DC, on Twelve Occasions between 24 December 1941 and 14 January 1942*, Joint Chiefs of Staff file copy, accessed on 15 May 2020, https://www.jcs.mil/Portals/36/Documents/History/WWII/Arcadia3.pdf. Included are minutes of meetings by the CCS and the Joint Planning Committee on northwest Africa, dated 13 January 1942. These documents are in US Serial ABC-4; British Serial WW (JPC); ABC-4/2A and WW(JPC)- 2A.
10. Craven and Cate, *Army Air Forces*, I:115.
11. James Parton, *Air Force Spoken Here: General Ira Eaker and the Command of the Air* (Maxwell AFB, AL: Air University Press, 2000), 128.
12. Parton, *Air Force*, 128–29.
13. Davis, *Spaatz*, 71.
14. Parton, *Air Force*, 188. The Eighth planned for 185,000 officers and men, and 4,000 aircraft on 1 January 1944.
15. Eric Hammel, *Air War Europa: America's Air War against Germany in Europe and North Africa, Chronology, 1942–1945* (Pacifica, CA: Pacifica Press, 1994), 38–39.
16. Craven and Cate, *Army Air Forces*, I:614.

17. Report of Lt. General Ira C. Eaker on US Army Air Forces Activities in the United Kingdom Covering the Period 20 February 1942 to 31 December 1943, to Commanding General ETOUSA, A5853/1054-1106.
18. Parton, *Air Force*, 130.

Notes for Chapter 5

1. Document in AFHRA A5842/993. Marginalia states, "Given to Eaker, enclosed in ltr to Chaney, January 31, 1942." A missing transmittal page was probably titled, "Initial Directive to Bomber Commander in England, of 31 January 1942." Parton, *Air Force*, 507n6.
2. Office of the Director of Intelligence, *Target Priorities of the Eighth Air Force: A Resume of the Bombardment Directives and Concepts Underlying Them*, Headquarters, Eighth Air Force, 15 May 1945, B5054/1707-1723, 170.
3. Henry H. Arnold, *American Airpower Comes of Age: General Henry H. "Hap" Arnold's World War II Diaries*, ed. John W. Huston, 2 vols. (Maxwell AFB: Air University Press, 2002), I:281–83, editorial comments by General Huston.
4. Roland G. Ruppenthal, *Logistical Support of the Armies, May 1941–September 1944*, vol. 4 of United States Army in World War II, European Theater of Operations (Washington, DC: Department of the Army, Office of the chief Historian, 1959), 14–22. By March of 1942, RAINBOW-5 was totally obsolete (28).
5. Stephen E. Ambrose, *The Supreme Commander: The War Years of Dwight D. Eisenhower*, (Jackson: University of Mississippi Press, 1999), 46–47, 48, 55.
6. AHFRA A5835/875. The *Letter of Instruction* is from the Headquarters United States Army Forces in the British Isles, dated 25 February. There is also an endorsement above the Instructions, as follows:

    American Observers Group, High Eyco, Bucks. dated 20 March 1942

    Plan For Initiation of US Army Air Forces Bombardment Operations in the British Isles.

    1. The Directive: The directive from the Commanding General, US Army Forces in the British Isles under which this plan was submitted, follows: . . .
7. Parton, *Air Force*, 134, 142.
8. Arnold, *Air Power*, I:283, editorial comments by General Huston. Eisenhower found Chaney's office a mess, unable to understand how to further the war effort. Ike remarked that either Chaney did not understand Washington or Washington did not understand him. See inter alia: Hansell, *Air War*, 64; Eisenhower, *Crusade*, 49–50; Ambrose, *Commander*, 45–48.
9. Davis, *Spaatz*, 71–72.
10. Alfred Goldberg and Richard Overy, presentation at Joint Royal Air Force and United States Air Force Seminar, Royal Air Force Museum, Hendon, London, 29 October 1990, *Air Power History* 38, no. 3 (Fall 1991): 38–48.
11. Craven and Cate, *Army Air Forces*, I:639; Hammel, *Europa*, 44. The Eighth's four subordinate commands were bomber, fighter, air support, and Air Service.

12. Executive Order 9082 of 9 March 1942.
13. Ray S. Cline, *Washington Command Post: The Operations Division*, vol. 2 of The War Department, The United States Army in World War II (Washington, DC: United States Army, Center of Military History, 1990), 91.
14. Cline, *Washington*, 90, 91.
15. Cline, *Washington*, 107–8.
16. Hammel, *Europa*, 48–49.
17. Hammel, *Europa*, 42.
18. Craven and Cate, *Army Air Forces*, I:563–66.
19. John S. D. Eisenhower, *General Ike: A Personal Reminiscence* (New York: Free Press, 2003), 79.
20. Craven and Cate, *Army Air Forces*, I:563, 566.
21. Hammel, *Europa*, 41, 42, 46. The quick approval makes one think that, perhaps, the wheels were greased ahead of time.
22. Hammel, *Europa*, 42, 43.
23. Craven and Cate, *Army Air Forces*, I:615, 639.

Notes for Chapter 6

1. Letter, War Department, Headquarters Army Air Forces, 5 May 1942, A5842/977; Curtis LeMay and Bill Yenne, *Superfortress: The Boeing B-29 and American Airpower in World War II* (Yardley, PA: Westholme, 2006), 42.
2. Davis, *Spaatz*, 75. Brigadier General Haywood S. Hansell referred to the Luftwaffe as the "intermediate target," the destruction of which would allow the "effective bombardment of economic targets"; Goldberg and Overy, presentation, 44.
3. Letter, Headquarters United States Army Air Force Observers Group (Chaney's command) to Commanding General, United States Army Air Forces in the British Isles (Spaatz, in Washington), Subject: Study of General Arnold's Letters, 26 April 1942, A5842/977.
4. Craven and Cate, *Army Air Forces*, I:310–11.
5. DeWitt S. Copp, *Forged in Fire: Strategy and Decisions in the Airwar over Europe, 1940–1945* (Garden City: Doubleday, 1982), 380.
6. Davis, *Spaatz*, 71, 74–75.
7. Davis, *Spaatz*, 76, referencing Spaatz's command diary for 15 May 1942.
8. Eisenhower, *Crusade*, 49; Arnold, *Global Mission*, 308.
9. Hammel, *Europa*, 47.
10. Eisenhower, *Crusade*, 49–50.
11. Arnold, *Global Mission*, 315.
12. Eisenhower, *Crusade*, 66, 68.
13. Hammel, *Europa*, 47; Davis, *Spaatz*, 72.
14. Craven and Cate, *Army Air Forces*, I:653.
15. Craven and Cate, *Army Air Forces*, II:41, 61.
16. Craven and Cate, *Army Air Forces*, I:564.
17. Craven and Cate, *Army Air Forces*, I:564. Hansell, *Air War*, 61–62 tosses out a half dozen "uncertainties" that had already been resolved or nearly so.

18. *FRUS*, docs. 262–68; the conference papers and meeting minutes are documents 259 to 309. Craven and Cate, *Army Air Forces*, I:570; Arnold, *Global Mission*, 323; Hammel, *Europa*, 49. The conference had no code name, a consequence of its unscheduled timing.

19. Emphasis the author's; Chief of Staff, United States Army (Marshall) to the President, *FRUS*, doc. 301.

20. Roosevelt-Churchill meeting, *FRUS*, doc. 267.

21. Hammel, *Europa*, 48–49.

22. Eisenhower, *Crusade*, 51.

23. Letter, Arnold to Eisenhower, 22 June 1942, Arnold Papers, reel 200.

24. Carlo D'Este, *Eisenhower: A Soldier's Life* (New York: Henry Holt, 2002), 309.

25. Ambrose, *Commander*, 71.

26. Eisenhower, *Crusade*, 71; D'Este, *Eisenhower*, 334–35.

27. Eisenhower, *Crusade*, 70.

28. Eisenhower, *Crusade*, 69.

29. Hammel, *Europa*, 64; Perret, *Winged*, 257.

30. Arnold, *Global Mission*, 321.

31. Dik Alan Daso, *Hap Arnold and the Evolution of American Air Power* (Washington, DC: Smithsonian Institution Press, 2000), 180.

32. David R. Mets, *Master of Airpower: General Carl A. Spaatz* (Novato, CA: Presidio Press, 1998), 125; Davis, *Spaatz*, 82. Spaatz even landed at the challenging Bluie West I, a Marston Mat strip located at the dead end of a narrow fjord, to assess the airfield.

33. Davis, *Spaatz*, 82–83.

34. Craven and Cate, *Army Air Forces*, I:623–24. The AAF was deficient (as in completely devoid) in air intelligence as it had been too busy creating a bombardment theory to think about the intelligence necessary even for target selection. Meanwhile, the RAF had developed a superior air intelligence capability but did not have the bomber force capable of taking advantage of it. Ehlers, *BDA*, 211 and passim. The citation speaks specifically to BDA but applies across the broader air intelligence spectrum, as he and other experts acknowledge elsewhere.

35. Hammel, *Europa*, 45.

36. Davis, *Spaatz*, 43–56, passim; 71.

37. Many in the RAF were also unhappy about night area bombardment. In the late 1930s and through 1940, the RAF sought to practice daylight bombing with its better accuracy, as discussed between Jack Slessor and Haywood Hansell in November of 1940. It was because the RAF bombers were close to defenseless against Luftwaffe fighters that the service switched to night bombardment. Goldberg and Overy, presentation, 43-44.

38. Davis, *Spaatz*, 53.

39. Hansell, *Air Plan*, 53. GEE and OBOE were primarily navigation systems but could be modified for quasi-precision bombardment.

40. Edward T. Russell, *Leaping the Atlantic Wall: Army Air Forces Campaigns in Western Europe, 1942–1945*, vol. 4 of The U.S. Army Air Forces in World War II (Washington, DC: Air Force History and Museums Programs, 1999),

1–2. See also Arnold's interview with the *Daily Telegraph* of 19 October 1943, B40505/12.
41. Arnold, *Global Mission*, 149.
42. Craven and Cate, *Army Air Forces*, I:651.
43. Davis, *Spaatz*, 85.
44. Arnold, *Airpower*, I:314, editorial comments by General Huston.
45. Arnold, *Global Mission*, 44; Coffey, *Hap*, 78.
46. Perret, *Winged*, 143.
47. Perret, *Winged*, 136.
48. Perret, *Winged*, 138.
49. A major in 1940, Norstad attained four stars in 1952, at age 45.
50. Hughes, memoirs, 21–23.
51. Curtis served in the Eisenhower administration the 1950s, holding important positions in the civil aviation arena and winning the Collier Trophy for the greatest achievement in aviation for 1957.

Notes for Chapter 7

1. Kit C. Carter and Robert Mueller, *United States Army Air Forces in World War II: Combat Chronology, 1941–1945* (Washington, DC: Center for Air Force History, 1991) (hereafter *ComChron*) July 1942; Hammel, *Europa*, 51; and Craven and Cate, *Army Air Forces*, I:644, all cite 1 July 1942 for arrival of the 97th. Davis, *Spaatz*, 85, gives the date as 2 July.
2. Hammel, *Europa*, 54; Craven and Cate, *Army Air Forces*, I:642. Moreover, HqAF reduced the planned number of combat groups for the Eighth from sixty-six by March '43 to fifty-four by that April but increased to 137 groups by 31 December. Hammel, *Europa*, 52.
3. Craven and Cate, *Army Air Forces*, I:656.
4. Davis, *Spaatz*, 83, 88.
5. Davis, *Spaatz*, 90.
6. Daso, *Hap*, 69. Arnold admitted to "unreasonableness," at 163; "can-do" and "take-charge" attitudes, and a "light-hearted" but "well-guarded" sense of humor at 68.
7. James M. Scott, *Black Snow: Curtis LeMay, the Firebombing of Tokyo, and the Road to the Atomic Bomb* (New York: W. W. Norton, 2022), 14.
8. Postscript, 10 June 1942 letter to Kenney when CG, 4th Air Force, papers of General of the Air Force Henry H. Arnold, Reel 200, MS Div, LoC (hereafter Arnold Papers).
9. Daso, *Hap*, 227.
10. Perret, *Winged*, 137; Daso, *Hap*, 176.
11. Scott, *Black Snow*, 17.
12. Laurence F. Kuter and Laurence S. Kuter, "The General vs. the Establishment: General H. H. Arnold and the Air Staff," *Aerospace Historian* 21, no. 4 (December 1974): 186.
13. Arnold, *Airpower*, II:9, editorial comments by General Huston.
14. Scott, *Black Snow*, 17.

15. Document titled: Brief of Report on Operations of US Army Air Forces in United Kingdom, 1 December 1942–31 December 1943 (submitted by General Eaker), in three pages, signed "Pesler."
16. Hammel, *Europa*, 47–50, for the chronology.
17. The cable arrived 28 June.
18. Craven and Cate, *Army Air Forces*, I:658.
19. Copp, *Forged*, 267.
20. Parton, *Air Force*, 165–67.
21. Copp, *Forged*, 267.
22. Davis, *Spaatz*, 90.
23. Craven and Cate, *Army Air Forces*, I:658–59. One surviving crewman committed suicide after the raid.
24. Davis, *Spaatz*, 90.
25. *Narrative*, A5805/592, 593.

Notes for Chapter 8

1. Eisenhower, informed of the decision on 22 June, called it "the blackest day in American history." Ambrose, *Commander*, 73.
2. Hammel, *Europa*, 53.
3. Craven and Cate, *Army Air Forces*, II:211; Hammel, *Europa*, 53; *ComChron*, July 1942.
4. Herman S. Wolk, *Cataclysm: General Hap Arnold and the Defeat of Japan* (Denton, Texas: University of North Texas Press, 2010), 213.
5. Miller, *Masters*, 62–63. L. Douglas Keeney, *The POINTBLANK Directive: The Untold Story of the Daring Plan That Saved D-Day* (Oxford, UK: Osprey Publishing, 2012), states on 99 that "Spaatz immediately pulled out of the Eighth . . . his best squadrons of fighters and heavy bombers and sent them to North Africa." This is incorrect: full groups were transferred between air forces, not individual squadrons. Spaatz did not have the authority to "pull out" units and transfer them anywhere; he obeyed those orders from Washington. Most of the groups transferred had their orders to the Eighth changed before they ever became officially attached to the Eighth. Last, Spaatz was continually distressed over losing groups to North Africa. Keeney cites no source for his statement, for there can be none.
6. Parton, *Air Force*, 169–70.
7. Letter, Arnold to Spaatz, 25 August 1942, Arnold Papers, reel 200 (one of several from Arnold dated that day). Correspondence was always between "Arnold" and "Tooey," the West Point way.
8. Letter, Arnold to Spaatz, 25 August 1942, Arnold Papers, reel 200 (replying to Spaatz's letter of 21 August), discussing a "readjustment" in BOLERO.
9. Hughes, memoirs, 24.
10. Parton, *Air Force*, 173; Davis, *Spaatz*, 98; Hammel, *Europa*, 56; *ComChron*, August 1942; Craven and Cate, *Army Air Forces*, I:661. See Perret, *Winged*, 246, for 108 Spitfires escorting 12 bombers.
11. Parton, *Air Force*, 120, 172.

12. Perret, *Winged*, 245.
13. *ComChron*, August 1942.
14. Parton, *Air Force*, 173.
15. Sauter, "So Near Heaven and Surrounded by Hell: The Character and 1942–1943 Military Career of World War II Pilot Frank A. Armstrong, Jr.," *North Carolina Historical Review* 88, no. 2 (April 2011): 173.
16. Perret, *Winged*, 246.
17. L. Douglas Keeney, *The Air War against the Luftwaffe, 1943–1944: The Untold Story of the Air War against Germany and How World War II Hung in the Balance* (Campbell, CA: Fastpencil, 2011), 4. This is a reproduction of a long-lost USAAF report classified SECRET in 1945. Keeney obtained a "worn and nearly unreadable" copy sixty-five years later and, with a team of students, historians, and technicians, was able to reconstruct it, thereby making a serious contribution to the history of the air war in Europe. See Ehlers, "Bombers," 11, for the ULTRA tidbit.
18. Letter, HQs VIII Bomber Command to Commanding General, 8th Air Force, "Narrative Report of First Bombardment Mission," 19 August 1942, papers of Lieutenant General Ira C. Eaker, box 1:16, MS Div, LoC (hereafter Eaker Papers).
19. Letter, HQs VIII Bomber Command to Commanding General, 8th Air Force, 25 August 1942, Eaker Papers, box 1:16.
20. Miller, *Masters*, 63.
21. Davis, *Spaatz*, 100–101.
22. Davis, *Spaatz*, 101.
23. Letter, Arnold to Spaatz, 19 August 1942, Arnold Papers, reel 214.
24. Davis, *Spaatz*, 101.
25. Miller, *Masters*, 44. Eisenhower was an excellent bridge player and one wonders how the bridge team of Ike and Tooey did against the others at ETOUSA and USSTAF.
26. Davis, *Spaatz*, 105–6.
27. Davis, *Spaatz*, 105.
28. Davis, *Spaatz*, 104–5.
29. Spaatz interview, 27 June 1945, A5535/304.
30. Robert H. Ferrell, ed., *The Eisenhower Diaries* (New York: W. W. Norton, 1981), 94–95.
31. Eisenhower, *Crusade*, 56.
32. Parton, *Air Force*, 169–70.
33. Letter, Arnold to Spaatz, 26 August 1942, Arnold Papers, reel 214.
34. I. B. Holley Jr., "An Air Force General: Laurence Sherman Kuter," *Aerospace Historian* 27, no. 2 (June 1980): 89.
35. William W. Ralph, "Improvised Destruction: Arnold, LeMay, and the Fire-bombing of Japan," *War in History* 13, no. 4 (October 2006): 508 and passim. The difference with Norstad was that the recipients knew without question that it was Norstad who was their correspondent.
36. Parton, *Air Force*, 171.

37. John T. Correll, "The Third Musketeer," *Air Force Magazine*, December 2014, 58.
38. Doolittle (General, USAFR [Ret.]) and Carroll V. Glines, *I Could Never Be So Lucky Again* (New York: Bantam Books), 55.
39. Parton, *Air Force*, 139–40.
40. Correll, "Musketeer," 59.
41. Correll, "Musketeer," 58.
42. Richard Overy, *The Bombers and the Bombed: Allied Air War over Europe, 1940–1945* (New York: Viking/Penguin, 2013), 88.
43. Davis, *Spaatz*, 32.
44. Daso, *Arnold*, 175. After retirement Eaker was frequently asked about his final relationship with Arnold by interviewers, but Eaker always remained silent on this point, refusing to criticize Arnold.
45. The books were *Army Flier* (New York: Harper and Bros., 1942); *This Flying Game* (New York: Funk & Wagnalls, 1943), and *Winged Warfare* (New York: Harper and Bros., 1941).
46. Parton, *Air Force*, 115.
47. Davis, *Spaatz*, 4, 19, 33, 35.
48. Parton, *Air Force*, 170–72.

Notes for Chapter 9

1. Directive for Commander-in-Chief, Allied Expeditionary Force (as approved CCS 36th Meeting on 13 August 1942), Arnold Papers, reel 214.
2. Craven and Cate, *Army Air Forces*, I:63.
3. Davis, *Spaatz*, 91.
4. Spaatz interview, 27 June 1945, A5535/299-300.
5. Overy, *Bombers*, 105, asserts that Arnold ordered Spaatz to join Eisenhower in North Africa, to "make him overall commander of all American air forces in Europe." Overy misunderstands: it was Eisenhower's decision, not Arnold's, whether Spaatz would go to North Africa and what he would do there. Arnold had no authority to assign any officer to Eisenhower's staff without the latter either first concurring or requesting it.
6. Davis, *Spaatz*, 101.
7. Parton, *Air Force*, 165–67.
8. Parton, *Air Force*, 448. Eaker, 51 at retirement, was expected to follow Spaatz as the second United States Air Force chief of staff, which would have meant the highly merited fourth star.
9. Letter, Eaker to Major General George Stratemeyer, Chief of the Air Staff, 21 August 1942, Eaker Papers, box 1:16
10. Hammel, *Europa*, 56–58.
11. Richards, *Portal*, 309. Harris's short autobiography omitted almost all references to the AAF.
12. Sir John Slessor, *The Central Blue: The Autobiography of Sir John Slessor, Marshal of the RAF* (New York: Frederick A. Praeger, 1957), 429–30. Slessor highlights Churchill's visceral hatred of the idea of too many casualties.

13. Henry Probert, *Bomber Harris, His Life and Times: The Biography of Marshal of the Royal Air Force Sir Arthur Harris, Wartime Chief of Bomber Command* (Toronto: Stoddart Publishing, 2001), 243.
14. Dudley Saward, *Bomber Harris: The Story of Sir Arthur Harris, Marshal of the Royal Air Force* (New York: Doubleday and Company, 1985), 60.
15. Saward, *Harris*, 167.
16. Probert, *Bomber*, 245.
17. Eisenhower, *Crusade*, 63.

Notes for Chapter 10

1. Key decisions dates are in Hammel, *Europa*, 55–59.
2. Davis, *Spaatz*, 127.
3. See Doolittle and Glines, *Lucky*, 277, where Doolittle almost ruined his relationship with Ike before it had even begun.
4. Doolittle and Glines, *Lucky*, 283.
5. Davis, *Spaatz*, 109.
6. Overy, *Bombers*, 123.
7. Parton, *Air Force*, 183.
8. Spaatz interview with USSTAF historian, 27 June 1945, A5535/300–301
9. Spaatz interview with USSTAF historian, 27 June 1945, A5535/301.
10. Davis, *Spaatz*, 109.
11. Miller, *Masters*, 63.
12. Stout, *Men*, 63. Colonel Frank Armstrong, CO of the 97th BG, was one of those whose leadership qualities were too exceptional to lose, so Eaker (a longtime friend) relieved him of command and reassigned him to PINETREE as the A-3; Parton, *Air Force*, 184.
13. Spaatz interview, 27 June 1945, A5535/301. The historian opined that the relationship was "built on mutual respect through reasonableness," to which Spaatz agreed.
14. Letter, Spaatz to Arnold, 24 August 1942, Arnold Papers, reel 214 (replying to Arnold's letter of the nineteenth).
15. Memorandum, Arnold to Marshall, dated 19 August 1942 on front page top right, but under Arnold's closing signature was also the date, 21 August 1942, Arnold Papers, reel 214. Arnold's figures are questionable, in hindsight, especially the numbers for the Luftwaffe during and after TORCH. Recent scholarship has determined that, by TORCH, the Germans had air superiority over Algeria and Tunisia not because of numbers but because they were simply better than the Allies.
16. Letter Arnold to Spaatz, 26 August 1942, Arnold Papers, reel 214.
17. Memorandum, Arnold to Marshall, dated 19 August 1942 on front page top right; under Arnold's closing signature was the date, 21 August 1942; and letter, Arnold to Spaatz, 3 Sept 1942, Arnold Papers, reel 214.
18. Letter, Arnold to Spaatz, 3 Sept 1942, Arnold Papers, reel 214.
19. Letter, Spaatz to Arnold, 27 August 1942, Arnold Papers, reel 214.

20. Letter, Spaatz to Arnold, 27 August 1942, Arnold Papers, reel 214. Flying officers spoke almost reverentially of their ground crews, the "unsung heroes of the Eighth Air Force." Harry H. Crosby, *A Wing and a Prayer: The "Bloody 100th" Bomb Group and the US Eighth Air Force in Action over Europe in World War 2* (New York: HarperCollins, 1993), photo following 112. Crosby was group navigator for the 100th for most of the war.

21. Davis, *Spaatz*, 111.

22. Hammel, *Europa*, 163.

23. Letter, Arnold to Spaatz, 19 August 1942, Arnold Papers, reel 214.

24. Arnold to Spaatz, 19 August 1942, Arnold Papers, reel 214.

Notes for Chapter 11

1. Craven and Cate, *Army Air Forces*, II:279.

2. Cable, Spaatz to Arnold, 31 August 1942, Arnold Papers, reel 214.

3. Cable, AGWAR Washington, REF 118, to Headquarters ETOUSA, 26 August 1942, Classification: URGENT SECRET, Arnold Papers, reel 214.

4. Hansell, *Air War*, 58.

5. Letter, Arnold to Spaatz, 3 September 1942, Arnold Papers, reel 214.

6. Letter, Spaatz to Arnold, 27 August 1942, Arnold Papers, reel 214.

7. Hansell, *Air War*, 58. Whether Arnold and Marshall possibly colluded in Hansell's written orders is unknown, but the omission of specific instructions is curious. Hansell "had learned to be secure and at ease in the corridors of influence and power," which may have aided him to see so quickly the broad opening the instructions allowed him and the ease with which to do so. Ralph N. Nutter, *With the Possum and the Eagle: A Memoir of a Navigator over Germany and Japan* (Novato, CA: Presidio Press, 2002), 39, for Hansell's background.

8. Kreis, *Fog*, 150.

9. James R. Cody, "Air War Plans Division-42," chap. 3 in *AWPD-42 to Instant Thunder: Consistent, Evolutionary Thought or Revolutionary Change?* (Maxwell AFB: Air University Press, 1996), 15, http://www.JSTOR.com/stable/resrep13787.9.

10. Cody, "Air War," 18.

11. Hansell, *Air Plan*, 107. See also Keeney, *War*, 10–12; McFarland and Newton, *Command*, 82. Thinking was universal in the AAF in 1942 that no fighter could ever escort the heavies to Berlin and back, a position carved into stone at ACTS in the 1930s.

12. Hansell, *Air War*, 58–59.

13. Davis, *Spaatz*, 111.

Notes for Chapter 12

1. Parton, *Air Force*, 177.

2. Craven and Cate, *Army Air Forces*, II:115, 225–26.

3. From ETOUSA (Eisenhower) to AGWAR (for General Marshall), of 5 September 1952: Memorandum For: The Chief of Staff, September 8, 1942; Subject: Cable Number 1812 from General Eisenhower, Arnold Papers, reel 214.
4. Parton, *Air Force*, 174–75. Information on missions between 19 August and 2 October 1942 is pulled from Hammel, *Europa*, 57–65.
5. Arnold, *Global Mission*, 486.
6. Hammel, *Europa*, 57–67, passim; *ComChron*, September and October 1942.
7. Parton, *Air Force*, 178.
8. Hammel, *Europa*, 66. And yet no one questioned the wisdom of future unescorted missions into Germany.
9. Curtis E. LeMay and Beirne Lay Jr., *Strategic Air Power: Destroying the Enemy's War Resources*, vol. 2 of Impact: Destruction from the Air (Harrisburg, PA: National Historical Society for the Air Force Historical Foundation, 1989), xii.
10. Letter, from Spaatz to Arnold, 31 October 1942, B5054/1297.
11. a. Letter, Arnold from Spaatz, 30 October 1942, B5054/1297. b. Message 1812, Eisenhower to Marshall 5 September 1942: "It is my purpose to use all of the US Air Force now in the UK in TORCH if necessary." c. Memorandum for: The Chief of Staff, Subject: Cable 1812, Sept. 5, 1942: "I believe that this cable is of such great and immediate importance as to warrant the presentation of its contents to the President and to the Joint Chiefs of staff. /s/ H.H. Arnold"; Arnold Papers.
12. Letter, Spaatz to Arnold, B5054/1294–99.
13. Craven and Cate, *Army Air Forces*, II:259, 260.

Notes for Chapter 13

1. Hughes, *Memoirs*, 25.
2. Craven and Cate, *Army Air Forces*, II:242.
3. Craven and Cate, *Army Air Forces*, II:245.
4. Craven and Cate, *Army Air Forces*, II:237, 242.
5. Ehlers, *Targeting*, 133–34.
6. Jeremiah S. Heathman, *The Bombing of Brittany: Solving the Wrong Problem* (Ft. Leavenworth, KS: School of Advanced Military Studies, US Army Command and General Staff College, 2010), 49.
7. Copp, *Forged*, 313.
8. Copp, *Forged*, 310.
9. Davis, *Spaatz*, 112.
10. Copp, *Forged*, 335.
11. Hughes, memoirs, 25.
12. *Narrative*, A5805/592, 607.
13. *ComChron*, October 1942; Craven and Cate, *Army Air Forces*, II:238.
14. Eisenhower, *Crusade*, 85.
15. Craven and Cate, *Army Air Forces*, II:239.
16. Heathman, *Brittany*, 9.
17. Heathman, *Brittany*, 14.

18. Gordon Williamson, *U-Boat Bases and Bunkers, 1941–45* (Oxford, Osprey Publishing, 2003), 13, 41.
19. Craven and Cate, *Army Air Forces*, II:243.
20. Copp, *Forged*, 313; Davis, *Spaatz*, 113.
21. Craven and Cate, *Army Air Forces*, II:312. The RAF found mining the ports much more effective.
22. LeMay and Lay, *Strategic*, xii; see also Ehlers, *Targeting*, 132; Copp, *Forged*, 313.
23. Parton, *Air Force*, 183; Copp, *Forged*, 312.
24. Spaatz letter to Arnold, 31 October 1942 in B5054/1293.
25. Hammel, *Europa*, 80; *ComChron*, October 1942; Spaatz letter to Arnold, 31 October 1942 in B5054/1293.
26. Copp, *Forged*, 312.
27. Craven and Cate, *Army Air Forces*, II:312.
28. Copp, *Forged*, 312.
29. Heathman, *Brittany*, 17. In autumn of 2022 this author visited the St. Nazaire pens, which were still structurally sound and in use by local government and civic organizations.
30. Heathman, *Brittany*, 22.

Notes for Chapter 14

1. Material for this paragraph, unless otherwise noted, is found in Parton, *Air Force*, 187–88.
2. Ehlers, *Targeting*, 142.
3. Spaatz to Arnold, 31 October 1942, a single-page postscript added to a five-page letter, B5054/1299.
4. The 6 November trip to Gibraltar is found in Hansell, "Kuter," 92.
5. Copp, *Forged*, 324.
6. A personal acquaintance of the author's was the engineer on one such Fortress.
7. Headquarters 4th Combat Bomb Wing (H) Instruction 80-7 of 18 November 1943, B0895/240. Castle would be promoted to brigadier two days later.
8. Muir S. Fairchild, AWPD-42: Requirements for Air Ascendancy (War Department, Army Air Forces, Air Staff, copy 12, Air University Library).
9. Eisenhower, *Crusade*, 72, 73; Ambrose, *Commander*, 79.
10. Eisenhower, *Crusade*, 93.
11. Letter, Arnold to Marshall, 19 August 1942, Arnold Papers, reel 214.
12. Parton, *Air Force*, 198.
13. Keeney, *War*, 8.
14. Parton, *Air Force*, 198–99.
15. Davis, *Spaatz*, 140.
16. Davis, *Spaatz*, 141.
17. Peter A. Costello, *A Matter of Trust: The History of Close Air Support* (Maxwell AFB, AL: Air University Press, 1997), 8.
18. Matthew G. St. Clair, "Allied Air Operations in North Africa," in *The Twelfth Air Force: Tactical and Operational Innovations in the Mediterranean Theater*

of Operations, 1943–1944 (Maxwell AFB: Air University Press, 2007), 5–8. General Larry Kuter would write a new doctrine in less than two weeks.

19. Copp, *Forged*, 335, 336.
20. Spaatz, letter to Arnold, 31 October 1942, B5054/1295.
21. Chris Hansen, *Enfant Terrible: The Times and Schemes of General Elliott Roosevelt* (Tucson: Able Baker Press, 2012), 234, 243.
22. Copp, *Forged*, 339.
23. Overy, *Bombers*, 124–25.

Notes for Chapter 15

1. Letter from General Hansell, CG,1st Wing to CG, VIII Bomber Command, 16 January 1943, B5054/1200–1201.
2. LeMay, *Mission*, 235.
3. LeMay, *Mission*, 233–35. For some months the box was a work in progress, changing as improvements were sought or as more bombers began flying the missions. Later missions with hundreds of bombers from a dozen or more groups flew deep into Germany in multiple series of combat boxes. Per several sources, Brigadier General Frank Armstrong, now commander of the 306th BG, collaborated with LeMay in working out the box.
4. LeMay, *Mission*, 231–32.
5. LeMay, *Mission*, 236–39, 240–44; McFarland, *Pursuit*, 170–75.
6. LeMay, *Mission*, 255–58.
7. Roger A. Freeman, *The Mighty Eighth War Manual* (London: Cassell, 2001), 52–53.
8. LeMay, *Mission*, 237–38, 240–44. The evolution of the lead crew system in all its complexity may be found in Crosby, *Wing and a Prayer*. Crosby ended the war a group and lead navigator. Ralph Nutter was lead navigator for LeMay in the 305th and for Brigadier General Haywood Hansell. See Nutter, *Possum*.

Notes for Chapter 16

1. Arnold, *Airpower*, II:434, editor's note.
2. Perret, *Winged*, 248. The Eighth bombed Germany for eleven months before a long-range escort appeared.
3. Arnold, *Diaries*, I:435, editor's note.
4. Sinclair's quotation is in Arnold, *Diaries*, I:436, editor's note; the gist of his note to the PM is in Parton, *Air Force*, 193.
5. Combined Chiefs of Staff Memorandum 166/1 of 21 January 1943.
6. Hansell, *Air War*, 72.
7. Hansell, *Air War*, 117.
8. Hansell, *Air War*, 72.
9. Hansell, *Air War*, 73.
10. Overy, *Bombers*, 109.
11. Slessor, *Central Blue*, 448.
12. Slessor, *Central Blue*, 448.

13. Harris, *Bomber*, 144.
14. Hansell, *Air War*, 78. His problem was (correctly) that Hitler was not suffering, and unless the people were willing to rise up—which they were not—it would be and to a large extent was a feckless enterprise.
15. Keeney, *POINTBLANK*, 9. See, too, Keeney, *War*, 12–15.
16. Eaker was ordered to "proceed at earliest practicable time to Casablanca for Conference." Dick Hughes was senior duty officer on the thirteenth and noted on his copy that he had been informed by General Chauncy, Eaker's chief of staff, by telephone. Hughes's copy is in the Eaker Papers, box 1:16.
17. Herman S. Wolk, "Decision at Casablanca," *Air Force Magazine*, January 2003, https://www.airforcemag.com/article/0103casa/; Perret, *Winged*, 243. Some accounts (Parton, *Air Force*, 218; LeMay, IMPACT, xv) say the president was under pressure by the PM vice having already agreed to his argument.
18. Parton, *Air Force*, 25.
19. Parton, *Air Force*, 221–22. Later told that he had "saved the B-17s," Churchill responded that if so, it was because he had not opposed them.
20. B5054, pages 677–90.
21. As in fact happened; RAF Bomber Command incurred higher losses than USSTAF post–March 1944.
22. Parton, *Air Force*, 222.
23. McFarland and Newton, *Command*, 93 and 271n30.
24. Copp, *Forged*, 359–60.
25. Arnold, *Diaries*, I:439, editor's note. Craven and Cate, *Army Air Forces*, I:301–3. The PM was soon complaining to his own generals again about the Americans not bombing Germany.
26. Arnold, *Global Mission*, 397.

Notes for Chapter 17

1. *Narrative*, A5805/592-605.
2. Memorandum for CG, VIII Bomber Command from CG, 1st Bombardment Winged (Hansell), 26 January 1943, B5054/1196–99; Hammel, *Europa*, 96; *ComChron*, January 1943.
3. Hammel, *Europa*, 97; *ComChron*, January 1943.
4. Parton, *Air Force*, 231.
5. Nutter, *Possum*, 60. The redeployment of German fighters held critical consequences for the German presence in those theaters.
6. Charles Griffith, *The Quest: Haywood Hansell and American Strategic Bombing in World War II* (Maxwell AFB: Air University Press, 1999), 114.
7. Craven and Cate, *Army Air Forces*, II:600.
8. Copp, *Forged*, 366–67.
9. Copp, *Forged*, 367.
10. Parton, *Air Force*, 234, 233.
11. Nutter, *Possum*, 61.
12. Parton, *Air Force*, 233.
13. Parton, *Air Force*, 239.

14. Hammel, *Europa*, 100–102, 106.
15. Craven and Cate, *Army Air Forces*, II:308.
16. Letter, Eaker to Arnold, 15 February 1943, Arnold Papers, reel 214. Eaker had been flying combat missions for seven months and was still talking about "showing early success" in the future.
17. Wolk, *Cataclysm*, 111. Comment to General Haywood Hansell from General Lauris Norstad when Hansell was commanding general of XXI Bomber Command in late 1944, but would easily be applicable to Arnold and his famous impatience by 1943.
18. Letter, Stratemeyer to Eaker, 23 February 1943, Eaker Papers, box 1:16; Parton, *Air Force*, 242.
19. Hammel, *Europa*, 99–106, 123. Of the 107 reaching Bremen, 16 were shot down.
20. Arnold, *Global Mission*, 434–41.
21. The Monroe Doctrine was alive and well.
22. Holley, "Kuter," 88.
23. Kuter and Kuter, "General," 185.
24. Kuter and Kuter, "General," 187–88.
25. Herman S. Wolk, "The Founding of the Force," *Air Force Magazine*, September 1996, 62–67, 64.
26. Kuter and Kuter, "General," 186.
27. Holley, "Kuter," 89.
28. Memorandum to General Arnold, 12 June 1943 [from Colonel O'Donnell], Arnold Papers, reel 214.
29. Electronic Message, Office of Origin: Commanding General, Army Air Forces, to Commanding General, Eighth Air Force, London, 26 June 1943, Arnold Papers, reel 214.
30. Letter, Eaker to Giles, 31 July 1943, Eaker Papers, box 1:16.

Notes for Chapter 18

1. Gladwell, *Mafia*, 76–77; Nutter, *Possum*, 38–39.
2. Nutter, *Possum*, 75.
3. Overy, *Bombers*, 125–26. Hansell had also recognized the need for escorted bombers to the target and return by February 1943.
4. Parton, *Air Force*, 242.
5. Letter, Eaker from Stratemeyer, 6 March 1943, Eaker Papers, box 1:16.
6. Letter from Headquarters, 2d Bombardment Winged, 11 March 1943, Brigadier General James P. Hodges, Commanding, B5054/1188–93. When developing the *Historical Narrative* for the Eighth in 1944, the researchers were unable to locate any records of training done in the States for the Eighth. *Narrative*, A5805/592/596.
7. Letter, Brigadier General Haywood S. Hansell, Commanding General, 1st Bombardment Wing, to Eaker, "Tactical Lessons Learned from Operations," 13 March 1943, B5054/1178-5. Emphasis added.

8. Secret Radiogram, Emmons to Arnold, Eyes Only, 7 July 1943, Eaker Papers, box 1:17.
9. Eaker Papers, box 1:18.
10. Griffith, *Quest*, 115; Hammel, *Europa*, 108–9.
11. Griffith, *Quest*, 115.
12. Hammel, *Europa*, 109.
13. Griffith, *Quest*, 115.
14. Griffith, *Quest*, 115; Hammel, *Europa*, 112.
15. Hammel, *Europa*, 112; the yards were out of commission for only three months.
16. Parton, *Air Force*, 243.
17. Keen, *Eyes*, 10–11.
18. Memorandum: General Andrews from General Eaker, April 9, 1943, Eaker Papers, box 1:17; Keen, *Eyes*. Hall was a rare World War I aviator who managed to fly as a squadron and group combat commander in World War II. His personal dislike of the 325th RW's CO possibly prevented reconnaissance B-26s from the 25th BG/654th BS from spotting the Wehrmacht armored force buildup in the Ardennes in early December 1944, just prior to the Battle of the Bulge.
19. Memorandum: Commanding General ETOUSA; signed Major General Ira C. Eaker, 30 March 1943, Eaker Papers, box 1:17.
20. Missions flown were numbers 31 to 48 inclusive.
21. Hansell, *Air Plan*, 121.
22. Arnold, *Diaries*, II:22, editor's comments. It was too often Eaker writing multiple pages of detail while Arnold wanted to read two things only: more missions and more bombers per mission.
23. Undated Memorandum, Eaker to Arnold, written between 28 and 31 March 1943, Eaker Papers, box 1:17.
24. Copp, *Forged*, 376.
25. Parton, *Air Force*, 247–48.
26. Craven and Cate, *Army Air Forces*, II:616.
27. Craven and Cate, *Army Air Forces*, II:260.
28. Copp, *Forged*, 380–81,
29. Copp, *Forged*, 381.

Notes for Chapter 19
1. Perret, *Winged*, 257.
2. Craven and Cate, *Army Air Forces*, II:260. This described the situation in January of 1943, but it was just as apt for much of that year.
3. Cable, Eaker to Commanding General, ETOUSA, Subject: Reply to Cablegram R 9124, June 4, 1943, Eaker Papers, box 1:17.
4. Arnold, *Diaries*, II:46, editor's comment.
5. Perret, *Winged*, 281.
6. Craven and Cate, *Army Air Forces*, II:
7. Craven and Cate, *Army Air Forces*, II:309.
8. Stout, *Men*, 104.

9. Parton, *Air Force*, 261–62; Copp, *Forged in Fire*, 387–88.
10. Nutter, *Possum*, 67.
11. Copp, *Forged in Fire*, 388.
12. Craven and Cate, *Army Air Forces*, II:331.
13. Keeney, *War*, 18–19.
14. Nutter, *Possum*, 69. Captain Ralph Nutter had been the mission's lead navigator in the same aircraft with Anderson.
15. A-2 Headquarters Eighth Air Force Daily Journal, 25 June 1943, Item 7, B5059/382–83. The photos of 10 March 1942 proved nothing as the plant could easily have been decommissioned between then and August of 1942. The crashed FW's inspection plate was not determinative.
16. Kreis, *Fog*, 140; Ehlers, *Targeting*, 165; Keeney, *War*, 6.
17. Biddle, *Rhetoric*, 223.
18. Biddle, *Rhetoric*, 207.
19. Letter contents are in Copp, *Forged*, 388.
20. Giles to Eaker in Parton, *Air Force*, 271.
21. Coffey, *Hap*, 311.
22. Parton, *Air Force*, 168, 214, 261–62.
23. Griffith, *Quest*, 104–5.
24. Perrett, *Winged*, 246–47.
25. Miller, *Masters*, 65–66.
26. Hammel, *Europa*, 122.
27. Hammel, *Europa*, 128–38. Keeney, *War*, foreword.

Notes for Chapter 20

1. Hansell, *Air War*, 81.
2. Office of the Combined Chiefs of Staff, Plan for the Combined Bomber Offensive from the United Kingdom, Trident Conference, May 1943, Papers and Minutes of Meetings, CCS Doc. 217 at 23, https://www.jcs.mil/Portals/36/Documents/History/WWII/Trident3.pdf, accessed 2 August 2020. See also Hammel, *Europa*, 132, 134, 136–37.
3. Copp, *Forged*, 399.
4. TRIDENT Document 242/6.
5. Trident Conference, May 1943, Papers and Minutes of Meetings, edited and published by the Office of the Combined Chiefs of Staff, 1943, accessed 17 June 2020 at hpps://www.jcs.mil/Portals/36/Documents/History/WWII/Trident3.pdf.
6. Copp, *Forged*, 414–15.
7. Letter, Eaker to Arnold, 18 May 1943, Eaker Papers, box 1:17
8. Parton, *Air Force*, 278.
9. Perret, *Winged*, 41.
10. Perret, *Winged*, 141.
11. Parton, *Air Force*, 116.
12. Perret, *Winged*, 44–45.
13. Parton, *Air Force*, 114.

14. Parton, *Air Force*, 114–16; more on Lovett at 268–71.
15. Arnold, *Global Mission*, 195–96.
16. Spaatz interview, 27 June 1945, B5535/299.
17. Arnold, *Diaries*, II:21–23, editor's commentary.
18. Craven and Cate, *Army Air Forces*, II:338.
19. Craven and Cate, *Army Air Forces*, II:309; *ComChron*, May 1943; Hammel, *Europa*, 137–38.
20. Miller, *Masters*, 143. Miller thinks it may have been a "confidence born of necessity" since there were no long-range fighters, anyway.
21. Letter, Major General Follett Bradley to Arnold, 14 June 1943, Arnold Papers, reel 200.
22. Parton, *Air Force*, 241.
23. Parton, *Air Force*, 242.
24. Letter, Major General Follett Bradley to Arnold, 14 June 1943, Arnold Papers, reel 214.

Notes for Chapter 21

1. Overy, *Bombers*, 127–28. See also Parton, *Air Force*, 271. Per Overy this period was when Arnold began to "lose confidence" in Eaker. Colonel Brian D. Vlaun, USAF, opines that Eaker "probably crossed the line on 12 July 1943" in a letter to Arnold in which the former acknowledged that it "might appear" that he was opposing an idea from Washington although it "seemed sound from there"; see Vlaun, *Selling Schweinfurt: Targeting, Assessment, and Marketing in the Air Campaign against German Industry* (Annapolis: USNI Press, 2020), 231n21.
2. Cable, Arnold from Eaker through Devers, 12 June 1943, Eaker Papers, box 1:17.
3. Copp, *Forged*, 400.
4. Cable, Arnold to Eaker, 5 June 1943, Eaker Papers, box 1:17.
5. Copp, *Forged*, 404.
6. Arnold, *Diaries*, II:25, General Huston's commentary.
7. Cable, Eaker from Giles, 11 June 1943, Eaker Papers, box 1:17.
8. Cable, Arnold from Eaker, through Devers,12 June 1943, Eaker Papers, box 1:17.
9. Copp, *Forged*, 401.
10. Arnold, *Diaries*, II:24, General Huston's comment.
11. Copp, *Forged*, 402.
12. Letter, from Eaker to Major General Idwal H. Edwards, Chief of Staff, ETOUSA, 19 June 1943, Eaker Papers, box 1:17.
13. Keeney, *War*, 6–7.
14. Parton, *Air Force*, 290.
15. Parton, *Air Force*, 273.
16. Letter, Arnold to Eaker, 28 June 1943, Eaker Papers, box 1:17.
17. Parton, *Air Force*, 273.
18. Parton, *Air Force*, 273.

19. Letter, Eaker to Arnold, 29 June 1943, Eaker Papers, box 1:17; Arnold, *Diaries*, II:26, editor's commentary.
20. Letter, Eaker to Arnold, "Eyes Only," 28 June 1943, Eaker Papers, box 1:17.
21. Letter, Arnold to Eaker, 7 July 1943, Eaker Papers, box 1:17.
22. Parton, *Air Force*, 121, 123–24.
23. Hammel, *Europa*, 13; Arnold, *Global Mission*, 376.
24. Stout, *Men*, 157.
25. Stout, *Men*, 157–58. Advanced versions of the P-47 appeared in spring of 1945 with even larger internal tanks which, with two wing tanks, allowed them to go anywhere the bombers could. Information on P-47 variants are at https://www.368thfightergroup.com/P-47-2.html, accessed 28 June 2023.
26. Hammel, *Europa*, 159.
27. Hammel, *Europa*, 12–13; see also 159; Stout, *Men*, 157; *ComChron*, July 1943.
28. Craven and Cate, *Army Air Forces*, II:678–80. Also: Hammel, *Europa*, 12–13; Perret, *Winged*, 263.
29. Arnold, ever pragmatic, was changing his mind on long-range escorts. He later wrote, "I should have preferred never to send any unescorted bomber over Germany," but he is being misleading; in *Global Mission*, 149.
30. Parton, *Air Force*, 278.

Notes for Chapter 22

1. Eaker's draft of the CBO, as approved by the Combined Chiefs, with transmittal note to General Devers is at https://www.alternatewars.com/WW2/CBO_1943/CBO_Eaker.htm, accessed on 15 September 2022.
2. Overy, *Bombers*, 117.
3. Denis Richards, *Portal of Hungerford: The Life of Marshal of the Royal Air Force Viscount Portal of Hungerford* (London: Wm. Heinemann, 1977), 313.
4. Overy, *Bombers*, 117.
5. Hansell was kind enough to do just that, in *Air Plan* at 163.
6. Richards, *Portal*, 313.
7. Overy, *Bombers*, 118.
8. Hammel, *Europa*, 134, 135, 137; *ComChron*, May 1943.
9. Hammel, *Europa*, 141; *ComChron*, June 1943.
10. Hammel, *Europa*, 142; *ComChron*, June 1943; Copp, *Forged*, 407.
11. Craven and Cate, *Army Air Forces*, II:670-671; *ComChron*, June 1943; Hammel, *Europa*, 142. Craven and Cate opined that the number of defenders shot down "might" have approximated the claims of the force gunners. It did not, and never did.
12. After noting the "philosophy of General Eaker . . . who is a champion" of the self-defending bomber, Hammel details the 13 June 1943 mission to Bremen, in which the Eighth suffered heavy losses and the death of Brigadier General Nathan Bedford Forrest III. He observes that, on this mission "ranking proponents of [HADPB] are given more than ample justification for reassessing the need for" long-range fighter escorts. Hammel, *Europa*, 127, 142.

13. See Parton, *Air Force*, 240–41. The reluctance to negatively affect gunners' morale by reducing the number of claimed kills unconsciously reinforced the promise of the self-defending bomber.
14. Miller, *Masters*, 161.
15. Craven and Cate, *Army Air Forces*, II:717.
16. Richards, *Portal*, 314.
17. Harris, *Bomber*, 220–21.
18. Miller, *Masters*, 161.
19. Craven and Cate, *Army Air Forces*, II:714.

Notes for Chapter 23

1. Kreis, *Fog*, 176; Hammel, *Europa*, 147.
2. Kreis, *Fog*, 176.
3. Kreis, *Fog*, 176–77.
4. McFarland and Newton, *Command*, 85.
5. Copp, *Forged*, 277.
6. Here, "losses" include not only combat losses but also end of tour returns to the US and reassignments to organizations outside of the Eighth.
7. Copp, *Forged*, 437.
8. Letter, Colonel Jacob Smart to Arnold, 15 August 1943, Arnold Papers, reel 214.
9. Hammel, *Europa*, 157–61.
10. Hammel, *Europa*, 157.
11. McFarland and Newton, *Command*, 109. See Miller, *Masters*, 180, for the weather break opening the way for Blitz Week.
12. Hughes, memoirs, 39–42, AFHRA 40505.
13. Hammel, *Europa*, 157; *ComChron*, July 1943.
14. Baron Manfred von Richthofen, https://quotessayings.net/topics/richthofen/, accessed 4 September 2020. The quotation is also found with "rubbish" in place of "nonsense": sign on the Ready Room wall of Marine Fighter/Attack Squadron 251 at MCAS Beaufort, SC, during the Vietnam War.
15. Copp, *Forged*, 418. There was no determination on whether the mission counted toward the canine's twenty-five for a ticket home.
16. Craven and Cate, *Army Air Forces*, II:676.
17. Craven and Cate, *Army Air Forces*, II:676; Hammel, *Europa*, 157.
18. Hammel, *Europa*, 157.
19. Copp, *Forged*, 418. Copp has 199 heavies over targets, a not uncommon situation when several sources are utilized for the same operation.
20. The Messerschmitt fighters were, officially, BF-109s—BF for the original production facility, the Bayerische Flugzeugwerke, near Augsburg, Germany (Bavaria). Allied airmen inevitably referred to the aircraft as "Me-109" after its designer, Willie Messerschmitt.
21. Craven and Cate, *Army Air Forces*, II:675.
22. Hammel, *Europa*, 13. The victories were the nine kills on mission 78 and the twenty-four kills on mission 80.
23. McFarland and Newton, *Command*, 153.

24. Copp, *Forged*, 419.
25. Copp, *Forged*, 442.
26. Copp, *Forged*, 437.
27. Intelligence Memorandum, VIII Bomber Command, from Assistant Chief of Staff, A-2, VIII Bomber Command, 3 August 1943, Signed by Colonel Harris Hull, GSC and the Assistant Chief of Staff, A-2, B5115/671–73.
28. One report on the German B-17s was in cablegram R-1236 (n.d.) wherein the author wrote that perhaps the "Germans were hoping that we will be at once both excited and jittery and start shooting down our own planes." Subordinate reasons for the hostile bombers included learning the markings on the US bombers, and "studying gun positions and angles and sphere of fire and so forth"; Eaker Papers, box 1:18.
29. Hammel, *Europa*, 12.
30. Craven and Cate, *Army Air Forces*, II:682. Craven and Cate, Hammel, and *ComChron* usually give the total number of aircraft dispatched, as well the number of those that reach the target; Copp is too often unclear. This work figures losses only as a percentage of bombers reaching the target area.
31. Richard Overy, *The Bombing War: Europe, 1939–1945* (London: Allen Lane, 2013).
32. McFarland and Newton, *Command*, 122. Milch could turn out all the airplanes he wanted, but there would be fewer pilots to fly them.

Notes for Chapter 24

1. Memorandum, Lovett to Arnold, 19 June 1943, Arnold Papers, reel 215. Miller, *Masters*, 144.
2. Miller, *Masters*, 162.
3. Copp, *Forged*, 177n.
4. Stout, *Men*, 157.
5. Davis, *Spaatz*, 18.
6. Gilles memo, Arnold Papers, reel 215.
7. Arnold, *Diaries*, II:27; Overy, *Bombers*, 171; Miller, *Masters*, 144. Overy gives an abbreviated description of the event while stating the P-51 did not see service over Germany until spring 1944; the first Mustangs began escorting on 5 December 1943, although not in large numbers. Overy provides an excellent discussion of the background and overall issues with the long-range escorts.
8. Perret, *Winged*, 260–61.
9. See Overy, *Bombers*, 173, for confirmation of what every author has written—namely, that Eaker was psychologically wedded to the self-defending bomber myth as well as the "security of the force" concept, where a large number of bombers could ensure protection for all.
10. A few Liberators landed at RAF Nicosia, Cyprus, but the others were gone, downed over Romania or ditched in the Mediterranean, along with eight interned in Turkey.
11. Arnold, *Diaries*, II:30, editor's commentary by Major General Huston.
12. Arnold, *Diaries*, II:31, commentary by General Huston. Spaatz's letter was written after JUGGLER and conditioned his comment on the air forces

being used against "vital targets"; Miller, *Masters*, 161. This illuminated a concern that assignment to theater commanders would result in the strategic bombers being employed in tactical roles, something also disquieting to the air commanders in England and to Arnold re: B-29s in Asia.

13. Arnold, *Diaries*, II:31–32.
14. Overy, *Bombers*, 149; *ComChron*, August 1943.
15. Craven and Cate, *Army Air Forces*, II:685.
16. Memorandum, General Arnold from Colonel Jacob Smart, 16 August 1943, Arnold Papers, reel 214 (hereafter "Smart Memorandum"). Smart, from Arnold's advisory council, summarized for the chief key points from a series of meetings he had attended with Eaker, Anderson, Devers, Edwards, and the RAF's ACM Harris in England.
17. Smart Memorandum.
18. Smart Memorandum.

Notes for Chapter 25

1. Hansell, *Air War*, 85. If this is correct, an Eaker-Anderson assessment of flying this mission in early summer may been unfavorable for some reason (or reasons), with Anderson working up Blitz Week instead.
2. Keeney, *War*, 5. Schweinfurt was not included as a target, apparently, just the Messerschmitt plants. Eaker averred later that while in Washington, "I was pushed into it before we were ready; I protested it bitterly."
3. Perret, *Winged*, 264. Hughes's side is at pages 30–32, unpublished memoirs, AFHRA 40505.
4. Craven and Cate, *Army Air Forces*, II:683.
5. Perret, *Winged*, 264.
6. Letter, Eaker to Spaatz, 19 July 1943, Eaker Papers, box 1:16. Portal's suggestion is in Parton, *Air Force*, 292.
7. Craven and Cate, *Army Air Forces*, II:683.
8. Eighth Air Force Cable A 565 E, of 12 August 1943, Eaker to: Brereton, Ninth Air Force; Mediterranean Air Command; North African Air Force (Spaatz); and North African Strategic Air Force (Doolittle); Eaker Papers, box 1:16.
9. The Ninth Air Force strike hit the Wiener-Neustädter Flugzeugwerke Plants (WNF), part of the Messerschmitt company; Hammel, *Europa*, 168–69.
10. Overy, *Bombing War*, 340.
11. Overy, *Bombing War*, 340. Jeremy Harwood, *World War Two from Above: An Aerial View of the Global Conflict* (Minneapolis: Zenith Press, 2014), 148, for "commemorated."
12. Overy, *Bombing War*, 340. The 376 B-17s was the largest strike yet, although only 315 reached the targets. The 4th Wing had just been redesignated the 3rd Bombardment Division and the 1st Wing the 1st Bombardment Division; both retained their original designations for this strike.
13. Miller, *Masters*, 195.
14. Harwood, *World War*, 150.
15. Miller, *Masters*, 196.

16. Harwood, *World War*, 150. The five-hour delay is in Perret, *Winged*, 266; others call the delay as three or three-and-a-half hours (e.g., Copp, *Forged*, 428).
17. Miller, *Masters*, 195–96.
18. Parton, *Air Force*, 299.
19. Copp, *Forged*, 427.
20. Miller, *Masters*, 199. Schweinfurt was the worst of his sixty-nine recorded missions, Major General Lewis Lyle would say years later.
21. Harwood, *World War*, 148.
22. This strike may be the most written about mission in military aviation history; readers seeking full (and often competing) details will easily find them elsewhere, including a number of first-person accounts.
23. Keeney, *War*, 29.
24. Craven and Cate, *Army Air Forces*, II:684–85.
25. Arnold, *Global Mission*, 495.
26. Harwood, *World War*, 152, states that the strike also "wrecked the building turning out jigs for the top-secret Messerschmitt Me-262 jet fighter"; Hammel, *Europa*, 170; Copp, *Forged*, 428; Overy, *Bombers*, 150.
27. Copp, *Forged*, 428.
28. Bomber gunners claimed an astonishing 288 Luftwaffe fighters downed, almost as many as the entire German defending force that day. Actual kills were 47, per Luftwaffe records. Miller, *Masters*, 202.
29. Parton, *Air Force*, 300–302; Overy, *Bombers*, 150; *ComChron*, August 1943; Copp, *Forged*, 428. Overy gives a good summary but is alone in stating that only fifty-five of LeMay's bombers returned to England from North Africa; the agreed-upon number was eighty-five and *ComChron* would be the definitive source here.
30. *ComChron*, August 1943; Hammel, *Europa*, 170, has 183 B-17s over the target and omits the number dispatched. Parton, *Air Force*, 310, has eighty-eight direct hits on two of the buildings.
31. Harwood, *World War*, 152, gives as a contributing cause of off-target drops confusion over the direction of attack as General Williams changed the approach just short of the target. He added that one-hundred-plus B-17s were DBR (152). See also Copp, *Forged*, 427–28; Craven and Cate, *Army Air Forces*, II:686; Overy, *Bombers*, 151.
32. Harwood, *World War*, 152.
33. Ehlers, *Targeting*, 171–72. RE8 as a component of Allied intelligence is discussed on 125, 162–63, 164, 166.
34. Ehlers, *BDA*, 172.
35. Parton, *Air Force*, 311.
36. Miller, *Masters*, 200.
37. McFarland and Newton, *Command*, 128.
38. Parton, *Air Force*, 311. Copp, *Forged*, 428, asserts that more powerful ordnance would have created more devastation. Parton cited Speer in writing the shortage of bearings was "so acute" that the Germans sent emissaries to Switzerland and Sweden to purchase more, despite the six months' supply cached in the woods.

39. Miller, *Masters*, 200; Overy, *Bombers*, 138.
40. Copp, *Forged*, 429.
41. McFarland and Newton, *Command*, 128.
42. Hammel, *Europa*, 170.
43. Harris, *Bomber*, 220–21 for panacea and Schweinfurt; 181–83 for the Peen-emünde raid; Denis, *Portal*, 313–14. Parton, *Air Force*, 311–12 for Harris, Portal, and Schweinfurt.
44. *ComChron*, August 1943; *ComChron*, September 1943; Hammel, *Europa*, 171–79. The overall code name for Hitler's "vengeance weapons" and their developmental and testing facilities was CROSSBOW; operational launching sites were NOBALL targets.
45. Allan Williams, *Operation Crossbow: The Untold Story of the Search for Hitler's Secret Weapons* (London: Random House, 2013).
46. Stout, *Men*, 145.

Notes for Chapter 26

1. Craven and Cate, *Army Air Forces*, II:279–80.
2. Miller, *Masters*, 41.
3. Craven and Cate, *Army Air Forces*, II:280.
4. Craven and Cate, *Army Air Forces*, II:282–83.
5. Craven and Cate, *Army Air Forces*, II:282.
6. Davis, *Spaatz*, 115.
7. Craven and Cate, *Army Air Forces*, II:284.
8. Arnold, *Global Mission*, 448–50; Davis, *Spaatz*, 267–68.
9. Davis, *Spaatz*, 268–69; Mets, *Master*, 176; Overy, *Bombing War*, 308.
10. Arnold, *Global Mission*, 448–49.
11. Mets, *Master*, 177. The meeting was generated by the British to clarify another matter, but Arnold took advantage to place his plan before the BCS. Welsh forwarded it to Portal in London.
12. Davis, *Spaatz*, 269; Parton, *Air Force*, 331–33.
13. Goldberg and Overy, presentation, 49.
14. Hammel, *Air War*, 180; Copp, *Forged*, 432.
15. Because of a difference in airspeeds, the Liberators were often used in diversionary raids; if teamed with Fortresses, they had to fly as the last echelon.
16. Arnold, *Global Mission*, 450.
17. Arnold, *Global Mission*, 450. By this time Air-Sea Rescue included both the RAF's service and a newly established USAAF rescue service.
18. Arnold, *Global Mission*, 449–50; *ComChron*, September 1943; Hammel, *Europa*, 170; Harwood, *World War*, 152–53; Craven and Cate, *Army Air Forces*, II:688; Harwood, *World War*, 152. Overy, *Bombing*, 341, has sixty-five bombers downed, a loss rate of 19 percent, while Parton, *Air Force*, 306, states 14 percent lost.
19. Arnold, *Global Mission*, 450. The company was (and still is) AB SKF, an international company founded in 1907 with the home office in Gothenburg, Sweden.

20. Robert J. Mrazek's *To Kingdom Come: An Epic Saga of Survival in the Air War over Germany* (New York: New American Library, 2012) tells in detail of the Stuttgart raid, including Anderson's supposed responses to Arnold's queries about mission results.
21. Miller, *Masters*, 204.
22. Overy, *Bombers*, 174.
23. Hammel, *Europa*, 20.
24. Copp, *Forged*, 433.
25. Arnold, *Diaries*, II:52.
26. Parton, *Air Force*, 307.
27. Copp, Forged, 435.
28. Keeney, *War*, 35.
29. Copp, *Forged*, 436–38.
30. Keeney, *War*, 35. Arnold's first letter was 25 September, the second was the twenty-sixth. On the twenty-seventh he cabled about German aircraft production; see Keeney, *War*, 35n197.

Notes for Chapter 27

1. Hammel, *Europa*, 191; *ComChron*, October 1943.Thirty-four heavies were damaged.
2. Keeney, *War*, 36.
3. Roger A. Freeman, *The Mighty Eighth War Diary* (Osceola, WI: Motorbooks International, 1993), 121.
4. Hammel, *Europa*, 194.
5. Keeney, *War*, 37.
6. Report, VIII Fighter Command Operation of 10 October 1943, by Fighter Command A-2 Section, B5032/1526–27; Hammel, *Europa*, 195.
7. Miller, *Masters*, 11, says the aiming point was the railroad yards "and an adjacent neighborhood of workers' homes," but then adds "declassified mission reports and flight records clearly list the 'center of town' as the AP." Records for the 94th BG have the AP as a "built up section of North East tip of Marshaling yards." Keeney, *POINTBLANK*, 36, has "major railroad center" for the target; Hammel, *Europa*, 195, has "rail targets and canals" as the AP.
8. Twelve B-17s were shot down over Germany; the thirteenth crash-landed in England at a different airfield.
9. Keeney, *POINTBLANK*, 49.
10. Copp, *Forged*, 439.
11. Arnold, *Diaries*, II:48.
12. Parton, *Air Force*, 319–20.
13. Parton, *Air Force*, 320.
14. Parton, *Air Force*, 313.
15. *ComChron*, October 1943. Of course, the "real" pressing question was, or should have been, "Never mind the aircraft numbers, how many *rated pilots* do the Germans have?" The response would have been, "Fewer and fewer every day."

16. *ComChron*, October 1943; Copp, *Forged*, 439–40; Hammel, *Europa*, 196.
17. Hammel, *Europa*, 191. The problem for the Germans was not in the numbers of fighters but in pilots to fly them. The Allies did not pick up on the crucial pilot shortage quickly enough.
18. Crane, *American*, 43. Dr. Crane adds that German fighter pilots flew until "killed or maimed. . . . Less than 10 percent of German fighter pilots survived the war."
19. Keeney, *POINTBLANK*, 62.
20. Immediate Interpretation Report No. K.1785, CIU, RAF Medmenham, 17 October 1943, B5032/1193–94.
21. *ComChron*, October 1943; Hammel, *Europa*, 196; Stout, *Men*, 151.
22. Kreis, *Fog*, 201–2n. The last quotation is from Craven and Cate, *Army Air Forces*, II:9; Perret, *Winged*, 260; Overy, *Bombers*, 151, cites losses of 65 bombers out of an "attacking force" of 229, losses of over 28 percent.
23. *ComChron*, October 1943; Hammel, *Europa*, 196.
24. Overy, *Bombing War*, 341.
25. Ehlers, *Targeting*, 172, in part quoting from "ACIU K Section Report Number K.1785 Schweinfurt" of 20 October 1943. An RAF Spitfire covered the strike as the Eighth's 7th PR Group flew no missions to Schweinfurt in October 1943; Keen, *Eyes*, 317–19.
26. Ehlers, *Targeting*, 172.
27. Copp, *Forged*, 441.
28. Copp, *Forged*, 441.
29. Overy, *Bombing War*, 151.
30. Overy, *Bombing War*, 341; Kreis, *Fog*, 202.
31. Copp, *Forged*, 442.
32. Parton, *Air Force*, 318.
33. Erhart, *Intelligence*, 202.
34. Stout, *Men*, 152.
35. Keeney, *POINTBLANK*, 74–75.
36. Ralph, "Improvised Destruction," 525.
37. Miller, *Masters*, 236.
38. Hammel, *Europa*, 206.
39. Hammel, *Europa*, 215.
40. Parton, *Air Force*, 319.
41. *ComChron*, October 1943; Hammel, *Europa*, 198. Hammel has eighty-six bombers hitting the primary at Düren, vice ninety-seven in *ComChron*. The difference is that eleven of the ninety-seven still couldn't find the target and therefore bombed Aachen, leaving eighty-six at the primary.
42. Hammel, *Europa*, 209.
43. Eaker continued to believe with his British counterpart, "Bomber" Harris, that day/night "round-the-clock" bombing would be sufficient to "knock out the industrial props" of the Germans. Overy, *Bombers*, 338. True, perhaps, but that would do little to satisfy the CBO requirement to ensure air superiority for D-Day.
44. Keeney, *POINTBLANK*, 31.

45. Copp, *Forged*, 444.
46. See Copp, *Forged*, 413–14, 424; Parton, *Air Force*, 126; Miller, *Masters*, 144.
47. Copp, *Forged*, 413–14.
48. Miller, *Masters*, 204.

Notes for Chapter 28

1. Craven and Cate, *Army Air Forces*, II:566–67. The authorization was document CCS 217/1 of 24 October 1943.
2. Parton, *Air Force*, 323. There was no explanation of whether the "axiom" actually worked that way.
3. Stout, *Men*, 154–55.
4. Parton, *Air Force*, 323. The CBO projected a success rate of 66.67 percent; the numbers and targets are broken down on 323.
5. Overy, *Bombers*, 317, provides a chart of these data compiled from AFHRA sources.
6. *ComChron*, December 1943.
7. Coffey, *Hap*, 291–92.
8. Arnold, *Diaries*, II:31–32.

Notes for Chapter 29

1. Davis, *Spaatz*, 268.
2. This episode is captured by Davis in *Spaatz*, 263–68.
3. Copp, *Forged*, 445.
4. Davis, *Spaatz*, 266–67.
5. Parton, *Air Force*, 331.
6. Overy, *Bombers*, 174. The document was also transmitted to the membership of the CCS on the same date.
7. These were the 7th PR Group and the 25th Bomb Group (Reconnaissance) under Brigadier General Elliott Roosevelt's 325th Reconnaissance Wing.
8. Davis, *Spaatz*, 267.
9. McFarland and Newton, *Command*, 147.
10. Davis, *Spaatz*, 268.
11. Davis, *Spaatz*, 268.
12. Memorandum by the United States Chiefs of Staff, "Integrated Command of US Strategic Air Forces in the European-Mediterranean Area, Doc. No. CCS 400 of 18 November 1943," in US Secretary and Office of the Combined Chiefs of Staff, *Sextant Conference, November–December 1943: Papers and Minutes of Meetings, Sextant and Eureka Conferences* (Washington, DC: Office, US Secretary and Office of the Combined Chiefs of Staff, 1943), 94, https://www.jcs.mil/Portals/36/Documents/History/WWII/Sextant_Eureka3.pdf (hereafter, *Sextant*).
13. Memorandum by the United States Chiefs of Staff, "Integrated Command of US Strategic Air Forces in the European-Mediterranean Area," Doc. No. CCS 400, 18 November 1943, in *Sextant*, 94–95. The POINTBLANK Directive was

a part of the CBO and stated that "the highest priority for every combat mission flown into Occupied Europe by every Allied fighter and bomber was to defeat the Luftwaffe" to eliminate the German Air Force threat to OVERLORD. Keeney, *POINTBLANK*, 40.

14. Memorandum by the United States Chiefs of Staff, "Integrated Command of US Strategic Air Forces in the European-Mediterranean Area," Doc. No. CCS 400/1 of 26 November 1943, in *Sextant*, 95.

15. Davis, *Spaatz*, 269.

16. Davis, *Spaatz*, 269, 271.

17. Memorandum by the British Chiefs of Staff, "Integrated Command of US Strategic Air Forces in the European-Mediterranean Area," Doc. No. CCS 400/1 of 26 November 1943, in *Sextant*, 100–101. See also Davis, *Spaatz*, 269, for the "diametrically opposed" comment.

18. Arnold, *Global Mission*, 473–75.

19. Of the crucial 6 December meeting, Arnold omits any mention either in his autobiography or his edited diary, including especially his intense criticism of Eaker to the Group. Ditto for Portal's biographer.

20. Combined Chiefs of Staff, Minutes of 134th Meeting, Sextant Conference, Mena House, Cairo, Egypt, 4 December 1943. Portal's complete reclama at 472–75.

21. Davis, *Spaatz*, 270.

22. Miller, *Masters*, 244.

23. CCS, Minutes of 134th Meeting, Arnold's rebuttal at 475–76.

24. Davis, *Spaatz*, 271.

25. CCS, Minutes of 134th Meeting, 476.

26. CCS, Minutes of 134th Meeting, 482.

27. CCS, Minutes of 138th Meeting, Sextant Conference, Mena House, Cairo, Egypt, 7 December 1943, 503.

28. CCS, Minutes of 138th Meeting, 504.

29. Discussion, "Integrated Command of US Strategic Air Forces in the European-Mediterranean Area," Doc. No. CCS 400/2 of 4 December 1943, in *Sextant*, 97.

30. Appendix, "Integrated Command of US Strategic Air Forces in the European-Mediterranean Area," in *Sextant*, 98–99.

Notes for Chapter 30

1. Davis, *Spaatz*, 272; Parton, *Air Force*, 335. The reference to "Tedder" was Air Chief Marshal Sir Arthur Tedder, air officer commanding, Mediterranean Air Command. On 4 February 1944 the designation was changed to United States Strategic and Tactical Air Forces (USSTAF), Europe, reflecting the inclusion of the Ninth Air Force.

2. Eisenhower, *Crusade*, 216.

3. Portal had apparently already witnessed too much of Major General Brereton. Davis, *Spaatz*, 276.

4. Spaatz Command Diary, December 1943; Daily Journal Entry for 9 December 1943, B5535/274-275.

5. Davis, *Spaatz*, 278. Davis writes that Spaatz was not ever, even once, in his papers or postwar interviews critical of Eaker's performance as commanding general of the Eighth Air Force.

6. Letter, Devers to Eaker, 15 December 1942, Eaker Papers, box 1:17.

7. Davis, *Spaatz*, 272.

8. Copp, *Forged*, 363; Parton, *Air Force*, 239.

9. Parton, *Air Force*, 336.

10. Parton, *Air Force*, 336. Lieutenant General Barney McK. Giles later claimed that "the decision"—presumably for Eaker to go to the Mediterranean—was made by Arnold "after consultation with Eisenhower"; McFarland and Newton, *Command*, 149.

11. Parton, *Air Force*, 336; Davis, *Spaatz*, 274–75. At the time Kuter was writing many of Arnold's cables; possibly it was he who drafted this one.

12. Parton, *Air Force*, 336.

13. Arnold, *Global Mission*, 441.

14. Parton, *Air Force*, 336–37; Coffey, *Hap*, 331.

15. McFarland and Newton, *Command*, 282n91.

16. Craven and Cate, *Army Air Forces*, II:749.

17. Coffey, *Hap*, 331. Coffey may have been attempting to make Arnold look a bit better than he did. No other author writes of Arnold's "notorious inability" to express himself in writing. Coffey, 333, lays Eaker's assignment to MAAF solely at the feet of Eisenhower.

18. Craven and Cate, *Army Air Forces*, II:749.

19. Davis in *Spaatz*, 273–80, discusses in some detail this correspondence.

20. Spaatz Command Diary, December 1943; Daily Journal Entry for 19 December 1943, B5535/279–80.

21. Spaatz Command Diary, December 1943; Journal Entry for 9 December 1943, B5535/275.

22. Spaatz Command Diary, December 1943; Journal Entry for 19 December 1943, B5535/278.

23. Spaatz Command Diary, December 1943;, Journal Entry for 23 December 1943, B5535/278.

24. Cable, Eaker from Eisenhower, 25 December 1943, Eaker Papers, box 1:17.

25. Miller, *Masters*, 245.

26. Letters, all in Eaker Papers, box 1:17.

27. Letter, Devers to Eaker, 21 December 1943, Eaker Papers, box 1:17.

Notes for Chapter 31

1. Hammel, *Europa*, 207; *ComChron*, November 1943.

2. "USSTAF" was by command of Lieutenant General Spaatz in directive, Headquarters, United States Strategic Air Forces Europe, of 4 February 1944. The "T" was to stand for "Tactical," added after the Ninth (Tactical) Air Force was placed under Spaatz's administrative control.

3. Printed in full in Metts, *Master*, 191.

Notes for Postscript

1. Parton, *Air Force*, 346.
2. Parton, *Air Force*, 370.

Bibliography

General

The ladies at the Air Force Research and Historical Agency gave much welcomed assistance by providing digital files of documents from the Eighth Air Force during the years 1942–1945. Reference books, countless official and candid unofficial photographs unavailable anywhere else, air and groundcrew memoirs, and many other materials—not excluding a stunningly impressive amount of knowledge about the Eight's air war and its people and subordinate organizations—reside in the Roger A. Freeman Research Center at the National Museum of the Mighty Eighth Air Force in Pooler, Georgia. These resources were liberally consulted as the director of the center, Dr. Vivian Rogers-Price, provided research assistance in addition to being an exceptional source of factual knowledge. Staff members Judy Roddy and Tiffany Bueno were always ready to provide much-needed help with databases and computer manipulations. By far the best and most interesting were the veterans of the Eighth who used to serve as docents or who were visitors and spent time in the center sharing their experiences of England and the Eighth. The museum is close by the Savannah–Hilton Head International Airport, originally Savannah Army Air Field (AAF) where the Eighth Air Force was born in January 1943.

The assistance of the AFHRA in providing copies of official documents was both outstanding and greatly appreciated. In the endnotes, most AFHRA documents are identified by the reel's designation of a capital letter and five digits, followed by a backslash (/) and the document's page number(s). Page numbers usually correspond to the counter on the PDF viewer. Exceptions are for a few that display a "Frame Number" at the bottom of the document, used in lieu of the viewer counter (example: C0140/2934).

As this volume was being drafted, a detailed "Combat Chronology" of AAF missions worldwide from 1942 through 1945 was located on a Rutgers University website hosted by the Computer Sciences Department and relied upon by the author as it listed every mission flown in each theater for each day of the war: https://people.cs.rutgers.edu/~mcgrew/wwii/usaf. During the editing process, this source was removed from the internet. However, Kit C. Carter and Robert Mueller's The Army Air Forces in World War II, Combat Chronology, 1941–1945 with essentially identical information concurrently became available on the internet at https://archive.org/details/AFD-100525-035/page/n9/mode/2up. Data from either are cited in endnotes and identified only as "*ComChron*, month year" without ultimate source distinction.

The Manuscript Division, Library of Congress, could not have been more helpful or nicer in providing facilities, materials, and documents. I was told several times that their first responsibility was to the researchers. And this one was particularly grateful.

Notes

AFHRA: Air Force Research and Historical Agency, Maxwell Air Force Base, Alabama

MS Div, LoC: Manuscript Division, Library of Congress, Washington, DC

NMMEA: National Museum of the Mighty Eighth Air Force, Pooler, Georgia

Maxwell AFB: Maxwell Air Force Base, Montgomery, Alabama

Unpublished Manuscripts

Harris, Elbert F. "An Account of My Experiences in the Eighth Air Force in World War II. Norman Malayney Collection-2077. NMMEA.
Hughes, Richard D'Oyly. Untitled memoirs. Reel 40505/188-258. AFHRA.
Wendling, Jack. *A Bomber Tour Revisited: Recollections of an 8th Air Force Pilot of the Air War in Europe.* Copy in the author's possession.

Postwar Interviews with Commanding General, USSTAF

Spaatz, General Carl A. Interview by Bruce C. Hopper, PhD (historian for USSTAF). Park House, Teddington, London, 20 May and 27 June 1945. Reel A5535/297-318 and A5535/247-262. AFHRA.

Academic Research

Anderson, Barry J. *Army Air Forces Stations: A Guide to the Stations Where US Army Air Forces Personnel Served in the United Kingdom During World War II.* Maxwell AFB, AL: Research Division, USAF Historical Research Center, 31 January 1985.

Ballew, Brian P. *The Enemy Objectives Unit in World War II: Selecting Targets for Aerial Bombardment that Support the Political Purpose of War.* Fort Leavenworth: US Army Command and General Staff College, 2014.

Beagle, T. W. *Operation Pointblank: Effects-Based Targeting, Another Empty Promise?* Maxwell AFB, AL: Air University Press, 2001.

Bishop, Benjamin W. (Colonel, USAF). *Jimmy Dolittle: Cincinnatus of the Air.* PhD diss., Air University, 2016.

Cline, Ray S. *Washington Command Post: The Operations Division.* Vol. 2 of The War Department, The United States Army in World War II. Washington, DC: United States Army, Center of Military History, 1990.

Culbertson, Charles N. (Lieutenant Colonel, USAF). *Air Intelligence and the Search for the Center of Gravity.* Report. Maxwell AFB, AL: Air War College, Air University 1988.

Ehlers, Robert S. *BDA: Anglo-American Air Intelligence, Bomb Damage Assessment, and the Bombing Campaigns against Germany, 1914–1945.* PhD diss., Ohio State University, 2005.

Ennels, Jerome A., Robert B. Kane, and Silvano A. Wueschner. *Cradle of Airpower: An Illustrated History of Maxwell Air Force Base, 1918–2018.* Report. Maxwell AFB, AL: Air University Press, 1 October 2018.

Finney, Robert T. *History of the Air Corps Tactical School: 1920–1940.* Maxwell AFB, AL: Research Studies Institute, USAF Historical Division, Air University, 1955.

Heathman, Jeremiah S. (Major, USAF.). *The Bombing of Brittany: Solving the Wrong Problem.* Ft. Leavenworth, KS: School of Advanced Military Studies, US Army Command and General Staff College, 2010.

Laine, Howard David. *AWPD-1: America's Pre–World War II Plan for Bombing Germany.* Master's thesis, Virginia Polytechnic University, May 1991.

Owens, John Patrick (Major, USAF). *The Evolution of FM 100-20, Command and Employment of Air Power (21 July 1943): The Foundation of Modern Air Power Doctrine.* Master's thesis, US Army Command and General Staff College, 1989.

Rauch, John T. *Assessing Airpower's Effects: Capabilities and Limitations of Real-Time Battle Damage Assessment.* Maxwell AFB, AL: Air University Press, 2004.

Rigole, Julius. *The Strategic Bombing Campaign against Germany during World War II.* Master's thesis, Louisiana State University, 2002.

St. Clair, Matthew G. *The Twelfth Air Force: Tactical and Operational Innovations in the Mediterranean Theater of Operations, 1943–1944.* Maxwell AFB, AL: Air University Press, 2007.

Stewart, Paul D. T. (Group Captain, RAF [Ret.]). *Medmenham: Anglo-American Photographic Intelligence in the Second World War.* PhD diss., University of Northampton, 2019.

Sutterfield, Jon (Major, USAF). *Eighth Air Force Bombing 20–25 February 1944: How Logistics Enabled "Big Week" to Be "Big."* Master's thesis, Air Command and Staff College, Air University, April 2000.

Tate, James P. (Lieutenant Colonel, USAF [Ret.]). *The Army and Its Air Corps: Army Policy Toward Aviation, 1919–1941.* PhD diss., Air University, June 1998.

Vlaun, Brian D. (Major, USAF). *Selling Schweinfurt: Targeting, Assessment, and Marketing in the Air Campaign against German Industry.* Annapolis: USNI Press, 2020.

Professional Papers and Seminars

Campbell, James B. "Origins of Aerial Photographic Interpretation, US Army, 1916 to 1918." *Photogrammetric Engineering & Remote Sensing* 74, no. 1 (January 2008): 77–93.

Carter, Kit C., and Robert Mueller. *United States Army Air Forces in World War II: Combat Chronology, 1941–1945.* Washington, DC: Center for Air Force History, 1991. https://archive.org/details/AFD-100525-035/page/n9/mode/2u.

Ehlers, Robert S., Jr. (Colonel, USAF, [Ret.]). "Air Intelligence and the Bombing of Nazi Germany." Unpublished article. Capstone Course for the Bachelors Degree in Intelligence and Security Studies, ISSA 4303, Angelo State University, TX. Accessed 19 December 2013. http:/angelo.edu/courses/syllabi/202120/22990.pdf/.

Davis, Richard, G. *Bombing the European Axis Powers: A Historical Digest of the Combined Bomber Offensive, 1939–1945.* Maxwell AFB, AL: Air University Press, 2006.

Davis, Richard, G. (Office of Air Force History). "Royal Air Force / United States Air Force Cooperation." Royal Air Force / United States Air Force

Cooperation Seminar, RAF Museum, Hendon, London, 29 October 1990. *Proceedings of the Royal Air Force Historical Society*, no. 9, 1991.

Fay, Elton C. "Air Strength of the United States." *Annals of the American Academy of Political and Social Science* 29, no. 9 (May 1955): 30–37.

Goldberg, Alfred, and Richard Overy. Presentation at Joint Royal Air Force and United States Air Force Seminar, Royal Air Force Museum, Hendon, London, 29 October 1990. *Air Power History* 38, no. 3 (Fall 1991): 38–48.

Guglielmo, Mark. "The Contribution of Economists to Military Intelligence during World War II." *Journal of Economic History* 68, no. 1 (March 2008): 109–50.

Hallion, Dr. Richard. "The USSAF Role." Chap. 5 in *Air Intelligence Symposium Bracknell Paper No 7*. London: Royal Air Force Historical Society and Royal Air Force Staff College, 1997.

Holley, I. B. (Major General, USAF [Ret.]), and John Terraine. "Land/Air Operations in the Mediterranean and Northwest Europe." Presented at the Joint Royal Air Force / United States Air Force Seminar, Royal Air Force Museum, Hendon, London, 29 October 1990. *Air Power History* 38, no. 4 (Winter 1991): 30–42.

LeMay, Curtis E. (General USAF [Ret.]), and Beirne Lay Jr. (Colonel USAFR [Ret.]). *Strategic Air Power: Destroying the Enemy's War Resources*. Vol. 2 of Impact: Destruction from the Air. Harrisburg, PA: National Historical Society for the Air Force Historical Foundation, 1989.

McGrew, Charles. *Combat Chronologies of the US Army Air Forces*. Accessed early summer 2021. paul.rutgers.edu/~mcgrew/.

"Photographic Reconnaissance in World War II." Seminar, Royal Air Force Museum, Hendon, London, 10 June 1991. *Proceedings of the Royal Air Force Historical Society*, no. 10, 1991.

Putney, Dr. Diane. "USAAF Intelligence and the European War: Daylight Strategic Air War in Europe." Chap. 6 in *Air Intelligence Symposium Bracknell Paper No 7*. London: Royal Air Force Historical Society and Royal Air Force Staff College, 1997.

Russell, Edward T. *Leaping the Atlantic Wall: Army Air Forces Campaigns in Western Europe, 1942–1945*. Vol. 4 of The U.S. Army Air Forces in World War II. Washington, DC: Air Force History and Museums Programs, 1999.

Storlie, Chad. "Manage Uncertainty with Commander's Intent." *Harvard Business Review*, November 3, 2010. https://hbr.org/2010/11/dont-play-golf-in-a-football-g.

Government Publications

Aandahl, Frederick, William M. Franklin, and William Slany, eds. *Foreign Relations of the United States, The Conferences at Washington, 1941–1942, and Casablanca, 1943.* Washington, DC: US Government Printing Office, 1958. https://history.state.gov/historicaldocuments/frus1941-43.

Office of Air Force History. *Condensed Analysis of the Ninth Air Force in the European Theater of Operations: An Analytical Study of the Operating Procedures and Functional Organization of Tactical Air Power as Developed by the Ninth Air Force in the War of Western Europe.* Washington, DC: United States Air Force, 1984.

Rostow, W. W. "The Beginnings of Air Targeting." Adapted from *OSS/Research and Analysis War Diary.* Vol. V of CIA Historical Review Program. Washington, DC: Center for the Study of Intelligence, Central Intelligence Agency, 22 September 1993.

Rostow, W. W. "Waging Economic Warfare from London: The Enemy Objectives Unit." *Studies in Intelligence* 36, no. 5 (1992): 73–80.

Ruppenthal, Roland G. *Logistical Support of the Armies, May 1941–September 1944.* Vol. 4 of United States Army in World War II, European Theater of Operations. Washington, DC: Department of the Army, Office of the Chief Historian, 1959.

United States Marine Corps. "Marine Corps Planning Process." *Marine Corps Warfighting Publication (MCWP)* 5, no. 1 *(24 August 2010).*

Warner, Michael. "The Collapse of Intelligence Support for Air Power, 1944–1952." Center for the Study of Intelligence, Central Intelligence Agency. *Studies in Intelligence* 49, no. 3 (2007). Released in full.

Documents

Fairchild, Muir S. Fairchild (Major General, Director of Military Requirements). AWPD-42: Requirements for Air Ascendancy. War Department, Army Air Forces, Air Staff. Copy no. 12.

Combined Chiefs of Staff. Minutes of 134th Meeting, Sextant Conference. Mena House, Cairo, Egypt, 4 December 1943.

Combined Chiefs of Staff. Minutes of 138th Meeting, Sextant Conference. Mena House, Cairo, Egypt, 7 December 1943.

History of Directorate of Intelligence, United States Strategic Air Forces in Europe, January 1944—May 1945. Authorized by Brigadier

General George C. McDonald, Assistant Chief of Staff, A-2, USSAFE, 8 September 1945.

Joint Chiefs of Staff, 602. "Integrated Command of US Strategic Air Forces in the European-Mediterranean Area." Appendix. 26 November 1943.

Proceedings of the American-British Joint Chiefs of Staff Conferences. Held in Washington, DC, on Twelve Occasions Between 24 December 1941 and 14 January 1942. Joint Chiefs of Staff file copy. Accessed on 15 May 2020. https://www.jcs.mil/Portals/36/Documents/History/WWII/Arcadia3.pdf.

United States Bureau of the Census. *Those Who Served: America's Veterans from World War II to the War on Terror.* Washington, DC, June 2020.

US Secretary and Combined Chiefs of Staff. *Sextant Conference, November–December 1943: Papers and Minutes of Meetings, Sextant and Eureka Conferences.* Washington, DC: Office, US Secretary and Office of the Combined Chiefs of Staff, 1943. https://www.jcs.mil/Portals/36/Documents/History/WWII/Sextant_Eureka3.pdf.

Autobiographies and Diaries

Arnold, Henry H. (General, Air Force). *American Airpower Comes of Age: General Henry H. "Hap" Arnold's World War II Diaries.* Edited by John W. Huston. 2 vols. Maxwell AFB, AL: Air University Press, 2002.

Arnold, Henry H. (General, Air Force). *Global Mission.* New York: Harper & Row, 1948.

Babington-Smith, Constance. *Air Spy: The Story of Photo Intelligence in World War II.* New York: Harper and Brothers, 1957.

Crosby, Harry H. *A Wing and a Prayer: The "Bloody 100th" Bomb Group and the US Eighth Air Force in Action over Europe in World War 2.* New York: HarperCollins, 1993.

Doolittle, James H. (Lieutenant General, USAFR), and Carroll V. Glines. *I Could Never Be So Lucky Again.* New York: Bantam Books, 1991.

Eisenhower, Dwight D. *Crusade in Europe.* New York: Doubleday, 1948.

Hansell, Haywood S., Jr. *The Air Plan That Defeated Hitler.* Atlanta: Higgins-McArthur/ Longino & Porter, 1972.

Hansell, Haywood S., Jr. *The Strategic Air War against Germany and Japan: A Memoir.* USAF Warrior Studies. Washington, DC: Office of Air Force History, 1986.

Harris, Sir Arthur T. (Marshal of the Royal Air Force). *Bomber Offensive.* London: Collins, 1947.

Johnson, Kenneth B. *A Spy in the Sky: A Photographic Reconnaissance Spitfire Pilot in WWII*. Yorkshire: Pen and Sword Books, 2019.

Jones, R. V. *The Wizard War: British Scientific Intelligence, 1939–1945*. Brattleboro, VT: Echo Point Books, 2017.

LeMay, Curtis E. (General, USAF [Ret.]), with McKinley Kantor. *Mission with LeMay: My Story*. Garden City: Doubleday and Company, 1965.

LeMay, Curtis E. (General, USAF [Ret.]), and Bill Yenne. *Superfortress: The Boeing B-29 and American Airpower in World War II*. Yardley, PA: Westholme, 2006.

McLaughlin, J. Kemp (Brigadier General, USAFR). *The Mighty Eighth in WW II: A Memoir*. Lexington: University Press of Kentucky, 2000.

Nutter, Ralph N. *With the Possum and the Eagle: A Memoir of a Navigator over Germany and Japan*. Novato, CA: Presidio Press, 2002.

Powys-Lybbe, Ursula. *The Eye of Intelligence*. London: William Kimber & Co, 1983.

Slessor, Sir John (Marshal of the Royal Air Force). *The Central Blue: The Autobiography of Sir John Slessor, Marshal of the RAF*. New York: Frederick A. Praeger, 1957.

Thompson, Robert L. *Flying in the Coffin Corner*. Tucson: White Winged Press, 1995.

Secondary Sources: Books

Ambrose, Stephen E. *The Supreme Commander: The War Years of Dwight D. Eisenhower*. Jackson: University Press of Mississippi, 1999.

Avery, Thomas Eugene. *Interpretation of Aerial Photographs*. 3rd ed. Minneapolis: Burgess Publishing, 1977.

Biddle, Tami Davis. *Rhetoric and Reality in Air Warfare: The Evolution of British and American Ideas about Strategic Bombing, 1914–1945*. Princeton: Princeton University Press, 2003.

Cody, James R. "Air War Plans Division-42." Chap. 3 in *AWPD-42 to Instant Thunder: Consistent, Evolutionary Thought or Revolutionary Change?* Maxwell AFB: Air University Press, 1996. http://www.JSTOR.com/stable/resrep13787.9.

Coffey, Thomas M. *Decision Over Schweinfurt: The US Eighth Air Force Battle for Daylight Bombing*. New York: David McKay Co., 1977.

Coffey, Thomas M. *Hap: The Story of the US Air Force and the Man Who Built It, General Henry H. "Hap" Arnold*. New York: Viking Press, 1982.

Copp, DeWitt S. *Forged in Fire: Strategy and Decisions in the Airwar over Europe, 1940–1945.* Garden City: Doubleday, 1982.

Costello, Peter A. *A Matter of Trust: The History of Close Air Support.* Maxwell AFB, AL: Air University Press, 1997

Crane, Conrad C. *American Airpower Strategy in World War II: Bombs, Cities, Civilians, and Oil.* Lawrence: University Press of Kansas, 2016.

Craven, Wesley Frank, and James Lea Cate, eds. *The Army Air Forces in World War II.* 3 vols. Chicago: University of Chicago Press, 1952.

Crosswell, D. K. R. *Beetle: The Life of General Walter Bedell Smith.* American Warrior Series. Lexington: University of Kentucky Press, 2012.

Daso, Dik Alan. *Hap Arnold and the Evolution of American Air Power.* Washington, DC: Smithsonian Institution Press, 2000.

Davis, Kenneth S. *Eisenhower: Soldier of Democracy.* Old Saybrook, CT: Konecky & Konecky, 1945.

Davis, Richard G. *Carl L. Spaatz and the Air War in Europe.* Washington, DC: Center for Air Force History, 1993.

D'Este, Carlo. *Eisenhower: A Soldier's Life.* New York: Henry Holt, 2002.

Downing, Taylor. *Spies in the Sky: The Secret Battle for Aerial Intelligence during World War II.* Boston: Little, Brown, 2012.

Ehlers, Robert S., Jr. *The Mediterranean Air War: Airpower and Allied Victory in World War II.* Modern War Studies Series. Lawrence: University Press of Kansas, 2015.

Ehlers, Robert S. Jr. *Targeting the Third Reich: Air Intelligence and the Allied Bombing Campaigns.* Modern War Studies Series. Lawrence: University Press of Kansas, 2009.

Eisenhower, John S. D. *General Ike: A Personal Reminiscence.* New York: Free Press, 2003.

Ethell, Jeffrey L. *Bombers of World War II.* Ann Arbor, MI: Lowe and B. Hould, 2001.

Ethell, Jeffrey L., Robert Grinsell, Roger Freeman, David A. Anderton, Frederick A. Johnsen, Bill Sweetman, Alex Vanags-Baginskis, et al. *The Great Book of World War II Airplanes.* Tokyo: ZokishaPress, 1984.

Ferrell, Robert H., ed. *The Eisenhower Diaries.* New York: W. W. Norton, 1981.

Freeman, Roger A. *B-17 Fortress at War.* New York: Charles Scribner's Sons, 1977.

Freeman, Roger A. *The Mighty Eighth: A History of the Units, Men and Machines of the US 8th Air Force.* Osceola, WI: Motorbooks International, 1991.

Freeman, Roger A. *The Mighty Eighth War Diary*. Osceola, WI: Motorbooks International, 1993.

Freeman, Roger A. *The Mighty Eighth War Manual*. London: Cassell, 2001

Freeman, Roger A. *Raiding the Reich: The Allied Strategic Bombing Offensive in Europe*. London: Arms and Armour Press, 1997.

Gladwell, Malcolm. *The Bomber Mafia: A Tale of Innovation and Obsession*. Dublin: Penguin Books, 2022.

Greer, Thomas H. *The Development of Air Doctrine in the Army Air Arm, 1921–1941*. Washington, DC: Office of Air Force History, 1985.

Griffith, Charles. *The Quest: Haywood Hansell and American Strategic Bombing in World War II*. Maxwell AFB, AL: Air University Press, 1999.

Hammel, Eric. *Air War Europa: America's Air War against Germany in Europe and North Africa, Chronology, 1942–1945*. Pacifica, CA: Pacifica Press, 1994.

Hansen, Chris. *Enfant Terrible: The Times and Schemes of General Elliott Roosevelt*. Tucson: Able Baker Press, 2012.

Harwood, Jeremy. *World War Two from Above: An Aerial View of the Global Conflict*. Minneapolis: Zenith Press, 2014.

Haun, Phil, ed. *Lectures of the Air Corps Tactical School and American Strategic Bombing in World War II*. Lexington: University Press of Kentucky, 2019.

Henry, Paul F. "William E. Kepner: All the Way to Berlin." Chap. 6 in *Makers of the United States Air Force*, ed. John L. Frisbee. USGPO, Washington, DC: Air Force History and Museums Program, 1996.

Ivie, Tom. *Patton's Eyes in the Sky: USAF Combat Reconnaissance Missions, North-West Europe, 1944–1945*. Surrey, England: Classic Publications, 2003.

Jane's Information Group. *Jane's All the World's Aircraft, 1945/6*. London: Sampson Low Marston, 1946.

Keen, Patricia Fussell. *Eyes of the Eighth: A Story of the 7th Photographic Reconnaissance Group, 1942–1945*. Sun City, AZ: CAVU Publishers, 1996.

Keeney, L. Douglas. *The POINTBLANK Directive: The Untold Story of the Daring Plan That Saved D-Day*. Oxford, UK: Osprey Publishing, 2012.

Keeney, L. Douglas. *The War against the Luftwaffe, 1943–44: The Untold Story of the Air War against Germany and How World War II Hung in the Balance*. Campbell, CA: Fastpencil 2011.

Keeney, L. Douglas. *The War against the Nazi U-boats, 1942–1944*. Campbell, CA: Fastpencil, 2012.

Kreis, John F., ed., *Piercing the Fog: Intelligence and Army Air Forces Operations in World War II*. Washington, DC: Air Force History and Museums Program, 1996.

Lake, Jon. *The Great Book of Bombers*. London: Salamander Books, 2002.

Matloff, Maurice, and Edwin M. Snell. *Strategic Planning for Coalition Warfare, 1941–1942*. Washington, DC: Center of Military History United States Army, 1990.

Mauer, Mauer, ed. *Combat Squadrons of the Air Force, World War II*. Washington, DC: USAF Historical Division, Air University, Department of the Air Force, 1969.

McFarland, Stephen L. *America's Pursuit of Precision Bombing, 1910–1945*. Washington, DC: Smithsonian Institution Press, 1995.

McFarland, Stephen L., and Wesley Phillips Newton. *To Command the Sky: The Battle for Air Superiority over Germany, 1942–1944*. Washington, DC: Smithsonian Institution Press, 1991.

Mets, David R. *Master of Airpower: General Carl A. Spaatz*. Novato, CA: Presidio Press, 1998.

Miller, Donald L. *Masters of the Air: America's Bomber Boys Who Fought the Air War against Nazi Germany*. New York: Simon & Schuster, 2006.

Mrazek, Robert J. *To Kingdom Come: An Epic Saga of Survival in the Air War over Germany*. New York: New American Library, 2012.

Overy, Richard. *The Bombers and the Bombed: Allied Air War over Europe, 1940–1945*. New York: Viking/Penguin, 2013.

Overy, Richard. *The Bombing War: Europe, 1939–1945*. London: Allen Lane, 2013.

Parton, James. *Air Force Spoken Here: General Ira Eaker and the Command of the Air*. Maxwell AFB, AL: Air University Press, 2000.

Perret, Geoffrey. *Winged Victory: The Army Air Forces in World War II*. New York: Random House, 1993.

Persico, Joseph E. *Roosevelt's Centurions: FDR and the Commanders He Led to Victory in World War II*. New York: Random House, 2013.

Price, Alfred. *Targeting the Reich: Allied Photographic Reconnaissance over Europe, 1939–1945*. London: Greenhill Books/Lionel Leventhal 2003.

Probert, Henry. *Bomber Harris, His Life and Times: The Biography of Marshal of the Royal Air Force Sir Arthur Harris, Wartime Chief of Bomber Command*. Toronto: Stoddart Publishing, 2001.

Richards, Denis. *Portal of Hungerford: The Life of Marshal of the Royal Air Force Viscount Portal of Hungerford*. London: Wm. Heinemann, 1977.

Saward, Dudley. *Bomber Harris: The Story of Sir Arthur Harris, Marshal of the Royal Air Force*. New York: Doubleday and Company, 1985.

Schrader, Karl R. *A Giant in the Shadows: Major General Benjamin Foulois and the Rise of the Army Air Service in World War I*. Maxwell AFB, AL: Air University Press, 2013.

Scott, James M. *Black Snow: Curtis LeMay, the Firebombing of Tokyo, and the Road to the Atomic Bomb*. New York: W. W. Norton, 2022.

Sherry, Michael S. *The Rise of American Air Power: The Creation of Armageddon*. New Haven: Yale University Press, 1987.

Smith, Graham. *The Mighty Eighth in the Second World War*. Newberry, England: Countryside Books, 2001.

Stanley, Roy M. (Colonel, USAF [Ret.]). *World War II Photo Intelligence*. New York: Charles Scribner's Sons, 1981.

Stout, Jay A. *The Men Who Killed the Luftwaffe: The US Army Air Forces against Germany in World War II*. Lanham, MD: Stackpole Books, 2010.

Taaffe, Stephan R. *Marshall and His Generals: US Army Commanders in World War II*. Lawrence: University Press of Kansas, 2011.

Tate, James P. *The Army and Its Air Corps: Army Policy Toward Aviation, 1919–1941*. Maxwell AFB, AL: Air University Press, 1998.

Thomas, Lowell, and Edward Jablonski. *Bomber Commander: The Life of James H. Doolittle*. London: Sidgwick & Jackson, 1977.

Williams, Allen. *Operation Crossbow: The Untold Story of Photographic Intelligence and the Search for Hitler's V Weapons*. London: Random House, 2013.

Williamson, Gordon. *U-boat Bases and Bunkers, 1941–45*. Oxford, UK: Osprey Publishing, 2003.

Wolk, Herman S. *Cataclysm: General Hap Arnold and the Defeat of Japan*. Denton: University of North Texas Press, 2010.

Yenne, Bill. *Hit the Target: Eight Men Who Led the Eighth Air Force to Victory over the Luftwaffe*. New York: New American Library, 2015.

Secondary Sources: Articles

Air Force Historical Research Agency. *The Birth of the United States Air Force*. 9 January 2008.

Cahill, William M. "Technology Not Realized: Army Air Forces Radar Employment in the Early Pacific War." *Air Power History* 56, no. 2 (Summer 2009): 14–27.

Correll, John T. "The Air Force on the Eve of World War II." *Air Force Magazine*, October 2007.

Correll, John T. "Daylight Precision Bombing." *Air Force Magazine*, October 2008.

Correll, John T. "Targeting the Luftwaffe." *Air Force Magazine*, March 2018.

Correll, John T. "The Third Musketeer." *Air Force Magazine*, December 2014.

Ehlers, Robert S., Jr. (Colonel, USAF [Ret.]). "Bombers, 'Butchers,' and Britain's Bête Noire: Reappraising RAF Bomber Command's Role in World War II." *Royal Air Force Air Power Review* 14, no. 2 (Summer 2011): 5–18.

Felice, Carman P. (Major, USAF). "The Men and Machines, Part V: Air Operations in World War I." *Air Power Historian* 5, no. 1 (January 1958): 38–53.

Glines, Carrol V. "In Pursuit of Pancho Villa." *Air & Space Forces Magazine*, February 1, 1991. https://www.airandspaceforces.com/article/0291villa/.

Glock, John R. (Captain, USAF). "The Evolution of Air Force Targeting." *Air and Space Power Journal* 26, no. 6 (November–December 2012): 146–74.

Grotelueschen, Mark E. "Joint Planning for Global Warfare: The Development of the Rainbow Plans in the United States, 1938–1941." *Army History* 97 (Fall 2015): 8–27.

Hansell, Haywood S., Jr. "General Laurence S. Kuter, 1905–1979." *Aerospace Historian* 27, no. 2 (June 1980): 91–94.

Haulman, Daniel L. "Precision Aerial Bombardment of Strategic Targets: Its Rise, Fall, and Resurrection." *Air Power History* 55, no. 4 (Winter 2008): 24–33.

Holley, I. B., Jr. "An Air Force General: Laurence Sherman Kuter." *Aerospace Historian* 27, no. 2 (June 1980): 88–90.

Hopper, Bruce C., PhD. "American Day Bombardment in World War I." *Air Power Historian* 4, no. 2 (April 1957): 88–97.

Kuter, Laurence F., and Laurence S. Kuter. "The General vs. the Establishment: General H. H. Arnold and the Air Staff." *Aerospace Historian* 21, no. 4 (December 1974): 185–89.

Meilinger, Phillip S. (Colonel, USAF [Ret.]). "The Prescient Planners of AWPD-1." *Air Force Magazine*, July 2011.

Ralph, William W. "Improvised Destruction: Arnold, LeMay, and the Firebombing of Japan." *War in History* 13, no. 4 (October 2006): 495–522.

Sauter, Dale. "So Near Heaven and Surrounded by Hell: The Character and 1942–1943 Military Career of World War II Pilot Frank A. Armstrong, Jr." *North Carolina Historical Review* 88, no. 2 (April 2011): 164–88.

Tillman, Barrett. "Back to Schweinfurt." *Air Force Magazine*, August 2018.

Tillman, Barrett. "Hard Targets: An Attempt to Destroy German U-boats in Their Pens Was Fraught with Peril and Frustration." *Air Force Magazine*, February 2015.

Trimble, Michael M. "Air Force Strategic Bombing and Its Counterpoints from World War I to Vietnam." *Joint Force Quarterly* 91 (2018): 82–89.

Werrell, Kenneth P. "The Strategic Bombing of Germany in World War II: Costs and Accomplishments." *Journal of American History* 73, no. 3 (December 1986): 703–13.

Wolk, Herman S. "Arnold Races the Clock: The Battle of Japan." *Air Power History* 56, no. 1 (Spring 2009): 35–45.

Wolk, Herman S. "Decision at Casablanca." *Air Force Magazine*, January 2003.

Wolk, Herman S. "The Founding of the Force." *Air Force Magazine*, September 1996.

Wolk, Herman S. "Ike and the Air Force." *Air Force Magazine*, January 2006.

Index

A

A-20 (Boston/Havoc), 64–65
AAF (Army Air Forces), 16, 19–20, 30–31, 35–37, 39–41, 62–66, 70–71, 82–85, 92–93, 98, 107, 119, 127–32, 140–41, 151–52, 172–74, 189–91, 223–25, 227–28, 259
AAFIB (Army Air Forces in Britain), 33–34, 41
ABC conversations, 22–25, 36
  ABC-1, 23–25, 30
  ABC-2, 24
ACTS (Air Corps Tactical School), 8–9, 11–17, 19, 25, 27–28, 63, 83, 129–30, 141, 164–65, 194
  attended by Spaatz, Eaker, 15
AEF (American Expeditionary Force), 3–4, 6
Afrika Korps, 31–32, 51, 259
Air Corps (USAAC), 8, 11–21, 24, 172, 222
Air Corps Tactical School. *See* ACTS
aircraft, 1–3, 5–7, 12–14, 24–27, 63–65, 70–72, 87–88, 90–93, 113–16, 119–24, 136–40, 147–49, 154–57, 159–61, 163–64, 173–75, 178–83, 201–5, 213–17, 226–29
  damaged, 155, 160, 175, 202–3
  factories, 27, 205, 213, 228, 233, 235
  German, 5–7, 27, 30, 54, 92, 107, 120, 202–5, 215, 217, 219, 233, 235, 239, 241
  production, 25, 27, 41, 67, 181, 205
aircrews, 6, 44–45, 61, 63, 65, 136, 146–49, 155, 160–61, 163, 179–80, 203, 217, 251–52, 280
  new, 107, 111
  qualified, 116, 138, 161, 170
air power, 3–4, 8, 11, 13, 15, 23–26, 43, 46, 85, 95, 97, 118, 128, 261, 263
  strategic, 3–5, 8, 11, 23, 25, 46, 85, 108, 118, 128, 250, 261, 263
Air-Sea Rescue (ASR), 201, 229
air superiority, 7, 23, 43, 55, 90, 131–32, 134, 171, 190, 194, 242
air supremacy, 40, 43, 50, 67, 89, 95–96, 131, 171, 190–91, 193
Algeria, 215–16, 218, 259
Algiers, 119
Allied air forces, 7, 31, 118–19, 128, 131, 134, 232, 242–43, 264, 270, 272–73

D

La Pallice, 106, 170, 191
Lorient, 106, 108, 110, 135, 150
St. Nazaire, 106, 110–11, 121–23, 173, 191
yards, 150, 162, 170, 191, 201
ULTRA, 71, 197–98, 205, 238
USAAC (United States Army Air Corps). *See* Air Corps
US Strategic Air Forces, 257, 260–61, 267–68

V

V-1 flying bomb, 221, 280
V-2 rocket, 221
Vandenberg, Hoyt S., 73
Vegesack, 146, 150, 185, 252
Vichy, France, 31, 120
VIII Bomber Command. *See* Eighth Air Force, VIII Bomber Command
VIII Fighter Command. *See* Eighth Air Force, VIII Fighter Command

W

WAC (Womens Army Corps), fig. 16
Walker, Kenneth N., 12, 15, 19, 25
WDGS (War Department General Staff), 4–5, 12, 39, 41, 44, 141
Welsh, William L., 225
WIDEWING, 75, 97, 166, 224, 243, 280
Wiener-Neustadt, 198, 213–14
Wilhelmshaven, Germany, 136, 138, 185, 191–92, 201
Williams, Robert A., fig. 5
Wilson, Donald, 12, 15, 27, 171
Winant, John G., 53, 152, 172, 274
    Navy Cross, 53, 172
women, 9, 32, 141, 259, 271. *See also* WAC
World War I, 1, 5, 8–9, 11, 17, 33, 57–58, 92, 222
WPD (War Plans Division), 39–40
Wright Field, 13

Y

Yankee Doodle (B-17), 70